# PECULIAR SATISFACTION

# Peculiar Satisfaction

## THOMAS JEFFERSON AND THE MASTERY OF SUBJECTS

*Melissa Adler*

FORDHAM UNIVERSITY PRESS NEW YORK 2026

Fordham University Press also publishes its books in a variety of electronic formats. Some content that appears in print may not be available in electronic books.

Visit us online at www.fordhampress.com.

For EU safety / GPSR concerns: Mare Nostrum Group B.V., Mauritskade 21D, 1091 GC Amsterdam, The Netherlands, gpsr@mare-nostrum.co.uk

Library of Congress Cataloging-in-Publication Data available online at https://catalog.loc.gov.

Printed in the United States of America

28 27 26 5 4 3 2 1

First edition

*To Valerie Adler, my grandmother and my first librarian, who modeled independence in thinking and reading as a practice of freedom.*

*For my dad, Dick Adler, and my mom, Peg Michalski, who are in my head and heart always.*

*For library, archives, and museum workers who honor and uphold diversity, equity, inclusion, accessibility, and decolonization.*

*For S & G, with hope and love.*

# Contents

PROLOGUE ix

NOTE ON LANGUAGE, SPELLING, NAMING, AND CITATIONALITY xxiii

Introduction: "These Precious Monuments of Our Property and Our History" 1

**PART 1 – ARCHIVES**

1 Information as Revolutionary Action 31

2 Archives and the Making of American History 55

3 Haunted Ontologies 83

**PART 2 – LIBRARIES**

4 "A Blueprint of His Own Mind": Jefferson's Libraries 115

5 The Racial Aesthetic of Jefferson's Library Catalog 149

6 From Geography to History 173

**PART 3 - MUSEUMS**

7 Jefferson's "Indian Hall" and the Doctrine of Discovery 197

8 How the American Antelope [*sic*] Became a Document 220

Coda: Afterlife of Information 241

ACKNOWLEDGMENTS 257

NOTES 261

BIBLIOGRAPHY 301

INDEX 325

# Prologue

I take it as self-evident that readers who have selected this book on Jefferson, libraries, archives, and museums are familiar with the Library of Congress Classification system. Even if you are not fully aware of the way that it has conditioned the possibilities for your searches for information and how you do research, I would wager that you do know that this classification organizes books into disciplines in most academic libraries. Perhaps you have experienced a "peculiar satisfaction" in browsing for books in a particular section of the library, as did Thomas Jefferson when he viewed the books on his own shelves at his home at Monticello. Some readers are likely aware that the Library of Congress was installed in the first year of Jefferson's presidency and that he sold his personal collection to the Library of Congress after the existing congressional library was burned in the War of 1812. Jefferson's personal library became the core collection for the federal library of the new United States in the early nineteenth century. Today the Library of Congress is not only the largest library in the world, but it also sets many of the standards by which libraries around the globe organize their materials. We are connected to Jefferson through our libraries, and when we consult library catalogs, we "can see the books through Jefferson's eyes."[1] Throughout this book I will show how his vision for libraries and other cultural and educational institutions continues to shape our encounters with information. The institutions and practices associated with the collection, storage, and retrieval of information sustain a very Jeffersonian America, with all of its complexity and contradictions.

Scholars and professionals in the field of library and information studies will be keenly aware of the technical aspects of the Library of Congress Classification, and it is also probably safe to say that they are most at home in the

Z section, labeled "Bibliography. Library Science. Information Resources." Museum scholars and workers will find their books at the very other end of the classification, in A—"General works," and specifically classed under AM, which is designated for "Museums. Collectors and Collecting." If you are a historian of the United States, you've probably spent a lot of time in the E and F sections of your library, and if you're an archival studies scholar, you're likely well-versed in C—"Auxiliary Sciences of History"—especially the vast section on "Archives," in the range CD 921–4280. Rarely does a book fit neatly into one category, so most readers will find the books they seek across and beyond these sections.

This book, *Peculiar Satisfaction*, will have presented a conundrum for library catalogers, as it touches on all of the subjects described above and many more, including political theory, Jefferson studies, science and technology studies, Indigenous studies, whiteness studies, and the history of anti-Black racism in the United States. As much as I want to comment on its location in the library, I won't know where it will be placed until the book is in production—after it has been written and copyedited. Between the time I complete this book and the moment it reaches its readers, it will have been entered into copyright, the office for which is housed in the Library of Congress.[2] In fact, according to James Billington, Librarian of Congress from 1987 to 2015, "No subsequent legislation was more important to the Library than the 1870 law that finally transferred the 'copyright business' from federal courts to the Library of Congress. The law required all authors, poets, composers, artists, publishers and map makers to deposit in the Library two copies of every work registered in the United States—producing in time a vast permanent archives of American creativity for the benefit of future generations of researchers."[3] This book will also receive a "Cataloging in Publication" record around this time, based on information supplied by the publisher. It will feature basic descriptive metadata for the book—title, author, publisher, the ISBN (International Standard Book Number), and perhaps subject headings and shelf classifications according to the Library of Congress and the Dewey Decimal Classification (the editorial office of which is also housed in the Library of Congress). You might be able to find this information printed on the verso of the title page, or there may be a note indicating that this data is available online. When the book is published, more complete data will be entered into a shared master record that can be downloaded by the libraries that acquire the book so that their users can retrieve it and put it to use.

I can only speculate as to where this book will be shelved, but my guess is that it will be assigned to the E300s with the books on US presidents. The 330 range is designated for Jefferson's presidential administration and is subdivided into several categories. E331 refers to general works on the "Biography of Thomas Jefferson, 1743–1826." E332 applies to "General works. Jefferson as president and statesman" and is subdivided into dozens of subcategories, such as "Homes and haunts," "Journeys," and "Purchase of Louisiana, 1803." Some of these classes are subdivided again. "Writings," for example is divided into "Collected works," "Correspondence," "Individual works" (which includes subclasses for "Commonplace books, Literary bible," "Declaration of Independence," etc.), and so on. If it were up to me, I would probably class this book in the broader 331 (Biography), even though that category designation is an imperfect match. I resist calling this book a biography, but rather, I see it as a critical history that uses Jefferson as a lens for gaining understanding of the formation of libraries, archives, and museums. I have trouble containing his work to a class for works on Jefferson as president and statesman because so many aspects of Jefferson that I describe in these pages were personal. After all, it was questions about the crossing of his domestic, plantation, and political worlds in his library, archives, and museum practices that brought me to this project in the first place. Because the disciplines are spread out across a library space, placing this book among other books about US presidents will mean that scholars whose research focuses on libraries, archives, and museums are unlikely to find the book solely by browsing the stacks. By the same token, placing it with books about libraries, archives, or museums might result Jefferson scholars missing it.

Jefferson wrestled with similar dilemmas when he classified his own books. He described his method for arranging his books in correspondence with George Watterston, the third Librarian of Congress, when he transferred his collection from Monticello to the congressional library. Jefferson stated his preference for arranging his books by topic rather than alphabetical order and insisted that his system remain intact when the collection was installed for Congress. He described the challenges of interdisciplinarity—especially with regard to books about travel, which he said, "blend together the geography, natural history, civil history, agriculture, manufactures, commerce, arts, occupations, manners Etc. of a country." Nevertheless, Jefferson observed a "*peculiar satisfaction*" in classifying books according to subject, which derived from "seeing at a glance the books which have been written on [a subject], and selecting those from which we expect most readily the information we seek."[4] Every library cataloger is well aware of the central paradox of cataloging: in order to make materials accessible, i.e., to make a collection usable, texts have to be reduced to categories so that each book can occupy a space on a shelf for retrieval. At the heart of Jefferson's system is a set of acts of reducing complex works to single-subject categories, arranging those categories by associations according to his point of view, and making determinations about where the books belong. One could take his classificatory decisions as declarations about the books' contents and how they relate to his own information needs.

One of the core principles that grounded my first book, *Cruising the Library*, was that to classify is to make a statement—or in fact, a series of statements.[5] Take for example the Library of Congress's decision to classify the book *Dark Matters: On the Surveillance of Blackness*, by Simone Browne (Duke University Press, 2015), with the call number E185.86. This classification is defined by the Library of Congress as "United States—Elements in the Population—African Americans—Special topics—Social conditions. Social life and customs."[6] We could translate this classificatory decision into a series of declarative statements.[7]

First there is the set of statements regarding what the book is about:

*Dark Matters* is about the United States.
*Dark Matters* is about African Americans.
*Dark Matters* is about the social conditions and/or the life and customs of African Americans in the United States.

Looking more closely at the hierarchical arrangement of the Library of Congress Classification, we notice that other statements are being made here: African Americans are "elements in the population" of the United States; the "social conditions" and "social life and customs" of African Americans are to be regarded as a "special topic"; these social conditions are adjacent or related to religion (but not all religions), economic conditions, and the professions. The structure itself is making a series of statements regarding the techniques of order based on logical syllogism and specific understandings of relatedness, which result in broader, narrower, and related categories, as shown below.

| | |
|---|---|
| E | UNITED STATES |
| | Elements in the population |
| | African Americans |
| | Special topics |
| 185.62 | Intermarriage of races. Miscegenation. Mulattoes. |
| 185.625 | Psychosocial factors. Race identity. |
| 185.63 | African Americans in the Armed Forces |
| | [a list of cross references for different wars appears here] |
| | Crime. Delinquency see HV6197.A+ |
| (185.7) | Religion. Africa American churches |
| | For African American religions not limited to Christianity see BL1+ |
| | For Black Muslims see BP221+ |
| | For African American churches (General). African American clergy, etc. see BR563.B53 |

| | |
|---|---|
| | For missions to African Americans (Individual denominations) see BV2766.A+ |
| | For missions to African Americans (General) see BV2783 |
| | For individual Christian sects, denominations, local churches see BX1+ |
| 185.8 | Economic conditions |
| | For special aspects of economic conditions, see class H |
| | The professions |
| | see the individual profession |
| 185.86 | Social life. Social conditions and customs. |
| | Including family, women, youth, children, etc. |
| | Health. Physical condition |
| | see class R[8] |

The reductive classificatory statements fail to address Browne's description of the book's purpose:

> *Dark Matters* names the surveillance of blackness as often unperceivable within the study of surveillance, all the while blackness being that nonnameable matter that matters the racialized disciplinary society. It is from this insight that I situate *Dark Matters* as a black diasporic, archival, historical, and contemporary study that locates blackness as a key site through which surveillance is practiced, narrated, and enacted.[9]

We can also derive an infinite list of negative statements by thinking about where the book could be placed but is not. In other words, there are several things that the classification of *Dark Matters* in E185.86 is *not* saying:

> *Dark Matters* is about surveillance.
> *Dark Matters* is about technology.
> *Dark Matters* is about the State.
> *Dark Matters* is about Canada.
> *Dark Matters* is about human rights.

The significance of this series of what-is-*not*-being-said becomes more apparent when we compare it to related statements across the library. For example, *Surveillance as Social Sorting*, edited by David Lyon and the *Routledge Handbook of Surveillance Studies*, edited by Kirstie Ball, Kevin Haggerty, and David Lyon, are both shelved in JC596, defined as "Political theory. The State. Theories of the State.—Rights of the individual—Right to privacy."[10] Here individuals' and communities' rights to privacy are foregrounded in this section about political theory and the State.

Compare these both with the classification of Toby Beauchamp's *Going Stealth: Transgender Politics and U.S. Surveillance Practices*, which is shelved in HV7936.T4. The hierarchical chain for this class makes another set of statements: "Social pathology. Social and public Welfare. Criminology—Criminal justice administration—Police. Detectives. Constabulary—Special topics, A-Z—Television. Electronic surveillance."[11] Why is this book placed with books on social pathology, rather than with the books on political theory and rights to privacy? Or following the logic of the classification of *Dark Matters*, which locates that book within a minoritized category, should *Going Stealth* be shelved with other books on transgender issues in the HQ section, which is home to books about gender?

Practically speaking, the classificatory decisions for these books on the surveillance of Black and transgender people are given "special" treatment—resulting in a verification and reification of their minority status. *Dark Matters*, a book on the surveillance of Black people is shelved together with other books on a wide range of topics about the social conditions of Black life in the United States. *Going Stealth*, a book on the surveillance of transgender people is shelved with books on criminality and social pathology, seeming to suggest an assumed pathology of trans people that necessitates policing. These are very different kinds of statements that have material effects and have arisen out of political, social, and technical conditions. If a person is browsing the stacks in the section that contains books primarily about surveillance in the political theory section, where whiteness and cisgender are normative, they won't come across *Dark Matters* or *Going Stealth*.

Discursively speaking, this is a powerful set of statements with a long history that precedes the publication and categorization of these books, which I trace back to Jefferson's personal library at Monticello. In addition to thinking about what these statements are saying, it is important to consider what they are *doing*. These statements support the universalization of whiteness and binary gender by placing books that fall outside of these assumed norms in various "Other" locations across the library. In Foucault's terms, the condition described here is an effect of the ways that "discipline organizes an analytical space,"[12] and a recurring theme of this book will be the connections between discourse and information architectures, which facilitate access and contain statements of their own.[13] The example of the classification of *Dark Matters* is one of many across the library that demonstrate a "racial schematization of the visible field" and a visualization of the racialized field.[14] And as Beauchamp writes, "visibility works as a part of biopower to produce" categories, a phenomenon that is fundamental to the formation and function of classifications that inform and are informed by the visual field.[15] Placing Simone Browne's book with other books about African Americans within American history asserts particular "facts of blackness" and serves as an example of how racism is scripted and re-cited in systems.[16]

The questions that drive the present work have emerged out of my interest in Jefferson's influence in the formation of those classifications. I was aware that he had sold his private book collection to the Library of Congress after the War of 1812, and I wanted to discern whether some of the principles on which the classifications that organize our research libraries in the present are informed by his original catalog. My aim was to find a thread connecting the critical cataloging research of the present to the founding of the Library of Congress in 1800. Whereas *Cruising the Library* examined the history of the Library of Congress's current classificatory tools beginning around 1900, *Peculiar Satisfaction* looks to the moment in which the Library of Congress was established and to the person who oversaw its formation.

Jefferson's methods for arranging, preserving, and indexing documents provide rich data for understanding the significance of information organization in the founding of the republic. My project began as a study of his personal library catalog and has become a book about the principles upon which information institutions, architectures, and infrastructures much more broadly defined have been constructed. Large systems like the Library of Congress Classification continue to stand strong and reify the universality of certain Jeffersonian principles. Those principles are complex, and by placing Jefferson's use of information at his plantation at Monticello and in his public offices at the center of the story of the enduring contradictions and paradoxes of the American political landscape, we gain insight into the role of information in the formation and expansion of liberal democracy in the United States. The Library of Congress is just one of many different institutions that contributed to a discursive field that supplied the informational architecture for an early republic. This book will look at the durability of Jefferson's organizing principles in the histories of academic disciplines, public libraries, and state archives and museums.

In *Cruising the Library* I described the Library of Congress's classificatory techniques in Foucauldian terms, arguing that the Library of Congress is the kind of institution to which Foucault refers when he says that his central project is "to account for the fact that it is spoken about, to discover who does the speaking, the positions and viewpoints from which they speak, the institutions which prompt people to speak about it and which store and distribute the things that are said."[17] I still maintain this position, as the Library of Congress not only stores and provides access to information, but it also actively produces knowledge through its organizing techniques. It participates in and deploys state and cultural discourses. Among the techniques that it deploys is its classifications. Historicizing that work more fully by tracing the lineage of the Library of Congress's classifications for sexual perversion back to Jefferson's classifications for racialized and gendered subjects, and forward to the modulating categories in search engines and databases, necessitates a deeper examination of the ways in which repression is built into those systems. Doing so may reveal how the repressed returns.

My claim is not that Jefferson was the first American classificationist or archivist or "information scientist," nor that he acted alone in his classificatory experiments. Rather, my central argument is that Jefferson's inventions and adaptations of structures and technologies were instrumental in the formation of the United States, and that the systemization of racial categories was a key mechanism by which liberal democracy was established. Jefferson understood the importance of documentation and the organization of knowledge in all aspects of his life, and his influence on the foundation of cultural institutions exceeded that of his peers. Installing these principles in information systems—especially by contributing to the establishment of libraries, archives, and museums in spaces adjacent to government offices—made those principles stick and enabled their increasingly global reach.

Necessarily, I have been selective in choosing which documents and information practices are relevant to this research. I have consulted letters written to, by, and about Jefferson, newspaper articles and cartoons about him, his *Notes on the State of Virginia*, account books, commonplace books, Farm Book, Garden Book, political declarations, proposed bills, meeting notes, epitaphs, graveyards, architectural drawings, maps, classified library catalogs, and scientific notes and diagrams. Although Jefferson's name is attached to nearly all of the documents I have consulted, we see that not only is he one of many people in a large network that spans multiple discursive fields in various geographical and cultural contexts, but that so much of what we think we know about Jefferson and his milieu is the product of collective imaginaries that have been reinscribed in national memory. In this archive, we find a huge cast of collaborators, coconspirators, and coauthors, and by looking carefully, we can also locate traces of silenced and suppressed voices from a variety of perspectives. What we do not see or hear is often more important than what is explicitly written down, and so throughout this project I have been attentive to the omissions and erasures, which index the conditions of and *in*-formation.

Examining the past through a present lens is useful for thinking about how we are entangled with Jeffersonian information constructs and helping us to see ourselves in this ongoing history in the making. I am certainly not about to make any claims to know what it might have been like to be enslaved or displaced in Jefferson's time, nor can I gaze at Jefferson "from below"—from the position of people who lived and worked on his grounds and beneath his own living quarters. I can interpret the historical record from where I stand, however, as historians have always done. I have read hundreds of books and articles on Jefferson, from his period to the present, and nowhere is there ever a disinterested interpretation of the historical record. The facts of racialization and racism across Jefferson's archive are realities that have not yet been submitted to thorough analysis. As Vice President for Research and Saunders Director of the Robert H. Smith International Center for Jefferson Studies Andrew Davenport writes, "Modern interpreters of Jefferson do not revise history so much as they seek to restore perspectives that were cast aside during the institutionalization of Jefferson's reputation."[18] My primary purpose derives from my commitment to understanding the depths of the problems of marginalization in the information professions, institutions, and knowledge organization systems. A critical, anti-colonial twenty-first-century gaze is essential for making sense of settler colonialism's trajectories, and in the context of information, it helps to understand how various channels have carried settler colonial and imperial techniques into the very technologies with which we interact on a daily basis in our own information age.

Public institutions have long been sites where it can be imagined that people of all walks of life converge with information and where democratic discourse and dissent are possible. They have the potential to be spaces of appearance, which for Hannah Arendt is essential for political participation. "The presence of others who see what we see and hear what we hear assures us of the reality of the world and ourselves," she writes. And on the other hand, the shrinking public sphere results in the intensification of private feelings, which "will always come to pass at the expense of the assurance of the reality of the world and men."[19] For Arendt, "the term 'public' signifies the world itself, in so far as it is common to all of us and distinguished from our privately owned place in it. . . . To live together in the world means essentially that a world of things is between those who have it in common, as a table is located between those who sit around it; the world, like every in-between, relates and separates men at the same time."[20] The vision for equality depends on public forums where people can distinguish themselves from others, where a diversity of people and diversity of opinions appear together. The public realm for Arendt is a "common world" that "gathers us together and yet prevents our falling over each other, so to speak." The special feature about the institutions described in this book is that they all contain common holdings of collections of things in common spaces where people can gather (to varying degrees). These spaces epitomize the idea of a democracy "rooted in common love for, antipathy to, and contestation of public things." These spaces and their contents are essential to a functioning democracy. "Without public things," warns Bonnie Honig, "action in concert is undone and the signs and symbols of democratic life are devitalized."[21]

Arendt saw the diminishing space for politics and lamented, "What makes mass society so difficult to bear is not the number of people involved, or at least not primarily, but the fact that the world between them has lost its power to gather them together, to relate and to separate them."[22] A bind arises when the political conditions are such that the space of appearance is foreclosed or policed in such a way that political action is censored. As Judith Butler observes, "if politics is oriented toward the making and preserving of the conditions that allow for livability, then it seems that the space of appearance is not ever fully separable from questions of infrastructure and architecture, and that they not only condition the action, but take part in the making of the space of politics."[23] The public institutions and spaces described in this book take part in their own making, and when those institutions are themselves under threat, they become the battlegrounds on behalf of their own existence. For example, I heard from my graduate teaching assistants on the picket line that a strike for fair contracts is a fight for the institution itself, born out of an insistence that graduate students deserve a living wage so that they can focus on their research without distractions of poverty-level wages and mounting debt. Fighting for the right to protest on campuses is similarly a fight for the institution itself. It is an insistence that education is a public good and a public priority. It derives from the belief that institutions of higher education have value and should be allocated public money to ensure equity and diversity in our student bodies. It comes from the recognition on the part of those of us who have chosen academic professions that the classroom is still a space where radical ideas are up for discussion and liberation is possible and that campuses should be spaces where dissent is viewed as necessary to democracy. Like the graduate student I talked to on the picket line, I believe this is a freedom worth fighting for.

One of the most compelling aspects of public institutions is their role as sites of assembly for people who are not there to gather around any particular political cause or platform, but rather, they are there because they want to learn, be entertained, or perform an action like applying for a job or find a family history. The institutions and practices examined in this book provide essential *social* infrastructure— "the physical conditions that determine whether social capital develops." As Eric Klinenberg explains, "when social infrastructure is robust, it fosters contact, mutual support, and collaboration among friends and neighbors; when degraded, it inhibits social activity, leaving families and individuals to fend for themselves. Social infrastructure is crucially important, because local, face-to-face interactions—at the school, the playground, and the corner diner—are the building blocks of all public life."[24]

Former President of the American Library Association Emily Drabinski describes how public libraries operate: "In most communities, the public library is funded by a mix of federal, state and mostly local coffers—our taxes. Public sector employees manage and staff libraries, and pool these public funds to purchase materials to be held in common by the public and shared among members of the public. Everyone can share in resources that far exceed what any average individual could collect for their own use."[25] Public squares and publicly funded museums and historical societies are also vital to urban infrastructure. They are all undergirded by circulatory infrastructures organized by categories and formulas and driven by hardware and software. They are places where people exercise the most basic freedom to obtain access to information about whatever they need, attend a public talk on a topic that interests them, or use the space to rest or get out of the heat. They can also serve as spaces of common causes and gathering for activism. In this moment, when the gutting of public institutions is part of a full-frontal attack on democracy, there is a collective heightening awareness of how crucial they are. At the same time, we are presented with an opportunity to reimagine the common and think about how these institutions might be reconfigured more democratically. I am thinking along the lines of Michael Hardt and Antonio Negri's multitude and a "plural ontology of social being."[26] For Hardt and Negri, a common is defined as "the wealth of the earth and the social wealth that we share and whose use we manage together."[27] They raise questions about the private and the public, and contradictions of state ownership of institutions, all of which is relevant here but isn't pursued in detail. What is of primary importance here is the capacity to use our institutions in our shared struggles and to think about how to configure them in ways that expand our capacity for collective resistance through shared materials, occupying spaces, and cooperation.

## Overview of Chapters

This book is organized into three main parts, according to type of institution—archives, libraries, and museums. First, the introduction provides an account of the history of monuments and their removal in Charlottesville, Virginia, to enter into a discussion of the monumentality of documents and the information architectures by which they are organized and preserved. Part 1 is about Jefferson's archival practices, and my account begins in Chapter 1 by demonstrating his vision for shaping history as it was unfolding in the formation of the United States. I center the discussion around Jefferson's use of "information" as an action word in the context of the revolution and the establishment of a democratic republic. I also situate archives, libraries, and museums as memory institutions that are essential to political action. In Chapter 2, I examine Jefferson's role in the formation of American archives more fully and demonstrate his archival theory and practices. Julian Boyd, the person who directed the publication of Jefferson's papers at Princeton, regards Jefferson as "a progenitor of archival concerns in America," and so I account for Jefferson's development of techniques for preservation and access of government documents in the history of archival science and practice. Crucial to his historical method was the placement of Indigenous inhabitants outside of American history, while imagining that white Americans could start anew by separating from their European pasts. He also neglected Black lives and histories and registered the deferral of the end to slavery to future generations. In Chapter 3, I argue that classification is a technique of repression—one rooted in guarding against the conditions that can't be thought. Understanding the repressive nature of classification shows that censorship resides in the systems themselves. By looking at Jefferson's Farm Book, in which he entered information about the people he enslaved in a ledger book, along with livestock and crop production, I show that the repressive technique of reducing lives to subjects and arranging them according to a particular point of view is intrinsic to political repression and the subjugation of human life. I also examine techniques of deferral and distinction as they appear in his archive.

Part 2 features three chapters on Jefferson's libraries, beginning with Chapter 4, which provides an overview of his advocacy for the establishment of public libraries and his influence on the founding of the Library of Congress. I also explore the connections between his personal library catalog and the writing of *Notes on the State of Virginia*, as well as the way that he modeled his classificatory work on the method that Denis Diderot and Jean le Rond d'Alembert used to organize the *Encyclopédie* following Francis Bacon's division of knowledge into three faculties—Memory, Reason, and Imagination. Chapter 5 examines his classificatory decisions regarding books about slavery, Africa, and people of African descent. I discuss his decisions to place the works of Ignatius Sancho and Phillis Wheatley Peters at the bottom of the columns of the "Epistolary" and "Pastorals, Odes, Elegies" chapters, respectively. Jefferson read eighteenth-century aesthetic philosophy—especially works by Edmund Burke and William Hogarth—and so I contextualize his writings on blackness, the sublime, and morality to show that his organizing techniques were strongly influenced by racial aesthetics. Expanding the analysis of racial categories in the book catalog, Chapter 6 examines Jefferson's placement of books that describe Indigenous peoples in his Geography section. This framed a metanarrative of explorer and explored, self and other, national and alien, community and foreigner, past and present. By comparing Jefferson's library catalog and his writings about Indigenous peoples in *Notes on the State of Virginia*, we gain a deeper sense of how Indigenous peoples informed his worldview and how he put his views into discourse.

Part 3 delves into Jefferson's participation in natural history museums. Chapter 7 presents an analysis of Jefferson's treatment of the Indigenous material that Lewis and Clark sent to him from their expedition. I examine the museum he assembled in his entrance hall at Monticello, where he exhibited Indigenous artifacts to educate visitors. Jefferson's museum, perhaps more uniquely than his other information techniques, demonstrates the connection between information and the dispossession of Indigenous peoples of their land, objects, and knowledges, as well as the geographical metaphors like navigation, search, and discovery, that have become fundamental to information storage, retrieval, and seeking. In Chapter 8, I use correspondence between Jefferson and Charles Willson Peale, founder of the Philadelphia Museum, to demonstrate the ways that settler colonial, Euro-American science rendered animals into objects of observation and study. The case of the antelope is particularly revealing for the way the animal resists classification and capture, but also how the *thingification* of nature was scripted in and by the Lewis and Clark expedition and American expansion.

The book closes with a coda titled "Afterlife of Information," which returns to the discussion of monuments by considering the legacy of Jefferson's books and history-making practices. I turn to a comparison of the graveyard for his white family and the unmarked graves in the African American cemetery at Monticello, as well as his excavation of Monacan burial mounds. The grave sites serve as a stark reminder of the differential treatment of the people who lived at and near Monticello, while highlighting the importance of efforts to reclaim the stories of the people who were enslaved there by attuning to traces in the archival record, inviting oral histories, and using technologies to revise and augment collective memory about the people who lived and labored at Monticello, and the displaced Indigenous communities whose sacred spaces were violated for anthropological study, agriculture, and settlement.

## Note on Language, Spelling, Naming, and Citationality

I have chosen to maintain Jefferson's original spelling and punctuation. Jefferson had some quirky writing conventions, which include using lower case letters at the beginnings of sentences, and strange uses of commas and periods. Some of his stylistic and spelling choices reflected standards of his time, but some were peculiar even then. Apostrophes appear in many instances where today's readers might view them as errors.

Throughout the text, I also frequently use the words "America" and "United States" interchangeably but acknowledge the there are multiple Americas across Turtle Island. I use the terms "Indigenous," "Native American," "American Indian," and only use "Indian" on its own if that is the term used in quoted material. I live in Canada where a preferred term for Indigenous peoples is "First Nations," which is distinct from Métis and Inuit, so that language also appears as appropriate. Wherever possible I name a tribe or band instead of using the broader "Indigenous." I have also taken into consideration the precautions of Michif-settler scholar Max Liboiron, "It is common to introduce Indigenous authors with their nation/affiliation, while settler and white scholars almost always remain unmarked. . . . This unmarking is one act among many that re-centres settlers and whiteness as an unexceptional norm, while deviations have to be marked and named."[1] This condition parallels the classification structures that I describe throughout the book. As this is a book that addresses the processes by which Euro-American points of view have set standards for knowledge organization and citational practice, I have tried to heed Katherine McKittrick's guidance in the chapter, "Footnotes (Books and Papers Scattered about on the Floor)" in *Dear Science and Other Stories*[2]:

> The works cited are many and various divergent and overlapping texts, images, songs, and ideas that may not normally be read together. The works cited, all of them, when understood as in conversation with each other, demonstrate an interconnected story that resists oppression. We do not have to agree with all the works in the works cited. We do not have to like all of the works in the works cited. We do have to trust that the works in the works cited are helping us understand and talk about and theorize how to know the world differently. The praxis, then, is not about who belongs and who does not belong in the index or the endnotes; rather, it is about how we, collectively, are working against racial apartheid and different kinds and types of violence. . . . Thus, we might recognize black studies not as a citational project of naming and unnaming, but instead as sharing ideas about how to struggle against oppression. This has less to do with white men as embodied knowers and more to do with doing the work of liberation.

This project is primarily about the formation of categories in settler colonial and imperial projects, so I have wrestled with the problem of marked and unmarked categories in my own research and writing. In the end, I have decided to include information about tribal or band affiliations for scholars who have announced themselves as such in their writing.[3] I have also consulted Gabrielle Foreman et al., "Writing about Slavery/Teaching About Slavery: This Might Help," a community-sourced document, as a guide for language regarding slavery. Settler scholars' perspectives have also shaped narratives about the founding of the United States since Jefferson's time. Rather than universalize and naturalize this condition, I am stating here that most of the cited work in this book is the product of settler scholarship, a tradition to which Jefferson has directly contributed. Where authors have stated their settler positionality, I reproduce it in the text, and if I have not found an author statement, I have left them unmarked. Each of these choices is made with the awareness that people may change the ways that they want their affiliations to be described in writing over time. It may also be the case that I made some oversights in my research and failed to find information.

P.S. I am highly pleased with your Declaration. God preserve the united States.

We know the Race is not to the swift nor the Battle to the strong.

Do you not think an Angel rides in the Whirlwind and directs this Storm?

JOHN PAGE TO THOMAS JEFFERSON
20 JULY 1776

The angel would like to stay, awaken the dead, and make whole what has been smashed. But a storm is blowing from Paradise; it has got caught in his wings with such violence that the angel can no longer close them. This storm irresistibly propels him into the future to which his back is turned, while the pile of debris before him grows skyward.

This storm is what we call progress.

WALTER BENJAMIN
1940

yet on the whole I have preferred arrangement according to subject; because of the peculiar satisfaction, when we wish to consider a particular one, of seeing at a glance the books which have been written on it, and selecting those from which we expect most readily the information we seek.

THOMAS JEFFERSON TO GEORGE WATTERSTON,
THIRD LIBRARIAN OF CONGRESS
7 MAY 1815

# Introduction

## *"These Precious Monuments of Our Property and Our History"*

At a midnight hour in June of 1921, hundreds of leading professional men gathered around Thomas Jefferson's grave on top of Monticello mountain (see Figure 1), just outside Charlottesville, Virginia. They met to seal "the pledge of chivalry and patriotism with the deepest crimson of red American blood," and to enliven the Ku Klux Klan.[1] The Charlottesville *Daily Progress* reported that "the fiery cross, symbol of the Invisible Empire and of the unconquered and unconquerable blood of America cast an eerie sheen upon a legion of white robed Virginians as they stood upon hallowed ground and renewed the faith of their fathers."[2] Four months later, following a celebration that featured children who stood in the formation of the confederate flag, a monument to Thomas J. "Stonewall" Jackson was unveiled in what is now called Court Square Park.[3] Around the same time, the University of Virginia, founded by Jefferson in 1819, received money from the Klan to build a gymnasium. The president of the university, Edwin Alderman, delivered a speech in October of that year, praising Stonewall Jackson and declaring that "he passed without dispute, in the glory of unconquerable youth, into the inner circle of soldier-saints and heroes of the English race."[4] Alderman was regarded as so important by future administrators that he was the namesake of the university's main library from 1938 until 2024, when it was changed to the Edgar Shannon Library after renovations.[5]

Alderman also accepted, on behalf of the university, a monument to George Rogers Clark, a surveyor, Revolutionary War leader, and elder brother of William Clark of the Lewis and Clark expedition.[6] When the George Rogers Clark statue was unveiled at Monument Square, University Avenue,

Figure 1. Aerial view of Jefferson's house at Monticello and Montalto, overlooking Charlottesville, Virginia. Credit: ©Thomas Jefferson Foundation at Monticello.

in an area known as the Corner in Charlottesville, on 3 November 1921, Albert LeFevre, the university's Corcoran Professor of Philosophy announced in his speech:

> I present to the University of Virginia this monument of pride, enlightenment and inspiration—a monument erected as a memorial to the daring adventures of George Rogers Clark, the conqueror of the Northwest territory. This beautiful work of sculptural genius, like the noble statue of Lewis and Clark, awakens in us just pride, because it makes us ever mindful of the tribute we love to render to those great and heroic sons of the soil of Albemarle, sent forth on their high missions and fateful destinies by the prophetic wisdom of Thomas Jefferson.[7]

Clark and Jefferson were colleagues who held similar views on expansion. Indeed, as we will see in the chapters ahead, Jefferson acted upon his own contradictory views of Indigenous people and inscribed those views into early American policy. On the one hand Jefferson often spoke reverentially about Indigenous peoples, and on the other, he believed they stood in the way of American westward progress. For example, writing from his office as governor of Virginia in 1780, Jefferson wrote to George Rogers Clark to inform him that he had "directed the Lieutenants of the Counties of Washington, Montgomery, Botetourt, Rockbridge, and Green-Briar to assemble and concert, and immediately with a Portion of their Militia carry an Expedition into the Indian Country." Jefferson's directive was motivated by the drive to defend and expand American territory during the Revolutionary War—"Nothing is more desirable than total suppression of Savage Insolence and Cruelties," he wrote.[8] He was seeking Clark's assistance in this military mission to seize control of Indigenous land. The monument to Clark was erected over a hundred years later, after the Civil War, well into the Jim Crow era, and around the same time that particularly harsh, discriminatory laws were written to secure the disenfranchisement of Native Americans. The statue commemorated one of the leaders of the theft of Indigenous lands and the killing of the Indigenous peoples who inhabited and defended those lands. The erection of the statue in 1921 not only advanced the myth of the "vanishing Indian," but represented a revitalized movement based in the will to complete the removal of Indigenous people from Virginia.

On a Friday night in May 1924, members of the Klan burned a large cross at the top of Montalto, the "high mountain" that overlooks Monticello.[9] The fire lasted from 9:00 p.m. until 11:00 p.m. and was visible for miles from the height of 1,278 feet. Again, the *Daily Progress* reported on the event, this time saying that the "burning of the cross is supposed to have been part of a demonstration by the Ku Klux Klan in connection with their program," which was to be held the following day.[10] Those festivities included a parade on Main Street at 8:30 in the evening, followed by speakers on the circus lot in the Belmont neighborhood.[11] The following week, on 21 May 1924, the United Camp of Confederate Veterans held their thirty-seventh reunion in Charlottesville. A full day of events began with the veterans' visit to Monticello and concluded with a "grand ball" and reception in the University of Virginia gymnasium. The Klan paraded in full regalia through the city, ending in the African American Vinegar Hill neighborhood. The main event of the day was the unveiling of the Robert E. Lee statue in downtown Charlottesville, a few blocks away from Vinegar Hill, which was a prominent African American neighborhood.[12] Thousands of people came to watch.

According to Joshua Rothman, the 1920s iteration of the Klan at the height of the Jim Crow era was "the most insidious of them all," as the emplacement of the monuments described above seem to confirm.[13] The Charlottesville parades and monuments coincided with the Virginia General Assembly's 1924 passage of the highly discriminatory Racial Integrity Act, which redefined racial classification to prevent interracial sexual relationships, as well as the federal Immigration Act of 1924, which included the exclusion of Asians.[14] "Packaging its noxious ideology as traditional small-town values and wholesome fun," writes Rothman, "the Klan of the 1920s encouraged native-born white Americans to believe that bigotry, intimidation, harassment, and extralegal violence were all perfectly compatible with, if not central to, patriotic respectability."[15] The Klan of that era was also media-savvy, and the newspapers featured spectacular descriptions of the Klan's gatherings and events.

The spectacle of memorial events like these were created "in order to produce a certain kind of collective memory, generally at the scale of the city and in relation to the production of the nation."[16] The "grand dragon" had visited Charlottesville in August 1922 to meet with the Klan leaders to build momentum and concentrate power in their movement. The *Daily Progress* directly quoted the Klan's central tenets: "Protection to our women, that their honor may be preserved, and the racial purity of our decendants [*sic*] may be kept untarnished," the "preservation of our Free Public Schools, that our children may be taught American history, American traditions and American ideals, by Americans," and "Allegiance to the country, absolute and undivided, that we many never have to attempt to reconcile civil and political allegiance to America with ecclesiastical allegiance [*sic*] to an alien. It is still a fundamental truth that no man can serve two masters." The tenets unabashedly called for the "Rigid preservation of white supremacy," stating that, "The destinies of America shall remain within the white race." The article stated that, although the Charlottesville Klan was not the largest in Virginia, it could count some of the most influential citizens among its leaders. The Klan, according to the *Daily Progress*, was "here to stay."[17] By 1924 there were sixty local chapters in Virginia, and nationwide there may have been as many as four million members.[18]

■

On 11 August 2017, hundreds of white supremacists descended upon the University of Virginia in Charlottesville in their rally to "Unite the Right." That night, around twenty people—mostly University of Virginia students protecting justice, dignity, and equality—encircled and locked arms around the monument to Jefferson that stands in front of the Rotunda. The white supremacists then surrounded that group, bearing torches and chanting "white lives matter" and "you will not replace us."[19] Among the tragedies that took place the following day was the death of Heather Heyer, who was killed on the second day of the rally, when James Fields Jr. drove his car into a crowd of pedestrians. Two police officers died in a helicopter crash, and dozens of people were injured. One month after the Unite the Right rally, student protesters surrounded the Jefferson monument, carrying "Black Lives Matter" signs and banners, mounted the statue, and shrouded it in a black cloth. In April 2018, the day before the university's Founders Day, people spray-painted the words "racist" and "rapist" in red on the base of the statue.

The Unite the Right rally was motivated by the threat of the removal of the Robert E. Lee and Stonewall Jackson monuments, which became a rallying cry for the right-wing and reinvigorated white supremacist demonstrations in the heart of the city. Far-right leader and white nationalist Richard Spencer had previously led a parade around the Robert E. Lee statue and Lee Park (since renamed Market Street Park) in Charlottesville on 13 May 2017. Spencer described the intent of using torches—"It evoked a kind of mystical and even religious-like experience . . . it was a way to communicate with the dead."[20] As part of a dramatic rise in hate groups at the time, the Klan was building momentum across the country, but in Charlottesville the movement reached an intensity of symbolic power, matched by violence and destruction.[21] David Duke, a former "grand wizard" of the Klan, attended the Unite the Right rally and said that it represented a "turning point" for the movement.[22] The resurgence was also propelled by a desire among white supremacists to reclaim a "white republic" that they believed had been lost in the Civil Rights era of the 1960s.[23] That the scene of these rallies was in Thomas Jefferson's city is anything but accidental.

The removals of the Robert E. Lee and Stonewall Jackson monuments had been set in motion by a 2016 petition from high school student activist Zyahna Bryant. The Charlottesville city council voted to approve the action to take the statues down in April 2017, but a judge placed a stay on the decision in response to an appeal from local history groups and Confederate supporters. After litigation and debate, the Lee and Jackson statues were finally removed on 10 July 2021, followed by the removal of George Rogers Clark monument, which was located on the University of Virginia Grounds, and the statue of Meriwether Lewis, William Clark, and Lemhi Shoshone interpreter Sacagawea.[24]

■

On Saturday, 21 October 2023, folks associated with the Jefferson School African American Heritage Center in Charlottesville melted the Robert E. Lee statue in secret. It was "cut into fragments and dropped into a furnace, dissolving into a sludge of glowing bronze," in preparation for the metal to be remade into art.[25] The project's website reads:

> Swords Into Plowshares is our vision for transforming Charlottesville's Robert E. Lee statue into a new commissioned work of public art. In naming the initiative, we have drawn inspiration from the prophetic

> vision of Isaiah 2:4, which celebrates turning tools of violence into ones of peace and community-building. This project is already shaping the national conversation around toppled Confederate statues by modeling a community-engaged process of creative transformation—one that turns historic trauma into an artistic expression of democratic values and inclusive aspirations.[26]

As of this writing, Swords Into Plowshares is a coalition of Charlottesville-based organizations including the Memory Project at the University of Virginia's Karsh Institute of Democracy, the Institute for Environmental Negotiation, and Virginia Humanities. The project has received twenty-eight letters of support from leading organizations and individuals and has sought community input regarding the location for the new public art.

While some statues of famous men were removed in Charlottesville, others, like the one erected to Jefferson outside the Rotunda at the University of Virginia in 1910 will remain, but with context added, "to provide a more complete set of information."[27] The choice to allow the statue to stand is motivated by the conviction that Jefferson should be remembered as the founder of the university, and that a fuller picture of his story can offer an account of his ownership and use of the lives of hundreds of people. The Jefferson monument at the University of Virginia (see Figure 2)—the one encircled by social justice defenders and white supremacist protestors—features Jefferson standing on a pedestal on top of a bell, stately and strong, but unthreatening in his pose.[28] He holds an unrolled document in his hands, and on the outside of the bell are four angels who represent Liberty, Equality, Justice, and the Brotherhood of Man. The angel Equality is tearing up a document labeled "1776" and "primogeniture," while the Stamp Act is trampled beneath her foot (see Figure 3).

The university's President's Commission on Slavery has consulted with community members on various actions toward repair and reconciliation, including the 2020 construction of the "Memorial to Enslaved Laborers" (see Figure 4), which honors the people who "built and maintained" the university—more than four thousand enslaved people who lived and worked there between 1817 and 1865. The creation of this monument was a student-led effort. As described by former University of Virginia student, Thomas Soh:

> The shape of the memorial is in the form of a circle that is not fully completed to represent the broken shackle from which the 4,000 slaves that worked on the grounds were set free. Its strategic location also has significance, where its two paths lead to points of freedom;

Figure 2. Statue of Thomas Jefferson by Moses Jacob Ezekiel, Rotunda, University of Virginia, Charlottesville. Photo by author.

> the north path pointing towards the North Star and the lower path aligning with the sunset of March 3rd, the day the local slaves were set free by Union troops.[29]

As the contestation surrounding the removal, contextualization, and creation of monuments attests, commemorative statues and sculptures are extraordinarily powerful sites of national memory. These actions demonstrate that

Figure 3. Detail, "Angel of Equality," statue of Thomas Jefferson by Moses Jacob Ezekiel, University of Virginia, Charlottesville. Photo by author.

Figure 4. Memorial to Enslaved Laborers, University of Virginia, Charlottesville. Designed by Höweler and Yoon. Photo credit: WomenArtistUpdates, Wikimedia Commons.

memory matters, and practices of memorialization are not merely projections of fantasy, but that monuments contain and direct those fantasies, as well.

In light of the events described above, one might feel compelled to ask, what is it about the city of Charlottesville, the mountain that Thomas Jefferson called home, and the university that he founded that makes them gathering places for white supremacists? Some might wonder what Jefferson would think if he were alive today. These are questions that my friends and colleagues frequently put to me, and although they are certainly worth pondering, they are not issues on which I wish to take a position here. Although I have ideas on these questions, I am not sure it makes sense to assert a claim about what Jefferson would say about the resurgence of white supremacy in his city today, the far-right insurrection in the US Capitol building on 6 January 2021, or the election of Donald Trump to a second term of the US presidency. I do believe that he would have confidence in the government that he and his colleagues installed and the conviction that the fundamental tenets of freedom of speech, freedom of the press, equality, and democracy would ensure the safety of the nation.[30] In fact, he stated that any effort to destroy the government would stand as a "monument" to the government's strength and the permanence of its formative principles:

> We are all republicans: we are all federalists. If there be any among us who would wish to dissolve this Union, or to change its republican form, let them stand undisturbed as *monuments* of the safety with

> which error of opinion may be tolerated, where reason is left free to combat it . . .
>
> I know indeed that some honest men fear that a republican government cannot be strong; that this government is not strong enough. But would the honest patriot, in the full tide of successful experiment, abandon a government which has so far kept us free and firm, on the theoretic and visionary fear, that this government, the world's best hope, may, by possibility, want energy to preserve itself? I trust not.

Jefferson saw the republic itself as a monument—a testament to its own strength, and that it would stand as an example to other nations:

> a just & solid republican government maintained here, will be *a standing monument & example* for the aim & imitation of the people of other countries; and I join with you in the hope and belief that they will see from our example that a free government is of all others the most energetic, that the enquiry which has been excited among the mass of mankind by our revolution & it's consequences will ameliorate the condition of man over a great portion of the globe.[31]

Jefferson firmly believed in the pillars of good government, but he also held that a government's design was meant to be revisited. A republican government depended on the renegotiation and adaptation of its laws to ensure that they were applicable to the changes in society. Even as Jefferson envisioned a unified white population, he wanted the public realm to be a space for dissent among citizens, and he worried about consequences of uneducated masses gaining control of the country. In his day, in the moment of a revolution that was won by seizing lands and enslaving laborers, the aim of education was to inform and unite a white citizenry and to instruct the people according to a particular national imaginary. Disagreements would arise among members, even in a homogeneous public, but the vision was for those disputes to be settled in public, and that political participation of the citizens was essential for settling matters of how to improve and expand American liberal democracy. Dissent among mostly like-minded citizens, as long as it was directed toward a broadly shared vision of a United States, was not only welcome—it was essential for the functioning of the state. The guard against tyranny was an informed citizenry who could protest, call decisions into question, and unseat the leaders who made decisions that ran counter to the will of the citizenry.

Jefferson also believed that one generation did not have the right to bind the next and wrote to James Madison in 1789 that, on "similar ground it may be proved that no society can make a perpetual constitution, or even a perpetual law. The earth belongs always to the living generation."[32] Jefferson thought that constitutions and laws would "naturally" expire every nineteen years, a period of time that was roughly equivalent to a generation. "The tree of liberty must be refreshed from time to time with the blood of patriots and tyrants," he wrote. "It is it's natural manure."[33] Jefferson might regard the events in Charlottesville as "natural manure"—that it should not be surprising that blood has been shed in the conflicts surrounding fundamental questions about civil rights, freedom, and citizenship. He probably would have warned that the circulation of disinformation would have threatened democracy.

The eruption of violent conflict at the monument constructed in Jefferson's image in front of the Rotunda at the University of Virginia is perhaps a sign that Jefferson himself has come to stand for questions regarding the durability of liberal democracy and his own principles. Jefferson is firmly inscribed into national memory as a historical figure. He is also a container and a screen for a national imaginary, and as such, he is a highly contested site. Onto Jefferson people project their dreams, hopes, beliefs, anger, and fears, based on their own political, social, and economic positions. He has become representative—an abstraction, a medium, and a monument in and through which meaning is concentrated, but also a narrative device in the stories people tell about the United States and their relationship to country and nation. Those stories change over time, depending on who is doing the telling and the intended audience. The monuments to various figures in US history are sites that *in*-form by building historical memory into a statue, sculpted from materials that are meant to last. They are memorials to collective fantasy, put on display as grand statements about individuals, collectives, landmarks, and events. They are forever out of context, standing in artificially selected locations, and very often in isolation or removed from their original place and time. As memorial events and perspectives change, the collective memory associated with the monument also changes, and the monument becomes something of a palimpsest, on which narratives are inscribed and reinscribed. The spray-painting of "racist" and "rapist' literalized this phenomenon with the insistence on the narrative that foregrounds Jefferson as a person who enslaved Black lives and who had a sexual relationship with one of those enslaved persons, Sally Hemings.

## "Monuments of the Infancy of Our Country"

This book is, in fact, not exactly about monuments of the type described thus far. Rather, it is mostly about documents as most people conventionally understand them—papers, ledgers, books, and so on; the architectures that organize them, especially the classification systems and their categories and hierarchies; and the institutions that house them. It also examines the very concept of a document, leaning on documentation theory in the field of library and information studies to understand processes of datafication that are associated with the thingification of life, living beings, and communities.[34] The aim of this book is to consider the vast collections of documents that take the forms that we readily identify as informational and archival, as well as individual documents like the Declaration of Independence, as monuments to history. I will demonstrate Jefferson's role as crucial to the transformation of documents into monuments through archival practices of preservation and organization, as well as the formation of libraries and museums, and why these matter in the interlocking histories of information and the United States. Conducting this research has led me to understand the ways that the "modern invention of information" is imbricated with the formation of liberal democracy during the founding of the United States.[35]

In the long history of archives, scholars frequently point to the French Revolution to show how archives became monumentalized as they were nationalized and tend to view the United States as a latecomer to archival science because the US National Archives was not formally established until 1934. I suggest, however, that the American context was differently producing national archives as it was becoming a nation. The United States had to construct institutions of government and culture at the same time that it was becoming a country, and Jefferson was a leader in advocating for the establishment of archival practice, museums, and libraries to preserve historical memory around the same time that archival records in Europe were "transfigured from evidence into memorial," or as Eric Ketelaar puts it, "from muniments they emerge as monuments." The term "muniments" is a legal conceptualization that defines documents "as a title deed or a charter, by which rights or privileges are defended or maintained," and Ketelaar's point is that records that had previously been intended solely for administrative purposes became culturally significant in the late eighteenth century and passed into cultural patrimony—their preservation was meant to ensure that they endure for collective memory over time. Family and national documents were submitted to an anticipated "genealogical gaze" that viewed the histories of families as important in the production of national narratives for future generations. Documents pertaining to land and estates were useful to families and municipalities, but this shift toward monumentality meant that archival materials would also inform future historians about the formation of identities in the context of nation-making.[36] Michel Foucault takes note of this condition in his *Archaeology of Knowledge*:

> To be brief, then, let us say that history, in its traditional form, undertook to "memorize" the monuments of the past, transform them into documents, and lend speech to those traces which, in themselves, are often not verbal, or which say in silence something other than what they actually say; in our time, history is that which transforms documents into monuments.[37]

Perhaps even more than (or at least differently from) the early Dutch and French archivists, to whom Ketelaar attributes the emergence of a "paradigm of patrimony," Jefferson was keenly aware of the importance of saving and gathering historical documents for posterity. He possessed a "patrimonial consciousness" that informed his personal and professional documentary practices.[38] That consciousness was written into archival practices that sustain many of our present information institutions. Well before he drafted the Declaration of Independence, he was deeply engaged in the collection and preservation of the documented history of British America and actively documented history-in-the-making as the American Revolution unfolded. The American Revolution would give rise to an entirely new country, and along with the development of the new republic, archival practices were becoming institutionalized. Jefferson was in France at the time of the French Revolution and assisted in writing its Declaration of the Rights of Man and of the Citizen. He would have seen the libraries and archives there, but he possessed an archival impulse before his term as diplomat to France and understood the significance of documenting a nation's history as it happened.[39] Jefferson is genealogically tied to what Jarrett Drake notes of the early twentieth century—that archival professionals from the American South led the formation of a national archives to establish and prove genealogical claims. He identifies a "family fetish" in American archives that was designed to cultivate a documentary tradition that preserved kinship and common history among its white families. Drake writes, "Archives are a hidden terrain, then, in a much larger battleground of belonging."[40] Jefferson was a key player in implementing archival practices that simultaneously memorialized wealthy families and inscribed the unbelonging of people racialized as other than white by excluding them from History.

Indeed, Foucault identified a great rupture in history's "position in relation to the document" in the years between 1775 and 1825—a span of time that corresponds to Jefferson's professional life.[41] Foucault was referring to the formation of human sciences in that era, a moment that he viewed as a turning point in archival science. According to him, the human sciences arose in this moment, when "man constituted himself in Western culture as both that which must be conceived of and that which is to be known"—when man became the object of science. This was, in Foucault's analysis, "an *event in the order of knowledge*."[42] It is also at this time when specialized knowledges were formed to understand different aspects of human existence. As Roderick Ferguson writes, the "common denominator that unites the disciplines is, for Foucault, their interest in a particular type of historical errand oriented around the figure of man. . . . Western man would lay the groundwork for disciplining minority difference—making its activation concomitant with its regulation."[43] Foucault focused on late eighteenth- and early nineteenth-century European natural historians who became conscious of the role of documentation in organizing history, specifically during the French Revolution.

As we will see throughout this book, Jefferson, whose career maps almost too perfectly onto the years that Foucault specifies, was organizing American history by collecting, classifying, and preserving documents as the United States came into being. In 1775 Jefferson was elected to the Continental Congress, and the years that immediately followed were extraordinary for reasons that will be obvious to readers—the Declaration of Independence, revolution, war, the US Constitution and Bill of Rights, Jefferson's presidency, and the Louisiana Purchase are probably the first to come to mind. Notably, Jefferson died on 4 July 1826—the fiftieth anniversary of the signing of the Declaration of Independence, just beyond the year that Foucault identifies as the outer edge of the rupturing event in *The Order of Things*.[44] Jefferson wrote the Declaration at the beginning of the era that Foucault defines as the moment that conditioned the possibilities for the discursive formulation of Man. Jefferson himself viewed the revolutionary moment in America as a rupture. As Hannah Spahn explains, Jefferson insisted on the necessity of constructing a "narrative of American progress . . . premised on such moments of radical discontinuity with the past."[45] Spahn writes, "Jefferson's generation was instrumental in founding, along with the political institutions of the United States, a lasting culture of national memory."[46] His conception of time was a Newtonian one—at times paradoxical, and simultaneously forward- and backward-looking. And the mythical status we accord to the founders was of their own construction. The Jeffersonian/Newtonian method of self-historicization has persisted into the present, which explains some of the dangers of doing history, including the repetition of exceptionalist narratives about progress and revolution.[47]

Jefferson understood the significance of documents, perhaps more than others of his time, and his oeuvre invites inquiry into the role of documents in forming national histories. Documents can be *lieux de mémoire*, or sites of memory—not just metaphorically, and not only because they index the places that are meant to be remembered and how—but as memorials that have attained the status of monumental.[48] Jefferson was highly influential in the formation of information institutions adjacent to governing bodies, including public libraries, the Library of Congress, municipal and state archives, and museums. Their establishment was guided by the governing principles in which Jefferson believed so fervently. These institutions have been essential for enshrining those principles through information architectures constructed from collections, categories, and disciplinary techniques, as well as brick and mortar. These architectures ensure the durability of the organizing principles on which they are based and have monumentalizing effects.

This becomes clear in Jefferson's exchanges with Ebenezer Hazard, "America's first historical editor," especially in a 1791 letter regarding the necessity of collecting and preserving Virginia's historical papers.[49] Jefferson wrote, "I return you the two volumes of records, with thanks for the opportunity of looking into them. They are curious *monuments of the infancy of our country*."[50] A few years later, Jefferson penned a letter addressed to his mentor and colleague George Wythe that would be printed as a broadside and publicly posted. In it, Jefferson conveyed the reasons that Congress should invest in gathering and maintaining archival documents of the nation and the British colonies:

> Very early in the course of my researches into the laws of Virginia, I observed that many of them were already lost, and many more on the point of being lost, as existing only in single copies in the hands of careful or curious individuals, on whose deaths they would probably be used for waste paper. I set myself therefore to work to collect all which were then existing, in order that when the day should come in which the public should advert to the magnitude of their loss in these precious *monuments* of our property and our history, a part of their regret might be spared by information that a portion has been saved from the wreck which is worthy of their attention and preservation. In searching after these remains, I spared neither time, trouble, nor expence.[51]

Near the end of his life, in an 1820 letter to the historian Isaiah Thomas, Jefferson expressed his gratitude for Thomas's historical efforts in similar terms: "it is truly pleasing to hope that, by their attentions, the *monuments* of the character and condition of the people who preceded us in the occupation of this great country will be rescued from oblivion before they will have entirely disappeared."[52] In each of these instances, Jefferson explicitly equated historical documents with monuments, and it was with this spirit that he collected, cataloged, preserved, and circulated information in his personal and public domains. Jefferson devised and developed several techniques for cataloging his worlds, which coincided with his thinking about the posterity of national memory during and after the revolution. His archival actions anticipated the nineteenth-century heightening of large-scale public memorials to national figures, events, and places in urban spaces that cultivated emotional connections among citizens and the events of their nation's formation and victories.[53]

Donovan Schaefer is among the scholars who are examining the recent embattlement of monuments in political contest. In fact, his analysis provides a critical point of departure for conversations about the connection between information and processes of monumentalization. Schaefer observes that monuments—"construed as information in metallurgical form"—have earned "special protection as 'free speech,' with their destruction condemned as 'censorship.'"[54] In fact, his critique of the use of monuments in our current political arena resides in his assertion that people have reduced monuments to informational objects. He says that "monuments are fully integrated with and necessary to the projection of colonial power" but insists that a distinction must be made between statues and other textual materials like signs, posted documents, and plaques. "What is needed," writes Schaefer, "is a terminology that allows us to diagnose publics as formed not just by intellectual tissue but by material objects that have their own capacities to exert force independent of the register of information and ideas."[55] How should we talk about information, which is also material—not just a concept or an intangible entity with material effects? Information appears in form and substance in things like paper documents, code, landscapes, built environments, and bodies. My concern is that maintaining a distinction between information and its mediating technologies is to overlook the ways that social and technical conditions are always *in*-formation. Schaefer frames monuments in terms of a Foucauldian *dispositif*—"a thoroughly heterogeneous assemblage of discourses, institutions, architectural forms, regulatory decisions, laws, administrative measures, scientific statements, philosophical, moral and philanthropic propositions—in short, the said as much as the unsaid,"[56] which facilitates deeper discussions of how monuments are imbricated in relations of power. He notes that "even speech . . . has material-affective form," citing Donna Haraway's conceptualization of the "material-semiotic node" in *Simians, Cyborgs, and Women*, where she "locates information and objects on a single interactive plane."[57] My questions aim toward considering information as an agential, material participant in political movements and a deeper investigation of information and its architectures as sites of contest. It is true that information has taken on a particular function in liberal democratic governance, but does framing this as flattening overlook opportunities to find out how information has been constructed and how it operates in affective relations and relations of power?

Alongside Schaefer's conceptualization of monuments as *dispositif*, Alexander Weheliye's definition of racialization furnishes conceptual ground for this project: "Overall," writes Weheliye, "I construe race, racialization, and racial identities as ongoing sets of political relations that require, through constant perpetuation via institutions, discourses, practices, desires, infrastructures, languages, technologies, sciences, economies, dreams, and cultural artifacts, the barring of nonwhite subjects from the category of the human as it is performed in the modern west."[58] Not merely a biological or cultural descriptor, but "a conglomerate of sociopolitical relations that discipline humanity," racialization is a set of interlocking and persistent processes of hierarchization that happen in assemblages of power.[59] While it may seem counterintuitive to present a history of racialization while advocating for a strengthening of state-supported institutions, I believe strongly that this critique is necessary for establishing grounds on which to support libraries, archives, and museums with the aim toward expanding their potential to meet their stated values regarding equity of access to information for the functioning of a democratic society. Understanding how these institutions have been made alongside the making of Man and a "constitutive outside" comprised of Indigenous and enslaved peoples, as well as the more-than-human, including animals, is essential to that aim.[60]

Giorgio Agamben finds Carl Linnaeus's division of species curious especially because Linnaeus himself does not identify specific characteristics that differentiate the human from other animals, "other than the *ability* to recognize himself."[61] In *The Open*, Agamben observes that "Homo sapiens, then, is neither a clearly defined species nor a substance; it is, rather, a machine or device for producing the recognition of the human."[62] And it is through that device that Man rises to primacy (yes, in the sense of the ape who sees himself as human, and at the top of the hierarchy), and delineates a "state of exception." Agamben concludes that "the decisive political conflict, which governs every other conflict," in our culture, "is that between the animality and the humanity of man" and that the "anthropological machine was the motor for man's becoming historical." Indeed, it is a problem of biopolitics and techniques for drawing a distinction between Man and his others.[63] Agamben argues that life "must be ceaselessly articulated and divided" in modernity, that "in the machine of the moderns, the outside is produced through the exclusion of an inside and the inhuman is produced by animalizing the human, here the inside is obtained through the inclusion of an outside, and the non-man is produced by the humanization of an animal: the man-ape, the *enfant savage* or *Homo ferus*, but also and above all the slave, the barbarian, and the foreigner, as figures of an animal in human form."[64]

He also insists on the necessity of making sense of how these ontological machines work so that we can put a stop to their violence.

Yellowknives Dene scholar Glen Sean Coulthard's definition of settler colonialism is another useful point of departure for describing and contextualizing this project, especially for the ways that he describes domination in terms of structured discursive formations:

> A settler-colonial relationship is one characterized by a particular form of *domination*; that is, it is a relationship where power—in this case, interrelated discursive and nondiscursive facets of economic, gendered, racial, and state power—has been structured into a relatively secure or sedimented set of hierarchical social relations that continue to facilitate the *dispossession* of Indigenous peoples of their lands and self-determining authority.[65]

The institutionalization of information practices required the creation of categories by which information could be organized, "reinforcing and producing the human through a set of foreclosures, radical erasures, that are, strictly speaking, refused the possibility of cultural articulation."[66] Weheliye's aim is to "underscore just how comprehensively the coloniality of Man suffuses the disciplinary and conceptual formations of knowledge we labor under, and how far we have yet to go in decolonizing these structures."[67] Libraries, archives, and museums provide empirical evidence about their own ordering techniques and the ways that they continue to uphold the genres of being as delineated by colonial powers. They offer material for "thinking through the political and institutional dimensions of how certain forms of violence are monumentalized and others are relegated to the margins of history."[68] Colonial knowledge organization systems also demonstrate the concept of "ontological genocide."[69] In other words, the taxonomic techniques described here were integral to the "purposeful destructive targeting of out-group cultures so as to destroy or weaken them in the process of conquest or domination."[70]

Jefferson's "literacy situation" serves as a medium through which to work through concepts of coproduction and agency in conditions of enslavement, disenfranchisement, and colonization, as well as the paradox that arises in facilitating access to information.[71] Coproduction signals the ways that "social norms, policies, and institutional frameworks shape a context that make some technologies appear inevitable and others impossible."[72] Technologies and society are mutually constitutive: "One loops back in to reinforce, shape, or disrupt the actions of the other, although it should be understood that, because power is held unevenly, such multidirectional influences do not happen evenly."[73] As Andrew Woolford contends in his conceptualization of ontological genocide, "The material aspects of life that we define as physical and biological are enmeshed with the frames provided by our cultures, just as these cultures are co-constituted by our relations with our material world."[74] The framing devices that structure information contribute to the establishment of a regime of truth that secures colonial power. Information technologies are not simply inert devices that store information for retrieval and communication, but rather, the technologies themselves are a form of writing that activate and are inscribed by categories and conventions, convey the priorities and worldview of the people who create them, and "make the material world through interactions between the human and the other-than-human."[75] In Jefferson's information techniques we find classes of people who were designated as lamentable, chattel, comforts, or property, as opposed to people who counted as citizens; those *about* whom information was gathered and classified versus those *for* whom that information was collected, organized, and distributed—people who could claim ownership of information, and people who could not; and those who could claim access to human rights, and those who could not. The people who owned other people also owned and controlled information about those people. Gendered and racialized categories are not incidental to the organization of knowledge, but have been instrumental to the white, heteropatriarchal backbone upon which American information systems and literacy have been constructed and how they relate to present global standards. The very particularity of "universal" knowledge organization techniques and structures becomes apparent in the light of the complex interchange between Jefferson's many local classificatory grids and their global applications.

## "Heighten the Contradictions"

The conditions of our own present are mediated by an ever-increasing proliferation of information, much of which has been reduced to taglines and tweets that are, by their very nature, over-simplifying and polarizing. In so many online discussions of Jefferson in spaces like newspaper comment sections, I have seen extraordinarily reductive, emotionally charged claims that assert either that he was a monster or an idealized father figure. What this tells me is that people are very invested in Jefferson as a figure and use him to channel their own experiences and politics. Jefferson has become a monument and a site for spectacle and speculation about the fate of the nation. My hope is that digging into the complexities inherent to the establishment of libraries, archives, and museums will help us to reassert the guiding principles of liberty, equality, and justice from which they emerged, while exposing the ways that these institutions are also structured by an agenda intended to secure those principles for white men. I care deeply about these institutions, and like Jefferson, I believe in our own capacity to strengthen them as spaces for political participation, learning, and connection. However, there are lasting consequences embedded in the ideological and technical infrastructures that undergird access to information in these institutions. Those problems derive from assumptions about the people who were meant to be informed and those who were regarded as informational. By coming to terms with the ways in which these ordering principles have functioned in an ongoing settler colonial imaginary, we can collectively perform acts that undermine the oppressive regimes of truth on which they are based while preserving the essential tenets that guard freedom and aspire to equality. Libraries, archives, and museums are spaces from which one can assemble factual evidence that informs and gives shape to the conditions for political action. Fred Moten and Stefano Harney's call to "heighten the contradictions" in the context of museums and universities is useful for working through the paradoxical nature of cultural and educational institutions more broadly.[76] Their call to action is one that not only critiques but works toward collectively confronting the structures and institutions that support and sustain oppression. The wager is that the "logic of contradiction can actually serve as a principle of intelligibility and rule of action in political struggle."[77] As library historian Christine Pawley notes, "contradiction . . . is a condition that characterizes the field."[78]

Scholars like Sylvia Wynter and Gayatri Spivak have pointed to Foucault's limitations, which derive in part from the fact that he is of the systems that he analyzes. It has been widely observed that Foucault is limited in his analysis of the biopolitics of slavery in the context of colonialism and the early Americas. He was aware of the barriers to seeing the system from within, expressing the condition of trying to understand the rupturing event that resulted in the Enlightenment while still residing in an Enlightenment-era order of things: "This event, probably because we are still caught inside it, is largely beyond our comprehension."[79] Wynter's critique of Foucault's history of the human sciences centers on the "overrepresentation of Man"—"the ongoing imperative of securing the well-being of our present ethnoclass (i.e., Western bourgeois) conception of the human, Man, which overrepresents itself as if it were the human itself."[80] Wynter's analysis pairs well with Spivak's assessment of Foucault in dialogue with Gilles Deleuze on the topic of "intellectuals and power," in which she says that they cannot see their own failure in accounting for ideology in relations of power and their complicity in upholding divisions and ways of seeing through their intellectual frames and positions of authority. According to Spivak, Foucault "seems unaware that the intellectual within socialized capital, brandishing concrete experience, can help consolidate the international division of labor by making one model of concrete experience *the* model."[81] Foucault is not terribly unlike Jefferson, citing and reciting knowledge claims that uphold a universalized Western European Man, even as he contemplates the history of relations of power in the *order of things*. Both seem unable to account for their own desires in their intellectual pursuits about knowledge and power. But more importantly, in the context of the question of whether the subaltern can speak, Sally Hemings is just one of so many people that lived at Monticello that call us to listen, even if her testimony was never recorded and archived, even if she could not write (we have no conclusive evidence that she could or could not write), even if the historical record about her life is sparse. As Annette Gordon-Reed has painstakingly demonstrated, Sally Hemings's story speaks volumes, in spite of all the attempts from Jefferson himself to the historians who deny the truth of their relationship, to silence it.[82]

Still, Foucault is indispensable for research on Jefferson and information, and his work is best understood in dialogue with critical theorists that speak directly to the matters of racial capitalism, settler colonialism, and the exchange of women in early America. I will invoke his work throughout these chapters. The task of the observer of systems is to figure out how they function by ways of codes and distinctions.[83] This is a challenge, of course, because the researcher cannot step outside the system and see it objectively. Everything "is self-referentially observed and described."[84] This is not to suggest that objectivity is the goal, nor do I mean that we are not capable of knowing the self and others. Quite the opposite, really. As Karen Barad writes, "Practices of knowing and being are not isolable; they are mutually implicated. We don't obtain knowledge by standing outside the world; we know because we are *of* the world."[85] Placing distance between the self and others is a way of producing a false objectivity, and with it an illusion of neutrality and disinterest. The removal of the self from the world being observed can also deny the co-constitution of the world and self.

Information and communication systems have become naturalized so that most people are unaware of the ways that they condition what can be known and how. The objective, then, is to "observe the conditionings by which they distinguish and designate."[86] Niklas Luhmann suggests a method designed "to observe how other observers render invisible the paradoxes that get in their way." Intentionally situating oneself in the paradox is required, in part because it is impossible not to, but also because such a vantage point foregrounds the necessary condition of paradox itself. This presents an opportunity to see why "every projection, every setting of a goal, every formation of an episode necessitates recursive observation and why, furthermore, recursive observation makes possible not so much the elimination of paradoxes as their temporal and social distribution onto different operations."[87] The consequences of Jefferson's classificatory decisions in the context of the formation of the United States result in part from the fact that they were installed in the systems that circulated the information by which citizens were informed and over time have become reified with use and repetition across agencies and locations. The effect is the replication and amplification of whiteness by the figuration of racialized peoples in the margins, which mark them always as others that support and affirm the framework that universalizes Man.

Luhmann also identifies a significant shift in the production of ontologies in the eighteenth century from hierarchical stratification toward "functional differentiation," which operated through requisite function systems that featured "their own ways to transform equality into inequality and freedom into restraint."[88] The result was a new kind of paradox and "a new semantics of modernity" at the end of the eighteenth century. This helps to explain how our public institutions are simultaneously sites where the expansion of democratic processes and greater inclusion seem possible, while at the same time, such processes are inherently constrained by the structuring mechanisms that organize the functions of the institutions themselves. One needs only to read the classifications by which information on the shelves and in online spaces is organized to see how distinctions are written into information architectures and affect access. The paradox is that in order to obtain books about racialized, gendered, and sexualized others, one has to submit to a system that marks these subjects as "other," "special," "elements in the population," or even as "social pathology," as in the case of books about disability, addiction, poverty, and animal welfare, which are shelved in the HV section of the Library of Congress Classification. These divisions reflect the usefulness of knowledge about a subject in relation to a normative white knower and a state that has historically universalized Man. The classification maps the functions and implied disfunctions of each classified other. I will return to the paradoxical aspects of information and its technologies in Chapter 3.

## Architectures

To clarify what is meant by "information architectures," let's return to the Library of Congress. Any library space is defined by several types of architectures, but the Library of Congress is remarkable for its size, scope, and grandeur. The design of the library building, the over eight hundred miles of library shelves that contain twenty-four million books and other printed materials, the classifications, metadata, standards, and hardware that enable findability in the catalog and on the web, and the networks that connect libraries to one another and their users are interconnected architectures that facilitate access to information.[89]

In 1897 the library was moved into a new building—a spectacular work of architecture, aptly named the Thomas Jefferson Building (see Figure 5). The James Madison Memorial Building (opened in 1980) and the John Adams Building (opened in 1939)—are connected to the Jefferson building through underground tunnels. The Jefferson building is situated next door to the US Supreme Court and across the street from the US Capitol building, which is also connected to the library by a tunnel for efficient delivery of documents to members of Congress. The interior of the building is exquisitely decorated with statues of important historical figures, including Francis Bacon, Homer, and Christopher Columbus, as well as sculptures that symbolize the disciplines—history, philosophy, etc. Colorful mosaics and quotes from scholars and poets from Western history are inscribed in tiles along the walls and ceilings.[90] The details of the interior and exterior are too vast to describe here, but it suffices to say that the building presents itself as a magnificent temple to knowledge. When the Jefferson building opened, librarians of Congress

Figure 5. Thomas Jefferson Building, Aerial View. Photo credit: Carol M. Highsmith, Wikimedia Commons.

reclassified its holdings, developing the shelf classification system that we use today, based in part on Jefferson's core ideas about universality and progress. The Library of Congress, with its various types of architectures, is also a monument to Jeffersonian principles and the intimate relation between knowledge and government.

The Library of Congress is now the largest library in the world, but its operations began under Jefferson's presidency in 1801.[91] That early library was destroyed by British troops during the War of 1812, at which point Jefferson sold his personal library and offered his classified catalog to Congress. His collection and catalog were formative for the way that his priorities and tastes became inscribed into national memory, in what stands today as the largest federal cultural agency in the United States. The classifications that order books on library shelves and content in digital libraries are derived from Jefferson's own vision for his home library at Monticello and reflect his beliefs about universality and the intrinsic connection between information, self-mastery, and democratic republican government. Similarly, what I will demonstrate throughout this book, is that the hierarchies and categories that structure information in libraries, archives, museums, and government offices are monumental for their power to concentrate meaning into a single structure through processes of abstraction and universalization. Classificatory names and hierarchies serve as indicators of what counts as knowledge in the minds of the classifiers. It is through far less spectacular (and indeed, to most people, invisible) monuments to universal principles that the idealization of whiteness and property are extended into the daily lives of library visitors in the United States and around the globe.[92] Following Ronald Day, I look to modern library classifications to "expose the process by which language passes through the machinery of authoritative rhetorical devices and institutions for the purposes of ideological control."[93] Enlightenment-era politics and science gave rise to the possibility of a "universal library," and today's Library of Congress continues to espouse this idea as its aspiration and promise.[94] Now more commonly called "global classifications," the universal classifications that were designed to organize collections are enmeshed in the same universalizing discourses that produced and idealized Man as the proper human.

Jefferson's home and landscape architectures, as well as his architectural designs for the state buildings, and his vast array of information architectures inform our understanding of how he inscribed power and ideology into the built environment. His personal library catalog became the foundation for the catalog of the legislative branch of the United States; his ideas about archival preservation put a set of values and practices into motion; his museum was the result of expeditions and has a direct connection to national natural history museums; and his ideas about education, travel, political participation, and efficiency, were all integral to the formation of information infrastructures that facilitated circulation and communication. Knowledge organization systems like library classifications are often overlooked because they are invisible to most users, but it is precisely their hiddenness and their purpose as circulatory systems that make them particularly significant for understanding the ways in which knowledge was structured to secure relations of power in the late eighteenth century.[95] Rather than focusing on the content that can and cannot be retrieved, studying information architectures turns toward the ways in which hierarchies and naming techniques influence how people encounter information. There can be no question that the accumulation of texts across bureaucratic institutions, on library shelves, in print and online, organized around assumed norms, affect our consciousness and how research is done across the disciplines.

An information architectural component such as a classification is not spectacular, but it does the heavy support work, making the presentation and display of information possible, allowing the ordering principles to appear as natural, or creating the illusion that the information in front of us just ontologically happens to be as it appears. What these have in common with the monuments that are intended to be seen is that "the architecture of the memorial stages encounter."[96] Whereas Christina Sharpe cautions about the tendency for monuments to repeat and reify racial and sexual violence by putting scenes of destruction on display for visitors to contemplate, the structures that I will be describing throughout this book stage encounters with information by ordering the information that people seek and use. A library shelf, for example, displays books according to a classification system that has the violence of racism built into it, with alphabetized lists of racial, ethnic, and religious minorities in subcategories labeled "elements of the population" or "special topics." A state-sponsored museum displays material objects that were acquired, cataloged, and preserved by theft and the application of terms of ownership as defined by imperial powers. Imbued with the principles upon which they were constituted, the information architectures monumentalize the universalization of whiteness and heteropatriarchy by indexing particular actors, places, and events.

The desire to make information accessible to the people who want and need to use it is confounded by the fact that the standards for organizing information are still based on universalizing and racializing discourses associated with the founding of the United States. The operationalization of information in systems has been essential to circulating a national fantasy, and racial engineering has been central to the technologies that sustain that vision. My intervention is to unearth the processes by which capital, eighteenth-century natural philosophy, and state power converged in Jefferson's cataloging methods. My claim is that the information architectures that organize the materials held within these institutions are mechanisms by which cultural and political divisions endure, and close examination of Jefferson's information creation, management, and use reveals some of the processes by which problems associated with settler colonialism, racism, and heteropatriarchy have become systemic. The fact that these systems are mostly unseen by users means that information organization functions to conceal, even as it facilitates access to information. As we will see with Jefferson's classificatory impulse, information architectures are projections of a particular point of view, and when they are deployed in political contexts, that point of view frames the search, retrieval, and use of information. Cataloging, classification, search, and retrieval are all acts of memorializing and re-memorializing.

In an essay on books, architecture, and democracy, Barry Bergdoll has pointed to the potential for meaningful research that situates Jefferson's library within the context of monuments. He notes that Jefferson acquired most of the key French works on the concept of the monument, thus presenting a potential research topic with respect to Jefferson's library, as well as the "role of the monument in shaping civic virtues and public values."[97] I suggest that we might consider the very monumentality of Jefferson's libraries and other sites of information architecture. As a function of their role "between memory and history" information architectures mediate human encounters with information and affect our experiences of searching for and finding information.[98] The recording and ordering of memory affect how we do history, what counts as historical, and how historical narratives are produced. That is not to say that they do not allow for different uses or interpretations. As with any type of monument, people project their individual and collective fantasies and desires onto archival records, rare books, museum objects, and historical figures. They put them to use for the advancement of theory or their political positions in their own time, drawing them into narratives that serve their present purposes. Indeed, "no one historian's archive is ever like another's."[99] The historical record is open to a multitude of readings, and the possibilities for interpretations shift over time. "There is a deep politics to memory," writes Katharyne Mitchell, "and each age attempts to refashion and remake memory to serve its own contemporary purposes." Mitchell continues, "memory is sustained through the interplay between collective recollection and repetition." The repetitions of similar rituals in many places affirms a "highly idealized, composite image," which provides a framework upon which people form their own individual memories.[100] The capacity for remembrances to endure depends upon and reenacts relations of power. At the same time, the potential for narratives and counternarratives is ongoingly expansive, and different possibilities for their activation arrive with every generation and social movement. This is as true of information architectures as it is of monuments and memorials like statues and landmarks. Just as the collective projects of resistance have resulted in the removal and contextualization of statues erected to commemorate certain historical figures and events, community archivists, library workers, and their publics are revising, augmenting, decolonizing, and indigenizing the tools and techniques by which library, archives, and museum collections and education curricula are ordered. For example, the extraordinary Getting Word African American Oral History Project at Monticello, which "preserves the histories of Monticello's enslaved families and their descendants," features over two hundred oral history interviews that work toward a more complete story of the various lived experiences on Jefferson's plantation.[101]

Framing this project in terms of monumentality aids in the discussion about possibilities for action in response to what critical information scholars observe about the othering effects of information architectures in the present.[102] It serves as an intervention in navigating efforts toward dismantling the racializing structures that support white supremacy and American dominance in cultural and educational organizations in the United States and beyond. Is it enough to redescribe, add and subtract categories, or use the systems as opportunities to teach library and archives users about the coloniality of information?[103] Do revisions and contextualizations actually serve to reinforce certain structures and uphold Man? In some cases, might we need to do what seems impossible and melt them down altogether to make something else? These are conversations that I hope extend from the research presented in this book.

# PART 1

## *Archives*

# 1
# Information as Revolutionary Action

Consciously, or unconsciously, each maker of schemes puts into his work a part of himself, his background, his interests, and his prejudices, as well as the knowledge of his age.

—LEO LAMONTAGNE, *AMERICAN LIBRARY CLASSIFICATIONS WITH SPECIAL REFERENCE TO THE LIBRARY OF CONGRESS*

This event, probably because we are still caught inside it, is largely beyond our comprehension.

—FOUCAULT, *ORDER OF THINGS*

On 30 April 1775, Thomas Jefferson wrote to Ebenezer Hazard to commend him on his ambitious plan to gather and preserve the documentary heritage of the British colonies in North America. Jefferson stated that this early archival project was "an undertaking of great utility" for its potential to contribute "*to the information* of all those concerned in the administration of government," as well as any historian that would benefit from materials that a person "would otherwise acquire with great difficulty and perhaps not acquire at all."[1]

Jefferson used the word "information" in this letter in accord with an eighteenth-century definition, which associated the concept with the action of imparting knowledge by shaping the mind or character, or communicating to instruct.[2] It is rare that we hear the word "information" as an action word today, but in the context of building an archive while the colonies were bursting with revolutionary potential, Jefferson used the term as both a verb and a noun. Information is otherwise generally regarded as a thing—a set of facts or data, an insight found in a book or article, or a report on the weather, the census, or the actions of government. Information is something that can be stored, processed, managed, and retrieved. It can be acted upon—used, consulted, and consumed—or created in acts of production. It can be delivered in the news, circulated in libraries, or transmitted via broadcast media or over the internet. Things become informational by virtue of their usefulness to humans. "For something to be information," James Elmborg explains, "there must be a person who is informed. Information is therefore, literally, that substance which the informing material transmits to the person informed."[3] Even when information is intangible, it still has a thingness to it, as in the kind of information that circulates in gossip channels, or the images, facts, or ideas, stored in a person's memory. Information can be factual or untrue. Misinformation is still information, whether errors and untruths are transmitted intentionally or accidentally. And, as Michael Buckland writes, "'information-as-thing,' by whatever name, is of especial interest in relation to information systems because ultimately information systems, including 'expert systems' and information retrieval systems, can deal directly with information *only* in this sense."[4] Without things, there isn't material to process or be known.

Jefferson understood information in all of these ways, but in this letter to Hazard, Jefferson was conveying the concept of information as *revolutionary action*. By coupling it with "utility," Jefferson was also highlighting the usefulness of information for government and making history.

Ebenezer Hazard's plan for an archival program in the nascent and newly United States of America was intended not only to ensure the posterity of foundational colonial documents, but also to facilitate greater access to what Jefferson described as the "monuments of the infancy of our country" and "of our property and our history."[5] To accomplish this prodigious task, all of the important documents would have to be systematically gathered, copied, and bound in printed volumes, a project to which Jefferson contributed. Jefferson first wrote to Hazard in 1775, less than a year after he penned "A Summary View of the Rights of British America," a lengthy text that is widely regarded as the precursor to the Declaration of Independence. Using the tools and training of a lawyer's trade, Jefferson drew upon documentary evidence from the historical record to build his case against the Crown. In his application of this historical method in the "Summary View," he extended his narrative back to the Norman Conquest, and identified the 1651 treaty between the Crown and the Virginia colony, which established settlers' rights to land and trade. "Resolved, that it be an *instruction*," begins the "Summary View," announcing Jefferson's intention for how this document should be used by the delegates to the first Continental Congress.[6] "*History has informed us*," wrote Jefferson, "that bodies of men, as well as individuals, are susceptible of the spirit of tyranny."[7] As he would later do in the Declaration, he submitted an account of historical facts, up to and including the actions and inactions of the British Parliament and King George III, as evidence of the Crown's abuse of power. By outlining a series of "unwarrantable encroachments and usurpations" in detail, he established evidence of a pattern of systematic abuses.[8] History, for Jefferson, was informationally useful.

The Declaration of Independence is, in form and substance, a similarly well-reasoned argument beginning with several premises, including the "self-evident" truth that people are endowed with unalienable rights. It also presents historical evidence to show how this inviolable truth had been breached:

> The history of the present King of Great Britain is a history of repeated injuries and usurpations, all having in direct object the establishment of an absolute Tyranny over these States.
>
> To prove this let Facts be submitted to a candid world.

The defense of the Declaration proceeds with a catalog of offenses against the people living in the British colonies that demonstrate why, based on the facts and the truth of the premises, it had become "necessary for one people to dissolve the political bands which have connected them with another."[9] He would rely on this historical method throughout his career, and he continued to actively participate in the collection, preservation, access, and use of historical documents.

It is relatively plain to see that the Declaration of Independence has become a monument, having attained a particularly poignant status in this moment of celebration and reflection on the 250th anniversary of its signing. Hannah Arendt's reading of the Declaration places its significance in its form, signaling the way that this document is fundamentally grounded in action: "No doubt there is a grandeur in the Declaration of Independence," writes Arendt, "but it consists not in its philosophy and not even so much in its being 'an argument in support of an action' as in its being the perfect way *for an action to appear in words*." Citing Jefferson's reflections on the writing of the document, where he says that "it was intended to be an expression of the American mind," Arendt continues: "And since we deal here with the written, and not with the spoken word, we are confronted with one of the rare moments in history when the power of action is great enough to erect its own monument."[10] In Arendt's view, this action-put-into-words has become an object that has attained the status of a monument.

Jefferson wanted present and future Americans to learn from the lessons of the past, and archives held a unique potential for instruction. In his only published book, *Notes on the State of Virginia*, he wrote, "History by apprising them of the past will enable them to judge of the future; it will avail them of the experience of other times and other nations; it will qualify them as judges of the actions and designs of men; it will enable them to know ambition under every disguise it may assume; and knowing it, to defeat its views."[11] Jefferson believed that documentary evidence served as the most authoritative source of facts. In *Notes on the State of Virginia*, he famously wrote, "A patient pursuit of facts, and cautious combination and comparison of them, is the drudgery to which man is subjected by his Maker, if he wishes to attain sure knowledge."[12] The primacy with which he accorded recorded knowledge was tied to his extraordinary efforts to keep, preserve, copy, and facilitate access to primary historical records. His philosophy is evident in his early writings, and arguably, it was his own "pursuit of facts" that laid the groundwork for gaining independence and American expansion.[13] Documenting the history of the emerging republic was particularly urgent in the time leading up to and following the signing of the Declaration of Independence. Collection and preservation were methods that were imagined to counter or contain the precarity and uncertainty of the revolution. Jefferson knew that his personal archives would be read in ways that would affect the nation's progress. He cared about the founders' legacy, and he also held firmly in the belief that future generations would continue to improve the republic. For that to be possible, they would need to refer to the nation's history.

The same writings that demonstrate the utility of historical documents in furnishing the evidence upon which the United States would dissolve its political ties with Great Britain also reveal Jefferson's attitudes and beliefs about land, slavery, and Indigenous and Black peoples. In the "Summary View," he accused the king of reducing white Americans to slavery and imposing the institution of the importation and enslavement of Africans on the colonies. "The abolition of domestic slavery is the great object of desire in those colonies, where it was unhappily introduced in their infant state," wrote Jefferson, who, at the time of that writing, owned the lives and labor of 190 people.[14] In his original draft of the Declaration, Jefferson again referred to slavery—"[the king] has waged cruel war against human nature itself, violating it's most sacred rights of life & liberty in the persons of a distant people who never offended him, captivating & carrying them into slavery in another hemisphere, or to incur miserable death in their transportation thither"—but that language was edited out of the final, signed version.[15]

From these documents we also see that Jefferson and his colleagues believed the land to be the property of settlers. There is no mention of Indigenous rights to the land. Jefferson was unequivocal in his explanation of white settlers' rights in the "Summary View": "Their own blood was spilt in acquiring lands for their settlement, their own fortunes expended in making that settlement effectual; for themselves they fought, for themselves they conquered, and for themselves alone they have right to hold." He also blamed the king for causing war between the colonies and Indigenous peoples. The last item on the list of grievances in the Declaration states that the king "has excited domestic insurrections amongst us, and has endeavoured to bring on the inhabitants of our frontiers, the merciless Indian Savages, whose known rule of warfare, is an undistinguished destruction of all ages, sexes and conditions."[16] Referring to Indigenous people as "savages" served to mark a distinction between them and the "civilized" British Americans. What is strikingly absent from the Declaration or most other early American public papers is any account of the lives and experiences of the people who were disenfranchised, enslaved, displaced, and killed at the hands of European settlers. Jefferson's historical accounts effectively erased Black and Indigenous histories, marked time with British milestones, declared the land to be property, and selectively presented historical information to make a case for American independence.

Jefferson and his colleagues were doing more than producing, collecting, and storing information—they were part of a societal shift toward the making of an "information state" and a "fundamental shift in what political information means."[17] Randolph Head ascribes this shift to a European early modern notion of information that "involved a process of communication from world to political actors, which took place when traces of a past action or situation (increasingly in writing) informed a political actor in the present."[18] This suggests a change in the concept, management, and use of information that aligned with actions of the state, and at least a tacit understanding that actions can be transmitted and inform decisions across generations. The other effect of this change was to reify information as a thing, which also opened the possibility for it to be commodified. Head locates this conceptual shift in early modern Europe during a transition to archival "information states," where "the term 'information' gained a second, novel meaning: rather than being the process by which the world informed rulers, information became the raw material that entered the registry. Divided into categories and circulated in coded documents, information in a registry became a thing, a substance to be processed by the state."[19] Further to this point, Christine Pawley and Geoffrey Nunberg both provide explanations for another shift from information as action to information as thing in the mid-nineteenth century. Nunberg notes that it was at this time that information no longer referred to "the instruction derived from books, but the content of books from which the instruction is derived."[20] This change in purpose, perhaps more accurately described as the "datafication of information,"[21] resituated "the agency of instruction to the text and its producers" and reduced the reader "to the role of passive consumer of content."[22] In this analysis, according to Pawley, the concept of information "shifted from an effect to a cause, but a cause inextricably linked to books and reading."[23] It is probably most appropriate to say that this shift became firmly institutionalized in the eighteenth and nineteenth centuries, depending upon political and geographical conditions, with a concomitant shift in the formation and function of state libraries, archives, and museums. I suggest that the interlocking processes of capital and information management may best be understood in this revolutionary moment when planters were statesmen. Jefferson's particular investments in the founding of the nation and natural sciences were central to their institutionalization, and the cultivation of an information literate citizenry was essential for the functioning of the young republic.

Trained in law, educated among the Virginia planter elite, and invested in the natural sciences, Jefferson's information organization techniques were practical, but Jefferson the archivist also knew he was writing into the future. Thomas Jefferson's libraries, documentary records, and museum are instructive for understanding the ways that information conditions the possibilities for political action. I focus on Jefferson and his documentary techniques to show the ways that his information practices derived from life, his intimate and public relations, and his public offices. He was influenced by people and ideas that came before him, and as a polymath, he promiscuously borrowed techniques from a variety of traditions. His "infolust" was profound, but it was certainly not isolated, and he inherited many techniques from the Renaissance, a period that experienced an information explosion, due in part to a "new attitude toward seeking out and stockpiling information."[24] Early modern writers believed that improved information management techniques would protect against the loss of cultural memory. Jefferson inherited the notion that storing and cataloging information were vital to preserving personal, cultural, and national memory, and he produced, used, managed, and structured information in and across public, planter, and domestic domains. Information was instrumental to building the young republic, and the entirety of Jefferson's strategies, combined with communications with his friends and colleagues across the republic of letters, might be regarded as a "technology of collective fantasy."[25] Vincent Brown, historian of slavery and founder of Harvard's History Design Studio, articulates the ways that archives are sites of activity and activation:

> When we shift our emphasis from historical recovery to rigorous and responsible creativity, we recognize that archives are not just

> the records bequeathed to us by the past; archives also consist of the tools we use to explore it, the vision that allows us to read its signs, and the design decisions that communicate our sense of history's possibilities."[26]

Making sense of the principles on which knowledge was organized in the late eighteenth and early nineteenth centuries requires an investigation into the logics that drove the desire to classify, the desires underlying the categories themselves and their arrangements, and the ways that ideology is structured by those desires.

Following Roderick Ferguson, who thinks in terms of "critical possibilities," I too believe that creative and scholarly interventions hold potential to interrogate institutions and their practices—not only to report about institutions' failures to live up to their proclamations about diversity, inclusion, equity, and freedom, but how they also succeed, even if only provisionally. There are good models for using these institutions for the benefit of collective life.[27] Information is not only useful and essential for political and daily life, but encounters with information also continually alter us affectively and relationally. Perhaps the most important aspect of these institutions is their potential for facilitating expansive possibilities for circulation of information through and in minds and bodies, objects, images, and stories, and spaces and places across time. To be a participant in this web of relations—to be touched by information, and to be carried and inspired by ideas in all kinds of mediums, genres, and formats—can be a magical, if sometimes terrifying way of inhabiting the world. To be open to this kind of possibility is to my mind one definition of freedom. As Bonnie Honig writes, "we apprehend the adhesive and integrative powers of things and the dependence of all collected—not just of citizens and publics but also of crowds and commons—on things and their powers of enchantment."[28] We tend to think of information as utility, but informational things like books and interpretation can also be sources of enchantment, self-discovery, and expression—channels for desire, and points of connection. The processes that contribute to the operationalization of information, including the decisions about information entities that contribute to their utility, affect their circulation within and beyond the agencies that hold them.

Viewing information as a thing that participates in public realms—as something that is acted upon but also acts, and as essential to the expansion of *Dingpolitik* (politics of things), as well as *action* in and of itself—opens space for thinking with information in public institutions like national, state, and municipal public libraries, archives, and museums, as well as parallel spaces that emerge out of communities and collectives.[29] In his call for *Dingpolitik*, Bruno Latour expressed the need for an "object-oriented democracy" on the basis of the failure of matters of fact. "Fact" is not precisely synonymous with "information," but they can be thought together.[30] "Information, on its own, is an abstract concept with little factual value; rather, it is the labour, work, and material practices involved in documentation that transform abstract information into fact."[31] Latour's frame is useful for considering the consequences of divorcing information from action and agency, the flattening of our own encounters with information, and how we come to self-knowledge and knowledge about the world via informational things. Things, according to Latour, "are much more interesting, variegated, uncertain, complicated, far reaching, heterogeneous, risky, historical, local, material, and networky than the pathetic version offered for too long by philosophers." Latour also reminds his readers, via Heidegger, that "the old word 'Thing' or 'Ding' designated originally a certain type of archaic assembly."[32] The *Oxford English Dictionary* also reveals that "thing" was used as a verb once upon a time— "To plead the cause of, supplicate or intercede for, make intercession for; to bring to reconciliation." The *OED* also offers a definition that shows that, even in more recent history, it has been occasionally used as an action that impresses upon the thingness of a thing: "To view or express as a thing; to represent by means of material objects; to reify." In sum, information-as-thing is enriched if we think about the actions and agency of information and how it is activating through various kinds of encounters, especially in public institutions where people go to find things out. Information is among the public things that Bonnie Honig describes when she writes, "Public things constitute citizens equally, as citizens, or ought to, and can be made, sometimes, by way of actions in concert, to deliver on that promise."[33]

As Walter Benjamin attests, things that have agency also communicate. In what Hito Steyerl describes as the "weirdest" of Benjamin's writings, "On Language as Such and on the Language of Man," Benjamin considers things that are activated in language: "Man therefore communicates his own mental being (insofar as it is communicable) by *naming* all other things. . . . All nature, insofar as it communicates itself, communicates itself in language, and so finally in man."[34] What Benjamin's observations call to notice is that the boundaries between the named and person who names and anyone who puts that name and the object being named to use are not so easy to distinguish. As Steyerl explains, Benjamin is interested in the acts of translation that happen across and within things. "According to Benjamin," writes Steyerl, "things are never just inert objects, passive items or lifeless shucks at the disposal of the documentary gaze. But they consist of tensions, forces, hidden powers, which keep being exchanged. . . . Thus things can be interpreted as conglomerates of desires, wishes, intensities and power relations. And a *thing language*, which is thus charged with the energy of matter can also exceed description and become productive. It can move beyond representation and become creative in the sense of a transformation of the relations, which define it."[35] The interplay among things and the humans that name them carry potential for expansiveness of interpretation and making connections. I want to press this further to emphasize how necessary it is to have public spaces for these kinds of connections to be possible—places where humans collide with other humans and informational objects of various forms to create meaning, both individually and collectively.

Libraries, archives, and museums are cultural and educational spaces where public things like books, historical documents, and museum objects and artworks—the containers of information, and the technologies that mediate and circulate possibilities for information encounters—are assembled for human use and consultation. In this way, understanding the interaction of informational objects in more-than-human assemblages that exist in different types of public, common, and shared spaces offers a lens through which to consider the ways in which *information events* across time and space have given shape to collective memory, historical processes and methods, teaching and learning, and the institutions that house and activate the informational things that "furnish the world of democratic life."[36] Information is a kind of object that "moves through the application of specific media practices—practices that form nascent publics and shape their demands. Information is articulated to political visions of what might be. . . . In its movement and use, information makes promises that are much greater than 'finding things out.'"[37] Recognizing the materiality of information—not just as bits and bytes, but as that which is contained in documents and other forms, as well as that which acts—allows for an expansion of what it means to be informed. We might say that we are constantly in a state of processing information as it appears to us in everyday objects and events. More than that, though, humans and more-than-human worlds are also always in-formation, as our bodies mediate and transmit information through speech, acts, and being, and we are informed by our encounters with other humans, with every informational encounter. Scholars have described the ways in which humans have become datafied for corporate and government use. The idea that "we are data" drives home the ways that our online behaviors are tracked, counted, and fed into large data centers for the purposes of surveillance and marketing.[38] But on a much more humane level—one that I suggest we can embrace if we remember that "data are people," that what we do with information has a bearing on our own and others' lives, we can also find ways to live ethically and well in a world saturated with information, informational beings, and information communication technologies.[39]

## Information "Technologies of the Self" and Nation

It has become commonplace to identify Thomas Jefferson as a key figure in the installation of democracy and human rights on the basis of the universalization of the white, propertied, male subject. We also know that, in addition to being the principal author of the Declaration of Independence, which states axiomatically that "all men are created equal," many of his writings feature the rationalization of the enslavement, displacement, disenfranchisement, and elimination of African Americans and Indigenous peoples. Despite his stated abhorrence for the institution of slavery, Jefferson owned at least 607 enslaved lives over the course of his own lifetime. Some of Jefferson's most intimate interactions with people who were enslaved—most notably Sally Hemings—both informed and contradicted his political pronouncements, policies, and scientific conclusions. Less understood is the extent to which Jefferson produced, organized, and used *information* to construct a national imaginary—one that cultivated an idea of a citizenry in his vision, and to use Lauren Berlant's terms, circulated a "national fantasy."[40] For Jefferson, the acquisition, mastery, control, and circulation of information were "technologies of the self" that he projected from his daily life into his public offices.

In addition to drawing upon history to provide evidence of abuses, the Declaration of Independence also made assertions about self-governance. A newly forming and independent nation needed to be seen as equal to other already existing nations—capable of governing itself and participating in global affairs. It had become "necessary for one people to dissolve the political bands which have connected them with another" and assume "the *separate and equal station* to which the Laws of Nature and of Nature's God entitle them." For Jefferson and his colleagues, the United States of America would be a republic governed by and for the people. This required the truth of the statement that "all men are created equal," which carried the implication that men were capable of governing themselves. A nation of equals would direct the government for all, and that nation would be equal to other nations. Governing, then, required a liberally educated, well-informed, and ordered citizenry. Establishing and justifying the sovereignty of this newly independent nation and its people was essential, and marking non-white others as incapable of self-mastery was one way of confirming the salience and viability of the revolution, i.e., slavery was justified by the belief that Black people were incapable of self-governance. According to this logic planters could also believe in their own benevolence as they looked after the people who were enslaved as "inferior members of their own extended families."[41] Enrico Del Lago unpacks this line of thinking to explain the ways in which it upheld the institution of slavery and planter wealth: "Eighteenth-century Virginian planters referred to classical republicanism in order to uphold their justification of slavery, since in classical republican thought, independence, freedom and autonomy were related to virtue, while dependence and slavery were related to corruption."[42] Racist ideas about dependence, civilization, and self-governance ensured that certain people would remain excluded from liberal democratic processes and participation. People who were racialized as Black and Indigenous were also viewed as threats to an idealized order and the security of the nation.

Information, I argue, was differently deployed in Jefferson's era as a "technology of the self." Jefferson keenly understood that the development and use of information management techniques were mechanisms by which one would govern one's own conduct and the conduct of others. In the context of the emerging United States, accounting for every aspect of the republic was absolutely vital for ensuring its survival and success. Whereas Michel Foucault explains that *writing* is an ancient technique "in the culture of taking care of oneself," I suggest that reorienting the consideration of technologies of the self in terms of *information* points to the operationalization of writings across domestic, market, and political contexts. Information was essential to establishing a self-governing nation that relied upon the will of self-governing individuals. Jefferson's writings are abundant in correspondence about self-conduct and the conduct of others, and across his archive we see that "taking care of oneself" for Jefferson was "linked to constant writing activity."[43] Through his personal writings he actively pursued knowledge of the self, but his writing activity expanded into treatises, policy documents, statistical tables, scientific observations, maps, and diagrams. His personal attitudes and beliefs and his aesthetic values informed his worldview and public life. Jefferson's library catalog is just one of the many informational techniques that Jefferson created at home and then imported into federal offices. Writings were now becoming technologies that were used to inform and instruct an educated public, to govern, and to organize labor and daily life in the early republic. Understanding information as a concept and as material reality is essential to understanding the history of modern governmentality in the United States.

My approach to studying Jefferson's information management techniques is to find the metanarratives embedded in his cataloging and classification codes, i.e., his metadata, his decisions, methods, and mediums for acquiring, collecting, and circulating information, and the mechanisms by and purposes for which he put information to use. I look for the ways in which a "National Symbolic" has been inscribed and memorialized in the information architectures that organize the contents of libraries, archives, and museums. For Lauren Berlant, a "National Symbolic" resides in "the order of discursive practices whose reign within a national space produces, and also refers to, the 'law' in which the accident of birth within a geographic/political boundary transforms individuals into subjects of a collectively-held history."[44] The "accident" of Jefferson's birth into a land-owning elite, and his subsequent roles as political leader, planter, and lawyer is important for understanding his information practices and how they contributed to the formation of collective memory.

## "History Now Organizes the Document"

Jefferson's personal attachments crossed with his political ambitions, and most of his documentary techniques and information technologies were put to use and tested at Monticello. The classifications created by the likes of Carl Linnaeus and Charles Willson Peale, as well as the aesthetic theories advanced by Edmund Burke, William Hogarth, and Henry Home, Lord Kames, and Anthony Ashley Cooper the third earl of Shaftesbury, and the natural and political sciences of people such as the Compte de Buffon, Francis Bacon, Isaac Newton, and John Locke provided the intellectual and conceptual frameworks upon which Jefferson established his own ideas about slavery, citizenship, universality, freedom, happiness, and natural rights. My primary interest in Jefferson's archive resides in his ordering techniques within the materials, how that order matters in making and doing history, and the intimate relationship between the discipline of history, the history of discipline, and organizing information. In Jefferson's era, documents, and more importantly, the organization of those documents, entered into the consciousness of the people making history. As Foucault shows in his *Archaeology of Knowledge*, history came to organize the document. In this moment, history "divides [the document] up, distributes it, orders it, arranges it in levels, establishes series, distinguishes between what is relevant and what is not, discovers elements, defines unities, describes relations."[45] Jefferson and his peers learned from, adapted, and refined existing methods, and supplanted some of them with new ones. I am foregrounding the ordering techniques that situated his documents in an archival and informational field to show that information was disciplined before information science became a discipline. In other words, Jefferson is important for understanding and deepening the history of the "modern invention of information."[46] It should be noted that Jefferson did not use the word "discipline" to describe fields of study. These were not yet regarded as such. He frequently referred to the proper discipline of students, however, and the order of the academic subjects and student discipline should be viewed as co-emergent in this time.

Sylvia Wynter has significantly revised Foucault's account of history, suggesting that the changes that he defined as a rupture were actually refigurations of the events following the invasion of the Americas in 1492. Wynter identifies two critical moments, which incited two versions of Man—what she refers to as Man1 and Man2.[47] Man1 appears in early colonial conquest, when colonizers divided the world between the discovered and the civilized, and geography was projected onto ideological grounds, mapping a "space of otherness." For Wynter, this moment was critical for producing an Other that was outside the "grace" of Judeo-Christian regions, and was deemed irrational and less than human, and therefore expendable. Viewing the "new world" as uninhabitable and uninhabited contributed to a secularism that replaced God's word with science and sensory perception, the foundations of which were laid in natural historical, geographic, and ethnographic studies in colonized lands.

Wynter's revisions of Foucault's histories of biopolitics and knowledge formations show that, even if we identify the French and American revolutions of the eighteenth century to be critical moments in the history of documentation and scientific production, the classificatory techniques that became inscribed in those technoscientific practices had already been in the making for two hundred years, beginning with the division between rational and irrational. European countries were taking censuses of their populations in the Americas long before Jefferson signed the United States' first official census from his position of secretary of state in 1790, and colonial powers produced racializing discourses based on a rational/irrational divide to justify the extermination of Indigenous peoples. As Denise Ferreira da Silva explains, "What Wynter uncovers is that the conditions of possibility—the context of emergence of the refiguring of the 'discourse of race' Foucault locates in the nineteenth century—in fact resides in the division of the Human into the rational European and its irrational (American, African, Asian, Australian, etc.) Others."[48] In the Americas, Jefferson's information techniques were indeed a turning point—a reinscription of Man1 and a prerequisite for Man2 because of the way that "genres of being" were encoded into systems and government-adjacent institutions.

Jefferson's archive helps us to make sense of how informational things were structured according to a political rationality around the time of the formation of the United States. In Jefferson's classificatory practices we gain access to a view of how "the field of normative reason from which governing [was] forged."[49] Following David Lloyd and others, my research has been a project toward understanding how "the constitutive relation between the concepts of universality, freedom, and humanity and the racial order of the modern world is grounded in the founding texts of the disciplines that articulated them."[50] The cultural institutions I am describing here are agencies of the state, and they were designed to serve the men who governed, as well as educate an informed citizenry. The "we" of "we the people," was never an inclusive term, and indeed it depended on the universalization of Man and the unfree conditions of slavery for it to be imagined. The people, or the public, are not given, "but are rather constituted by the lines of demarcation that we implicitly or explicitly establish."[51] Framing the Declaration of Independence and the US Constitution for an imagined "we" was a potent discursive act. As Judith Butler writes, the "discursive move to establish 'the people' in one way or another is a bid to have a certain border recognized, whether we understand that as a border of a nation or as the frontier of that class of people to be considered 'recognizable' as a people."[52] What's at stake in our libraries, museums, and public squares is related to this question of recognizability. Public libraries are sites where drag story times have been possible and even flourished, and they are also spaces that allow participants in anti-2SLGBTQIA+ groups into their public auditoriums to deny and "debate" the reality of the existence of trans and queer children and adults. While the library is a space that aims to be welcoming to all, it is not necessarily experienced as welcoming by everyone equally. If the space is one where the defense of the freedom to read queer and trans books can happen while people's existence is in question, then the library's mission toward equality is uneven and sometimes undermined.

Wendy Brown's analysis helps to explain how public institutions are simultaneously sites of failure and promise: "Liberal democratic practices and institutions almost always fall short of their promise and at times cruelly invert it," writes Brown, "yet liberal democratic principles hold, and hold out, ideals of both freedom and equality universally shared and of political rule by and for the people."[53] Political participation is under threat and undermined in part because of the privatization of public spaces and public forums under neoliberal reason, a condition that is accelerating by design under fascism. Public spaces like libraries and museums, where the things are collected for the education and amusement of their publics, are complicated. As Honig writes, "At their best, public things gather people together, materially and symbolically, and in relation to them diverse peoples may come to see and experience themselves—even if just momentarily—as a common in relation to a commons, a collected if not a collective."[54] It is in these spaces where humans are essential to "the world's ongoing reconfiguring."[55]

One of the guiding aspirations for this project is that it might furnish ground for action. I draw inspiration from the conceptualization of information as revolutionary action, combined with the current turn toward "information activism" among communities that have long been neglected, omitted, and erased in memory institutions like archives, libraries, and museums.[56] This book exposes the strengths and limitations of Jefferson's vision, with an eye toward understanding the continuing contradictions and tensions inherent to universalizing discourses associated with access to information. The dissonances across these institutions, as well as their shortcomings with regard to living up to their roles in the collective American striving toward equality and freedom "have also been the material for a political imaginary exceeding liberal democratic precepts."[57] As Wendy Brown articulates this point, "In addition to harboring an ideal in excess of itself, liberal democracy's divide between the formal principles and concrete existence provides the scene of paradox, contradiction, and at times, even catachresis that social movements of every kind have exploited for more than three centuries."[58] Information is the stuff of history- and citizenry-making, as well as the creation of national imaginaries. Whereas Jefferson's vision was limited to a white settler republic, we can see that democratic institutions can hold potential for expansive public worlds, as well as the limits to that aspiration. The possibilities for revising and disrupting authorized collective memory through collective action and collective organizing have extended to and out of community archives, parallel libraries, and independent museums. By focusing on action, my aim is to insist on information as a public good, rather than a commodity, and to highlight the ways that information is central to doing, making, and thinking in the world. The public places described here are full of information-related activity. I choose to see events like drag queen story hours in public libraries as evidence that the democratic experiment has been working. Our cultural institutions have increasingly become spaces that invite participation for diverse publics, and I suspect that the reason that they have become targets of right-wing vitriol is because democracy was in fact seen to be expanding in these places. Whereas Jefferson encouraged dissent among citizens, fascism sees dissent as betrayal.[59] And whereas public institutions have been working toward equity, diversity, and inclusion, fascism actively exploits and exacerbates a "natural fear of difference."[60]

## Infra-structuring Events

Many of Jefferson's local and personal systems have grown into regional, national, and international information infrastructures in sets and series of events, designs, and modification that gave rise to very large interconnected systems and institutions. Information infrastructures are particularly useful historical sites, as Shannon Mattern explains: "Historical communication infrastructures offer artifacts like pneumatic tubes, gutta-percha-coated telegraph cables, old postal roads, technologies for the production and dissemination of early print forms, palimpsests of writing on city walls, ruins of ancient amphitheaters and old libraries."[61] Infrastructures that tend to come to mind are the public works that facilitate, ease, or obstruct transport and flows of people, goods, and resources—roads, ports, border walls, rails, pipelines, etc. Within and beneath the systems of transport and exchange are infrastructures that both mediate and respond to human and material flows in processes of maintenance, redesign, disuse, and repair. "Infrastructures—as structuring mechanisms materialized—enact a particular configuration on human and non-human motions, and constitute an intent, ideal, or practice imposed."[62] Collectively, the technologies that have been made and remade over time and space contribute to critical historical sensibility that can inform our current production and use of the built environment, including information and its mediating technologies.

*Infra* is a Latin word meaning below or beneath. One might think of a substrate— metaphorically as "something upon which something else 'runs' or 'operates.'"[63] Susan Leigh Star and Karen Ruhleder problematize the metaphor that "presents an infrastructure as something that is built and maintained, and which then sinks into an in-visible background," because an infrastructure that fades into the background or lays hidden beneath the circulating things, hides the relationships across the social and the technical.[64] *Infra* can also mean *within*. It is the *beneath*ness combined with *within*ness that conveys the significance of infrastructure. Infrastructure is a relational concept—architectures become infrastructural in relation to resources and humans whose circulation and flow are facilitated by the structures beneath and within.[65] Infrastructures become infrastructural through social and political processes, as they are "sunk into other structures, social arrangements, and technologies." Star identifies several definitional components of infrastructures—they are embedded in systems and networks, which contributes to the vastness of their reach and scope, and they are inscribed in conventions of practice where they embody the standards by which information practices are institutionalized. All of these elements are the result of design and use within a community. They don't just exist on their own. They have to come into existence through practice. Star also suggests that an infrastructure is learned as part of membership, that the "taken-for-grantedness of artifacts and organizational arrangements is a *sine qua non* of membership in a community of practice," and structured practices like information retrieval become naturalized within that community.[66] In order for meaning to adhere across different places, times, and communities, it has to be repeated in multiple locations or circulated among them. Thus, I regard the systems and institutions described here as continually *becoming infrastructural*. As Paul Edwards writes, "to be modern is to live within and by means of infrastructures . . . they are the connective tissues and circulatory systems of modernity."[67] I am especially curious about the ways that system designs function by way of categories, how they connect resources and people and put things into relationship, and the human and more-than-human relations through which they circulate. In Mattern's description of libraries as infrastructure, she points to "the way a library's collection is stored and made accessible shapes the intellectual infrastructure of the institution," and she argues that library workers and patrons need to "develop . . . new critical capacities to understand the *distributed* physical, technical and social architectures that scaffold our institutions of knowledge and program our values."[68]

In Jefferson's information universe we can observe how his techniques and technologies became large, connected, circulatory systems, co-constructed with other actors of his era, that transmit different kinds of information across publics and governing bodies. Seeing Jefferson's milieu as socio-technical, we find that we are still very much entangled with his information infrastructures. We continue to co-construct these systems in our applications of the present. How should we deconstruct the troubling aspects of systems while preserving certain principles and affordances that most of us hold dear—reading as a practice of freedom, equity of access to information, public education, the right to assemble, and so on? Do these infrastructures continue to reinforce fictions about the founding fathers to the exclusion of people and communities who were marginalized and excluded from their earliest constructions? To what extent do infrastructural racism and inequality in information systems and institutions undermine their aspirations to equity and inclusion?

Jefferson developed and applied a multitude of techniques to serve different purposes in the project of advancing the republic, the state of Virginia, and his plantation, manifesting "an assortment of local attempts to impose classificatory grids on a variety of colonised populations, to particular though coordinated ends."[69] Patrick Wolfe's comparison between settler colonialists' treatment and racialization of Black and Indigenous peoples is instructive here: "As opposed to enslaved people, whose reproduction augmented their owners' wealth, Indigenous people obstructed settlers' access to land, so their increase was counterproductive. In this way, the restrictive racial classification of Indians straightforwardly furthered the logic of elimination."[70] Wolfe suggests that these practices reveal how race is "made in the targeting. . . . Black people were racialized as slaves; slavery constituted their blackness. Correspondingly, Indigenous North Americans were not killed, driven away, romanticized, assimilated, fenced in, bred White, and otherwise eliminated as the original owners of the land but as Indians." Of course, people and communities exceed these constructions, but the classifications provided infrastructure for statecraft. The essential point for Wolfe is that "*invasion is a structure not an event*."[71] The logic of elimination includes the removal of the structures that support Indigenous knowledge and life—from kinship relations and rituals to language and land. Indeed, as J. Kēhaulani Kauanui writes, "Understanding settler colonialism as a structure exposes the fact that colonialism cannot be relegated to the past."[72] At the same time, thinking in terms of structure elides the fact that it was in fact humans who produced structuring techniques that have become naturalized in society. The *structure* that Wolfe describes was created and repeated, beginning with the first European encounters with Indigenous people in what are now called the Americas. And as Sai Englert observes, "the very categories of 'settler' and 'indigenous' should not be understood as pre-existing and immutable realties, nor should they be understood as universal or stable across time and place. Instead, these are political categories, created, institutionalised and policed always anew," and it is "through the process of dispossession, displacement, exploitation and/or elimination that the indigenous and the settler are made and reproduced—the former as its target and the latter as its beneficiary."[73] This is an important point and one that I will examine more fully in other chapters.

The selection and ordering of books are among the "literacy events [that] end up bioculturally shaping the ways we are embodied by the world and the ways we embody it."[74] Jefferson certainly knew this. The many lists of books that he assembled were like today's bestseller lists. He was very much like the librarians of the nineteenth and twentieth centuries who recommended the best reading for moral and social uplift. He was cultivating community and nationhood by sharing a culture of reading and taste and securing a bond among white readers. His catalog outlines the ways that he viewed the subjects in his books in relation to that imagined community, as well as his own personal tastes and preferences. Readers were white settlers, and very often elites, and rather than including Black readers in their community, they read books *about* Black people, Africa, and Africans by white authors. Jefferson's book classification is an ontologized expression of his worldview, and sharing his reading lists was a technique of securing bonds of friendship and nationhood. I view his reading and knowledge organization practices as *(infra-)structuring events* and as information actions.

As Nathan Snaza puts the point, "worlds are evental 'all the way down,'" and as such, instead of focusing on dismantling large-scale systems, one can turn toward the "thresholds where perception and attention are agitated and shift," where "coloniality and its violences adhere in the mind-bogglingly diffuse encounters and 'events.'"[75] In this formulation, any scene presents opportunities to "pay 'maximal' attention, and bring what you can to the event."[76] Applying this approach in the context of libraries, archives, and museums holds so many possibilities for "smaller, seemingly 'minor' forms of anti-antiblack and decolonial agitation."[77] In any given moment we can ask, "What can we do now, here, to break the homogenizing pattern so other futures may arrive?"[78] What conditions made this particular event possible, and how might we intervene to change its course toward freedom?

The events that contribute to information becoming a thing include the creation and application of classificatory apparatuses that situate information objects according to their usefulness and in relation to other information objects. Structures like those devised by Thomas Jefferson produce conditions for finding and using information. Even though the current Library of Congress appears to be structured very differently from Jefferson's original design, it carries forth his universalizing ideas about readers and reading by building "others," "elements of the population," and "special topics" around a structure based on the assumption that readers were white, male, Christian, and middle class. The re formation of the Library of Congress classification into hierarchical structures across academic disciplines has in fact reified divisions according to social, political, geographic, and economic categories. And with every application of that system by library catalogers who classify books and locate them on library shelves, that system becomes stronger. What we have is an "evental ontology of the world," one in which the library space and the subjects within it are "always becoming in and as events."[79] The people that interact with these systems are affected by these information events. These events have shaped how we do research and how we find information about everyday activities. The transfer of Jefferson's classified catalog to the library of the United States Congress was a structuring event that codified subjects at the same time that it codified a federal cultural institution in law. The present Library of Congress Classification is reiterated across libraries around the world, which means that every library that uses this system is engaging in ontological events that shape information worlds and the encounters that are possible. And when people use these libraries, the systems are reactivated with their engagement.

Understanding information as actions, events, things, *and* structures also aids in thinking about how Jeffersonian reason informs a "historical ontology of ourselves." Foucault, in his essay "What is Enlightenment?" (a response to Immanuel Kant's essay with the same title), implores, "We must never forget that the Enlightenment is an event, or a set of events and complex historical processes, that . . . includes elements of social transformation, types of political institutions, forms of knowledge, projects of rationalization of knowledge and practices, technological mutations that are very difficult to sum up in a word."[80] Foucault calls for "historical investigation into the events that have led us to constitute ourselves and to recognize ourselves as subjects of what we are doing, thinking, saying."[81] The events and objects that constitute our lives become infrastructural over time, meaning that we become attached to them without necessarily recognizing them and the ways that they structure encounters with the self and others. As Berlant observes, "You can never simply lose your object if it's providing a foundational world infrastructure for you." And if that object has informed a worldview based in white supremacy, that infrastructure is hard to undo. "You can't decide not to be racist, not to be misogynist, not to be ambivalent about your anchors or fixations," writes Berlant. "But you can use the contradictions the object prompts to loosen and reconfigure it, exploiting the elasticity of its contradictions, the incoherence of the forces that overdetermine it."[82]

Here, a much-overlooked 2004 paper by Ron Day is essential reading. In "Community as Event," Day describes two models of community—"one founded upon constitutional power and one founded on constituent power—that give rise to various forms of agency and identity: the modern state or nation, cultural or social senses of community, and last, but not least, the organization of the self."[83] He argues that considering information and communication as *events* in community through the framework of ontology positions information and communication in political philosophy. Day differentiates between the Habermasian "communicative reason" from which constitutional forms of government derive with another impetus for democracy—that which begins with what is "'in-common': affects, language, and at least for humans, a temporality beginning with a shared sense of finitude." For Day, the formation of community from a multitude stands in contrast to "the people"—a selective "we" that derives from constitutional reason. The "multitude and the ontological horizons of the multitude," writes Day, "may not in general exclude all that which is outside of 'man' or the human."[84] The constituted community is both impossible and "always already" because, in a Derridean sense, "it *comes* to us from the future." Derrida indeed states that the "we" of the Declaration of Independence "speaks 'in the name of the people.' But this people does not yet exist, before this declaration. They do *not* exist as an entity, the entity does not exist *before* this declaration, not *as such*."[85] In fact the signatories of the Declaration represented a people that they brought into being through writing on behalf of an imagined future constituted community. At the same time, "community is a function of an always already in-common ontological ground."[86] State archives, libraries, and museums are derived from and contain both kinds of community—that which is formed from common affective experience and shared events and resources, as well as what is recognized as being of and for "the people," from their inception during the birth of the republic into an imagined future.

In 2004, before social media became normalized in our everyday lives, Day observed that the "in-common of affect" that circulates in and through mass communication is also made available for state and corporate capitalization and suggested that new political techniques are required to reappropriate the in-common. In response to his question—"how can we think of information and communication technologies in relation to the in-common of in-formation?"—Day calls for thinking against information in the modern sense. Specifically, he problematizes information's participation in progressive, linear time, as well as the conceptualization of information as resource—conditions that derive from and feed state capitalism. Information and communication technologies can instead "be viewed in terms of their coresponsibility regarding affects, language, and ultimately time." These elements can be positioned in relation to the emergence and poesis of community and being, and "in contrast to the constituted State."[87] This is an extraordinary observation, especially insofar as it applies to our collective current moment. To what extent do libraries, archives, and museums bear responsibility in facilitating community formation through affective connection? To what extent have they been doing that all along? What limits the formation of community in-common? How do individuals, including workers, bear responsibility in guarding and cultivating community? As I write, American libraries, archives, museums, and universities are being faced with impossible decisions and conditions resulting from the threat of and actual cuts to federal funding, the dismantling of Diversity, Equity, and Inclusion initiatives, and the policing of books, reading, and programming. What I am already seeing is an astounding coming together of community and defenders of intellectual freedom. By the time this book is published, I expect we will know more about what is possible.

The systematization of philosophical reasoning in American academic and cultural institutions might best be understood in terms of ontology as defined by information scientists and practitioners—as a tool for structuring information via the operationalization of relationships among and properties of entities. If, however, as Zoe Todd suggests, "'ontology' is just another word for colonialism," then we must inquire into how to reconcile colonial structuring techniques with Black, Indigenous, queer, disabled, feminist, and diasporic ways of knowing. In a conversation about the trajectory of Sylvia Wynter's life and work, David Small and Wynter briefly discussed the possibility of "ontological sovereignty," suggesting that in order to even consider this, we "would have to move completely outside our present conception of what it is to be human, and therefore outside the ground of the orthodox body of knowledge which institutes and reproduces such a conception."[88] The notion of "ontological sovereignty," which they agreed that at the turn of the twenty-first century was something we did not really know how to talk about, anticipates current conversations about data sovereignty, especially for Indigenous and Black peoples. These conversations are centered around having control over one's own information, privileging Indigenous and Black knowledges and their formations, and reconceptualizing concepts like data and knowledge.[89]

Information management is a set of techniques that multiply discursive fields. On the one hand it organizes existing discourses in various contexts, but more significantly, it has its own discursive field, which shapes how other fields of knowledge are collected, consulted, and circulated. The methods of organizing knowledge are mostly hidden, residing beneath documents, and presenting those documents to users in ways that may seem natural. The organizing techniques convey their own authorized discourse which derives from practice, scientific principles, and particular kinds of expertise.

When we consider the ways in which a system like a library catalog, designed in a particular context, at Jefferson's home at Monticello, served as a foundation for what has become a set of global standards, we begin to realize the magnitude and reach of Jefferson's influence, and how our information infrastructures not only transmit information, but knit worlds together, very often to the exclusion of people who do not accord with a particular agenda. This is especially important in light of the figuration of kinship in his own life—that he and Sally Hemings, his deceased wife's enslaved half-sister, had four children that lived to adulthood, that those children were all enslaved, and that he did not document the lives of Sally and their children, other than in business-related contexts, such as "slave rolls" in his Farm Book[90] (see Figure 6). In contrast, the documented historical record includes many letters and other writings about and from his white family. Indeed, as Saidiya Hartman writes, "The libidinal investment in violence is everywhere apparent in the documents, statements and institutions that decide our knowledge

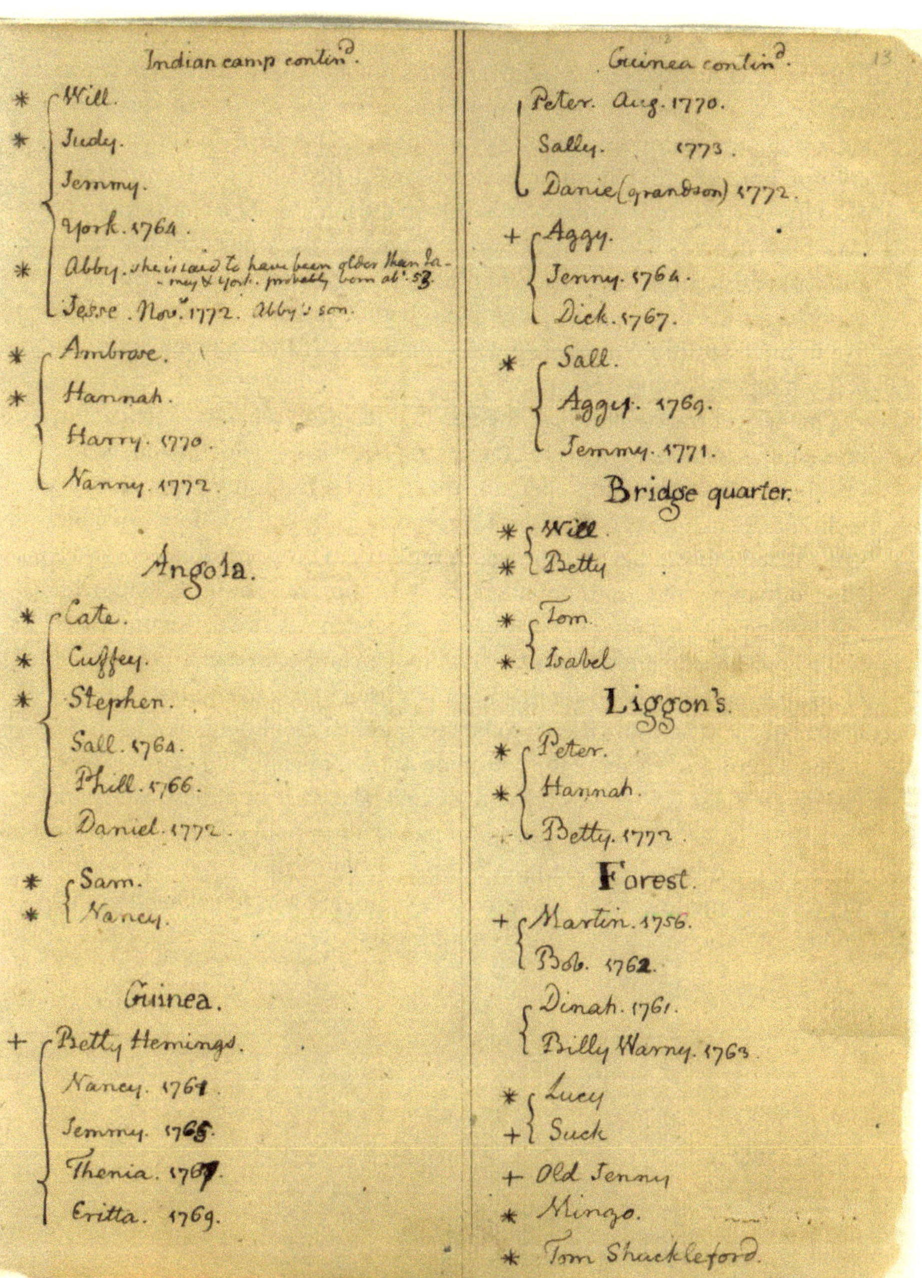

Indian camp contind.

* Will.
* Judy.
Jemmy.
York. 1764.
* Abby. she is said to have been older than Jammy & York. probably born abt. 58.
Jesse. Novr. 1772. Abby's son.

* Ambrose.
* Hannah.
Harry. 1770.
Nanny. 1772.

Angola.

* Cate.
* Cuffey.
* Stephen.
Sall. 1764.
Phill. 1766.
Daniel. 1772.

* Sam.
* Nancy.

Guinea.

+ Betty Hemings.
Nancy. 1761.
Jemmy. 1765.
Thenia. 1767.
Critta. 1769.

Guinea contind.

Peter. Aug. 1770.
Sally. 1773.
Danie (grandson) 1772.

+ Aggy.
Jenny. 1764.
Dick. 1767.

* Sall.
Aggy. 1769.
Jemmy. 1771.

Bridge quarter.

* Will.
* Betty

* Tom.
* Isabel

Liggon's.

* Peter.
* Hannah.
Betty. 1772.

Forest.

+ Martin. 1756.
Bob. 1762.

Dinah. 1761.
Billy Warny. 1763.

* Lucy
+ Suck
+ Old Jenny
* Mingo.
* Tom Shackleford.

Figure 6. Thomas Jefferson's Farm Book, "Roll of slaves, 1774." Sally Hemings was born in 1773 and is listed here as a member of Betty Hemings's family, living at Guinea, John Wayles's plantation. Wayles was Martha and Sally's father. When he died in 1773, Martha and Thomas (who were married in 1772) inherited some of the people enslaved by Wayles, including Betty and her children, including Sally. They went to Jefferson's home and plantation, Monticello, in 1775. Farm Book, 1774–1824, page 13. Original manuscript from the Coolidge Collection of Thomas Jefferson Manuscripts, Massachusetts Historical Society.

of the past."[91] Documentation affects how people are remembered and how their histories are told. The classificatory techniques that organize knowledge inform and are informed by a colonial imaginary and are driven by a will to knowledge in institutions. Throughout Jefferson's personal documents, preservation practices, and instruments it is clear that he understood the centrality of archives to preserving a nation's history in the making. The connections between this master's house, the Library of Congress, the University of Virginia, and national archives and museums illustrate the extent to which the personal collecting and cataloging practices of this particular person have been formative in the establishment of organizing principles in archival collections and their arrangement and description.

One way of working through the fact that Jefferson remains such a central figure in national memory is to closely read the ways in which a Jeffersonian imaginary is inscribed and operationalized in the institutions, practice, and technologies of our everyday lives. Ferguson suggests that the "forms in which minoritized subjects become the agents rather than the silent objects of knowledge formations and institutional practices . . . illustrate how imagination and institution come together to yield new types of peoples and communities. . . . In this moment in which minority difference can be used as an instrument of an archival mode of power that inscribes itself here and yonder, to 'revolutionize' minority culture means to be less huddled around the herculean feat and more considered about the activation of minor details."[92] Focusing on the mundane, the small acts of work and life that take place in public institutions, such as collecting books for queer and trans kids in public libraries, insisting on land-based pedagogy, attuning to unarchivable knowledges like whisper networks, or melting down monuments to conquest and remaking them into anti-racist public art, are all interventions that matter.

# 2

# Archives and the Making of American History

> If we think of the archive not simply as an institution but as a social formation, we might say that the United States is the archival nation par excellence.
>
> —RODERICK FERGUSON, *THE REORDER OF THINGS*

> If Jefferson stands as a synecdoche for the American archive, it is not merely his status as "founding father," or proprietor of the most famous domiciliary archive in US history—Monticello—but also because he was himself . . . a compulsive archivist.
>
> —JONATHAN ELMER, "THE ARCHIVE, THE NATIVE AMERICAN, AND JEFFERSON'S CONVULSIONS"

> the lost cannot be recovered; but let us save what remains: not by vaults and locks which fence them from the public eye and use, in consigning them to the waste of time, but by such a multiplication of copies, as shall place them beyond the reach of accident.
>
> —THOMAS JEFFERSON TO EBENEZER HAZARD, 1791

In a letter written just after the signing of the Declaration of Independence, one of Jefferson's dearest friends, John Page, invoked an angel of history:

> P.S. I am highly pleased with your Declaration. God preserve the united States.
>
> We know the Race is not to the swift nor the Battle to the strong.

> Do you not think an Angel rides in the Whirlwind and directs this Storm?

Page's words are uncanny for the way they presage Walter Benjamin's oft-cited passage about the angel of history in his 1940 "Theses on the Philosophy of History":

> The angel would like to stay, awaken the dead, and make whole what has been smashed. But a storm is blowing from Paradise; it has got caught in his wings with such violence that the angel can no longer close them. This storm irresistibly propels him into the future to which his back is turned, while the pile of debris before him grows skyward.
>
> This storm is what we call progress.

One could be forgiven for imagining for a moment that Walter Benjamin was intervening in the conversation between Jefferson and Page when he wrote about the angel of history, as if to caution them, or perhaps to alert us retrospectively of an ongoing mounting catastrophe. That would have been all but impossible, of course, as Page's letter would have been held in an archive in the United States. Benjamin was writing from and about the conditions in which he lived. His theses were among the last of Benjamin's published writings before his death by suicide during Hitler's reign.

The question that John Page put to Jefferson seems to suggest that the American Revolution was guided by a divine intervention—as if to say that they were a protected and chosen people—as if to say that they were riding toward destiny.[1] Benjamin's angel is caught in a whirlwind of catastrophe. Hardly directing the storm, his angel is hurled forward with his back turned toward the future. Benjamin writes, "Where we perceive a chain of events, he sees one single catastrophe which keeps piling wreckage upon wreckage and hurls it in front of his feet. The angel would like to stay, awaken the dead, and make whole what has been smashed." In both Page's and Benjamin's cases *the storm is what we call progress.* Could Benjamin and Page be referring to the same angel at different moments in history? Whose angel is this?

Aimé Césaire seems to be in dialogue with Jefferson, Page, and Benjamin on the question of progress when he writes: "I hear the storm. They talk to me about progress, about 'achievements,' diseases cured, improved standards of living," countering with his observations on the mechanisms of colonialism: "I am talking about societies drained of their essence, cultures trampled underfoot, institutions undermined, lands confiscated, religions smashed, magnificent artistic creations destroyed, extraordinary possibilities wiped out."[2] It matters how one is situated in the colonialist design, and despite the limitations to seeing from within a given system, as we necessarily are, viewing it from multiple vantage points grants access to the paradoxes and complexities inherent to information architectures constructed over time in the United States and beyond.

It was in a letter to Page in this revolutionary moment that we also have one of the first of Jefferson's writings that convey his aims toward expansion and elimination of Indigenous communities. Writing from Philadelphia on 5 August 1776, Jefferson responded to Page's communications regarding the progress of the revolution—specifically, the war between Haudenosaunee (Six Nations) and settler soldiers in Virginia—what Jefferson referred to as the "storm" that had been "brewing" there:

> I am sorry to hear that the Indians have commenced war, but greatly pleased you have been so decisive on that head. Nothing will reduce those wretches so soon as pushing the war into the heart of their country. But I would not stop there. I would never cease pursuing them while one of them remained on this side the Misisippi. So unprovoked an attack and so treacherous a one should never be forgiven while one of them remains near enough to do us injury. The Congress having had reason to suspect the Six nations intended war, instructed their commissioners to declare to them peremptorily that if they chose to go to war with us, they should be at liberty to remove their families out of our settlements, but to remember that they should not only never more return to their dwellings on any terms but that we would never cease pursuing them with war while one remained on the face of the earth: and moreover, to avoid equivocation, to let them know they must recall their young men from Canada, or we should consider them as acting against us nationally. This decisive declaration produced an equally decisive act on their part: they have recalled their young men, and are stirring themselves with anxiety to keep their people in quiet, so that the *storm we apprehended to be brewing* there it is hoped is blown over.
>
> Early days![3]

I use the correspondence above to highlight the importance of the bonds of friendship in revolutionary America and the formation of the United States. John Page and Thomas Jefferson had a uniquely close friendship, and Jefferson's letters to Page contain some of his fullest and most honest opinions. Page wrote to Jefferson, shortly after the Declaration of Independence was signed, from a place of admiration and affection, as a compatriot in the quest to build a republic. They regarded one another as kin, bound by their commitment to the project of gaining independence from the British monarchy and establishing a new nation.

The trope of the "founding fathers" is repeated so often that people may take for granted the fact that these men were indeed forming something of a family of would-be American citizens.[4] The bond between Jefferson and Page derived from their membership in the planter elite. They were both from wealthy Virginian families, formed a connection at the College of William and Mary, and stayed deeply attached until Page's death in 1808. Alliances like this extended across a network of aristocratic families in Virginia and other colonies. These strong attachments also reinforced the strength with which they fought against anyone who interfered with their aims to build a new republic. The letter quoted above shows that even in the "early days" of the war against Britain, Jefferson and his friends and colleagues were specifically and brutally targeting Indigenous communities with the aim of claiming the land and establishing their own territory. Jefferson already uses the word "remove" in this early letter to refer to the elimination of Haudenosaunee peoples from their own land to make room for white settlement.

A year earlier, in what Jonathan Elmer identifies as a key early American archival moment, Jefferson inscribed the full text of a speech of the Haudenosaunee-Mingo leader known as Chief Logan, in his Memorandum Book. Logan was living among the Shawnees when his family was murdered by settlers.[5] Logan exacted his revenge and then "sent by a messenger" a speech directed to Lord Dunmore, which Jefferson later cited in *Notes on the State of Virginia* as an example of Indigenous eloquence:[6]

> Colo. Cresap, the last spring, in cold blood and unprovoked, cut off all the Relations of Logan; not sparing even my women or children. There runs not a drop of my blood in the veins of any human creature. This called on me for revenge. I have sought it; I have killed many; I have fully glutted my vengeance. For my country I rejoice at the beams of peace, but do not harbor a thought that mine is the joy of fear. Logan never felt fear. He will not turn on his heel to save his life. Who is there to mourn for Logan?—Not one.

Elmer notes that Jefferson's transcription of the speech was one of several instantiations of the story, and that well before Jefferson included it in *Notes on the State of Virginia*, the speech had circulated widely. In a response to challenges of the accuracy of the charge against Michael Cresap two decades after the incident (that Cresap was the person who directed the killing of Logan's family), Jefferson recalled that the version that appeared in *Notes* was a repetition of several versions that appeared elsewhere over the course of a dozen years. After the campaign, which ended in Lord Dunmore's War and the signing of the Treaty of Camp Charlotte on 19 October 1774, Dunmore's "officers brought the speech of Logan, and related the circumstances of it. These were so affecting, and the speech itself so fine a morsel of eloquence that it became the theme of every conversation" in Williamsburg and beyond. The speech was published in the *Virginia Gazette*, which Jefferson preserved (more will be said about Jefferson's collection and preservation of newspapers later in this chapter). The story, "flew thro' all the public papers of the continent, and thro' the magazines and other periodical publications of Great Britain; and those who were boys at that day will now attest that the speech of Logan used to be given them as a school-exercise for repetition."[7] In addition to the usefulness of this story as evidence of Logan's oratorial skills, it also supplied material upon which to base narratives of the end of the Indigenous peoples and the beginnings of the white settler republic. Or, as Elmer puts it (invoking Niklas Luhmann to revise his theory of distinction), "the figure of the sovereign and the last Indian exemplify the effort of cultural semantics to stabilize—include as excluded—the consciousness of society's 'drastic differentiation' from its environment."[8]

Any Jefferson historian will tell you that trying to make sense of his archive is a humbling exercise, not only because of its vastness, but because of Jefferson's various communication strategies, which seem designed to confound his future historian—ranging from flattery to encryption to self-censorship. As Millicent Sowerby, who reassembled and annotated his personal library catalogs, wrote of the man: "Thomas Jefferson, like Tennyson's brook, goes on forever. There is no stopping him, no coming to an end either of himself as a personality or to the discoveries to be made concerning him. He himself never ceased to grow, and consequently our knowledge of him can never be considered complete."[9] He has perplexed historians for centuries, earning the name "American Sphinx" for his elusiveness.[10] The study of Jefferson's information practices is an inexhaustible pursuit, as he used many types of information and documents for different purposes (very often contradicting himself) in his roles as scientist, statesman, and private citizen inhabiting multiple worlds.

■

In this chapter my focus is on Jefferson's archival impulse and his ideas about history. The first half of the chapter presents a theoretical and contextual lens through which to view the formation of archives in the United States, and the second describes Jefferson's archival practices. It is a response to Foucault's call fifty years ago for critical archaeological inquiry into the archive itself—that what is "needed is a ramified, penetrative perception of the present, one that makes it possible to locate lines of weakness, strong points, positions where the instances of power have secured and implanted themselves by a system of organisation dating back over 150 years."[11] Jefferson's archive is a rich source from which to mine the types of evidence Foucault suggests is needed to understand how knowledge functions in relations of power. Following scholars who have identified Jefferson as the architect of "Indian Removal" policies, as a statesman who enacted laws according to the international Doctrine of Discovery throughout his career, and as a planter who owned over six hundred people in his lifetime, I examine the archival practices that Jefferson used, developed, and improved to record the history of the United States.

The concept of progress was core to Jefferson's philosophy of history. As Henry Commager writes in the foreword to the publication of Jefferson's *Garden and Farm Books*, "Nowhere does the American emphasis, nay, concentration, on the practical emerge more clearly than in American concepts of progress."[12] The "newness" of the "new world" in the eyes of the early Americans was something onto which the future could unfold, where the land could be improved through scientific methods, the settler population would increase, and the young republic governed by the people would grow and flourish. In a letter to Joseph Priestley, just after entering the office of the president, Jefferson wrote with great optimism about the newness of the republic and the hope for the future, again using the metaphor of a storm:

> as the *storm is now subsiding* & the horison becoming serene, it is pleasant to consider the phaenomenon with attention. we can no longer say there is nothing new under the sun. for this whole chapter in the history of man is new. the great extent of our republic is new. it's sparse habitation is new. the mighty wave of public opinion which has rolled over it is new. but the most pleasing novelty is it's so quickly subsiding, over such an extent of surface, to it's true level again. the order & good sense displayed in this recovery from delusion, and in the momentous crisis which lately arose, really bespeak a strength of character in our nation which augurs well for the duration of our republic.[13]

This newness was related to an early American *now*—one that was rich with possibility. He was aware that he was standing in a historical moment—one he called the "Revolution of 1800"—a phrasing that suggests a newly significant turn.

Note again, Jefferson's use of a storm as metaphor, and the clearing of the horizon, with the invocation of history. The "Revolution of 1800" was another beginning, a new chapter in "the history of man." His faith in the young nation was renewed by its rejection of John Adams for a second term in office, which Jefferson viewed to be a rejection of the Federalists and a reason to hope for progress. In that moment, Jefferson looked to a future when slavery would be abolished, formerly enslaved people would be sent to Africa, the present United States would expand westward, and Indigenous peoples would either be assimilated into white society, removed to areas yet unsettled by Americans of European descent, or eliminated if necessary. In Jefferson's vision for the future, progress relied upon homogeneity and whiteness. In other words, the progression of settler colonialism and empire expansion through time has necessarily meant ongoing catastrophe and resistance for people racialized as other than white.

Jefferson took pains to collect, preserve, and narrate history, and he also understood that his writings would be consulted by future generations. "When studying his conscientiously preserved collection of papers," writes Hannah Spahn, "readers should keep in mind that it was significantly shaped by this special temporal constellation: the writer and collector's expectation that later generations of historians would read and judge it with an eye on its moral content."[14] He wanted future Americans to learn from the lessons of the past. Archives had a capacity for instruction, and as Jefferson invested so much hope in the education of the citizenry, he wanted the archival record to provide the best lessons. By situating Jefferson as a central figure in the formation of American archival science, I examine some of the key relationships and actions that contributed to establishing a national archives in the United States.[15]

## Ebenezer Hazard's Archives

Jefferson corresponded and collaborated with Ebenezer Hazard, whom some historians regard as the United States' first archivist. According to Fred Shelley, "Ebenezer Hazard (1744/45–1817) was the first American to attempt to preserve the documentary heritage of the nation."[16] Hazard began compiling the *Historical Collections* in or around 1772 or 1773 while he worked in a bookshop. He was cognizant of the fact that history was unfolding all around him and that preserving it for future generations was crucial. He knew that important records of the colonies were scattered about in precarious circumstances, rendering them vulnerable to loss by carelessness, fire, or other disasters. Hazard's letter to Jonathan Trumbull, dated 3 August 1774, shows that Hazard had future historians in mind when he began compiling the colonies' documents:

> I wish to be the means of saving from oblivion many important papers which without something like this collection will infallibly be lost. . . . [Some papers] are intimately connected with the liberties of the people; others will furnish some future historian with valuable materials. The time will doubtless come when early periods of American history will be eagerly inquired into, and it is the duty of every generation to hand to its successor the necessary means of acquiring such knowledge, in order to prevent their groping in the dark, and perplexing themselves in the labrinths of error.[17]

On 30 April 1775 Jefferson wrote to Hazard in response to his proposal for producing an archival historical collection. That proposal included a list, compiled by Jefferson, of seventy-five colonial documents that should be included in the bound archival collection.[18] As mentioned in Chapter 1, Jefferson also secured eighteen subscribers from Virginia, and their names appear in the document. Jefferson expressed his support for the project:

> Your letter of Aug. 23. 1774 and Proposals for collecting and publishing the American state papers I have received. It is an undertaking of great utility to the continent in general, as it will not only contribute to the information of all those concerned in the administration of government, but will furnish to any historical genius which may happen to arise those materials which he would otherwise acquire with great difficulty and perhaps not acquire at all. Any thing in my power I will most gladly contribute to the compilation. I will direct office copies of our charters, resolutions of assembly &c. and of our treaty with the commonwealth of England to be immediately made out, and will forward them by the best means I can.[19]

In 1778 Hazard appealed to Henry Laurens, the president of the Continental Congress, for official "Patronage and Assistance" in developing the archives. His aims were to obtain funding and for members of Congress to recommend to the state governors that he be granted free access to the records of their states and permission to copy their documents. Congress resolved on 20 July 1778 to advance Hazard one thousand dollars and that he be allowed to view and copy public records without expense. In his letter to Laurens, which was read before Congress, he wrote:

> The Design of it is to furnish Materials for a good History of the United States, which may now be very well done; for so rapid has been

> our political Progress that we can easily recur to the first Step taken upon the Continent, and clearly point out our different Advances from Persecution to comparative Liberty, and from thence to independent Empire.[20]

Although the promise was not fulfilled in the end, the "value of the resolution of Congress lay, of course, in the recognition by the national government of its responsibility and duty in making archives and historical manuscripts safe and available and in financing their publication."[21] Hazard planned for the collections to comprise five printed volumes, but only two were published, in 1792 and 1794, due to financial and time constraints. Hazard had less time to devote to the project while he was serving as postmaster general beginning in 1782 and later as a surveyor of the postal roads. After being discharged from the office of postmaster general by President Washington, he was able to send two volumes to a printer in 1791. He sent a sample of the material to Jefferson, who quickly responded with what Frank Cogliano regards as "a mission statement for all documentary publishing projects"[22]:

> I return you the two volumes of records, with thanks for the opportunity of looking into them. They are curious monuments of the infancy of our country. I learn with great satisfaction that you are about committing to the press the valuable historical and state-papers you have been so long collecting. Time and accident are committing daily havoc on the originals deposited in our public offices. The late war has done the work of centuries in this business. The lost cannot be recovered; but let us save what remains: not by vaults and locks which fence them from the public eye and use, in consigning them to the waste of time, but by such a multiplication of copies, as shall place them beyond the reach of accident.[23]

Alexis de Tocqueville regarded the *Historical Collections* as essential, and in an appendix to his *Democracy in America* he supplied several bibliographic references. "At the head of the general documents which it would be advantageous to examine," he wrote, "I place the work entitled: *Historical Collection of State Papers and Other Authentic Documents, intended as materials for an history of the United States of America*, by Ebenezer Hazard."[24]

Jefferson reflected on his early efforts to document and preserve Virginia's history in a 16 January 1796 letter to his mentor and colleague George Wythe. The letter reveals his anxieties about the loss of important material and the various possible threats to archival preservation. Ultimately, he reiterates the belief that the best defense against the ravages of time, fire, and environmental factors was to make multiple copies:

> Very early in the course of my researches into the laws of Virginia I observed that many of them were already lost, and many more on the point of being lost, as existing only in single copies in the hands of careful or curious individuals, on whose deaths they would probably be used for waste paper. I set myself herefore to work to collect all which were then existing, in order that when the day should come in which the public should advert to the magnitude of their loss in these precious monuments of our property and our history, a part of their regret might be spared by information that a portion has been saved from the wreck which is worthy of their attention and preservation. In searching after these remains, I spared neither time, trouble, nor expence. . . . But . . . the question is What means will be the most effectual for preserving these remains from future loss? All the care I can take of them, will not preserve them from the worm, from the natural decay of the paper, from the accident of fire, or those of removal when it is necessary for any public purpose. . . . Our experience has proved to us that a single copy, or a few, deposited in MS in the public offices cannot be relied on for any great length of time. The ravages of fire and of ferocious enemies have had but too much part in producing the very loss we now deplore. How many of the precious works of antiquity were lost while they existed only in manuscript? Has there ever been one lost since the art of printing has rendered it practicable to multiply and disperse copies? This leads us then to the only means of preserving those remains of our laws now under consideration, that is, a multiplication of printed copies.[25]

The letter above was reprinted as a broadside by a committee of the Virginia House of Delegates in November of that year. The broadside was meant to persuade, but the General Assembly was not convinced of the efficacy of the project:

> The persons appointed, by an act of the last session, to superintend an edition of all legislative acts concerning lands, having perused the foregoing letter, written in answer to an application to the author for his copies of the acts, more compleat than any which can be elsewhere procured, and supposing that the General Assembly, upon reconsideration of the subject, might wish to enlarge the work, declined entering upon the business, until the sentiments of that honorable body shall be known.[26]

From an archival studies standpoint, Jefferson's letter to Wythe, reprinted as a broadside, is incredible for its attention to all the potential dangers to historical records. According to Julian Boyd, this was the letter that led to the compilation and publication of the William Hening's *Statutes at Large*, and it is this piece of writing that entitles "its author to rank as a progenitor of archival concerns in America."[27] This is a defining moment in the history of US government archives, and it is clear that Jefferson was devoting great amounts of time and resources at least as early as 1775 to the project of preserving the documented history of the early republic.

## Preservation and Access

At a celebration and symposium commemorating Jefferson's contributions to the Library of Congress and the 200th anniversary of the founding of the United States, Frederick Goff, former custodian of the Jefferson Collection at the Library of Congress proclaimed: "Jefferson was not only a maker of history. He preserved a great deal of the fabric of that history, and for this we are duly grateful."[28] Goff was particularly impressed by Jefferson's preservation of his contemporaries' newspapers. Jefferson understood not only the importance of newspapers in informing a wide public about the events and ideas of the day, but he also knew that they recorded history as it was being made. As Goff noted, Jefferson very intentionally secured and preserved complete or semi-complete runs of over sixty newspapers of his era. This was an early archival project, and arguably, the fact that many of these volumes of newspapers, along with thousands of manuscripts associated with the early republic are now housed in the Library of Congress and elsewhere, can be credited to Jefferson's archival drive.

Present-day archivists are primarily concerned with preservation and facilitation of access to archival materials. Even before he wrote the Declaration of Independence, Jefferson was preoccupied with these concerns as well, and making copies and assembling volumes were two of the principal archival methods that he used. As Fred Shelley has pointed out, "The thought of an extensive, fireproof storehouse, one safe from natural dangers, for public records and private manuscripts had not yet come into men's mind."[29] Archival collections were made accessible by printing multiple copies, compiling materials together, and distributing them, rather than by transporting scholars to a central location. Public records were maintained in local offices, but there was not yet a pervasive attitude about the importance of preserving those documents for posterity, nor had standard practices been established. In fact, people were suspicious of government efforts to store historical records, and the "French Revolution was yet to proclaim the theory that all citizens had the *right* to see public records."[30]

Jefferson's rationale for copying and printing resembles twenty-first century digitization projects, which are generally explained in terms of preservation and access. Copying a manuscript to a high-quality digital file is meant to preserve the content of the archival record, even if the materiality of the original is impossible to transmit in the process. Placing digital content in publicly accessible digital archives and libraries facilitates access for anyone with access to the Internet and hardware, and in some cases a subscription. As with bound volumes that can be reprinted, digital archives are simultaneously meant to deliver materials to distributed historians and public users and to prevent the loss of historical information. At the same time, it is unlikely that all of the contents of all of the archival collections will be digitized. Archivists very often select representative materials for their digital collections, while the bulk of the collections are available only in manuscript form.

An archival tradition certainly didn't begin with the American Revolution, and of course, many of the techniques that Jefferson and his colleagues used were borrowed from previous eras. For example, the Austrian Hapsburgs made paper copybooks—a technique that Jefferson further developed—after 1523 "to systematically record correspondence between the ruler, the regional administration, and the territories it supervised."[31] Elizabeth Eisenstein's description of some of the archival methods that were developed in response to the "knowledge explosion" of the sixteenth century provide important historical context.[32] The printing press not only contributed to the massive increase in the volume of informational materials, but it was also instrumental in developing techniques to manage all of that information, especially in the form of reference books. This era was important in the beginning of standardization, particularly for reference guides and visual aids, such as calendars, dictionaries, maps, charts, and diagrams. Reorganizing texts and reference guides by "rationalizing, codifying, and cataloguing data" affected the ways people read, but it also contributed to a reshaping of knowledge, and contributed to the formation of disciplines and social groups.[33]

In her history of the printing press as an "agent of change," Eisenstein asserts, "Of all the new features introduced by the duplicative powers of print, preservation is possibly the most important."[34] She cites Jefferson as the primary example of an eighteenth-century archival impulse, which was driven by his belief in the importance of information in democratization. Making copies both preserved information and ensured public access to historical records. This was essential to early modern science and Enlightenment-era thinking. His massive personal and public archives stand as a testament to this belief. Like other Enlightenment thinkers, Jefferson placed an emphasis on primary sources. As Cogliano points out, the "philosophical historians" of his era "assumed that human nature was universal across time and space, and that lessons could therefore be drawn from across history."[35] It was this belief that contributed to the cultivation of universal histories and universal libraries, as well as the universalization of Man as the writer, subject, and keeper of histories.

Jefferson was aware of preservation techniques for original documents and applied them in protecting manuscript copies of Virginia's early laws: "some of them will not bear removal, being so rotten that in turning over a leaf it sometimes falls into powder. These I preserve by wrapping & sewing them up in oiled cloth so that neither air nor moisture can have access to them."[36] He also worried about fire, vermin, and other threats to the preservation of documents. Indeed, Jefferson had firsthand experience of losing precious books and papers. At the age of twenty-seven, six years before he drafted the Declaration of Independence, his childhood home at Shadwell, and all of the books and family papers within, burned in a fire:

> My late loss may perhaps have reached you by this time, I mean the loss of my mother's house by fire, and in it, of every paper I had in the world, and almost every book. On a reasonable estimate I calculate the cost of the books burned to have been £200 sterling. Would to god it had been the money; then had it never cost me a sigh![37]

At the time of the fire, Jefferson was just beginning to build his home at Monticello, across the Rivanna River from Shadwell. Perhaps it was the loss of his family's papers and books in the 1770 Shadwell fire that brought the importance of preservation into focus for him, or maybe it was the instability and unknown future in the revolutionary years, but however one interprets Jefferson's motivations, he was acutely aware that history was being made and that future generations would want to have a record of it. As Rebecca Brannon writes, Jefferson understood that he "could literally shape his legacy through the shaping of his papers—and so he did."[38] He actively cultivated a narrative claiming his own authorship of the Declaration late in life. And, as Andrew O'Shaughnessy explains:

> As he had with the Declaration of Independence, Jefferson wrote bills with a view to instruct, explain, and persuade, beginning with a preamble introducing the purpose, objectives, and principles of the proposed legislation. He similarly undertook the seemingly dull task of writing the minutes of the Board of Visitors. This ensured that his version became the final record of their meetings.[39]

Jefferson put things in writing with a view to how they would be seen and used in the future. Lyman Butterfield, associate editor of Jefferson's papers wrote, "No other President except the second Roosevelt has possessed so strong an archival instinct; and however badly his papers have been manhandled since, Jefferson himself left them in beautiful order."[40] As meticulous as he was in copying the letters that he wrote and storing and cataloging the letters he sent and received, he did not encourage their publication in his lifetime. When Jefferson died, he left his personal papers to his grandson, Thomas Jefferson Randolph. After Randolph's death, most of the papers stayed in the Randolph family until 1898. Jefferson's great-grandson, Thomas Jefferson Coolidge acquired over eight thousand pieces and gave them to the Massachusetts Historical Society.[41] Cogliano notes that, in "transmitting to posterity such a substantial documentary legacy Jefferson sought to shape his posthumous reputation. He made an error, however, in not publishing his papers during his own lifetime, or leaving detailed instructions for how they should be handled. In so doing Jefferson lost control over his documentary legacy and, by extension, his reputation."[42] Cogliano suggests that he may have had personal reasons for wanting his archives to be published posthumously. But as Butterfield suggests, if "he had had anything to keep secret, he could and presumably would have destroyed it; yet there is no evidence that he ever destroyed a scrap of paper except his correspondence with his wife. That belonged to him, but everything else was preserved for the public to scrutinize in the future with all the curiosity that it wished."[43] Butterfield goes on to describe the wide array of types of materials that Jefferson kept, most certainly with the intention of preserving them for future historians:

> In the Princeton file there are literally hundreds of scraps of paper saved by Jefferson, and among them are some of the most entertaining and occasionally significant pieces in the whole body of his archives. There are mathematical calculations; designs for machines and furniture and landscape details; recipes for macaroni and other dishes; itineraries; agricultural and meteorological data; tables of useful information; book lists; and notes and memoranda on an incredible variety of subjects, from the use of Archimedes' screw at Kew to snuff, Sophocles, and specific gravity.[44]

Near the end of his life, in a detailed response to Hugh Taylor regarding historical documents, Jefferson discussed some of his archival holdings. His philosophy about archives comes through strongly, as he states that "it is the duty of every good citizen to use all the opportunities, which occur to him, for preserving documents relating to the history of our country."[45] He describes what he had in his possession: "some folio volumes. two of these are the proceedings of the Virginia company in England; the remaining 4. are of the Records of the Council of Virginia from 1622. to 1700."[46] Jefferson then offers an account of the trajectory of a compiled history of Virginia, showing that for him copying *is* archiving. He traces their passage through different private libraries until he acquired them, and then explains that he will deposit them in the University of Virginia library so that they can be protected:

> they contain the records of the Virginia co. copied from the Originals, under the eye, if I recollect rightly of the Earl of Southampton, a member of the company, bought at the sale of his Library by Doct^r Byrd of Westover, and sold with that library to Isaac Zane. these volumes happened, at the time of the sale to have been borrowed by Col^o R. Bland, whose library I bought, and with this, they were sent to me. . . . I shall deposit them in the library of the University, where they will be most likely to be preserved with care.

Finally, he describes in detail the contents of four other volumes, which he believed to be the original records of the Virginia Council. He had purchased Sir John Randolph's "library in a lump" from Randolph's executors, and the council records were included. Of the volumes, Jefferson wrote:

> I found the leaves so rotten as often to crumble into dust on being handled. I bound them therefore together that they might not be unnecessarily opened. and have thus preserved them 47. years. if my conjectures are right they must have been out of the public office about 80 years. I shall deposit them also, with the others in the same library of the University where they will be safer from injury than in a public office.[47]

Jefferson took on the role of archivist and went to lengths to preserve and protect not only his own personal papers, but the foundational and administrative documents of public offices. He seems to have known that "there is no political power without control of the archives."[48] In the end, as with his book collection and other possessions that he organized and insisted should maintain a certain order after their sale or his death, his papers became disordered and dispersed across several locations. Nevertheless, the techniques that he used to organize the information pertaining to his public and private lives contain and convey information about Jefferson's worldview, perhaps even more effectively than the contents of the archives themselves.

Jefferson not only kept and preserved papers. His archival and organizing impulse was expressed in several genres. Elmer reads Jefferson's *Notes on the*

*State of Virginia* as an attempt to formalize an archival project. In this reading, Jefferson is an archivist who "takes up his proper position vis-a-vis all that is heterogeneous, unverifiable, or convulsive in the archive, he will secure the needed formal closure of the one, not through projection onto the objective archive, but through introjection of the very limits to knowledge presented by his own finitude and particularity."[49] Jefferson assembled all of the historical information in the forms of statistical tables, literary description, drawings, technical language, conjecture and predictions, and laws in one document, in order from natural to civil history.

Jefferson's home was an archival repository until he deposited certain documents in his possession at the University of Virginia, or until people removed them from his estate after his death.[50] Jefferson acquired legal and legislative volumes from various sources. Some were gifts, some he purchased, and some came from the libraries of family members, friends, and colleagues. He was so deliberate in his aims to collect the documented history of the United States that he even "rescued" one volume of Virginia laws from a tavern where it had been used like "waste paper" to scribble on. He owned several filing presses of a standard size to hold boxes of papers, which were all ordered and labeled according to use. In March of 1785 Jefferson obtained a copy press, a portable device made by James Watt that produced a reversed copy of a written document by placing pressure onto thin, translucent paper. As James T. Rogers suggests, it "must have been a bother to use," as Jefferson would have had to write the original document with a "special ink containing sugar or gum arabic and then place the document under a leaf of dampened tissue paper in the press. The machine squeezed the two sheets together hard enough to transfer a reversed copy of the original to the tissue paper. Anyone wanting to read it had to hold it up to the light and peer through the back side."[51] Nevertheless, it did save him time, and within a few months Jefferson ceased writing and storing summaries of his outgoing letters because he could preserve the entire contents in copies. He shared his enthusiasm for the usefulness of the press in a September 1785 letter to James Madison: "Have you a copying press? If you have not, you should get one. Mine (exclusive of paper which costs a guinea a ream) has cost me about 14. guineas. I would give ten times that sum that I had had it from the date of the stamp act."[52] He used this method of copying until he encountered the polygraph, which was one of many technologies that Jefferson used to save time and maintain accuracy (see Figure 7).

Among the archival technologies that Jefferson used, the polygraph (not to be confused with the lie detector), an improvement from the copy press, was perhaps the most instrumental for the preservation of letters: "it is for copying with one pen while you write with the other & without the least additional

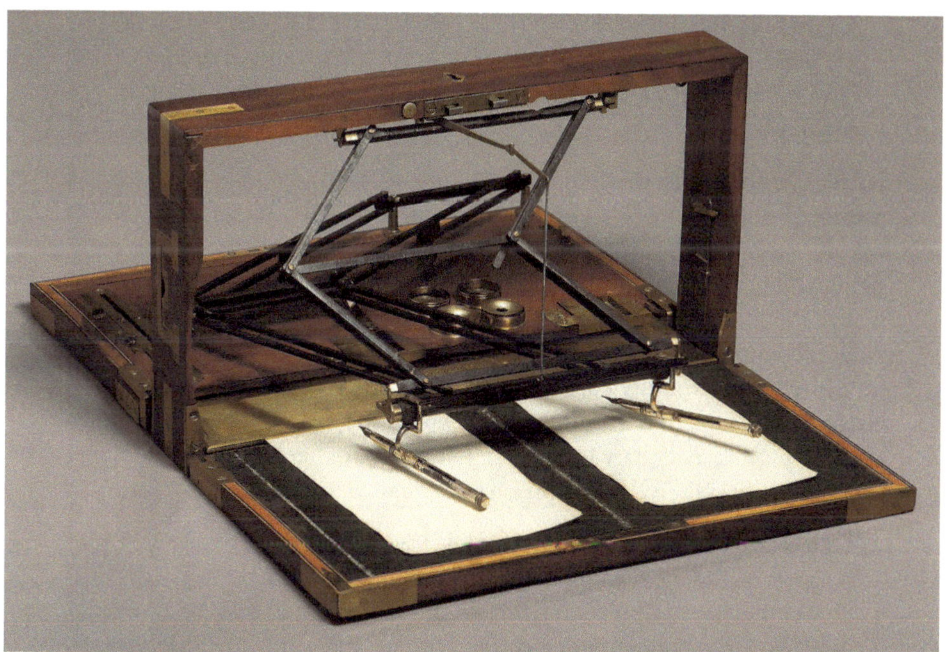

Figure 7. Hawkins's Patent Polygraph, owned by Jefferson. American Philosophical Society. Gift of Nicholas P. Trist, 1850.

embarrasment or exertion to the writer."[53] In other words, when Jefferson sat at his writing desk, he wrote with one pen, and an attached parallel pen simultaneously made a copy.

This way he could send a letter and keep a copy for his own records. Jefferson called it "the finest invention of the present age."[54] The instrument was invented by John Isaac Hawkins and developed and produced by painter and natural historian Charles Willson Peale, who opened one of the first natural history museums in the United States. Jefferson and Peale exchanged numerous letters about the device, with Jefferson making recommendations to Peale for improving it:

> Your favor of Sep. 14. was recieved in due time, and my small Polygraph continuing impracticable for the first half dozen lines, though perfect as to the rest, I have brought it on here to be forwarded to you for correction. it's size is perfect, & the best possible, not having a hair's breadth too much or too little. I should prefer however the double spring for holding the paper in place, as more convenient. you will also percieve that one of the pen cases has exfoliated so as

> not to hold the nib well. I will pray you to make the writing machinery perfect, that constituting the comfort of the machine. As Capt Elwood is expected here in a day or two, & is careful, I will send it by him.[55]

Jefferson's interest in copying went beyond archival methods. Copying also presented matters of intellectual property ownership. As secretary of state he was the administrator of patent and copyright laws under the 1790 acts and signer of the 1793 Patent Act. Today his 1813 letter to Isaac McPherson remains a source of debate among copyright law defenders and detractors who differently interpret the quote as useful for their point of view. My own interest in this letter is primarily connected to concerns about Jefferson as an archivist and intellectual. Whether Jefferson would support or oppose present-day copyright law is secondary to the fact that he would likely say that "copyright law should always serve free expression, and not vice versa."[56] Jefferson wrote:

> Stable ownership is the gift of social law, and is given late in the progress of society. It would be curious then, if an idea, the fugitive fermentation of an individual brain, could, of natural right, be claimed in exclusive and stable property. If nature has made any one thing less susceptible than all others of exclusive property, it is the action of the thinking power called an idea, which an individual may exclusively possess as long as he keeps it to himself; but the moment it is divulged, it forces itself into the possession of every one, and the receiver cannot dispossess himself of it. Its peculiar character, too, is that no one possesses the less, because every other possesses the whole of it. He who receives an idea from me, receives instruction himself without lessening mine; as he who lights his taper at mine, receives light without darkening me. That ideas should freely spread from one to another over the globe, for the moral and mutual instruction of man, and improvement of his condition, seems to have been peculiarly and benevolently designed by nature, when she made them, like fire, expansible over all space, without lessening their density in any point, and like the air in which we breathe, move, and have our physical being, incapable of confinement or exclusive appropriation. Inventions then cannot, in nature, be a subject of property. Society may give an exclusive right to the profits arising from them, as an encouragement to men to pursue ideas which may produce utility, but this may or may not be done, according to the will and convenience of the society, without claim or complaint from anybody.[57]

In this passage Jefferson was arguing that ideas and inventions cannot be considered by natural right to be the stable property of any particular person. Sharing ideas, allowing them to circulate and expand and build upon one another, was essential for the instruction and improvement of the citizens. Copying not only preserved the cultural record but facilitated its expansion and the progress of enlightenment.

According to Justin Hughes, the present debates among intellectual property lawyers and public commentators are clouded by ahistorical readings that repeat the commonly held belief that the alignment of ideas and intellectual content with property is a recent phenomenon. In truth, the concepts of intellectual property and literary property are seventeenth-century British constructs, which were codified in the Statute of Anne in 1710. Arising out of the Stationer's Company in England, the drafting of the law reflects the problems of defining rights of authors and publishers in terms of property. John Locke was among the members of Parliament who participated in the debate, writing a statement in 1694 that bears a striking resemblance to our present copyright law, that "it may be reasonable to [Stationer's Company members] to limit their *property* to a certain number of years after the death of the author, or the first printing of the book, as supposed, fifty or seventy years."[58] Jefferson was born into a British America that was actively pursuing definitional and political clarity with regard to intellectual property. He would become professionally invested in these questions, especially when he occupied the office of the secretary of state, the position from which he administered patent law, which took up a lot of his time.

Jefferson's friend and colleague James Madison was a key contributor to copyright policy, which was debated after the war in the March 1783 Confederation Congress. Madison was on the committee appointed "to consider the most proper means of the cherishing genius and useful arts . . . by securing to the authors or publishers of new books their property in such works." 1783 was a crucial moment for Madison and Jefferson. As we will see in Chapter 4, they had just been boarding in the same house and likely talked about Madison's proposal for a library for Congress. It is also highly probable that they had extensive conversations about the issue of copyright. In any case, the matter was referred to the states, and in 1785 Madison presented a bill before the Virginia House of Delegates, stating that books were the "exclusive property" of their authors. Madison reintroduced patent and copyright at the federal level during the Constitutional Convention, where he framed the clause in terms of progress and learning, arguing that copyright protections would encourage creative production. Section eight of Article One of the constitution reads, "The Congress shall have Power. . . . To promote the Progress of

Science and useful Arts, by securing for limited Times to Authors and Inventors the exclusive Right to their respective Writings and Discoveries."[59] As Siva Vaidhyanathan writes, this "fit with the overall Madisonian project for the Constitution. If the federal government were to operate as the nexus of competing interests, each interest would need to approach the public sphere with reliable information. Information could be deemed reliable only if it were subject to public debate. Ideas could be judged beneficial only if they had stood the tests of discourse and experience."[60] Jefferson was not a direct contributor to the US Constitution because he was serving as minister to France at the time. He did include his opinions of the articles in letters that he sent to colleagues, including Madison. Whereas he initially insisted that claiming ownership of information and ideas limited progress, he eventually softened his position, writing to Madison in August 1789: "Monopolies may be allowed to persons for their own productions in literature and their own inventions in the arts for a term not exceeding ____ years but for no longer term and no other purpose."[61] Hughes sees Jefferson's changing mind as adaptive and political: "While Jefferson may not have flip-flopped per se, he definitely elaborated on his views or reframed his position in certain letters, perhaps for whomever the recipient was."[62] He also would have had to adapt his views to policies as they were enacted, especially if he occupied the office that enforced them. He came to accept the utility of patents in encouraging ingenuity and invention, but he believed they should be in effect for a limited time.

One way to understand intellectual property is via property law regarding land. At issue with copyright is the concern over whether intellectual property can or should be regarded as real or chattel property, or in other words, whether the products of intellectual labor are moveable things or are more akin to the ownership of land. Indeed, the very notion of intellectual production as property was the culmination of processes and policies that imposed *thingness* through *form* onto intellectual creation. The entitlements derived from real and chattel property law include the rights to exclude others from the resource, powers to transfer property to others, and privileges of use. Rights to intellectual property seem less natural than rights to tangible property, and therefore, boundaries that identify a piece of intellectual content are created to fulfill requirements for ownership. As Wendy Gordon writes, because "intellectual property has no physical boundaries that can be crossed, it must perforce use something other than entry to distinguish between those uses of the property the owner can control and those she cannot."[63] Gordon continues, "In the law of real property, physical boundaries are essential to organizing transactions. To have a market, the objects to be bought, sold, and licensed must be clearly identified."[64] Copyright law is one of the mechanisms by which information became a thing to be traded, bought, and sold. By identifying intellectual creations as property and by constraining property to recorded knowledge, or information fixed in a tangible medium, like books and maps, but not ideas, methods, or processes, information became a transactional thing, giving rise to the economic functions of copyright. "Jefferson . . . dissented from the conventional wisdom" of his time, in what appears to be resistance to the thingification of "the action of the thinking power called an idea," but he "nevertheless influenced the philosophy of copyright and intellectual property."[65]

On 6 September 1789, just before the end of his term in France, Jefferson delivered one of his most famous declarations on generational sovereignty in a letter to Madison, and although the letter is generally cited in the context of primogeniture, it offers insight into his views of intellectual property, as well:

> The question Whether one generation of men has a right to bind another, seems never to have been started either on this or our side of the water. . . . I set out on this ground, which I suppose to be self evident, '*that the earth belongs in usufruct to the living*': that the dead have neither powers nor rights over it. The portion occupied by any individual ceases to be his when himself ceases to be, and reverts to the society. . . . Then no man can, by *natural right*, oblige the lands he occupied, or the persons who succeed him in that occupation, to the paiment of debts contracted by him.[66]

By invoking the legal term "*in usufruct*" in reference to the stewardship of property belonging to someone else, Jefferson maintained that the role of the founding fathers was to establish a republic in which the coming generations of educated citizens would be in control of their own property and destiny. They would not be bound by the past, but rather, each generation has an obligation to future progress. He wrote these lines just before returning to the land he owned in Virginia, where he struggled under the weight of his deceased father-in-law's debts, which he inherited when he and Martha Wayles Skelton married. It seems he felt chained by the obligations put to him by the dead, who collaborated with the law to limit his own freedom to enjoy what he believed was his by natural right. "Jefferson the revolutionary was dedicated to liberating the 'living generation' from the 'dead hand of the past' and the old structures of knowledge and power controlled by 'kings, nobles, and priests.'"[67] The passage above conceals the tragedy of the fact that the land that he called his own was stolen land, and the construction of his house, the fruits of the tobacco and wheat fields, and the nails made in his factory, were the products of the labor of stolen people. For Jefferson to use the language of bondage to refute the notion that "one generation of men has a right to bind another" is particularly scalding, considering the fact that he was just about to embark on his return to Monticello, where the enslaved population had been working in his absence for over half a decade, and where Sally will lose any rights to freedom that she may have enjoyed in France. It was in this letter that Jefferson calculated the term of a generation, arriving at nineteen years—the number of years that would guide his thinking about when a nation should revisit its constitution. He also revised his ideas about copyright to align with the duration of a generation, and to base the law on reason, rather than English precedent: "Establish the principle also in the new law to be passed for protecting copyrights and new inventions, by securing the exclusive right for 19. instead of 14. years."[68]

Jefferson's combined interests in copying, sharing, preserving, and expanding are crucial for the expansion of the nation. His letter to George Wythe includes an outline of what Jefferson thought would be a best practice:

> I think therefore that there should be printed at the public expence, an edition of all the laws ever passed by our legislatures which can now be found; that a copy should be deposited in every public library in America, in the principal public offices within the state, and some perhaps in the most distinguished public libraries of Europe, and that the rest should be sold to individuals, towards reimbursing the expences of the edition.[69]

His position regarding the possession of ideas was directly tied to his belief in scientific progress, and scientific and technological progress were regarded as essential for building the nation. Therefore, these practices are intertwined and show how fundamental the principles of preservation and access are to Jefferson's efforts toward unifying a national imaginary.

## Claims to History

Returning to Hazard's *Historical Collections*, we find another expressed relationship between the formation of an archival tradition, nation formation, expansion, and land. There is a wealth of information in Hazard's preface that gives insight into the impetus for his historical project, beginning with the observation that the American colonies' separation from Great Britain had made the newly independent states worthy of recognition. It was upon this basis that they were deemed to deserve a history of their own:

> Secluded from the rest of the World, the Anglo-American Colonies were viewed merely as the Dependencies of Great Britain; and little

> more of them, comparatively, was known, than at what time they were discovered, and by whom: But when they dared to assert their Claims to Freedom, and in Defence of them to oppose the Parent State, whose Power even Europe dreaded—when they compelled her to consent to their Emancipation, and to acknowledge them as Independent States—they were then thought worthy of more respectful Attention, and an Acquaintance with their History was fought for with Avidity. But although the public Mind was anxious for Information, it could not be easily obtained: the Histories which had appeared, relating to a few individual States only, were not sufficient to gratify the inquisitive, and were, in general, written so long since, as not now to prove satisfactory; and Materials for furnishing a more comprehensive View of the Subject were much dispersed, and not with the Reach of many. To remove this Obstruction from the Path of Science, and, at the same Time, to lay the Foundation of a good American History, is the Object of the following Compilation. It was the Compiler's original Intention to visit each State in the Union, and to remain there a sufficient Time to form a *complete* Collection of such Material for its History as had escaped the Ravages of Time and Accident.[70]

A statist history and archives of the United States emerged through the cultivation of a narrative for posterity. The archive inscribed imperial universality and contained history to literacy, the written word, and the privileging of documents. The notion that peoples and communities are not entitled to their own histories if they are regarded as a "dependency" within an empire indicates how Indigenous, Black, and other minoritized peoples were viewed in historical terms. Sovereign states are deemed worthy of having a history of their own, and the history of any community that has been positioned as dependent on the sovereign state will be variously documented or omitted from the record and told from the point of view of the sovereign. This tradition also established the qualification of having history as being a written history. "The *history* for Man," as Sylvia Wynter observes, is "narrated and existentially lived as if it were the *history-for* the human itself."[71] The centrality of written documents in libraries and archives has ensured settler colonial dominance and rationalizes claims that any people who were not literate in English and who did not write their histories down were not considered to possess their own histories. Documents would serve as evidence of sovereignty. The distinction between *being* historical and *having* a history is essential for the settler colonial conceptualization of sovereignty, and the lines between these were drawn at the level of literacy and writing. It is related to Daniel Heath Justice's observation that "not to have literature is, in some ways and to some eyes, to be less than fully human, certainly to be less 'civilized.'"[72] The emphasis on written evidence is one way of rationalizing a narrative that distinguishes "savagery" from "civilized." A masculinist, statist, imperialist conception of literacy was written into an emerging documentary tradition in the United States.

This becomes painfully clear when we look at some of the earliest documents that were added to the collection. Under the 1778 act of Congress authorizing support for the collection of historical documents, Hazard sent a letter to Samuel Huntington requesting particular materials associated with "Colonel Campbell's Report of the Expedition against the Cherokees." The request cited a report that indicated that "various Manuscripts, Copies of Treaties, Commissions, Letters, and other Archives of the Nation" had been "found in Okanastota's Baggage which he left behind in his Fright." Oconostota was a Cherokee chief who died in 1782 or 1783, just a few years after his village had been destroyed in 1780. Americans saw this as an opportunity to take and preserve his papers to document this moment of conquest, which they understood as integral to the history of the revolution. Huntington forwarded the letter describing this theft to Jefferson, indicating, "If any of the Manuscripts &c. to which his Letter refers, will in your Excellency's Opinion be useful or worthy of Notice in the Pages of History, I am perswaded you will be so kind as to forward them agreeable to his Desire, whenever Leisure from more important Concerns shall permit."[73] Then, at Jefferson's request, Campbell sent some of the papers, and later that year Jefferson sent them on to Congress. Today these materials are housed in the Library of Congress.[74] These communications and the archival descriptions of the documents sanitize the details of the events reported in the content that they are discussing, and they certainly do not contain the Cherokees' point of view. This campaign against the Cherokees was an extraordinarily destructive one, as described by Jefferson in a previous letter to Huntington, dated 17 February 1781:

> It was determined to carry the war into their country rather than await it in ours, and I have it in my power to inform you, that thus disagreeably circumstanced the issue has been successful. The Militia of this State and north Carolina penetrated into their country, burnt almost every town they had amounting to about 1000 houses in the whole, destroyed 50,000 bushels of grain killed 20 and took 17 prisoners. The latter are mostly women and Children.[75]

As early as 1776, Jefferson had recommended the removal of the Cherokees and other tribes that supported the British troops to land west of the

Mississippi. (Recall the letter to Page regarding Six Nations at the beginning of this chapter.)

These exchanges reveal the connection between the founding of American archives and genocidal violence, both for what it records and what it doesn't record. "The archive is, in this case, a death sentence, a tomb, a display of the violated body, and inventory of property," as Saidiya Hartman puts this point—"an asterisk in the grand narrative of history."[76] Jefferson and his colleagues' drive to preserve the documents associated with the bloody massacres of the Cherokees must be understood as integral to the American archival imaginary, which was constructed on the basis of universal Man and an expendable other. J. J. Ghaddar writes, "Colonizers love archives, and nothing is more common in the colonial world than the enthusiastic, if rather callous, figure of the academic or artist going about the self-appointed task of preserving—not Indigenous peoples themselves, but a record of them."[77] I will say more about the role of information in empire expansion in chapters on Jefferson's libraries and museum and how he recorded and organized information about Indigenous peoples. Indeed, the vastness of the types of record keeping and the repetition of racializing processes in the documentary record were key to solidifying the rationalization of expansion at any cost.

Another set of documents, this time related to the Lewis and Clark expedition, shows Jefferson's views about archival practice in the context of governing. Julian Boyd provides a thorough account of the case in which Jefferson insisted that certain papers from the expedition belong to the government. There were questions of a distinction between private and public ownership, as well as parts versus the whole. In Jefferson's view, the entirety of Lewis and Clark's journals should be archived. He was worried that the death of Benjamin Barton, who had been preparing the Lewis and Clark journals for publication, might cause them to be lost. In a letter to his friend José Corrêia da Serra, a Portuguese naturalist, Jefferson first described the contents of Meriwether Lewis's journals, which included ten or twelve bound volumes of hand-written observations during the expedition, possibly another book with descriptions of plants and animals, a collection of Native American vocabularies, observations of longitude and latitude, and a map spread across many pages:

> These constitute the whole. they are the property of the government, the fruits of the expedition undertaken at such expence of money and risk of valuable lives. they contain exactly the whole of the information which it was our object to obtain for the benefit of our own country and of the world. but we were willing to give to Lewis and Clarke

> whatever pecuniary benefits might be derived from the publication, and therefore left the papers in their hands, taking for granted that their interests would produce a speedy publication, which would be better if done under their direction. but the death of Cap$^{t}$ Lewis, the distance and occupations of General Clarke, and the bankruptcy of their bookseller, have retarded the publication, and rendered necessary that the government should attend to the reclamation & security of the papers . . . their safest deposit as fast as they can be collected, will be the Philosophical society, who no doubt will be so kind as to recieve and preserve them, subject to the orders of government; and their publication, once effected in any way, the originals will probably be left in the same deposit. . . . as to any claims of individuals to these papers, it is to be observed that, as being the property of the public, we are certain neither Lewis nor Clarke would undertake to convey away the right to them, and that they could not convey them, had they been capable of intending it.[78]

Of this commentary Julian Boyd proclaimed, "No archivist ever stated so emphatically the right of the Government to recover its own, no private citizen ever pursued that object with such unwearied diligence. It is true that Jefferson utilized the agency of our oldest learned society to accomplish his object. But the real instrument was the right of the Federal Government to reclaim and secure 'these precious monuments of . . . our history.'"[79] Jefferson's main concern was preventing the scatter and loss of the documents, but he also wanted the publication to reach a wider readership, including European politicians and natural historians, who had propelled ideas that the American landscape and climate produced degeneracy in its flora and fauna. Depositing the documents as a whole would bring them together in one place, and eventually publication would make them more broadly accessible. Arguably, this set the stage for acquiring archival documents pertaining to interactions with Native Americans and their languages and transferring them as property of the national government. And again, these archival actions are best understood alongside his *Notes on the State of Virginia*, in which he used archival evidence to defend his claim that Virginia's lands were lawfully obtained rather than stolen from the Indigenous communities that lived there for centuries: "That the lands of this country were taken from them by conquest, is not so general a truth as is supposed. I find in our historians and records, repeated proofs of purchase, which cover a considerable part of the lower country. . . . The upper country we know has been acquired altogether by purchases made in the most unexceptionable form."[80] This account ignores any facts that call into question the ethics of the methods by which land was obtained from Indigenous communities. Jefferson, the archivist could determine what counted as history and how it should be preserved, and Jefferson the historian could consult the archive to tell the story that he wanted to be told—a history of purchases of lands rather than coercion or theft. Jefferson the governor, secretary of state, and president, could authorize decisions about land acquisitions.

Jean O'Brien uses the frame of "firsting and lasting" to describe the ways that Indigenous people have been written out of history. Settlers had several ways of claiming firsts, which strengthened claims of ownership. The Doctrine of Discovery established the grounds for this practice, with its explicit assertion of the "first discovery" clause, which granted the first European country to "discover" new lands unknown to other European countries sovereign rights to the land. Once that country had occupied that land by establishing a fort or settlement, it gained the sole right to purchase land from the Indigenous people to whom the land belonged. The whole notion of discovery is based in the fiction of being the first to set eyes on land, and from this way of thinking comes the belief that the first one there gets to claim it. "Firsting" continues its force as a principle by which land, artifacts, and knowledge are claimed, even when the land, artifacts, and knowledge in fact were of Indigenous peoples first. Firsting had its complement, "lasting," which affirmed the myth of the vanishing Indigenous people. Settlers could perform mournfulness over the loss of cultures, while pretending that they were not responsible for the death and destruction of entire communities. The *Last of the Mohicans* is an obvious example, as that book reflected the pervasive belief that Indigenous peoples would eventually disappear. This was, of course, a self-serving narrative, as it rationalized the theft of Indigenous peoples' lands, and the removal of Indigenous communities from those lands to make way for American expansion and settlement. O'Brien writes:

> Historical narration implicitly argued that Indians can never be modern because they cannot be the subjects of change, only its victims. This discourse locates Indians in an ahistorical temporality that relegates Indian history to a degeneracy narrative marred by racial mixing and cultural loss. Conversely, non-Indian New Englanders reserve to themselves the authorship of recorded time, which is subject to a

> progress narrative wherein racial mixing and cultural dynamism are asserted as the privilege of whiteness.[81]

This explains why Logan and other figures of the "last Indian" in the American archive is both contradictory and durable. Indeed, Elmer interprets Jefferson's account of Chief Logan described in the beginning of this chapter, "as the earliest influential instance of a peculiarly enduring trope—the last of the X, the Indian facing and bewailing his people's extinction."[82] He also suggests that Logan's speech was source material for *Last of the Mohicans*. These are archival and literary mechanisms of ordering empire by way of making and narrating distinctions. Chapter 3 considers the weight of repression in Jefferson's archive, as well as the ways that repressive classificatory acts shape colonial archival imaginaries.

# 3
# Haunted Ontologies

> As the vehicle of progress, modern politics redirects time and transforms it into history.
>
> —CATHERINE HOLLAND, *THE BODY POLITIC*

> Indeed I tremble for my country when I reflect that God is just: that his justice cannot sleep for ever; that considering numbers, nature, and natural means only, a revolution of the wheel of fortune, an exchange of situation, is among possible events. . . . I think a change already perceptible, since the origin of the present revolution. The spirit of the master is abating, that of the slave rising from the dust, his condition mollifying, the way I hope preparing under the auspices of heaven, for a total emancipation.
>
> —THOMAS JEFFERSON, *NOTES ON THE STATE OF VIRGINIA*

Jefferson and his history-minded colleagues set a settler colonial archival imaginary into motion by making decisions about what to record, how to preserve documents, and what counted and did not count as American history. Michelle Caswell conceptualizes an "archival imaginary" as "the dynamic way in which communities creatively and collectively re-envision the future through archival interventions in representations of the shared past. Through the archival imaginary, the past becomes a lens to the future; the future is rooted in that which preceded it."[1] Early American archival practices played a crucial role in framing and sustaining an archival imaginary by putting materials to work toward particular uses of history and memorialization in the founding of the United States. Jefferson operationalized his ideas about degeneration, amelioration, and progress in the construction of the archive in choreographing American memory. His visions for the future generations of Americans to abolish slavery, the end of Indigenous lifeways, and the progress of civilization across the westward expanse are embedded in the structures by which archival knowledges are acquired and organized, and those structures affect the ways that stories are accessed, interpreted, and told. As Walter Benjamin writes, archives, and artifacts—what he calls "cultural treasures"—have violent origin stories:

> They own their existence not only to the efforts of the great minds and talents who have created them, but also to the anonymous toil of their contemporaries. There is no document of civilization which is not at the same time a document of barbarism. And just as such a document is not free of barbarism, barbarism taints also the manner in which it was transmitted from one owner to another.[2]

Benjamin was cautioning about histories that referred to the progress of humanity, which was the type of history that Jefferson advanced. As Theodor Adorno attests, the belief in progress as a historical "fact" carries danger. This is not to say that Benjamin and Adorno eschewed the idea of progress altogether, but rather, that historiography driven by Enlightenment reason is fraught with paradox that constrains progress within the context of domination and conquest. The aspiration to freedom requires the unfreedom of others. The challenge according to critical theorists like Benjamin and Adorno is to "*call attention to that very paradox*" if we are to use the tools of Enlightenment thinking toward nonviolence and reconciliation—to reaffirm the "ideals of freedom and equal respect as central to 'our' Enlightenment inheritance . . . by radically transforming them from within."[3] Amy Allen summarizes Adorno's view of historical progress as fact: "the idea that humanity has progressed in the past and that our present form of life is the result of such progress—stands in the way of progress as a forward-looking moral-political imperative, because such a belief leads to an 'idolization of history' that blinds us to its own ideological bases."[4] Allen uses the works of the Frankfurt school theorists, siding with Adorno and Foucault, to show how we can submit History to historicization to work toward a post- and decolonial critical theory. She suggests that "the realization of freedom requires the uncovering of the conceptual and normative violence implicit in the norm of freedom itself, such as uncovering how the autonomy of the subject depends on the domination of inner nature or the disciplining of the body or the denial of full subjectivity to those who are deemed wholly Other or abject."[5] Allen finds in Adorno and Foucault (and to a lesser extent Benjamin), direction for an idea of progress that does not ascribe to a forward-looking utopian vision, nor a backward-looking view of the arrival of Man, but "a more radically open-ended, futural conception of freedom, where we leave open the possibility that there may well be some future in which our own normative commitments and ways of thinking of ordering things will have been transcended, and thus will have come to seem impossibly strange."[6] Libraries, archives, and museums have inherited the strangeness of Jefferson's various cataloging techniques, and the peculiarity of his archival and historiographic methods.

Many of Jefferson's documents and organizing principles reveal the violence associated with the advancement of "civilization" in the United States. Considering how the seemingly originary place at Monticello was being developed in tandem with the founding and expansion of the nation brings clarity about the formation of early American archives. By "reading colonial records through an archival lens," and more broadly, by studying settler colonial history and history-making through an information studies lens, this opens space for thinking about the ways in which history is cultivated, constructed, passed from one generation to the next, and sometimes lost, erased, or omitted.[7] One might say that it is a meta-archival or meta-informational project invested in understanding the production of information in history and history in information. I insist, borrowing from Caswell, that the abstraction of archives into a general concept of "the archive" is a methodological error that overlooks archival labor and the human more generally.[8] Markus Friedrich concurs: "The view of archives as a reified institution must not obscure the fact that archives are constituted by countless activities and actions." He adds, "we are interested less in 'the archive' as an institution than in 'archiving' and 'archival work.'"[9] As Jefferson's case demonstrates, collecting and classifying are personal endeavors that take place in and are informed by culture. Abstracting "the archive" from archival collections and the people who curate them hides the personal and political motivations underlying the drive to acquire and give order to documents. It gives the illusion that the structures we have were inevitable, that the dehumanizing categories and structures are of the system, rather than produced by people. It also diminishes the fact that humans can and do perform archival and information work based on more socially just principles, especially in places like community archives.[10]

The theoretical, political, and practical implications of the relationship between the concept of the archive and archives as place become especially resonant in Jefferson's archive/s. Jacques Derrida reminds us that the Greek root of the word "archive" has two simultaneous meanings. It refers to places of origin: "*there* where things *commence*—physical, historical, or ontological principle," and it also refers to law: "*there* where men and gods *command*, *there* where authority, social order are exercised, *in this place* from which *order* is given."[11] He also explains that the meaning of "archive"—"its only meaning, comes to it from the Greek *arkheion*: initially a house, a domicile, an address, the residence of the superior magistrates, the archons, those who commanded."[12] The *Oxford English Dictionary* confirms that "arch" means "chief, principal, first in authority or order," combining the ideas of firstness, authority, and order.[13] It is no accident that "archive," "architect," and "archaeology" share the same root. The *OED* also indicates that "architect" refers to a master builder, or "One who designs and frames any complex structure; *esp*. the Creator."[14] Digging further into this definition, we arrive at the meanings of mastery, and although the term is considered a noun, the definitions signal actions associated with discipline and command: "The action of mastering a subject; Command or comprehensive knowledge of a subject, art, or process; pre-eminent skill in a particular sphere of activity." It also refers to "the state or condition of being master, controller, or ruler" or to ascendancy to power by way of a victory that results in "domination or subjugation."[15] The *OED* definitions signal intertwining processes of the master of academic subjects and the mastery and domination of people within their domain.

"Archaeology" is the study of beginnings.[16] An archive is, in this view, the institutionalization of origin studies, and the master determines the starting point. Hannah Arendt writes about the necessity of locating a revolution as a beginning:

> It is in the very nature of a beginning to carry with itself a measure of complete arbitrariness. Not only is it not bound into a reliable chain of cause and effect, a chain in which each effect immediately turns into the cause for future developments, the beginning has, as it were, nothing whatsoever to hold on to; it is as though it came out of nowhere in either time or space. For a moment, the moment of beginning, it is as though the beginner had abolished the sequence of temporality itself, or as though the actors were thrown out of the temporal order and its continuity.[17]

Citing Locke's famous "In the beginning, all the world was America," Catherine Holland suggests that the idea of America was loaded with symbolic power, signifying "the ancient ground on which the future will be forged, a fertile territory awaiting the cultivation and construction of a future purified of the contaminants of the European past."[18] The fantasy of this "new world" rested on a commitment to the belief that "America" was "terra nullius," devoid of civilization. It placed the natural world and the Indigenous inhabitants in a space and place without time or history, while imagining that new Americans could start anew by separating from their European pasts. The now of the revolution "started a new calendar" and reorganized time. The first Fourth of July serves as a reference point for recurring commemorative holidays. One of the last letters that Jefferson wrote, just over a week before he died, shows that he understood Independence Day as a moment by which the United States would keep time, and an "annual return of this day" would perpetually remind Americans to work toward the improvement of the human condition. Seeing the Declaration as a beginning, he could look to a future that would unfold after his passing:

> all eyes are opened, or opening to the rights of man. the general spread of the light of science has already laid open to every view the palpable truth that the mass of mankind has not been born, with saddles on their backs, nor a favored few booted and spurred, ready to ride them legitimately, by the grace of god. these are grounds of hope for others. for ourselves let the annual return of this day, for ever refresh our recollections of these rights and an undiminished devotion to them.[19]

The Italian Count Carlo Vidua met Jefferson when he toured America, and shortly after he wrote of the Declaration of Independence that "the document has become a national memorial which is publicly read each year, whose framed *facsimile* is found in almost every home and whose author is regarded as the living *Patriarch* of the American Republic."[20] Indeed, the Fourth of July continues to be the most spectacular American holiday, celebrated with fireworks, parades, and family gatherings.

Jefferson was archiving what he viewed as a beginning as the revolution was happening. The ancient view of archives applies all too well to Jefferson—the architect, master of the house on the "little mountain," public authority, and commander in chief. He designed Monticello and its surrounding landscape, as well as the University of Virginia and other buildings, based on European revivals of classical architecture. He was an archaeologist who studied Indigenous languages, burial grounds, and customs to discover the origins of the human race. He was a scientist who explained racial difference in biological terms and enslaved hundreds of people at his home. And he authorized and enacted genocidal policies toward Indigenous peoples in the name of expansion, progress, and civilization. Each of these aspects of Jefferson must be considered alongside his archive and the information architectures that confirmed and carried his authority. He was a master builder—an "architect of memory," an information architect.[21] Jefferson is important in the history of memory practices—specifically, the ways in which acts of committing to record are embedded in technical, social, and formal practices—which carry descriptions from his past into the future to be remembered.

Caswell notes that a common trope for archivists in the present is that "we preserve traces of the past for the future," and adds that "this assertion is our professional elevator speech, how we quickly explain the importance of what we do." But as she further explains, "this construction relies on a linear temporality that is rooted in dominant Western progress narratives."[22] The temporal diagrammatics of archival methods are associated with settler colonialism's investments in ideas about linear time and the progress of science and civilization.[23] Indeed, the "pedagogic temporality of the nation-state" is readily apparent throughout Jefferson's archive. Drawing from Charles W. Mills, Caswell describes the ways in which archives are informed by a "white temporal imaginary," which structures social feeling and thinking and produces "exclusionary gated moral communities protected by temporal, no less than spatial, walls. . . . White time," explains Caswell, "instantiates across multiple venues: in settler societies that deny history before colonization; in dominant expectations of productivity and proper use of time; and in carceral regimes of waiting and 'serving' time."[24] The distinction between the masters and the mastered are defined in part by a person's capacity to master time. The logic that Caswell locates in the twenty-first century resembles the logics outlined by Jefferson and his peers. She writes:

> White time asserts that the United States is an as-of-yet unfulfilled promise of democracy getting closer and closer to realization, rather than a foundationally and fundamentally white supremacist project that is proceeding as planned. Thus, white time is built not just on linear temporalities, but on grand notions of being in the midst of progress toward a post-racial (and therefore, according to dominant white logics, more just) future, even in the face of overwhelming evidence to the contrary.[25]

Kim TallBear, citizen of the Sisseton-Wahpeton Oyate, proposes that, instead of thinking in terms of a progress that aligns with linear time, we might "consider instead a spatial narrative of change—one in which we attend to all of our obligations upon a web or plane of relations." Linear narratives that appear to account for all, conflate "the universal (hu)man with settler-colonial culture and its assumed whiteness, masculinity, and straightness."[26] Temporal-spatial dimensions are important methodological considerations, as well, as the technologies and techniques for organizing knowledge change, become obsolete, and get repurposed over time. At the same time, thinking about the "temporal entanglements" embedded in information infrastructures draws attention to the fact that Jefferson was not only working within a particular socio-cultural-economic-political milieu, but that he inherited many techniques from the past, which echo into our present technologies, even if they are reconfigured, and even if we do not readily notice them.[27]

Technologies and formal procedures allow people to replace memories stored in the mind through abstraction, simplification, and substitution. The classifications and finding aids that facilitate information storage and retrieval are essential for the recall function of mediating technologies. As Geoffrey Bowker explains, we do not need to remember particulars if we have indexical systems that will guide our search for what we want to know, or what we want others to find out, i.e., "we classify in order to be able to forget."[28] We rarely remember complete stories, but we can reassemble them from an archive. What this and so many other projects demonstrate, however, is the "jussive nature of the archive," which "comes down to the question of what can and cannot be remembered," because of what is retained, how it's organized, and what is forgotten.[29]

## Redemption

Jefferson rarely invoked a god in public forums. In fact, he was disinclined to hold faith in a god whose existence could not be verified with empirical evidence. He famously cut references to supernatural events from his copy of the Bible, but he saw moral and historical value in the content regarding Jesus's life.[30] That he placed faith in God to correct the minds of master planters shows the inconceivability of emancipation if left to the hearts and minds of men. Still, he imagined an American future without slavery:

> Indeed I tremble for my country when I reflect that God is just: that his justice cannot sleep for ever; that considering numbers, nature, and natural means only, a revolution of the wheel of fortune, an exchange of situation, is among possible events. . . . I think a change already perceptible, since the origin of the present revolution. The spirit of the master is abating, that of the slave rising from the dust, his condition mollifying, the way I hope preparing under the auspices of heaven, for a total emancipation.[31]

Walter Benjamin's theses on history provide critical framing for Jefferson's imagined program for the eventual abolition of slavery. "Our image of happiness," writes Benjamin, "is thoroughly colored by the time to which the course of our own existence has assigned us . . . our image of happiness is indissolubly bound up with the image of redemption"[32] Jefferson hoped that generations to come would redeem his own with regard to slavery. The Declaration of Independence's statement regarding "the pursuit of happiness" is itself future-oriented. To be in pursuit of happiness suggests that it has not yet been attained. A given generation does not envy a more perfectly imagined future generation in this framework, in part because that imagined happiness serves as an index of its own redemption. "The past," too, says Benjamin, "carries with it a temporal index by which it is referred to redemption. There is a secret agreement between past generations and the present one." This is what Benjamin refers to as "Messianic time," or the "weak Messianic power" that the past has invested in the coming generations. Jefferson's deferral of action effectively cast responsibility off to children and grandchildren to correct the wrongs of the parent generation. Jefferson absolved his own revolutionary generation of responsibility with regard to slavery by passing blame to the cruelty, backwardness, and neglect of their "unfeeling brethren"—the British monarchy.[33]

There are several aspects of our twenty-first-century "now" that afford access to seeing this history in a new light. Police brutality, mass incarceration, school shootings, the impossibility of housing costs, and the death and destruction of more-than-human worlds due to industry and climate change have become normalized, and with them, the undeniable differential treatment and rights of racialized peoples in all of these realms. The recurrence and intensification of violence in our present demands a "view of history which gives rise to it [as] untenable."[34] Scholars have drawn attention to the connections between slavery, Jim Crow laws, and the racism of the present, which circulates across culture in information, bureaucracies, institutions, and everyday life. It is in this present moment that we can think about Jefferson's racism, because we can recognize an "image of the past" in the present "as one of [our] own concerns." As Benjamin explains, "To articulate the past historically does not mean to recognize it 'the way it really was'. . . It means to seize hold of a memory as it flashes up at a moment of danger." We see danger in our present, and the "same threat hangs over both: that of becoming a tool of the ruling class." In this kind of moment, which Benjamin describes as the "recognizability of the now," we are awakened to the "constellation of dangers" of maintaining the status quo.[35]

Rather than holding up the belief that any given generation is meant to redeem the past, perhaps it is more appropriate to recognize the pastness of the now. Michel-Rolph Trouillot speaks of the consequences of relegating slavery to the past: "What is obscene is not a relation to The Past, but the dishonesty of that relation as it would happen in our present. The trivialization of slavery—and of the suffering it caused—inheres in that present.

The 'past' fails to stay in the past."[36] Reconciliation and repair require accounting for what has happened and how slavery has been reinscribed. The angel of history can guide our attention. It is worth repeating the passage in full:

> Where we perceive a chain of events, he sees one single catastrophe which keeps piling wreckage upon wreckage and hurls it in front of his feet. The angel would like to stay, awaken the dead, and make whole what has been smashed. But a storm is blowing from Paradise; it has got caught in his wings with such violence that the angel can no longer close them. This storm irresistibly propels him into the future to which his back is turned, while the pile of debris before him grows skyward.[37]

The founding of the United States required a particular kind of history-making, which included formulating particular ideas about its past. The "construction of an imaginary past," however, "may itself involve the elision of the terms of its own construction, and such a denial may turn out to be necessary to the success of the new order."[38] As Niklas Luhmann observes, "Ever since history became a narrative . . . —that is, since the eighteenth century—describing history has been a semantical device presenting the unity of the past as a guarantee of the unity of the present."[39] The task is to observe the devices through which that history has been constructed.

The memorialized pastness recirculates stories of how the founding fathers fought for freedom and equality. This view of time suggests the possibility of "newness" in history. The moment of messianic rupture—redemption or revolution—is also a moment when past debts and complicities are thought to be cancelled out.

## Amelioration and Deferral

Jefferson believed, as did so many of his colleagues—even some of the most fervent abolitionists—that an end to slavery must be a gradual process.[40] In a letter dated 26 January 1789, he wrote, "that as far as I can judge from the experiments which have been made, to give liberty to, or rather, to abandon persons whose habits have been formed in slavery is like abandoning children."[41] As Hannah Spahn points out, "if the black slaves were depicted as 'naturally' dependent, like children or domestic animals, on the superior foresight of their (benevolent) owners, the postponement of abolition would appear, if not more justified, at least less cruel."[42] Amelioration, or the improvement of the institution of slavery, was variously viewed as a set of processes, depending on a person's point of view. For abolitionists, it was intended to pave the way toward a more humane treatment of people who were enslaved, and eventually their liberation. For many planters, however, amelioration was seen to be enough—if slavery could be improved, then it could also be defended. Although Jefferson was opposed to slavery and looked forward to a future America without it, he invested in several advances toward improving the conditions of slavery at his own plantation in part because of his belief in the promise of deferral. Slavery was a regressive institution in Jefferson's view, and he associated it with the tyranny and backwardness of the British monarchy. Jefferson asserted that slavery and the transatlantic slave trade were both "archaic, Old World systems foisted on Americans without their consent."[43] But, "in order to relegate slavery to the Old World," Jefferson and his colleagues "had to gloss over their recent past as agents of empire—and proponents of the slave trade—in the New."[44] The simultaneous future-looking and historicizing narratives of the slave trade were rhetorical tools that absolved themselves of responsibility in their present.

Lucia (Cinder) Stanton has documented the ways that Monticello was for a time a laboratory for labor management, techniques for which Jefferson adapted from the prison reform movement. Jefferson limited the use of corporal punishment and offered rewards as incentives for good work.[45] Improved conditions, Jefferson believed, would not only increase efficiency of production, but would be morally correct. Ameliorating the institution of slavery would bring a measure of humanization, while at the same time, planters would see a rise in profits. He believed that happier slaves would be more productive and docile. Improving the conditions of slavery may have logically seemed like an important step toward emancipation, but it also affirmed planters' authority. As Christa Dierksheide points out, the end goal of amelioration was to "broaden and protect the 'rights' and equality of slaveholding patriarchs." Planters viewed this as a source of progress. Whatever his intension, Jefferson "inadvertently wrote the language for slavery's perpetuation," with his plans for improving the lives of the people he enslaved.[46]

In Jefferson's mind, though, the path toward emancipation included several incremental processes, including the abolition of the transatlantic slave trade. Then the practice of slavery and treatment of enslaved people would be improved by several measures, including the reduction of violence, the introduction of incentives, and certain forms of care. For example, when Jefferson shifted his plantation's cash crops from tobacco to wheat, he also improved housing quarters so that families lived together in single units. The final stage of emancipation in Jefferson's view was the "repatriation" of Black people by sending them to Africa or the West Indies to form a colony.

The future America without slavery would ideally be a whitened populace made possible by exiling formerly enslaved people to another country. Without a slave trade to import people from Africa, and by sending Black people elsewhere, the slave population would disappear, according to this fantasy, and perhaps, eventually, an idealized whiteness would pervade.

Jefferson believed that too much was at stake in the early days of the republic and that the nation was too fragile to weather the conflict that would ensue from outlawing slavery. His vision for the republic demanded that abolition of slavery would wait, and in the meantime, the institution would have to be reformed. Unfortunately, as we know, the conditions of slavery worsened and the type of conflict that he predicted did materialize in the Civil War. The reality is that the domestic slave trade expanded dramatically after the end of the transatlantic trade, and the underlying truth of Jefferson's plan to abolish the transatlantic slave trade and his methods of amelioration at Monticello is that it served him financially. Keeping families together was a good business plan because they would continue to bear children, which would increase his labor force. In fact, he calculated his increase in "capital" in reproductive human property: "I consider a woman who brings a child every two years as more profitable than the best man of the farm."[47] Dierksheide notes that the "fact that Jefferson acquired many of the 607 slaves he owned in his lifetime through natural 'increase' undercut his understanding of slavery as a static and regressive 'blot' that would eventually be expelled from the nation."[48] His personal investment stands in contradiction to his public pronouncements.

In 1801, the first year of Jefferson's presidency, he wrote to James Monroe, "however our present interests may restrain us within our own limits, it is impossible not to look forward to distant times, when our rapid multiplication will expand itself beyond those limits, & cover the whole Northern, if not the Southern continent with a people speaking the same language, governed in similar forms, & by similar laws: nor can we contemplate, with satisfaction, either blot or mixture on that surface."[49] He believed that "race-mixing" posed a threat to the newly formed republican government. To his mind mixed-race people would render the country "a heterogeneous, incoherent, distracted mass," that would impede progress. As we know, however, his stated beliefs and his private lives did not align. It may be for this reason, suggests Dierksheide, that Jefferson could not publicly acknowledge his own mixed-race children born by Sally Hemings.

Jefferson was able to recognize the potential for rising conflict that would derive from slavery. He seems to anticipate Aimé Césaire's theory regarding the thingification of people, particularly in a passage on "Manners" in

*Notes on the State of Virginia*, knowing that this document would likely become public:

> There must doubtless be an unhappy influence on the manners of our people produced by the existence of slavery among us. The whole commerce between master and slave is a perpetual exercise of the most boisterous passions, the most unremitting despotism on the one part, and degrading submissions on the other. Our children see this, and learn to imitate it; for man is an imitative animal. This quality is the germ of all education in him. From his cradle to his grave he is learning to do what he sees others do.[50]

Jefferson predicted that this influence would limit the capacity for the nation to live up to its vision for freedom and equality. Indeed, Cesaire's observations speak back to Jefferson and are applicable in our present: "First we must study how colonization works to *decivilize* the colonizer, to *brutalize* him in the true sense of the word, to degrade him, to awaken him to buried instincts, to covetousness, violence, race hatred, and moral relativism." In a warning that turns colonialist language against colonizers, Césaire says that under the conditions of slavery, "the continent proceeds toward *savagery*."[51] Given Jefferson's predictions, he perhaps would have admitted that Césaire was correct.

## Repression

Jefferson's archive demonstrates Tavia Nyong'o's observation in the context of the dream of racial transcendence after the election of Barack Obama to the US presidency: "Our belief in the novelty of our contemporary moment is only a repression of our awareness of the history of such deferrals."[52] The methods by which he organized his documents contribute to a tightening and clarification of the concept of repression. Most commonly this term is used to refer to the use of force to control individuals or populations. Repression is the action or result of repressing something. To repress: "To put down by force, suppress (an enemy, lawbreaker, troublemaker, etc.); *to reduce to subjection*, subdue." The precision and specificity of language in the *Oxford English Dictionary* that defines repression as reducing to subjection strikes me as extraordinary for the way that it strikes at the heart of this research on Jefferson's information technologies, which is fundamentally invested in understanding the problem of reducing lives, literature, and knowledge to categories—that to master one's subjects, one has to reduce them, or that the very process of subjection requires the creation and ordering (both in giving orders and in sorting and ranking) of subjects. The repression of populations and their activities for the purpose of control depends upon classificatory techniques. The *withinness* and *beneathness* of information infrastructures described in Chapter 1 are intrinsic to mechanisms of repression.

The *OED* also provides a meaning derived from psychoanalysis: "To suppress (an unacceptable thought, memory, or desire) so that it becomes or remains unconscious, either deliberately or through an involuntary process." It also offers a definition for "repressed": "Of a thought or desire: kept suppressed and unconscious in a person's mind; (of a person, attitude, etc.) characterized by the repression of thoughts or desires, especially sexual ones." Knitting all of these dictionary definitions together, we come to understand "repression" as a condition that involves *reduction* for the purpose of *subjection*, as well as a censorship-suppression of thoughts and desires to the unconscious. What is repressed in the individual body and the body politic has materialized in the systems that govern our lives.

As much as a classification is a series of statements, it is also a technique of repression. In the context of archives, libraries, museums, and other sociotechnical systems, classifications frame the conditions of possibility for thinking in social spheres, and if we understand these conditions to be *organized by* repression, we gain an entirely different sense of the circulation of knowledge. Indeed, if information is trafficked along channels organized by the unconscious—by what can't be known or mastered—we discover that what we don't know or can't know is perhaps more significant that what we believe ourselves to know. The ways we encounter information and how we receive and interact with it are always driven at least in part by an unconscious. This is where the "*undercommons of the enlightenment*" reside—"where the work gets done, where the work gets subverted."[53] Censorship is generally regarded as the suppression or prohibition of content, but there are also ways in which we unconsciously censor material all the time—things that are unthinkable and unbearable to the conscious mind, or ideas that are too dangerous to register. Classification is instrumental to disciplinary discourse and plays an active role in outlining the circulation of knowledge. It is both a political and psychical technique of discipline and is an essential mechanism by which apparatuses are *structured by* repression.[54]

According to Peter Galison, Sigmund Freud did not simply believe that censorship of the cultural record was analogous to psychic repression, or that one could stand as a metaphor for the other. Rather, censorship was "both a psychic agency and a literal mechanism enlisted for political repression and stabilization."[55] Or as Derrida puts it, "repression is an archivization."[56] Hidden beneath a taxonomy's named categories and the relationships among them are the subaltern, horrors, and truths that threaten the security of a nation, a community, and an ideological framework. But taxonomies are written by people, and so they also reflect their creators' beliefs, their social and political investments, and their time and place. Buried in a classification may be thoughts that can't be named, ideas that can't be admitted into the historical record, the people who aren't considered human, or a person's own trauma or shame. In other words, as Derrida writes in *Archive Fever*, the unconscious is itself an archive that stores intentions and ideas—it holds and contains memory, even if it that memory is not recalled: "a repression also archives that of which it dissimulates or encrypts the archives."[57] Bowker and Star have described information architectures in terms of hidden infrastructures, noting that the classification systems that organize information are rarely seen by the public.[58] That research matters for thinking about how people are affected and informed by structures that escape their awareness. Indeed, the public consciousness and people's individual and collective encounters with information are shaped by the classifications that make the circulation of information possible.

These structures are not just hidden, but are doing a certain kind of "*work* performed by vision's unseen"—they contain repressed truths that are entirely irreducible and unfindable—submerged and dispersed across these ordered systems.[59] I am mindful of Jacqueline Rose's observations about Freud's questioning of visible evidence presented by the body—that one needed to penetrate beyond any visible symptom of disorder: "Freud's challenge to the visible, to the empirically self-evident, the 'blindness of the seeing eye'. . . can give us the strongest sense of the force of the unconscious as a concept against a fully social classification relying on empirical evidence as its rationale."[60] The task is to reveal the ways that Jefferson's classifications speak—to read each classificatory act as a statement, and to look for the unspoken and the unseen. It is not to get inside his head, but rather, to get inside the archival documents and view the structuring mechanisms of the archive as historical documents in and of themselves.

There are various conditions that produce unthinkability. One is cultural—certainly there were limits to what Jefferson could imagine because of the norms of the day. But the unconscious stores a different kind of thing that can't be thought. Trauma, guilt, grief, fear—so many affective experiences, thoughts, and desires. In Jefferson's documents we "have before us the production of the most *private* interiority in the midst of the *public* sphere."[61] Jefferson's Farm Book may be the source that most clearly stands as a classification that contains and represses knowledges and materializes in the lives of the people whom he enslaved. Jefferson started keeping his Farm Book in January 1774 and made his last entry in the book just over a month before he died, in May 1826. He recorded the activities associated with his plantations in Albemarle, Bedford, and Campbell Counties for fifty-two years. Some of the tables feature names and years of birth listed under the plantation at which they lived and worked—Monticello, Elk Hill, Lego, Shadwell, etc. Other tables are drawn to tally the allotments of blankets, shoes, linen, thread, beds, fish, beef, and other supplies. There is a page with the heading "Register of births," which divides the enslaved community according to gender and provides the first names of the child with his or her mother and the year of birth. There are lists devoted to counting the loaves of bread a person or family was given per week. Other pages provide lists of births and deaths in a single year. Very often names were grouped according to families. To categorize people in this Farm Book was to name them, group them, and prioritize them according to their tasks. It keeps them in their places, not only as slaves but as types of slaves. A person's rank determined how many blankets they were allotted in a given year, how much and what type of food they would eat, where they lived, and whether their families were likely to be separated. They were ranked according to their value as capital and producers of capital. But what isn't stated are all the aspects of their humanity—their emotions, their games, their interactions, their talents, their intellectual lives, and their dreams. To speak of the desires of the enslaved, it would seem, would be to admit their humanity and would undermine the slave system upon which the planters depended. The repressive nature of classificatory regimes means that censorship resides in the information infrastructures themselves. And it shows that this repressive technique of reducing lives to subject and arranging them according to a particular point of view is intrinsic to political repression and the subjugation of human life.

A classificatory act puts a subject into discourse by indicating what something is, how it ranks in relation to other entities, and how it ranks and relates to the classifier's priorities and worldview. As Saidiya Hartman writes, "The archive of slavery rests upon a founding violence. This violence determines, regulates and organizes the kinds of statements that can be made about slavery and as well it creates subjects and objects of power."[62] Along with the manifest statement about what something is, what it's about, or how it matters, is a multitude of possible statements that have not or cannot be enunciated. Galison's interpretation of Freud's theories of censorship and repression as techniques that re-territorialize the mind call forth opportunities to think about the interrelatedness of landscape, architecture, information, territory, and knowledge. These are not merely metaphors: the mind is a landscape; an information system's architecture takes up and organizes physical and intellectual spaces; the mind and information, including their hidden components, are inextricably connected and always in dialogue.

## Control and Concealment

Jefferson drew his own architectural plans for his home and the University of Virginia, as well as many public buildings. Jefferson's information architectures resemble those designs and similarly feature dynamics of concealment. One might say that his information architectures were among "Jefferson's many decades of architectural experiments in a slave society."[63] He intentionally hid the enslaved servants and their world from view, very often by stationing them underground, out of the field of vision from his pleasure gardens where he entertained guests. He used technologies like dumbwaiters and shelves mounted on a revolving door to lessen the physical presence of servants in the dining room. And he borrowed surveillance techniques from the prison reform movement to maximize his own field of vision and to create order across his plantation. Like Jeremy Bentham, he believed that corporal punishment was demeaning, and he thought that the enslaved workers would be more productive and better behaved if they believed they were being observed. At the University of Virginia, his architectural plan included zones specifically designed for students and the enslaved: "The enslaved were to live and work in the basements and in the work yards. . . . Students were to spend their time in their dormitory rooms and in classrooms and the library, places where the enslaved were to have little reason to venture."[64]

Collectively, his *Notes on the State of Virginia*, Memorandum Books, letters, drawings, and Farm Book reveal the ways in which he outlined bodies, spatial arrangements, and political ideology in various contexts for interconnected and diverging purposes. What could not be said or written down is as (or perhaps more) important than what was recorded, and the repressed content in Jefferson's documentary record might be considered the negative "blueprint of his own mind."[65] In its entirety, a classification is a projection of a person's conscious and unconscious minds, in the written and unwritten, the expressed and the repressed. We could easily replace Freud with Jefferson in Derrida's questions:

> Beyond every possible and necessary inquiry, we will always wonder what Freud (for example), what every "careful concealer" may have wanted to keep secret. We will wonder what he may have kept of his unconditional right to secrecy, while at the same time burning with the desire to know, to make known, and to archive the very thing he concealed. What was concealed? What did he conceal even beyond the intention to conceal, to lie, or to perjure? We will always wonder what, in the *mal d'archive*, he may have burned. We will always wonder, sharing with compassion in this archive fever, what may

> have burned of his secret passions, of his correspondence, or of his "life." Burned without him, without remains and without knowledge. With no possible response, be it spectral or not, short of or beyond a suppression, on the other edge of repression, originary or secondary, with a name, without the least symptom, and without even an ash.[66]

Jefferson logged and alphabetically indexed every letter he sent or received in what he called his "Summary Journal of Letters." Unfortunately, he did not begin his "epistolary record" until 1783, six years after his mother passed, but he continued to register his letters until just before his death. Jefferson wrote over 18,000 letters over the course of his lifetime. The letters that have survived as public records reveal performances of the roles from which he wrote. Each letter had its own intended reader, and he was always aware of the possibility of the letter getting in the wrong hands. As Annette Gordon-Reed and Peter Onuf write:

> Jefferson wrote in order to structure his own life, and to try to bring into existence the world as he wished it to be. . . . Transmitting this picture of family harmony to his daughter was one part aspiration, one part promise, and one part instruction. Of the astonishing array of Jeffersonian writing and record keeping—Farm and Garden Books, commonplace books, architectural plans, and Memorandum Books—letter writing was the principal means by which he imagined and structured his life.[67]

Perhaps Jefferson has captured so many imaginations because of what he has kept secret. On the one hand he was the most prolific and steadfast documentarian of his day, and yet he eludes interpretation. It's not just that he's from a different time and place so that our present condition makes it difficult to see him in his own light, but that he was indeed a most "careful concealer" whose archives burned—intentionally, as in the case of his correspondence with Martha, and unintentionally, as in the tragic Shadwell fire. More than that, he was very aware that his documents could potentially come into public view—that his privacy was never assured, that his documented life was not his own, and so he self-censored what he wrote. Take for example, his early correspondence about his romantic pursuit of Rebecca Burwell. In a letter to his friend John Page, Jefferson was worried that someone might have intercepted a previous letter and wished he'd been more fastidiousness in encrypting its contents:

> My letter of Jan. 19, may have been opened, and the person who did it may have been further incited by curiosity, to ask you if you had

> received such a letter as they saw mentioned therein; but God send, and I hope this is not the case. . . . I wish I had followed your example, and wrote it in Latin, and that I had called my dear *campana in die*, instead of a *αδνιλεβ*.
>
> We must fall on some scheme of communicating our thoughts to each other, which shall be totally unintelligible to every one but to ourselves. I will send you some of these days Shelton's Tachygraphical Alphabet, and directions.[68]

We can't know Jefferson's desires or Sally's, nor the desires of their children or the wider enslaved population at Monticello. We don't have access to the repressed material, and we can't possibly know how his own repressed desires shaped the contours of his archive—whether we're thinking of his unconscious or the documents, each of which can't be thought without the other. Citing Eric Ketelaar, Anne Gilliland and Michelle Caswell explain that "counter-archivalization," or the "'conscious or unconscious decision NOT to record or write down,' is an important cause for the record-that-never-was."[69] It cultivates the kind of impossible imaginaries that Gilliland and Caswell describe, leaving historians to speculate about what might have happened. Did Sally read and write? Were there letters that were destroyed? What were her feelings? What did she do during the course of a day, a year, her lifetime?[70]

Jefferson would have been able to control (at least to some extent) whether Sally Hemings would learn to write. He chose not to write anything of his life with Sally (or if he did, he chose not to retain those writings). We are told that Jefferson and his wife Martha enjoyed corresponding to one another but that he burned their letters after her death. There is also a rich documentary record of his correspondence with his white daughters and friends. Whereas his letters to friends and family suggest various expressions of intimacy, the family he had with Sally certainly did not fit into his proclaimed vision or his narrative: "They could never be a part of his imagined future for American families, because their existence did not promote the type of harmony Jefferson believed should reign in an ideal family."[71] Where and how the people in his life were documented reveals a system of categorization, as do the absences of documents. Indeed, across Jefferson's archive, the silences are as productive as the preserved writings. The life of his white family was documented in letters. The life of his extralegal family with Hemings was not. To write about it and allow this into the public record would have threatened the image of his legal family. His sons were all borne by Sally. Beverly, Madison, and Eston were placed in apprenticeships with their uncle John Hemings at ages of ten to twelve and worked as joiners and carpenters. Their daughter Harriet worked in the textile factory. We know this not from Jefferson's letters, but from his Farm Book and Memorandum Books—the texts in which he tabulated the duties and expenses associated with the enslaved inhabitants at Monticello and Jefferson's other plantations. We also know some of this from reports of descendants of Jefferson and Sally and others on the plantation—stories that were handed down to them and passed along to historians and reporters.

The content of the letters and his other writings are revealing in multitudes of ways, for they offer sets of contradictory positions and personas. The many sides of Jefferson that appear in these letters is one of the reasons historians struggle to arrive at any unified explanation of who this man was or what he truly believed. Jefferson is a rather untrustworthy documentarian in many respects, but if we isolate what he leaves us with and think through his informational texts for their categories and structures, we get a sense of his public-facing priorities and how he imagines an ideal republic should be organized. Therefore, Sally's appearance in the Farm Book does not reveal his heart, but it may reveal his reasoning and his vision for an ordered society, as guided by his head.[72] But from a classificatory standpoint, the various forms of the different information management genres he maintained also show us how he measured importance and how he viewed people and communities in relation to himself, his family, and the nation. Differentiating across these various forms and making choices about where to place people in the documentary record was one way that he maintained order and delineated each person's relevance to his own life and purpose. When Sally's name is written in his Farm Book, along with her siblings and cousins and mother and other enslaved people at Monticello, in the same pages as the accounts of supplies, livestock, and expenses and income, what matters for Jefferson is maintaining a sense of order, even if that order is something of an illusion.

Archivist at the Nelson Mandela Foundation Verne Harris argues that "the exercise of power hinges on control of information," but "records do not speak for themselves. They speak through the taxonomies which categorise them and the actors—from records managers to historians, bureaucrats to journalists, archivists to activists—most adept at using taxonomy."[73] All of these descriptors could be applied to Jefferson. But he did not only use, apply, and consult taxonomies; he mastered the techniques of organizing and created and developed knowledge organization systems for business, government, and personal use. Following Derrida, Spivak, and Hélène Cixous, Harris says that the "archive reaches *everywhere*—across the geopolitical spread of an empire into the depths of an individual's psychic apparatus." Indeed, "the archive is the very possibility of politics."[74]

As Derrida explains, the concept that is essential for understanding the historical suppression of writing and logocentrism itself is repression: "Repression, not forgetting; repression, not exclusion. Repression, as Freud says, neither repels, nor flees, nor excludes an exterior force; it contains an interior representation, laying out within itself a space of repression."[75] I am following Derrida's lead in my attempts to imagine the route to refiguring the systems that organize and delineate difference. Freud's "Note Upon the Mystic Writing-Pad" is relevant to this discussion because in it, he thinks of the psychic terrain as an apparatus that is written and rewritten; it's where memories are inscribed and stored. This writing pad is a technological metaphor for the ways that the psychic apparatus is structured and what it can do. A technology that resembles Jefferson's first copy press, the mystical writing pad is a wax tablet, covered by a thin sheet onto which impressions are written and through which those impressions are transferred to the wax pad. When the sheet is lifted the writing is erased from the sheet, but traces are left behind in the wax. And when the sheet is written on again, new traces will cover the old on the wax, like a palimpsest. Importantly, "the old inscriptions will cause what is being written to take certain paths, i.e., they condition the new traces."[76] The writing pad stands as a metaphor, but as Galison cautions, maintaining a distinction between political-technological apparatuses and the psychic apparatus might actually be unhelpful. Indeed, the psyche is a writing machine. If we understand writing, archives, and machines to be extensions or expressions of the psychic terrain, we might see the ways that knowledge organization systems indeed function like the unconscious. For Derrida, the "unconscious text is already a weave of pure traces, differences in which meaning and force are united—a text nowhere present, consisting of archives which are *always already* transcriptions . . . repositories of a meaning which was never present, whose signified presence is always reconstituted by deferral."[77] The same can be said of the systems that organize information. We can also say that Thomas Jefferson's psyche is inscribed in the systems that organized his public and private documents, and that those systems have been transmitted across generations. As Leo LaMontagne asserted in his 1961 history of library classifications, "Consciously, or unconsciously, each maker of schemes puts into his work a part of himself, his background, his interests, and his prejudices, as well as the knowledge of his age."[78]

A knowledge organization system, whether it is a planter's ledger or a book classification, puts sexuality into discourse by containing it, by addressing it without naming it, by designating what counts as knowledge. A classification delineates a given category's relationships to other categories, and it reveals the ways that those categories serve the interests of the classifier.

A ledger appears to be about accounting, nation-building, or plantation management, but it relies upon and supports the ordering and engineering of the sexes and race. It claims to be measuring the progress of freedom and expansion, but the liberty of white propertied men depended upon techniques of subjugation. The management of sex and sexuality was essential for the management of populations, whether it was an enslaved population on a plantation or a nation's population of free and unfree peoples. Subjugation was rationalized and operationalized through the formation of subject categories by reducing life and repressing knowledges.

Derrida understood this about archives—that examining the histories of institutionalized practices shows that archives have an underneath. Archives do protect and preserve cultural records, but they are also inherently destructive. The archive undermines itself in its striving toward unity and totality. Indeed, no archive is complete, and the classificatory techniques that structure and facilitate access necessarily decontextualize artifacts. Becoming archival not only refers to placing materials in archives, but it also includes their activation by researchers who put them back into their contexts and tell their stories. Archives are enciphered and encrypted, both in the sense that the meaning is coded, and that the housing itself is something like a crypt. Finding the truth of what has been archived is always informed by the repressed. And the force of the unconscious calls the authority of the order into question. The drive toward death, along with repressed desires and fears, are inscribed in the technologies through which memory traces become archival. In the case of colonial and government archives, the records sustain and affirm the state, while repressing memory that counters the colonial narrative. The illusion of unity mirrors and confirms the imagined unity of the state and its citizenry. But as Derrida explains:

> As soon as there is the One, there is murder, wounding, traumatism. *L'Un se garde de l'autre*. The One guards against/keeps some of the other. It protects itself from the other, but in the movement of this jealous violence, it comprises in itself, thus guarding it, the self-otherness or self-difference (the difference from within oneself) which makes it One.[79]

The archive "institutes itself as violence," which means that it carries great consequences for the memory of the Other.[80] The memory of Indigenous lives and dispossession and of enslavement are put into discourse in ways that reduce their humanity to numbers or lines in a ledger, rendering them enslaveable, discardable, and killable, without documented histories. This leaves historians to recover the traces of memory where they can and to assemble stories from fragments and silences. As Ferguson writes, "As an archival entity, the United States is simultaneously the fabled home that promises to put different peoples in their rightful places and the infamous regime that disciplines in the name of freedom. As such, it embodies the quintessential properties of all archives."[81] One of the aims of classification is to give order based on reason, but embedded in the order are the classifier's repressed ideas, motives, fears, and desires. The influence of the unconscious in information systems belies their purported rationality.

## Distinction

Wynter is an excellent observer of these types of systems and the processes of codification, but she is also aware of the ways in which her own experiences and capacity for seeing have been shaped by those same systems. Her use of Franz Fanon's sociogenic principle is key to understanding how Jefferson and his colleagues programmed racial distinctions into such systems, as well as the effects of those systems on the people being classified. Fanon, a practicing psychoanalyst who assessed the lived experience of being Black under colonialism, used the term "sociogeny" to augment Freud's theorization of ontogeny and phylogeny. For Fanon, the production of difference in culture contributes to a racialized person's experience in ways that Freud's terms could not explain. Wynter repeatedly articulates this in terms of code, as in her assertion that "a *sociogenic replicator* code *of symbolic life and death*" is built into society to mediate and differentiate between lives that matter and lives that are disposable.[82] Following Fanon, she writes, if "the prognosis for black self-alienation is to be favorable, the human must be redefined in terms of the hybrid phylogeny-ontogeny *cum* sociogeny mode of being that it empirically is, which is composed of descriptive statements or modes of sociogeny—in effect, of *genres* or *kinds* of being human, in whose always auto-instituted and origin-narratively inscribed terms we can alone experience ourselves *as* human."[83]

Put into dialogue with Luhmann's "theories of distinction," Wynter's body of research helps to explain how difference has been encoded into information systems. Because these systems are self-referential and feature the refinement of categories over time and the expansion of their reach and scope with use, they are best understood as autopoietic, or self-replicating information systems. Another way to describe this kind of system is to say that it is recursive, i.e., "it uses the results of its own operations as the basis for further operations."[84] As Cary Wolfe describes autopoietic systems, they continue their existence by responding to complexity "by reducing it in terms of the selectivity of a self-referential selectivity or code." More than that, however, autopoiesis produces a virtual reality with its own temporality and modality, which results in a condition of "openness from closure." This means that these systems should be understood as distinct from the environment that they describe, and that as these systems increase in internal complexity, they also increase "the system's connection and sensitivity to, and dependence on, the environment."[85]

Applying this theoretical frame to Jefferson's suite of information systems shows how the emergence of categories was important in formalizing distinctions that mattered in the early days of the republic, whether it was according to human populations, nations, or self and other. The categories by which access to information is facilitated in these systems have since become more deeply embedded with added refinements, and because they are replicated and applied across libraries, archives, and museums in physical and digital spaces around the world, they mediate what we come to know through a network of operationalized ontologies. These systems make contact possible by making information searchable and findable, and facilitating access to information that might otherwise be unavailable. It is important to understand how these categories and institutions have participated in naturalizing a "system of reality" as described by James Baldwin.[86] These systems inform people's relationship to what and how they come to be informed, but also differentially position members of society in relation to this system of reality, which was inscribed for the purposes of building a republic of white men. "Everything we know (scientifically, theoretically) and say (linguistically or in other forms of semiotic notation) about the body takes place within some contingent, radically nonnatural (that is, constructed and technical) schema of knowledge."[87]

Katherine McKittrick writes, "If we turn to the writings of Sylvia Wynter we can observe how the repetitive naming and critique of biological determinism is nested in a monumental system of biocentricity."[88]

Wynter, at length:

> In effect, because the systematically induced nature of black self-alienation is itself . . . only a function (a map), if an indispensable one, of the enacted institutionalization of our present genre of the human, *Man* and its governing sociogenic code (the *territory*), as defined in the ethno-class or Western bourgeois biocentric descriptive statement of the human on the model of a natural organism (a model that enables it to over-represent its ethnic and class-specific descriptive statement of the human *as if* it were that of the human itself), then, in

> order to contest one's function in the enacting of this specific genre of the human, one is confronted with a dilemma . . . one cannot revalorize oneself in terms of one's racial blackness and therefore of one's biological characteristics, however inversely so, given that it is precisely the biocentric nature of the sociogenic code of our present genre of being human that imperatively calls for the devalorization of the characteristic of blackness . . . in the same way as it calls, dialectically, for the characteristic of whiteness.[89]

Wynter continues, observing that the "invention of the global category of Human Others on the basis of the institutionalized inferiorization and subjugation of those human beings classified as *Indians, Native, Negroes* . . . was indispensable not only to the enactment of the new sociogenic code," drawing distinctions between in order to legitimate the expropriation of land and labor from people on the basis of race. Such processes also replicated the ongoing overrepresentation of whiteness—the "Western bourgeois genre or mode of being human, *as if* it were that of the human itself."[90]

## Hauntologies

Loss is an inherently disordering event—"the irreconcilable knowledge that the loved one is gone and will never return shakes the foundation of human stability and opens the body to its own potential disappearance even as it strums a new chord of sexual longing."[91] Citing Helen Macdonald's account of transferring her grief over the loss of her father toward falconry and its allure, Jack Halberstam asks how we might understand an epistemology that forms out of confronting loss and finding "a new constellation of desire and identification."[92] The grief from Jefferson's earlier losses of family members and friends, as well as the fire that took his childhood home and all of his books, were all transposed into his book catalog and other writings when the most unspeakable of all the tragedies hit home. Jefferson, at the edge of himself, cataloged his books to make meaning out of the world, to impose order in a moment of chaos.

Jefferson's knowledge organization techniques are perhaps best articulated through Derrida's concept of hauntology, which gives a frame and language for describing the processes at play when mourning becomes an impetus for organizing, acquiring, and controlling knowledge. I'll quote Derrida at length and then unpack what he is saying as it relates to Jefferson:

> First of all, mourning. It consists always in attempting to ontologize remains, to make them present, in the first place by *identifying* the

> bodily remains and by *localizing* the dead (all ontologization, all semanticization— philosophical, hermeneutical, or psychoanalytical—finds itself caught up in this work of mourning but, as such, it does not yet think it . . .) One has to know. *One has to know it. One has to have knowledge* [Il faut le savoir]. Now, to know is to know *who* and *where*, to know whose body it really is and what place it occupies—for it must stay in its place. Nothing could be worse, for the work of mourning, than confusion or doubt: one *has to know* who is buried where—and *it is necessary* (to know—to make certain) that, in what remains of him, *he remain there*. Let him stay there and move no more![93]

In particular, the relationship that Derrida identifies between *knowledge* and *place* is extraordinary for its explanatory power. Jefferson classified the objects across his own worlds at Monticello and in public offices, placing them in categories that identified their function, their location, their relevance to his life and purposes. He also classified human beings according to the same set of logics.

One thing that seemed to have a great therapeutic effect for Jefferson in his most extreme time of loss was a turn toward documentation and classification. As Dani Stuchel writes, "Archival things are the transitional or memorial objects through which we mediate our grief about and connection to the past, but they are also entities of a certain kind, dying a certain kind of death within our perception."[94] Fawn Brodie and Kevin Hayes have both observed that Jefferson's controlled and ordered practice of cataloging his books was an act of mourning. Indeed, his catalog and other record-keeping techniques can be understood in the context of memory, archiving, and loss. Twelve years before Martha's death, his mother and father's home at Shadwell burned to the ground, but what Jefferson seemed to have found most upsetting about the fire was the loss of his books and personal and professional papers. Jefferson's acts of mourning structured and were structured by experience, in ways that we cannot fully understand but can surely contemplate. As Avery Gordon writes, "Being haunted draws us affectively, sometimes against our will and always a bit magically, into the structure of feeling of a reality we come to experience, not as cold knowledge, but as a transformative recognition."[95] Surely, the relationship between mastery and control is rooted at least in part in mourning—the grief that comes with loss, the anxiety around the possibility of loss, the need to keep order so that things won't become lost.

Indeed, "Nothing could be worse, for the work of mourning, than confusion or doubt: one *has to know* who is buried where," and gathering and collecting and ordering are all techniques in trying to understand what happened.[96]

Jefferson turned to cataloging and classifying his books, as well as indexing and copying his letters, after Martha's passing. As Fawn Brodie writes of his letter indexing system, "this became a meticulous epistolary record lasting forty-three years, from November 11, 1783, to June 25, 1826."[97] Cataloging and indexing might have provided a sense of control and would have allowed him to take stock of the objects and correspondence that mattered most to him. And they would have ensured that the contents of the materials would have been recorded and remembered.

The tensions around loss and precarity in Jefferson's personal life had parallels at the national level, and a new republic brimming with the hope of great possibilities, with conflicting ideas about how to rear the young nation, required discipline and order. Social classes and strict family structures, along with the strength of kinship ties were believed to ensure the safety and security of the republic. Precarity and chaos were defining features before, during, and after the American Revolution. It would be no wonder that, at a time in which the nation's future was at stake, and with all of the emotional, political, and material investments hanging in the balance, Jefferson and his colleagues would go to lengths to control their environment and their comrades, as well as preserve their historical records. The fear of the loss of information continues to be one of the great drivers of the library, archives, and museum professions, and the people who work in the areas of conservation and preservation devote their careers to improving the techniques that ensure the posterity of historical documents and objects. We might consider the ways that preservation is connected to ontological commitments.

In the information sciences, "ontology" is a word for a kind of taxonomy, or a "specification of a representational vocabulary for a shared domain of discourse—definitions of classes, relations, functions, and other objects."[98] As a term borrowed from philosophy and operationalized for information storage and retrieval, "ontologies" are loaded with their own epistemological and material histories. When ontology, or the study of being and the organization of beings becomes operationalized and formalized in systems it becomes a device for organizing information, which in such a context is regarded as a thing. In other words, an ontology, according to computer and information scientists, is a tool for organizing things. Writing categories into systems, assembling and sorting entities in statistical tables, and creating formulas to determine who has access to rights are all examples of the informationalization and systematization of ontologies, and in each case, the information can be used to simultaneously rationalize and materialize the dehumanization of Others. Ontologies are now integral to all digital information and communication technologies, but I would suggest that we see their emergence in early political arithmetic and other documentary contexts. As John Cheney-Lippold notes, "ontologies are embedded within a set of power relations," and "the categories that are bred from those ontologies exercise a profound impact on how we as subjects encounter our world."[99] One way that racialization became a reality was through the ontologization of information and the informationalization of ontologies. Thinking with information and the ontological commitments that structure its transmission, while recognizing them as legacies of the documentation and accounting practices that were so integral to the functioning of the plantation, places information and communication technologies at the heart and circulatory system by which the ghosts of the plantation haunt our present and futures. McKittrick argues that "a plantation logic characteristic of (but not identical to) slavery emerges in the present both ideologically and materially," in institutions and practices like agriculture, mining, prisons, the city, resorts, and so on.[100] More specifically, Simon Gikandi addresses the classificatory effects of haunting: "Often posited as a moral stain on modern identity, slavery could inform and haunt almost all attempts to construct a transcendental set of categories in areas as diverse as moral philosophy, law, aesthetics, and political economy."[101] Surely we can add libraries, archives, and museums to Gikandi's set.

A distinction should be made between what has been encoded and what haunts us—who has done the coding and who has been coded. Hauntings are transmitted and received. In communication and information studies we know about the mathematical models for communication—that a message is sent, transmitted through channels, or *mediums*, and then that message is received. But the haunting exceeds the code with its materiality and set of expressions and effects. Haunting is a "particular way of knowing what has happened or is happening";[102] it resides underneath and around and above and beyond the code. Can we revisit, *reenact a new future*, that opens up lines of communication with the ghosts that most deserve to speak—spaces for the "whispers of absent authors, cryptic idioms, names without stories and stories without names, absent content, unknown contexts, the incessant movement of recontextualization, readings of content (past, present and future), readers excluded or obstructed, and so on"?[103]

As Gordon writes, "Following the ghosts is about making a contact that changes you and refashions the social relations in which you are located. It is sometimes about writing ghost stories, stories that not only repair representational mistakes, but also strive to understand the conditions under which a memory was produced in the first place, toward a countermemory, for the future."[104] We might apprehend the ways that categories register memory and how memories are put into relation to others, how certain ideas, events, places, and people are memorialized, and how some are registered to be forgotten after use. We archive something that we don't want to lose, that we want to remember, and we might repress that which we don't. The archive is a medium by which transferences of ghostly traces across generations occur. But the colonial archive contains very particular kinds of memories, and the archival absences must also be recognized as loss that must be grieved. Gordon describes the challenge of the work that needs to be done to retrieve the memory that has been repressed, whether that censorship has been a suppression of the cultural record or in the psychic apparatus, or both. How does one search for something that they don't consciously register as an absence? How do we find the stories of the missing, if we lack awareness that they ever existed in the first place? Indeed, "we need to know that something is missing in order to even begin to look for it or its dispersion of gestures anywhere, in the archive or in the imaginary zone."[105] The ghostly haunt provides a hint of what has been repressed, and it guides us in how to do the work.

Signaling Derrida's phrasing—"Haunting belongs to the structure of every hegemony"—Rinaldo Walcott writes:

> Emancipation as a mode of freedom is a hegemony that haunts. It is the persistence of Black life-forms that continually both show up and offer other possible ways of living a life beyond all bounds that makes evident the haunting nature of emancipation as a limit on what freedom might be. Black life-forms always find ways to exceed the boundaries of capital and other forms of containment as a way to imagine, build, and produce conduits that lead to collective self-referential lives.[106]

Exposing Jefferson's techniques shows how "the documents and ledgers and logs that narrate the brutalities of this history give birth to new world blackness as they evacuate life from blackness."[107] As a paternal figure who features so prominently in the American consciousness, and who also possessed "an archival imagination unmatched in his generation,"[108] Jefferson's archive is one that Stephen Best would likely describe as a scene toward which a "specifically forensic imagination should be directed."[109] Best insists that the questions to ask of archives are not so much about what can and cannot be retrieved, but rather, we should inquire into "what is born of the understanding of the archive as a scene of injury."[110] I am so intrigued by Best's use of the word "born" to talk about what comes from the archive. His response to various invocations of a "we" that gains a sense of belonging via shared violent origins, which can be traced back (even if they can't be found) to the archive is to insist that there can be no such claims to a "we" for Black culture, other than a "we" that is "structured by and given in its own negation and refusal."[111] To my mind, thinking of what is born from the archive, and what is born from particular interpretations and relationships to the archive in personal and collective histories, is precisely the right frame. The archive is both generative and annihilating, and the stories we tell, based on what the archive offers or denies, are crucial to understanding who we are in relation to one another and how, with, and to whom we belong. As Best suggests, there may be "pleasures to be found in a shared sense of alienation" among those who collectively refuse the colonial archive and its order.

Jefferson's plantation was revised and expanded over his lifetime, and on that plantation, he installed a factory for making textiles and nails—for clothing the people who were enslaved, for construction on the plantation, and for profit in an emerging industrial society. He invented and developed agricultural machinery to accelerate production. And Jefferson was one of the most outspoken advocates for converting the Indigenous population from hunters, gatherers, and growers to agricultural producers that resembled his idealized yeoman farmer. Jefferson not only maintained his own plantation, but he also advanced the idea that the republic would thrive if its citizenry owned and farmed the land. This became ideology and the expanding America was quickly populated and cultivated for farmland, thereby radically changing the landscape itself and the ways in which people related to the land. Rather than people seeing themselves as being with and of the land, the land carried newly symbolic weight, and a citizenry that could use and cultivate the land became the machinery by which the nation would gain its strength and expanse. He understood from boyhood that mapping and understanding the properties of the landscape was indeed essential to mastering it, outlining the methods for making claims to it, and cultivating a landed citizenry. Knowledge, infrastructures, and education are all informed by and inform settler colonialism's reliance on land acquisition. And the information architectures of the present remain grounded in the formulations that established the state in ongoing "invisibilized dynamics of settler colonialism."[112]

As Gikandi writes, "slavery functioned as the great unconscious in the infrastructure of modern identity."[113] He describes the affective experience of encountering the archives' repressions:

> Walking through the archive of empire and the colonial library, I discovered, as have other scholars before me, that the juxtaposition of such scenes—and the interpretive questions that they raise—was not unusual . . . it occurred to me that the strange and incomprehensible signs of a black presence in the making of high culture often tended

> to slip away, not because of the invisibility of the enslaved but because the construction of the ideals of modern civilization demanded the repression of what it had introjected—the experience or phenomenon that it had unconsciously assimilated. . . . Cultural or conceptual quarantines seemed to be necessitated by the common belief that the black, as unmodern, was either a source of shame or a toxin that threated the well-being of civilization.[114]

The "afterlife of the plantation" is materialized in today's information infrastructures.[115] As Nathan Snaza explains, the very social order that has become so naturalized and is so easily taken for granted "dulls us to particular aspects of our world," and diving into the order and its principles might bring understanding about how it functions and how it has been sustained over generations.[116] Dwelling in the very spaces in which the colonial imaginary is given shape and substance can unsettle knowledge by drawing attention "toward questions of how that particular social order was able to emerge and at what costs."[117]

Planters affected the lives of many—most violently, those of the enslaved and Indigenous people and nonhuman animals. Derrida asks us to turn toward the ghosts of the people who were taken, bought and sold, and killed for the sake of profit and empire:

> No justice . . . seems possible or thinkable without the principle of some *responsibility*, beyond all living present, within that which disjoins the living present, before the ghosts of those who are not yet born or who are already dead, be they victims of wars, political or other kinds of violence, nationalist, racist, colonialist, sexist, or other kinds of exterminations, victims of the oppressions of capitalist imperialism or any of the forms of totalitarianism."[118]

Unlike Jefferson, who wishes the previous generations would let loose of their hold on him, we must "learn to live *with* ghosts, in the upkeep, the conversation, the company, or the companionship, in the commerce without commerce of ghosts. To live otherwise, and better. No, not better, but more justly. But *with them*. . . . And this being-with specters would also be, not only but also, a *politics* of memory, of inheritance, and of generations."[119] We have inherited paradoxes and contradictions that inhere in the structures and spaces that facilitate access to information. To seize upon this moment of recognizability, one in which slavery and imperialism cannot be relegated to the past, is to reassemble public things, institutions, and information that promote political participation and action.

# PART 2

*Libraries*

# 4
# "A Blueprint of His Own Mind": Jefferson's Libraries

His library catalogue not only reflects how his mind worked, it also reflects Jefferson's state of mind in the summer of 1783.

—KEVIN J. HAYES, *THE ROAD TO MONTICELLO*

One of the most systematic of men, he was in character as a cataloguer.

—DUMAS MALONE, *THE SAGE OF MONTICELLO*

The collection was, in essence, Jefferson's Enlightenment, his encyclopedia if you will, built on Diderot's prescription "to collect all the knowledge that now lies scattered over the face of the earth, to make known its general structure to the men among [whom] we live, and transmit it to those who will come after us."

—CARLA HAYDEN, LIBRARIAN OF CONGRESS, "THE CHOICEST COLLECTION OF BOOKS"

Thomas Jefferson's book catalogs, divided into up to forty-four chapters, each of which contains an analytic order of its own, has been described as a "blueprint of his own mind."[1] The notion that a catalog is a visual outline of a person's intellectual terrain—one that maps his expectations, tastes, priorities, values, and desires—suggests that the division of knowledge according to subjects is both a scientific and aesthetic practice. Jefferson's catalog reveals the inner workings of the mind of a man who engineered the social and political landscape of the early American republic. It is also a projection of his vision for the United States. That catalog also became a template from which to build and organize lists of books to shape an informed citizenry, as Jefferson's subject classification method was repeated in a variety of libraries in his day, most notably, the Library of Congress, the University of Virginia, and the Library Company of Philadelphia.

Audre Lorde's famous essay strikes directly (if not intentionally) at the conceptualization of Jefferson's catalog as a blueprint. Lorde writes, "For we have, built into all of us, *old blueprints of expectations and response*, old structures of oppression, and these must be altered at the same time as we alter the living conditions which are a result of those structures. For the master's tools will never dismantle the master's house."[2] Lorde was a librarian before she devoted her life to poetry and activism, and surely, her library science training at Columbia University informed her critique of the tools and techniques of knowledge production.[3] As an African American lesbian and mother, she recognized the startling ways in which the systems that have been organizing people, books, territories, and nations are now built into our bodies, minds, and societies. Ruth Wilson Gilmore notes that Lorde's quote is repeated so often and out of context that a key message has been abstracted away. According to Gilmore, "The issue is not whether the master uses, or endorses the use of, some tool or another. Rather, who controls the conditions and the ends to which any tools are wielded?" Ownership is key, and our task is to "concentrate on fundamental orderings in political economy." Dismantling requires seizing the means of production, and recycling the materials of the master's house "to institutions of our own design."[4] Katherine McKittrick's observations are similarly striking and drive at the necessity of centering the human in thinking with the documentary tradition that recorded Black lives as capital: "I trust that the unindexed lies of our world and the evidence of what transpired are not *blueprints* for emancipation, or maps to our future, but instead are indicators of the ways in which the brutalities of racial encounter demand a form of human being and being human that newly iterates blackness as uncomfortably enumerating the unanticipated contours of black life."[5]

The classification for the colonial library and archive that has grown to be the largest library in the world was fashioned from Jefferson's worldview. Today the Library of Congress Classification is the system by which nearly all research libraries in North America, and many libraries in other parts of the world, organize their collections. Jefferson's convictions were inscribed in the system that was intended to organize information for the US Congress. And although the Library of Congress created a new system at the turn of the twentieth century and has expanded its reach to a broad, international public, traces of Jefferson's system remain. One of the aims of this project is to locate some of the "old structures of oppression" that haunt our library stacks and other informational spaces today through a close reading of Jefferson's arrangement of books into subjects, particularly those on race and Indigenous peoples.[6]

This chapter provides an overview of Jefferson's personal library practices, his advocacy for public libraries, and his participation in the formation of the Library of Congress and its collections. It also sets the stage for the next two chapters, which use the classified catalog that he offered with his books to the Library of Congress to perform close readings of Jefferson's ordering techniques about Africa, slavery, people of African descent, and Indigenous peoples and their land in the Americas. Library classifications are compelling historical sources because they demonstrate, in the form of hierarchies and naming conventions, the ways that people structure and prioritize subjects. Jefferson's library catalog is particularly important for the way that it entered into federal library practice and institutionalized his ordering principles. It affects the ways that information is retrieved and encountered, but for our purposes, I want to draw attention to the way that it gives form to history and other literatures, including the naturalization of racial divisions.

During his lifetime Thomas Jefferson acquired three personal libraries. The first was at his childhood home at Shadwell—the one that was destroyed by fire in 1770. The second, which "was probably the most substantial private library in eighteenth-century America," consisted of over 4,900 titles and 6,700 volumes.[7] This is the one that he sold to the US Congress. Between the sale of that library and his death in 1826, Jefferson built his "Retirement Library." In this chapter I begin by discussing his advocacy for public libraries and the Library of Congress. Then I provide important context about the development and use of his personal libraries, the Library of Congress, and the University of Virginia library. Although Jefferson did not live to see the establishment of local public libraries as we know them, he was involved in the development of several types of libraries, many of which he referred to as "public" libraries. In Jefferson's day the term "public" was used to describe institutions associated with government offices. The Library of Congress was a public library in this sense, as were governors' libraries. Jefferson also referred to the Albemarle Society Library as a public library, using the term "public" to refer to its being open to all citizens for a fee, as opposed to the more common model for subscription libraries that were only available to certain members of society.

The Thomas Jefferson Building of the Library of Congress, constructed in 1897, is one of the most elaborately designed buildings in the United States, with interior walls that contain mosaic tiles, paintings, and sculptures that collectively convey the deep connection between knowledge, history, and state power. The permanent exhibition at the Library of Congress, featuring Jefferson's books organized according to his own order, stands as a monument to his impact. Jefferson's role in promoting public libraries, his direct influence and leadership in the creation, organization, and collection development of the Library of Congress, and his attention to the academic library at the University of Virginia are reasons why Richard Adams has referred to him as "the father of American librarianship."[8]

## "Open to All"

Benjamin Franklin perhaps more immediately comes to mind in the history of libraries than Jefferson, as he is widely regarded as the first and most outspoken advocate for the distribution of useful knowledge in British America. He was a key figure in the development of subscription libraries, a precursor to the modern public library, and even before Franklin there had already been earlier iterations of libraries that made materials available to a limited population.[9] Early American subscription libraries were not intended to reach a wide and diverse public, but rather, the elite paid a fee to have access to books that were shared among the reading society. Franklin did aspire to form libraries that served a broader public, and as Richard Brown explains, he asserted "that books, despite being expensive, should be made more widely available through the establishment of public libraries."[10] Franklin promoted the value of cultivating "an informed citizenry by encouraging the 'more general Use and Esteem' of 'valuable Books,' which would 'have very good Effects on the Minds of the People . . . and furnish them with the most useful kind of Knowledge, that which renders Men benevolent and helpful to one another.'"[11] In contrast to their neighbors to the north, Virginian planters of the mid-eighteenth century were more reluctant to encourage literacy and access to literature for a broad population, but when Jefferson came of age politically, he used his official positions to drive discussions about education among Virginia's leaders. His own education provided him with an appreciation of the value of information, and he carried practices of list-making, note-taking, and cataloging that he learned in school into his personal and professional realms in adulthood.

From a young age Jefferson created reference works for his own personal use. He kept three commonplace books—one literary, one legal, and one on equity. His literary commonplace book, which he compiled between the ages of fifteen until thirty, was a notebook that he filled with passages quoted from the books he read. As Douglas Wilson explains, this notebook presents the preoccupations of a "very different Thomas Jefferson from the familiar figure of history."[12] Legend has it that Jefferson read all of the books in his father's library at Shadwell by age five, before he even started school. He received a classical education at the boarding school of Reverend James Maury and then attended the College of William and Mary beginning in 1760. As the literary commonplace book was a "product of Thomas Jefferson's formative years," informed by his early education, it "belongs principally to a time when he was young, unmarried, not yet established in the world, and not yet caught up in politics."[13] It is the earliest of his surviving notebooks.[14]

Several scholars have analyzed the contents of Jefferson's Literary Commonplace Book and have variously found evidence of misogyny, a preoccupation with loss and death, his poetic mind, his legal training, and so on.[15] Each of these themes matters because they provide insights into some of the ideas out of which his documentary practices emerged. His entries on life and death might signal anxiety about loss, for example, which one might read as one of the drivers of his personal and professional archival practices. To my mind, however, these passages can only provide limited evidence, for while the excerpts that Jefferson copied into his notebooks were likely important to him, it is very difficult to discern their relevance in relation to his life. What some scholars have identified as indicators of misogyny, others might interpret as evidence of heartbreak. Rather than analyze the contents or even the order of the commonplace book, then, I prefer to suggest that this was an early manifestation of Jefferson's encyclopedic inclinations that reveals the young cataloger's mind. A commonplace book is similar to a miscellany is similar to an encyclopedia is similar to a library, or *bibliographie*. A commonplace book is a type of catalog. All of Jefferson's information management techniques might be said to have originated in his note-taking practice that began when he was a boy at school.

His lifelong love of reading involved building communities of readers, and he actively shared reading lists at least as early as 1771, when he sent a list of books that he believed were essential to a gentleman's library to Robert Skipwith.[16] The list is revealing, particularly because it was written just six months after the Shadwell fire. He would have been preoccupied with rebuilding his own library, so it is likely that this list of books offers something of a blueprint of Jefferson's twenty-eight-year-old mind:

> I appeal to every reader of feeling and sentiment whether the fictitious murther of Duncan by Macbeth in Shakespeare does not excite in him as great horror of villainy, as the real one of Henry IV by Ravaillac as related by Davila? And whether the fidelity of Nelson, and generosity of Blandford in Marmontel do not dilate his breast, and elevate his sentiments as much as any similar incident which real history can furnish? Does he not in fact feel himself a better man while reading them, and

> privately covenant to copy the fair example? . . . Considering history as a moral exercise, her lessons would be too unfrequent if confined to real life. Of those recorded by historians few incidents have been attended with such circumstances as to excite in any high degree this sympathetic emotion of virtue. We are therefore wisely framed to be as warmly interested for a fictitious as for a real personage. The spacious field of imagination is thus laid open to our use, and lessons may be formed to illustrate and carry home to the mind every moral rule of life. Thus a lively and lasting sense of filial duty is more effectually impressed on the mind of a son or daughter by reading King Lear, than by all the dry volumes of ethics and divinity that ever were written.[17]

Jefferson seems to have appreciated a "feeling" for literature, as well as its capacity to evoke empathetic responses to characters and dramatizations of experiences outside of one's own life. He would likely have agreed with Aparna Tarc, who writes, "Literature can teach us of the unconscious yet deeply felt inner communions that take place in communicative encounter. Literature acknowledges interiority as it supports us to gain insight into the mysteries of the inner world. Literature attunes us to the emotional situation of language as it moves us to thinking."[18] Perhaps even more importantly, good fiction, in Jefferson's view, has an instructional quality, which might guide people through the dilemmas of daily life. Four years later he would assert the necessity of historical facts, but here, in this prerevolutionary moment, Jefferson emphasizes the instructional utility of fiction. It should be no surprise, then, that he had recently invoked Shakespeare's *Tempest* in one of the great tragedies of his life—the loss of his boyhood home and all of his belongings, including his books, to fire:

> To make the loss more sensible it fell principally on m[y books] of common law, of which I have but one left, at that time lent out. Of papers too of every kind I am utterly destitute. All of these, whether public or private, of business or of amusement have perished in the flames. I had made some progress in preparing for the succeeding general court, and having, as was my custom, thrown my thoughts into the form of notes, I troubled my head no more with them. These are gone, and "like the baseless fabric of a vision, Leave not a trace behind."[19]

The last line in the passage above belongs to Prospero, who famously said "My library was dukedom large enough."[20] This 1770 letter to Page and the 1771 list for Skipwith signal the cultivation of a shared reading habit. What began as relatively informal practices of commonplacing, listing, and talking about books with friends became integral to cultivating an informed republic.

Jefferson devoted much of his career to advocating for a public education that was available to all citizens.[21] In addition to insisting on the value of public schools that provided at least a basic education for all free white people, including girls, he asserted that books should be made available to all citizens. He proposed "A Bill for Establishing a Public Library" in 1779 when he was governor of Virginia, but as the editors of the Thomas Jefferson Papers indicate, this type of library was neither the public library to which we have become accustomed in the present, nor was it a subscription library like the one opened in Charlottesville, as described below. Written in the same year as the "Bill for the More General Diffusion of Knowledge," Jefferson's early proposal for a public library was meant to support the most elite of the educated in his proposed three-tiered system of schooling. This library would be located in Richmond, and three "visitors" would be appointed from the Virginia legislature to purchase materials for the collection and potentially hire a salaried "keeper" who would ensure the preservation of the books and maps. His intent was that the collection "shall be made useful by indulging the researches of the learned and curious, within the said library, without fee or reward, and under such rules for preserving them safe and in good order and condition."[22] This was a proposal for a public library insofar as it recommended that two thousand dollars be provided by the Virginia General Assembly annually, but this library was not meant to serve all members of the reading public. This proposal resembles future proposals that he and James Madison would write toward the establishment of the Library of Congress. Jefferson long held the view that a governing body should have a strong reference library collection to support the information needs of legislators in their deliberations of policy, and his proposal for a "public library" in Virginia is a precursor to proposals for the library for Congress.

## The 1783 Catalogue

Jefferson probably began cataloging his books in the mid-1770s and classified them according to Francis Bacon's framework around the time of his wife Martha's death, in around 1782. He was writing *Notes on the State of Virginia*, another encyclopedic project, alongside his book catalog.[23] Commonly referred to as his "1783 Catalogue," Jefferson organized his books according to the faculties of the mind (see Figures 8, 9, and 10), which were translated into categories for knowledge: Memory is *History*, or what is known—or what can be considered facts. He divided History into natural and civil histories. The faculty of reason is applied to *Philosophy*, or science, i.e., the advancement of knowledge. And Imagination is *Fine Arts* and literature.[24]

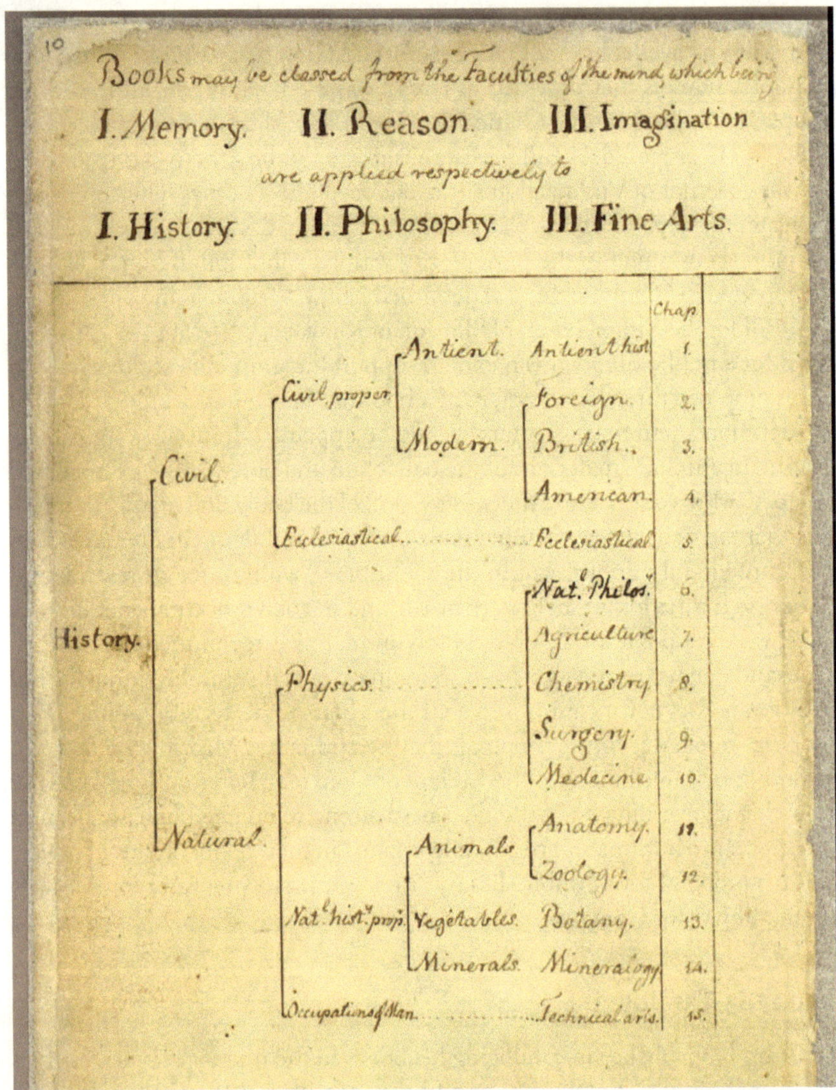


Figure 8. History classification, Thomas Jefferson's 1783 Catalog of Books, [circa 1775–1812]. Original manuscript from the Coolidge Collection of Thomas Jefferson Manuscripts, Massachusetts Historical Society.

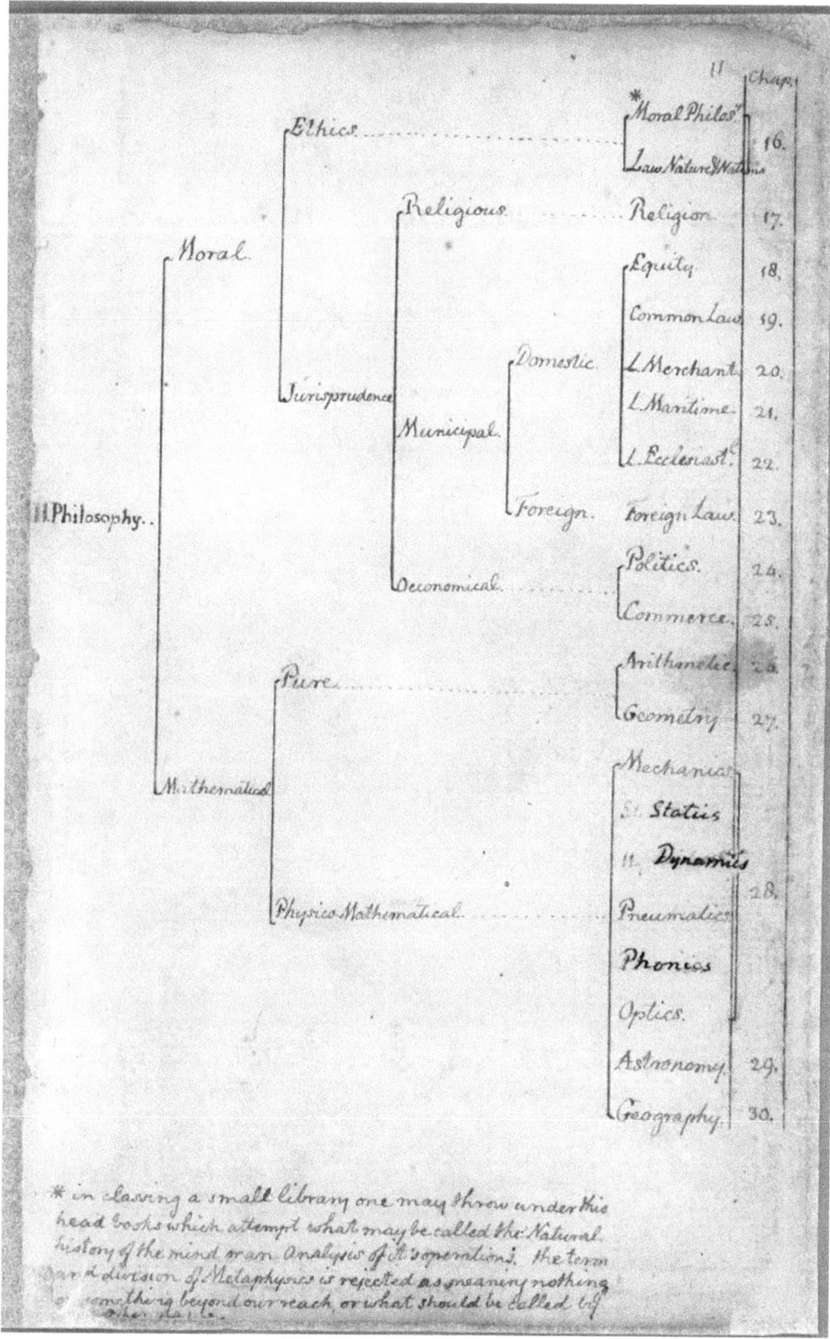


Figure 9. Philosophy classification, Thomas Jefferson's 1783 Catalog of Books, [circa 1775–1812]. Original manuscript from the Coolidge Collection of Thomas Jefferson Manuscripts, Massachusetts Historical Society.

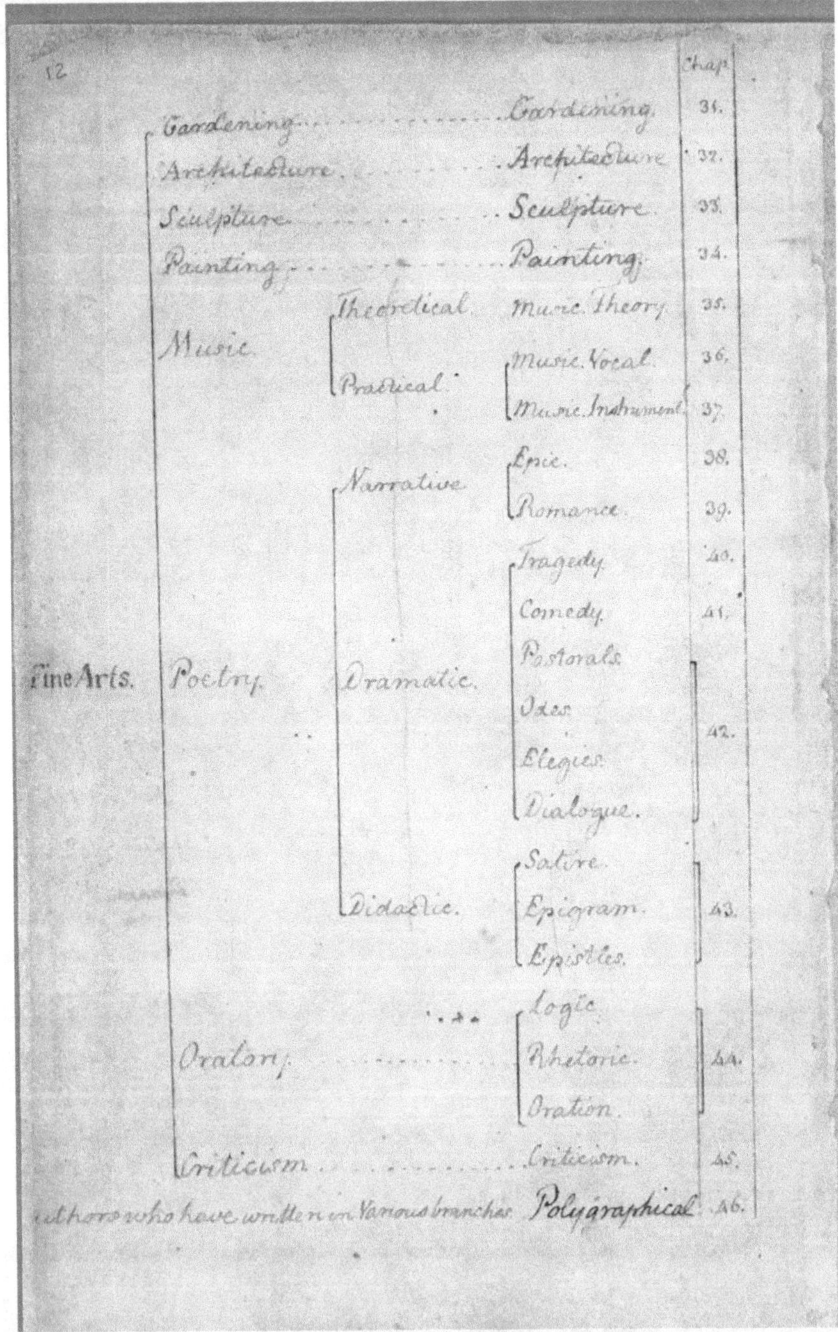

12

| | | | | Chap. |
|---|---|---|---|---|
| Fine Arts. | Gardening | | Gardening | 31. |
| | Architecture | | Architecture | 32. |
| | Sculpture | | Sculpture | 33. |
| | Painting | | Painting | 34. |
| | Music | Theoretical | Music. Theory | 35. |
| | | Practical | Music. Vocal | 36. |
| | | | Music. Instrumental | 37. |
| | Poetry | Narrative | Epic. | 38. |
| | | | Romance | 39. |
| | | Dramatic. | Tragedy | 40. |
| | | | Comedy | 41. |
| | | | Pastorals | 42. |
| | | | Odes | |
| | | | Elegies | |
| | | | Dialogue. | |
| | | Didactic. | Satire | 43. |
| | | | Epigram. | |
| | | | Epistles. | |
| | Oratory | | Logic | 44. |
| | | | Rhetoric. | |
| | | | Oration. | |
| | Criticism | | Criticism. | 45. |
| [A]uthors who have written in Various branches. | | | Polygraphical | 46. |

Figure 10. Fine Arts classification, Thomas Jefferson's 1783 Catalog of Books, [circa 1775–1812]. Original manuscript from the Coolidge Collection of Thomas Jefferson Manuscripts, Massachusetts Historical Society.

More precisely, Jefferson modeled his book classification on the method that Denis Diderot and Jean le Rond D'Alembert used to organize the *Encyclopédie*, following Francis Bacon's division of knowledge into the faculties of the mind. Dustin Gish and Daniel Klinghard have noted that the Baconian method aligned with the American project of revolution and the rejection of authority of the past, and it provided a way to contain and confront the unsettled environment and frontier.[25] Indeed, Jefferson regarded Bacon, John Locke, and Isaac Newton "as the three greatest men that have ever lived, without any exception, and as having laid the foundation of those superstructures which have been raised in the Physical and Moral Sciences."[26] D'Alembert's *Preliminary Discourse to Diderot's Encyclopedia*, described by Richard Schwab as "an adjustment of the rationalist spirit of René Descartes to the empiricism of Locke and Newton," would have provided an ideal guide for mapping Jefferson's intellectual terrain.[27]

For D'Alembert, a person's vantage point mattered: "The universe, if we may be permitted to say so, would only be one fact and one great truth for whoever knew how to embrace it from a single point of view."[28] The essential idea behind the encyclopedia was that it could provide the sum of all human knowledge, but in order for that to happen, phenomena had to be reduced to the essential facts and then connected together so that the truth of the universe could be discovered. Reduction, combined with the arrangement according to enchained relationships, was essential to this form of universalization. They differentiated their encyclopedias from alphabetically arranged dictionaries on the basis of visual-spatial metaphors:

> It is not the same with the encyclopedic arrangement of our knowledge. This consists of collecting knowledge into the smallest area possible and of placing the philosopher at a vantage point, so to speak, high above this vast labyrinth, whence he can perceive the principal sciences and the arts simultaneously. From there he can see *at a glance* the object of their speculations and the operations which can be made on these objects; he can discern the general branches of human knowledge, the points that separate or unite them; and sometimes he can even glimpse the secrets that relate them to one another.[29]

The phrasing "at a glance" signals the philosopher's capacity to control complexity through techniques of observation. It also calls to mind Jefferson's own "peculiar satisfaction" that derived from "seeing *at a glance* the books which have been written on [a subject], and selecting those from which we expect most readily the information we seek."[30] While Jefferson appreciated the variability of collections and their users, and recognized no rigid system could serve every reader, he also envisioned an overarching Baconian/encyclopedic design that could unify his personal collection and a national imaginary.

Bacon advanced the idea in the early seventeenth century that induction through experimentation and observation will advance knowledge and science, and he believed that inquiry would lead to the discovery of unifying principles. Essentially, his *Advancement of Learning* outlined a research agenda of topics which he grouped in these categories, grounded in the idea that the faculties of the mind drive these areas of study. Jefferson's encyclopedic prowess was in many ways the result of a set of intentional practices toward the cultivation of a scholarly self. Indeed, the world that he constructed at Monticello was a realization of Bacon's description of the essential components for a learned prince's intellectual apparatus:

> First, the collecting of a most perfect and general Library, wherein whatsoever the wit of Man hath heretofore committed to Books of worth, be they ancient or modern, printed or Manuscript, European or of the other Parts, of one or other Language, may be made contributory to your wisdom. Next, a spacious, wonderful garden, wherein whatsoever Plant...either wild, or by the Culture of Man, brought forth. . . . The Garden to be built about with Rooms, to stable in all rare Beasts, and to cage in all rare Birds . . . and so you may have in small compass, a Model of the Universal Nature made private. The third, a goodly, huge Cabinet, wherein whatsoever the Hand of Man by exquisite Art or Engine has made rare in Stuff, Form or Motion, whatsoever Singularity, Chance, and the Shuffle of things hath produced, whatsoever Nature has wrought in things that want life and may be kept; shall be sorted and included. The fourth, Such a Still-house so furnished with Mills, Instruments, Furnaces and Vessels, as may be a Palace fit for a Philosopher's Stone.[31]

Encyclopedic knowledge was not only a mastery of texts and information, but it also required and enacted the mastery of nature, the collection and display of objects and specimens, and a laboratory for experiments and observation, in addition to a "most perfect and general library." Jefferson's Monticello featured all of these components, and situated at the top of a mountain, from where he could view the landscape spread before him, this was an ideal place for a scientist-statesman who loved books. The encyclopedia—as a concept, object, visualization technique, and memory aid—was central to Jefferson's information worlds, and the exploration into that genre exemplifies the connection between the visual plane, classification, and information in the American Enlightenment. In Gordon S. Wood's estimation, "Jefferson had the most spacious and encyclopedic mind of any of his fellow Americans, including even Benjamin Franklin. He was interested in more things and knew more about more things than any other American. . . . He amassed nearly seven thousand books and consulted them constantly; he wanted both his library and his mind to embrace virtually all of human knowledge, and he came as close to that embrace as an eighteenth century American could."[32]

The first documentary evidence we have of Jefferson's interest in Diderot and D'Alembert's *Encyclopédie* comes to us in a letter from Jefferson dated 30 November 1780, to the Chevalier d'Anmours, consul of France in Virginia and Maryland. Serving as Virginia's governor at the time, Jefferson wrote that he was "exceedingly anxious to get a copy of Le grande Encyclopedie."[33] Just nine days later, the *Virginia Gazette* published an advertisement for the booksellers Amable and Alexander Lory: "To be sold, the Encyclopedy or Dictionary of Arts and Sciences, printed in French, with all the cuts belonging to the said work. Cash or tobacco will be admitted in payment, by applying to the subscribers."[34] On 27 February 1781, Jefferson sent a letter to John Fitzgerald along with notes of 15,068 pounds of tobacco, asking that he use it to purchase the twenty-eight-volume set for the use of the public office. Fitzgerald confirmed on the first of April that the purchase had been made.

When the set was delivered, Jefferson took it to his private residence and became so absorbed in the encyclopedia that, in July of 1782, Virginia legislators resorted to adopting a resolution to get the volumes out of Jefferson's private hands so that they could be made available to the public office: "The Commercial Agent is desired to take measures for getting from Mr. Jefferson the Encyclopaedia belonging to the state."[35] He still had the volumes at his home in late September of the following year, when Reverend James Madison, president of the College of William and Mary tried to borrow it from the governor's library. This is an extraordinary bit of information. His apparent refusal to return the *Encyclopédie* to the public office was occurring at the same time that he was revising *Notes on the State of Virginia* and his classified library catalog. I would wager that he was unwilling to give the encyclopedia over until he felt that his cataloging project was complete enough.

*Notes on the State of Virginia* was first and foremost an official state document, issued in response to a series of queries issued by François, Comte de Barbé Marbois.[36] Every state received a set of questions from the French diplomat, which were meant to supply France with information, but no one responded with the literary style and attention to detail that Jefferson did. Indeed, he turned this official document into a work of literature, shaped and informed not only by natural historians, but by the literary and philosophical works of Laurence Sterne, Edmund Burke, William Hogarth, and J. Hector St.

John de Crèvecœur, as well as the newly developed "political arithmetic" methods. Marbois was not asking for an account of the beautiful and the sublime, nor an explication of racial difference, but Jefferson took advantage of the opportunity to transform "what appeared to be the neutral task of documentation into an intellectual and patriotic discovery of the emergent nation."[37] He reordered Marbois's queries and made them into book chapters with new titles to frame a narrative about Virginia that progressed from accounts about nature to descriptions of culture.[38] *Notes on the State of Virginia* is simultaneously an account of law codes, a geographical narrative, an aesthetic treatise, and a discourse on race relations in eighteenth-century Virginia. It was also an attempt to set the record straight with regard to the Comte de Buffon's claim that the climate and landscape of North America were inferior to Europe's, and so Jefferson expounded upon the size and stature of the flora, fauna, and Indigenous peoples living and thriving in and around Virginia. It's such a genre-bending work that Jonathan Elmer suggests that Jefferson's "Notes are best grasped, in other words, neither as the finished archive nor as the heterogeneity of all that is archived, but as the record of a process of archiving itself."[39]

The years in which he was engaged in these writing projects were tumultuous ones for Jefferson. He was serving as governor of Virginia when he received the request for statistical information from Marbois, by way of Joseph Jones in 1780.[40] He started to write his responses soon after, but it was in the following years that he devoted time and attention to the task. Jefferson had escaped to Poplar Forest after he was nearly captured by British troops at his home at Monticello in June of 1781. He fell from his horse and was confined there for three to four weeks. He returned to his home at Monticello after his term as governor in 1781. Although he did send his responses to Marbois in December of 1781, he "substantially 'corrected and enlarged' the text . . . during the two and a half years between the time he sent Marbois his answers in December 1781 and his departure for Paris in July 1784."[41] During that time, his daughter Lucy was born, and Martha's health took a turn. (Another daughter Lucy had died in infancy in April 1781). Martha died due to complications after childbirth in September of 1782.

Jefferson completed the first iteration of his book catalog in March of 1783, approximately six months after Martha passed. Fawn Brodie suggests that cataloging his books was an act of mourning, or a "remedy for loneliness and despair."[42] Kevin Hayes expands on this assessment, writing, "Upon his wife's death [Jefferson's library] became a site of mourning. Upon his return in May 1783, it became a place of solitude where he could find order by devising his own personal, idiosyncratic scheme of knowledge. . . . Developed in the aftermath of his wife's death, his organizational scheme also offered a way to erect barriers to guard against the vagaries of life and death."[43] Or as Susan Manning puts it, "Here, perhaps, are the comforts of classification in the dark night of the soul."[44] For him the classification of his books was, at least in part, an act of mourning—systematizing his catalog was one way to gain a sense of control in a precarious world. The cross between public and private lives is very much written into his catalog. As Diane Ehrenpreis and Endrina Tay note, after Jefferson classified his books, he adhered to that system religiously. He did modify his categories over time, but the overall structure did not change. Indeed, he often recorded the titles of new books in between existing ones, preferring to squeeze the titles in according to his order than to add them at the end of a line or as an addendum.

His encyclopedic and cataloging projects intensified while Martha was ill, and even more after she passed. Their daughter Martha (Patsy) reported years later that during the months in which Martha's health declined, he devoted his time only to Martha's care and his writing: "When not at her bed side he was writing in a small room which opened immediately at the head of her bed."[45] According to Wilson, "The assiduous attention to his wife, and her death in September 1782, effectively suppressed his correspondence for several months, so the writing in which he had been engaged during this period may well have been connected with revising the answers to Marbois."[46] It is worth considering whether the devotedness with which he attended to his catalog and *Notes on the State of Virginia* had something to do with the emotional pain and loss he was experiencing, and that classifying books might be best understood as an act of control for memory-keeping by preserving knowledge and putting everything in its place to ensure some sense of security.

## A Library for Congress

James Madison, Jefferson's close friend and colleague, was chair of the committee that first proposed a library for the United States Congress in 1783, arguing that Congress should have at their command resources on the laws of nations and treaties, and that the lack of such information "was manifest in several important acts of Congress."[47] Along with his January 1783 proposal, Madison provided a list of suggested books, organized into broad categories. Having emerged from mourning and his massive cataloging projects, Jefferson lived in the same boarding house as Madison in Philadelphia during the four weeks that preceded that meeting of Congress. In March of 1783, he entered the date for the first version of his own newly organized personal book catalog. Jefferson and Madison surely had fascinating conversations about the order of books and the best reading for members of Congress during the months that they lived together.[48] They would have also been engaged in the conversations about copyright described in Chapter 2. Their exchange of ideas would have affected both of their book lists.[49]

In 1791, when Jefferson was secretary of state, he proposed a bill that revised the existing patent act. A provision for a national library was included in that proposal.[50] It was not until 1800, however, when Jefferson was vice president of the United States, that Congress voted to establish a library and appropriated $5,000 for the purchase of books. The first volumes were received in the early months of Jefferson's presidency in 1801. An Act of Congress of 26 January 1802 authorized Jefferson to appoint a librarian for the Library of Congress and also assigned the task of purchasing books with the remaining balance from the original $5,000 to a congressional committee. Jefferson appointed John Beckley, the clerk of the House of Representatives and a political ally, to the post of librarian, and by 14 April 1802 Jefferson submitted a list for approval by Congress. In his letter to Abraham Baldwin, chair of the library committee, Jefferson explained his reasoning for the recommended selections: "I have confined the catalogue to those branches of science which belong to the deliberations of the members as statesmen, and in these have omitted those classical books, antient and modern, which gentlemen generally have in their private libraries, but which cannot properly claim a place in a collection made merely for the purposes of reference." The entire list, written in Jefferson's hand is divided into several categories, beginning with "Law of Nature and Nations," followed by several applications of law, then "Political Arithmetic," "Geography," and "History."[51] At the bottom of the list Jefferson added a note recommending a collection development strategy for books about American history: "all the travels, histories, accounts &c. of America, previous to the revolution, should be obtained. it is already become all but impossible to make a collection of these things. standing orders should be lodged with our ministers in Spain, France & England, & our Consul at Amsterdam to procure every thing within that description which can be hunted up in those countries." The collection was initially arranged according to size, but by 1812, the catalog contained 3,000 titles and was reorganized according to the Baconian scheme, divided according to the faculties of the mind—Memory, Reason, and Imagination.[52] This resembled Jefferson's personal catalog, which was organized primarily by subject, and then by size within those subject categories.[53] In his role as president Jefferson advised on the selection of books, and most likely supervised the classification. He perhaps supplied his own catalog as a reference for the librarians to work from as they cataloged the books.

On 24 August 1814, the congressional library, housed in the US Capitol building, went up in flames as a casualty of the War of 1812. Jefferson was residing at Monticello at the time, facing inescapable debt, and so he suggested that Congress purchase his collection to replace the books that had been burned. His letter to Samuel Harrison Smith, in which he proposes selling his collection to Congress, resembles his 1770 letter to John Page for the way that he indicates that the destruction of books is the greatest of the losses: "I learn from the Newspapers that the Vandalism of our enemy has triumphed at Washington over science as well as the Arts, by the destruction of the public library with the noble edifice in which it was deposited."[54] After much debate, Congress voted to acquire Jefferson's collection of 6,487 volumes for just under $24,000 (over half a million in today's dollars), along with his classified catalog. Despite Jefferson's emphasis on the relevance of the collection to US policy, there were some members of Congress who opposed the purchase. Among the opponents' arguments against acquiring his collection was that it contained "irreligious and immoral books, works of the French philosophers who caused and influenced the volcano of the French Revolution which had desolated Europe and extended to this country."[55] His collection by this point had deviated from his original advice to limit a congressional collection to the "deliberations of statesmen."

Jefferson served as American minister plenipotentiary to France for five years, from 1784 to 1789. During that time Jefferson described himself as suffering from a "malady of Bibliomanie," a "disease" that caused him to purchase too many books.[56] While he was in France, he purchased a total of 1,850 books[57] and hundreds more for his American friends, including James Madison. According to Kevin Hayes, by selecting and shipping books to Madison, "Jefferson exerted a significant influence on the thought of his friend at a time when he was putting the final touches on the Constitution."[58] And when he reflected on his Paris years, Jefferson wrote, "While residing in Paris, I devoted every afternoon I was disengaged, for a summer or two in examining all the principal bookstores, turning over every book with my own hand, and putting by everything which related to America, and indeed whatever was rare and valuable in every science."[59] In that same letter, he continued:

> besides this, I had standing orders, during the whole time I was in Europe, in it's principal book-marts, particularly Amsterdam, Frankfort, Madrid and London, for such works relating to America as could not be found in Paris. so that, in that department, particularly, such a collection was made as probably can never again be effected; because it is hardly probable that the same opportunities, the same time,

> industry, perseverance, and expence, with some knolege of the bibliography of the subject would again happen to be in concurrence.[60]

Jefferson wrote these words years after he returned from France, in the context of selling his library to Congress, and so this passage was written in hindsight, as something of a sales pitch to his friend and colleague Samuel Harrison Smith, written with the hope that Smith would help him to persuade Congress to purchase his collection. Therefore, he was placing an emphasis on the books that directly pertained to the nation and diplomacy. In the United States and in Europe he had acquired books via various networks and channels, obtaining books in person from booksellers and in overseas shipments. He accumulated travel narratives, political treatises, history books, poetry and novels, and books on sciences and the fine and technical arts. He sold his classified collection to the US Congress with an eye toward seeing the collection as something that would mediate the conversations about the emerging nation, its priorities and threats, by supplying literature that included models and lessons on which to base decisions. When his books became the books for Congress, they became the printed resources upon which the congressional culture was informed.

Jefferson viewed the act of submitting his collection to the US Congress as a means to inscribe his legacy and political agenda into the intellectual and cultural realm of the nation. According to Endrina Tay, Fiske and Marie Kimball Librarian at the Thomas Jefferson Foundation, "Jefferson saw his carefully curated assemblage of literary treasures, many irreplaceable, as a reflection of who he was, the values he believed in, and how he wanted to be regarded by his fellow countrymen and by posterity—as the champion of a nation of enlightened and free men."[61] The method for organizing this collection was integral to its cohesion and value. As Hayes suggests, "In this respect, his careful library organization was more important than the individual books it contained. . . . Jefferson saw the sale of his highly organized library to Congress as an opportunity to determine how the new national library codified information."[62] And according to the former Chief of the Library of Congress's Rare Books and Special Collections Mark Dimunation, "His books, his collection, and its organization stood as the well source of fact from which he could pull together information and apply it to a changing world."[63] Historians agree that the collection was made exceptionally useful because of its classified catalog. "Only Jefferson," writes Dimunation, "possessed the prerequisites for this achievement—the bibliographic acumen, a comprehensive approach to knowledge, and, admittedly, his considerable means."[64] Jefferson could not have anticipated the reach of the Library of Congress's standards for organizing knowledge today, but the establishment of the United States' first federal cultural institution was instrumental in laying the groundwork for its present global knowledge organization systems. A *Washington City Chronicle* editorial dated 11 July 1829 confirms the usefulness of his cataloging system for the books for Congress: "It is, perhaps, the best that has yet been introduced. It is indeed, scientific, and by keeping all books upon the same subject together and under one head, it affords facilities that no other model hitherto adopted has been found to yield."[65] In addition to the analytic order, Jefferson also numbered the books according to shelf placement, which was arranged by size within subject chapters and disrupted the order of the catalog but maintained aesthetic unity. He had differently sized bookcases, which functioned as "stackable modular storage," allowing him to optimize shelf space.[66] The top shelves contained duodecimos and smaller volumes, next were octavos and quartos. Large folios were on the bottom shelves.

The Library of Congress is often regarded as the national library of the United States, but the truth is that its primary purpose is to serve as the library for the legislative branch of the United States government.[67] In its role as a public library as originally defined, it is an agency of the US government that serves the public interest. The Library of Congress is the oldest federal cultural agency in the United States, and its cataloging and classification standards have been developed in and for Congress and extended to an international network of public, academic, and special libraries.[68] The tension that derives from setting the standards for knowledge organization in libraries of all types in many parts of the world, while being a library meant to serve the US government is important in the story of American nation-building and expansion. The ongoing problem with the library's unwillingness to authorize the subject heading "Undocumented immigrants" to replace the heading "Illegal aliens" stands as a troublingly illustrative example of the library's relationship with Congress. Conservative members of the legislature intervened when a new heading was proposed in 2016, even writing legislation in an attempt to block the change. In November of 2021, the heading was cancelled and replaced with two different subject headings—"Illegal immigration" and "Noncitizens"—a change that many library workers and members of the public still see as inadequate and unjust. More recently, the Library of Congress changed the official subject headings "Mexico, Gulf of" and "Denali, Mount (Alaska)" to "America, Gulf of" and "McKinley, Mount (Alaska)" respectively, in response to President Trump's orders.[69] Whatever one's opinion about the changes, these cases demonstrate that the library is indeed an arm of the legislative branch, funded by Congress, and so its subject access terms sometimes reflect the US government's point of view. This was certainly the case in Jefferson's day, as well. Of his own books that he sold to the Library of Congress he said, "I do not know that it contains any branch of science which Congress would wish to exclude from their collection; there is, in fact, no subject to which a member of Congress may not have occasion to refer."[70] There was much debate about the efficacy of acquiring his books, and conservative members of Congress opposed the idea on the grounds that they included too much foreign literature or that it reflected a Democratic-Republican mindset.

From the moment Jefferson's collection and catalog were acquired in 1815, the Library of Congress adapted the classification to librarians' imagined needs of its readers. In an alteration that perturbed Jefferson, Librarian of Congress George Watterston revised Jefferson's system so that the titles were arranged alphabetically within each chapter. Gone was the precise intellectual order that revealed the inner workings of Jefferson's mind. Watterston's system was superseded in 1861 by one that incorporated a subject classification throughout, as librarians and users found the Jeffersonian plan too broad for the expanding collection. What seems to have been missed in the discussions of the applicability of Jefferson's system was that his original system was, in fact, narrower than people realized. Although he did not explicitly label subcategories within the chapters, patterns of subdivisions do become apparent upon close readings of his analytic arrangement. Subdivisions were present throughout the classification, but these intellectual associations were lost when Watterston reordered the titles alphabetically within the disciplines and genres. Watterston asked Jefferson about his modifications to the system, to which Jefferson replied, "you ask how I like the arrangement within the chapters? of course, you know, not so well as my own; yet I think it possible the alphabetical arrangement may be more convenient to readers generally, than mine which was sometimes analytical, sometimes chronological, & sometimes a combination of both."[71]

Jefferson continually updated and revised his classified catalog during his lifetime, and he modified and adapted the system for different contexts, including the University of Virginia. In fact, in September of 1824, near the end of Jefferson's life, book collector and Harvard professor George Ticknor observed that Jefferson had "prepared an entire catalog of seven or eight thousand volumes for the Library of the university, neatly written in his own hand, arranged according to subjects, with an index, and priced."[72] Jefferson willed his retirement library to the University of Virginia, but that expressed desire was not met. Instead, his books were sold at auction to pay the debts that he had left. Although the university was not the beneficiary of his collection, Jefferson's influence on the organization of the library was perhaps just as significant as the books themselves would have been. The placement of the library at the head of the Lawn in the Rotunda building was itself a statement. With the intentional absenting of a chapel, the Rotunda "represented a secular temple of reason that replaced revelation with empiricism."[73] Jefferson appointed the first two librarians, wrote the first set of rules and regulations, and not only advised on the collection, but compiled a list of 6,860 books for the library. By 1829 the university had acquired over 8,000 volumes—more than any other college or university, other than Harvard and Yale. He also sought recommendations for books from the faculty. Despite the vastness of the catalog, however, the library did not purchase any anti-slavery texts. As Andrew O'Shaughnessy writes, "the absence of abolitionist literature was a stunning omission and an indication of Jefferson's willingness to appease the proslavery interest in his late retirement to garner their support for the university."[74] This somewhat resembles the catalog that he sold to the Library of Congress, although it did include a few anti-slavery works. As I suggest in the Chapter 5, we can find patterns in that catalog that reflect a particular form of racism.

Jefferson was extraordinarily persuasive and set the tone and standard of practice for the library in the last years of his life. Upon appointing the student William Wertenbaker to the position of university librarian in 1826, Jefferson instructed him "to keep the books in a state of sound preservation, undefaced, and free from injury by moisture or other accident, and in their stated arrangement on the shelves according to the method and order of their catalogue." Just a few weeks before he died, Jefferson traveled by horseback to the university grounds to unpack the first shipment of books for the library. Wertenbaker recalled Jefferson's "manifested interest in getting everything rightly placed at an early date," and that with "feeble hands he helped to unpack the books and place them on the shelves, in the order and the way that he had chalked out in his mind."[75] Perhaps he was guarding against the type of rearrangement that had happened with his books at the Library of Congress. This was a chance to put things right and to secure his legacy in the order of the books.

## Charlottesville's "Public Library"

An exchange between Jefferson and John Wyche, just after Jefferson's retirement from the US presidency provides insight into his vision for a public library. Wyche had humbly approached Jefferson seeking approbation and advice regarding a newly formed Westward Mill Library Society in Brunswick County, Virginia. Jefferson's response included a reiteration of his views on the centrality of an educated citizenry to a successful government and the protection of human rights, this time in the context of a necessity of a public library system:

> I always hear with pleasure of institutions for the promotion of knolege among my countrymen. the people of every country are the only safe guardians of their own rights, and are the only instruments which can be used for their destruction. and certainly they would never consent to be so used were they not decieved. to avoid this they should be instructed to a certain degree. I have often thought that nothing would do more extensive good at small expence than the establishment of a small circulating library in every county to consist of a few well chosen books, to be lent to the people of the county under such regulations as would secure their safe return in due time. these should be such as would give them a general view of other history & particular view of that of their own country, a tolerable knolege of geography, the elements of Natural philosophy, of agriculture & mechanics. should your example lead to this, it will do great good.[76]

Jefferson offered his expertise to Wyche and his colleagues, admitting that "having had more favorable opportunities than fall to every man's lot of becoming acquainted with the best books on such subjects as might be selected," he would gladly share his knowledge with these men.[77] Jefferson's description of an ideal public library reflects a more progressive agenda than the prevailing ideas about public libraries, which, as described by Tom Glynn, were "public in the same sense that a public house or public conveyance was public. The term meant not that the collection was free but simply that it was available ostensibly to any member of the public, as opposed to one belonging to an individual or a closed, private organization such as a school."[78] Advocacy for public libraries had been more progressive in the northern states than in the South, but Jefferson advanced existing ideas farther by suggesting that counties should extend access to libraries to a broad public.

While governor of Virginia, Jefferson authored the Bill for the More General Diffusion of Knowledge that was intended to secure taxpayer supported basic education for all citizens of Virginia. Educating the entire free white population would help to ensure the rights and liberties of the citizenry. Children across all levels of wealth might be "disposed to become useful instruments for the public," and Jefferson believed that "it is better that such should be sought for and educated at the common expence of all."[79] This bill did not directly state that books would also be paid for by taxpayers, but his views on the efficacy of a general public education demonstrate an early conviction in the importance of literacy education for all citizens.

Although the first taxpayer supported library to open in the United States was established in 1833 in Peterborough, New Hampshire, after Jefferson died, his influence in the development of public libraries was significant.[80] He was involved in the formation of a subscription-based circulating library in Charlottesville, much like the one for which Wyche had sought his assistance. Very little documentation of the history of the Albemarle Library Society survives, but Wyche's description of the library in Brunswick County probably provides information that would have applied to the Charlottesville library:

> And without farther preface I will proceed to state to you that some fifteen or eighteen Months ago the Gentlemen (or some of them) of this Neighbourhood agreed to procure a collection of Books—establish a Library and form ourselves into a Society the stile & Title of which should be "The Westwardmill Library Society." We have accordingly drawn & ratified a Constitution contributed each Member a mite of ten Dollars for the purchase of Books & the most of the Money has allready been expended in that way—The Terms of admission are ten Dollars and the unanimous consent of the general meeting to form which a majority (at least) of all the members must be present we have some thoughts of applying to the Assembly for an Act of incorporation and under a belief that we shall do so I have taken the liberty of addressing you on the Subject & will If agreeable to you send a Copy of our Constitution and some of our fundamental Laws for your inspection & Correction And shall think myself very happy if by this means the Society shall gain your patronage and the advantages ensuing from your superior Information & experience though I have been & still am so much affraid you will treat it with neglect not to say contempt that the secret of my writing to you does & shall rest with my self untill I know the kind of reception you give this.

Wyche went on to describe the members of the society:

> Our Society is composed of Farmers, Mechanics Justicies of the Peace Ministers of the Gospel—Militia Officers Lawyers, Schoolmasters—Merchants—Postmasters one Member of Assembly & one member of Congress.[81]

Wyche regarded this as a diverse group of people from various walks of life. He also included the names and backgrounds of the board of directors, adding, "Query will such an heterogeneous body ever firmly & lastingly coalesce?"[82] It was seen as important that the board represented the different interests of people across the county, thus approaching the spirit of a public library, rather than being one that only served the planter elite.

A circulating "public" library of this type opened in Charlottesville in 1823. Frederick Winslow Hatch—founder and rector of Christ Church in Charlottesville, as well as tutor to Jefferson's grandsons—was among the leaders of the Albemarle Library Society. He posted a notice, mostly likely in Charlottesville's *Central Gazette*, notifying community members of a meeting to form a library. Jefferson sent his regrets but expressed his interest in supporting the library. Later, when the Library Society drafted a constitution, Jefferson weighed in on its terms, suggesting some modifications. Instead of allowing all shareholders to agree on book purchases, for example, these decisions would be better left to a committee, he thought. He also used this opportunity to express his long-standing belief that a library should be "open to all" citizens for a small fee, rather than limiting access to shareholders, with the "object being to diffuse instruction as extensively as possible." Non-shareholders would pay a fee by the week "for the use of a book in proportion to it's volume."[83] In that letter he requested four shares of the library and recorded the purchase at ten dollars per share in his Memorandum Book on the same day.[84]

The library was located at 2 Court Square (see Figure 11), across from the Charlottesville courthouse, in the part of town in which the leaders of Albemarle County gathered to meet and socialize.[85] In fact, it was two doors from the building at "Number Nothing" Court Square, which was built as a mercantile shop in the early 1820s, but was also the site of an auction block for the trade in human lives.[86] It is likely that Jefferson donated some of his books to the collection. He joined the committee that prepared a catalog of books. The final catalog featured a wide range of titles across genres and disciplines and included several novels, such as works by Tobias Smollett, Henry Fielding, and others. It also included volumes by Hannah More, an abolitionist and advocate for women's education. My searches did not find Hannah More's works in Jefferson's catalog, so this, along with the inclusion of novels (something Jefferson advised against for a public library of this type), may be an indication that the formation of the catalog was indeed a collaborative effort and that there was a will to provide a wide array of reading materials for the readership.[87] The catalog was approved on 5 April 1823 at a general meeting of the Albemarle Library Society, and on 22 January 1824, the Virginia General Assembly passed a bill making the Albemarle library company "a body politic and corporate."[88] The company would elect a president and board of seven directors, who would appoint a librarian. Valentine Southall was the first president, and William Meriwether was the first librarian.[89] The library operated at least until 1834.[90] A taxpayer-supported library was not yet in sight, but Jefferson's recommendation to offer books to all citizens does bring the

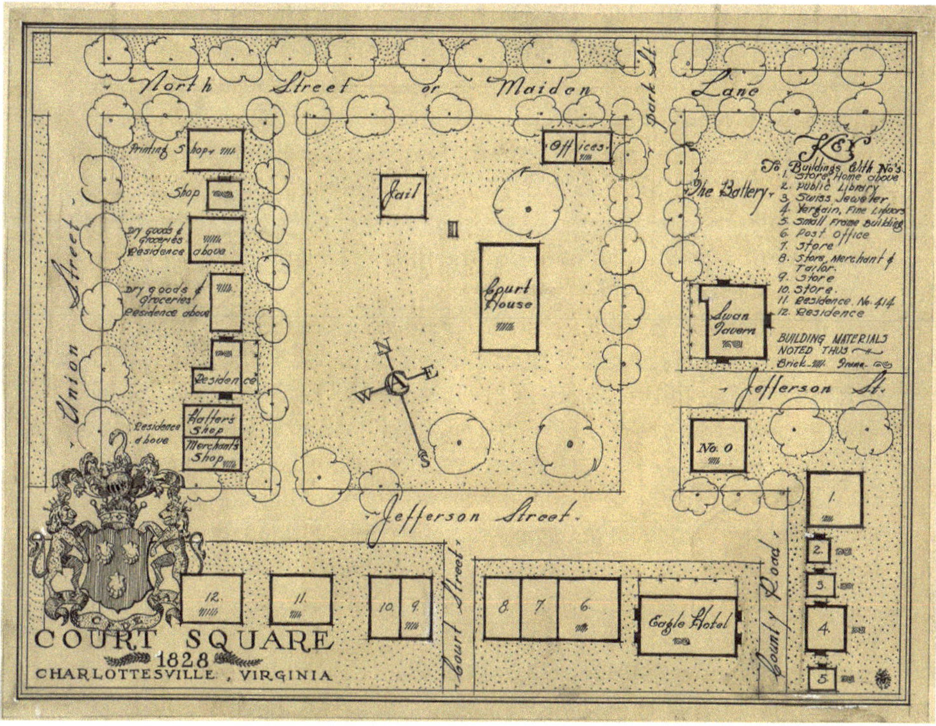


Figure 11. Court Square, Charlottesville, Virginia, 1828. University of Virginia Special Collections, MS 13633. The circulating library is building 2, in the lower right corner of the map.

subscription library nearer to a public library, at least for the idea that its books should be circulated among a broader public.

Sidney Ditzion, a library historian writing during and after World War II, framed the nineteenth-century formation of public libraries in terms of their value as "arsenals of a democratic culture," positioning that history in Jeffersonian origins: "The concepts of republicanism, risen from the enlightenment, advertised in the Revolution, strengthened in the philosophy of Jeffersonian and practiced in the era of Jacksonian democracy, were by mid-century deeply engraved in the popular mind. The doctrine of human rights, political equality, and residence of authority in the whole people, had become firmly fixed in the professed American credo."[91] But as Sam Popowich points out, writing from the field of critical librarianship, the "democratic ideals Ditzion imagined to be 'firmly fixed' in American society of the mid-19th century are ones which happily coexisted with legal slavery, not to mention the determined genocide of Indigenous populations across the entire continent."[92] In fact, Popowich turns Ditzion's frame inside out, and reveals the limitations to meeting that democratic ideal, reminding us that the protection of rights was bound to eighteenth-century ideas about natural rights of a universal Man that did not include racialized peoples. Indeed, as I show in the next two chapters, Jefferson owned books about Indigenous and Black peoples, and his classification of those books in his personal library, which would then be transferred to the Library of Congress, shows how the formation of categories functions in the interlocking processes of racialization and knowledge organization.

Public libraries have long been regarded as "cornerstones of democracy"—places where access to information is available to all, equally, but that narrative leaves out the history of the illegality of reading for Black people. They are sometimes referred to as the last public forum in which every member of society can freely assemble, pursue knowledge, and exchange ideas. Libraries have become essential spaces for many communities—people can use computers to look for and apply for jobs, contact friends and families online, find information about housing and social services, or produce creative work in makerspaces, in addition to checking out books and other materials. Indeed, the Ferguson Public Library will long stand out as exemplary of the promise of libraries to be a safe harbor in times of crisis because of its service to the community after the police killing of Michael Brown.[93] Public libraries stand at the heart of North American debates about rights, and (with a few exceptions) they try to guard against censorship and pressure from the public to select and deselect certain information resources. As Eric Klinenberg puts it, "the library is among the most critical forms of social infrastructure that we have," and it's "also one of the most undervalued."[94] He speculates that, perhaps this is "because the founding principle behind the library—that all people deserve free, open access to our shared culture and heritage, which they can use to any end they see fit—is out of sync with the market logic that dominates our time."[95] At the same time, however, funding for library buildings and resources are very often allocated along lines of wealth in American municipalities, meaning that libraries don't evenly live up to their stated purpose to serve everyone equally and equitably.

## Jefferson's Disciplinary Imagination

A formerly prevailing view among scholar librarians was that Jefferson's system was not intended to be a bibliographic tool, but rather, it was meant to organize a universe of knowledge. For example, the preface to the 1864 catalog of the Library of Congress stated: "It was never designed by its author as a bibliographical system, but rather as a scientific arrangement of the various branches of human knowledge. No further illustration of its defects need be given than the fact that in the last catalog of the Library of Congress the titles are distributed through a series of one hundred and seventy-nine distinct alphabets, arranged in an arbitrary sequence, and without an index."[96] This assessment, however, seems to be made about the Watterston version of Jefferson's catalog, in which the intellectual order was stripped away and replaced with an alphabetical one within each of the chapters. In light of Jefferson's other writings and emerging research into his information techniques, revisions are in order, and we should conclude that Jefferson did, in fact, intend his classification to be a tool for information storage and retrieval. He mapped his system to the interior of his private workspace at Monticello so that he and others could easily navigate the library according to their reading tastes. Jefferson also affixed labels to each of his books, "indicating the chapter of the catalogue to which it belongs, and the order it holds among those of the same format."[97] These labels provided what we refer to as call numbers today—notation that facilitates retrieval by shelf order. He also created an author catalog, indexing all titles alphabetically by name.

When he offered James Ogilvie full access to his library at Monticello in 1806, Jefferson described the layout of his library in detail:[98]

> I have great pleasure in finding an opportunity of making it useful to you. the key is at present in the hands of mr Dinsmore, at the place, who on sight of this letter will consider you as at all times authorised to have access to the library & to take from it any books you please . . . the arrangement is as follows. 1. Antient history. 2. Modern do. 3. Physics. 4. Nat. hist. proper. 5. Technical arts. 6. Ethics. 7. Jurisprudence 8. Mathematics. 9. Gardening, architecture, sculpture, painting, music. 9. Poetry. 10. Oratory. 11. Criticism. 12. Polygraphical. you will find this on a paper nailed up somewhere in the library. the arrangement begins behind the partition door leading out of the Book room into the Cabinet, & proceeds from left to right round the room; then entering the Cabinet it begins at the Eastern angle, & goes round that room. the presses not having been sufficed to contain the whole, the latter part of Polygraphics was put into the kind of closet at the first entrance of the book-room.[99]

This description and set of instructions reveal Jefferson's belief that a well-ordered system will ensure a library's usefulness. When he first built Monticello, with his books having burned at Shadwell, he needed to rebuild his collection. By 4 August 1773, he had already tallied 1,256 volumes in his Memorandum Book, noting that he also owned music books and kept books in Williamsburg:

| | vols. |
|---|---|
| In the Mahogany book case with glass doors | 510 |
| Walnut bookcase in N.W. corner of room | 180 |
| Walnut bookcase in N.E. corner of room | 224 |
| Shelves in N.W. corner of room | 151 |
| Shelves in N.E. corner of room | 131 |
| Lent out | 42 |
| Lying about | 18 |
| | in all 1256 vols. |

The counts are organized according to the part of the room in which they were shelved, so we gather a sense of what his library looked like. Importantly, this table shows that he let people borrow his books and probably made sure to register each loan. What's more, it appears that Jefferson intended his catalog and classification to be shared, used, and modified in other libraries. He sent lists of recommended books, often divided into categories or genres, to friends and colleagues on both sides of the Atlantic. He provided recommendations or instructions under his hand-drawn Baconian scheme in the 1783 catalog: "*in classing a small library one may throw under this head books which attempt what may be called the Natural history of the mind or an Analysis of it's operations."[100] This suggests that he intended for this system to serve as a template for other collectors wishing to organize their books by subject but that it was adaptable to libraries of different sizes and purposes. Jefferson's later vision toward his books being acquired by the University of Virginia retrospectively affirms that this early instruction may indicate that he had an eye toward standardization.

Jefferson's application of Diderot and D'Alembert's method to his book catalog demonstrates the role of encyclopedias in the formation of academic disciplines. As Richard Yeo notes, "encyclopedias have recorded and reinforced the divisions within knowledge, especially science, as much as they have evinced connections and interactions. . . . It is arguable that rather than being a force against specialization, as is often suggested, encyclopedias have reflected and facilitated the crystallization of natural knowledge into disciplines from the late eighteenth to the mid-nineteenth century."[101] Diderot and D'Alembert's adaptation of Bacon's system did not, however, suggest that there was something like a "gods-eye" view, or that any particular vantage point was better than another. Rather, they seemed to be anticipating Haraway's notion of "situated knowledges," which embraces the validity and possibility of seeing knowledge differently, depending on one's positionality:

> But as, in the case of the general maps of the globe we inhabit, objects will be near or far and will have different appearances according to the vantage point at which the eye is placed by the geographer constructing the map, likewise the form of the encyclopedic tree will depend on the vantage point one assumes in viewing the universe of letters. Thus one can create as many different systems of human knowledge as there are world maps having different projections, and each one of these systems might even have some particular advantage possessed by none of the others.[102]

They understood their system to be arbitrary, but they believed it to be useful and well-suited to the purposes of assembling and ordering the information universe. Jefferson held similar views about knowledge organization systems, which he expressed in different contexts. For example, in a letter written around the same time that he would have been preparing his collection for the Library of Congress transfer, he wrote a lengthy reflection on the arbitrariness of classification for natural history:

> Nature has, in truth, produced Units only thro' all her works. Classes, orders, genera, species are not of her work. her creation is of individuals. no two animals are exactly alike; no two plants, nor even two leaves or blades of grass; no two crystallisations. and, if we may venture, from what is within the cognisance of such organs as ours, to conclude on that beyond their powers, we must believe that no two particles of matter are of exact resemblance. this infinitude of Units, or individuals being far beyond the capacity of our memory, we are obliged, in aid of that, to distribute them into masses, throwing into each of these all the individuals which have a certain degree of resemblance; to subdivide these again into smaller groupes, according to certain points of dissimilitude observable in them; and so on, until we have formed what we call a system of classes, orders, genera, and species. in doing this we fix arbitrarily on such characteristic resemblances & differences as seem to us most prominent & invariable in the several subjects, and most likely to take a strong hold in our memories. . . . Nature has not arranged her productions on a single & direct line. they branch at every step, and in every direction, and he who attempts to reduce them into departments is left to do it by the lines of his own fancy.

Indeed, Jefferson viewed categorization and classification to be essential for scientific progress. A good classification scheme contains and controls the objects of study. He opposed the ideas of scientists like the Comte de Buffon, whose scientific practices followed from his belief that nature resisted classification:

> and so also the no-system of Buffon; the great advocate of individualism, in opposition to classification. he would carry us back to the days, and to the confusion of Aristotle and Pliny, give up the improvements of twenty centuries, and co-operate with the Neologists in rendering the science of one generation useless to the next, by perpetual changes of it's language.

Jefferson believed that one universal system was preferable to multiple systems, anticipating standardization. While he found value in the classifications of Blumenbach and Cuvier, for instance, at the end of the day, he advocated the Linnaean system:

> because it is sufficient as a groundwork; admits of supplementary insertions, as new productions are discovered, and mainly because it has got into so general use that it will not be easy to displace it, and still less to find another which shall have the same singular fortune of obtaining the general consent. during the attempt we shall become unintelligible to one another, and science will be really retarded by efforts to advance it.[103]

All to say, Jefferson was convinced of the efficacy of universal classifications, but he understood that they could be modified according to context. He was leaning toward a standard of practice, favoring Linnaeus because it had become so widely used that it afforded what we refer to today as interoperability. The Linnaean system could be somewhat flexible, but it was uniform enough that it could be applied in different disciplines in many locations. With regard to a catalog for a university library, he similarly expected that different professions will be likely to group books according to their disciplinary contexts and information needs:

> Where sciences are to be arranged in accomodation to the schools of an University, they will be grouped to coincide with the kindred qualifications of Professors in ordinary. for a library again, which was my object, their divisions and subdivisions will be made such as to throw convenient masses of books under each separate head. thus in the library of a Physician the books of that science, of which he has many,

> will be subdivided under many heads; and those of Law, of which he has few, will be placed under a single one. The Lawyer again will distribute his law-books under many subdivisions, his Medical under a single one.[104]

Suffering from pains that came with old age, Jefferson dictated the words above to his granddaughter, who transcribed them in a letter to Augustus Elias Brevoort Woodward, author of another encyclopedic work. Woodward's arrangement in his *System of Universal Science* seems to have brought Jefferson's thoughts about reorganizing his own catalog to mind, but at this point Jefferson was near the end of eighty-three years of life and became frustrated with the exercise. Jefferson thanked Woodward for sending his "system of universal science," referring to it as "a monument of the learning of the author and of the analysing powers of his mind."[105]

That Jefferson modeled his book classification on the *Encyclopédie* is important on several levels. For one, it indicates a transnational scientific practice that begins to take the shape of standardization. The exchange of ideas, with the imitation and emendations to the classificatory arrangements, would have amplified and reified the categorical divisions. The secularization of knowledge created a reliance on factual data and the suppression of anything that might be regarded as supernatural or myth. The concept of an encyclopedia derives from the Greek term for circle, and the encyclopedists also understood that they were reducing phenomena to their fundamentals in order to draw connections across the entire universe of knowledge. The *philosophes* believed that laws underlie each of the disciplines, and that a unity binds them together. Diderot and his colleagues were radical thinkers, and it is worth pointing out that Diderot engrossed himself in his encyclopedic project after being imprisoned and warned not to publish any other scandalous works. The form and content of the encyclopedia perhaps masked its subversive qualities. It is massive, with over seven hundred articles written by Diderot, Rousseau, Voltaire, and others. We don't know who all of the authors of the entries in the *Encyclopédie* are because they often collaborated orally and didn't always write things down.

The drama surrounding the production and prohibitions of the *Encyclopédie* and the punishments enacted upon its authors demonstrate just how threatening it was to the established order.[106] The turn away from metaphysics toward empiricism resulted in the subversion of religion by placing it within the realm of philosophy. As Robert Darnton writes, this "smacked of heresy because it seemed to subordinate theology to reason."[107] Jefferson also eschewed metaphysics and anything that could not be proven with empirical evidence. For his catalog, he modified Diderot's outline and made it even more radical, subordinating religion farther and giving it far less prominence in his book classification. The broad category of Philosophy (derived from the faculty of Reason) was divided into Moral and Mathematical Philosophy. Moral Philosophy was then subdivided into Ethics and Jurisprudence. And under Jurisprudence he created categories for Religious, Municipal, and Oeconomical. Religion falls under Religious Jurisprudence and is the subject of chapter 18 in his catalog.

The *Encyclopédie* was meant to be put in the hands of a general reading public. D'Alembert suggested that one day it might take the place of a library for a laymen, and for "all types of knowledge except his own particular domain for a professional scholar."[108] For Diderot and D'Alembert, the *Encyclopédie* surpassed existing dictionaries, which ordered concepts alphabetically, because it would "expound the true principles of things and will note their relationships, that it will contribute to the certitude and progress of human knowledge, and that by multiplying the number of true scholars, distinguished artisans, and enlightened amateurs, it will contribute new advantages to society as a whole."[109] As Darnton tells us, not only did the *Encyclopédie* attribute authority on knowledge to intellectuals committed to the Enlightenment, but it also was significant in opening the possibility for public education "and the emergence of the modern scholarly disciplines during the nineteenth century." For Darnton, the critical moment "took place in the 1750s, when the Encyclopedists recognized that knowledge was power and, by mapping the world of knowledge, set out to conquer it."[110] Taken together with Jefferson's role in the formation of the Library of Congress and the University of Virginia, the fact that Diderot and D'Alembert's framework underlies not only Jefferson's home library, but also these institutional libraries, Darnton's observations should be applied to American education, as well.

This encyclopedic project achieved its universality in part by repeating the racializing discourses that created irrational Others who were not the intended readers, nor were they likely to be contributing authors. Although Diderot and many of his colleagues were abolitionists, they agreed with many of the prevailing racializing discourses. According to Devin Vartija, the "*Encyclopédie* was coeval with Buffon's masterpiece Histoire naturelle, and. . . . Diderot and other encyclopedists relied heavily on Buffon not only for incidental articles but also for the epistemology that underpins the view of nature that dominates in the *Encyclopédie*."[111] The Comte de Buffon, director of the Jardin du Roi (now the Jardin des Plantes) advanced ideas that linked climate and geography to species development, writing in terms of "improvement" and "degeneration." He espoused the notion that the Americas were inherently less fertile places and that human and nonhuman animals were less likely to thrive. As Vartija writes, "The encyclopedists were instrumental in entrenching racial classification in Enlightenment thought, thus reinforcing the trend that began in earnest at the beginning of the century of including human beings in natural history." On the one hand, Vartija adds, the "*Encyclopédie* contains some of the most radical condemnation of slavery in French thought published up to that date, and, in numerous articles, slavery is vehemently condemned as a violation of natural rights."[112] At the same time, the encyclopaedists wrote about physical and biological differences in racialized terms. Vartija suggests that the secularized scientific studies of the human resulted in the development of racial classifications, which may help to explain how "eighteenth-century thinkers who were committed to a set of egalitarian Enlightenment values could contribute to a body of thought that would go on to have disastrous consequences," inflecting an emerging racial science on physical features with a "paternalist and Eurocentric aesthetic and moral judgments."[113] A Buffonian natural philosophy appears in several entries in the *Encyclopédie*, including Diderot's article on Indigenous peoples in the Americas, in which he espouses the view that non-Europeans have degenerated from whiteness. As for the classifications of African people, Diderot divides ethnic groups according to "biological" and aesthetic considerations. He classifies sub-Saharan Africans into two principal kinds—"Negres" and "Cafres," and like Buffon he attributes many physical features like skin color to climate and lifestyle.

Of course, we should also consider Francis Bacon, the person whose design Diderot, D'Alembert, and Jefferson imitated. Sarah Irving uses Bacon's own words to highlight his anxiety about colonialism—"I like a plantation in a pure soil; that is, where people are not displanted, to the end to plant in others. For else, it is rather an extirpation than a plantation."[114] Irving suggests that Bacon was invested in both the moral and epistemological implications of colonization. His interventions into organizing knowledge were intimately tied to the hope of advancing scientific knowledge by studying the natural history of the "New World." As Irving writes:

> The recovery of man's epistemic empire required knowledge collected in the New World. But it was vital that, in order for England to make use of that knowledge, it must be organised and administered properly. One of Bacon's primary concerns was with the proper use of knowledge for the purpose of state building. . . . A paradox emerges when we consider the project of restoring man's epistemic empire in the New World. The more knowledge is collected, the greater is the difficulty of

> its administration, because this task is conducted over a wider area and in a more diverse environment.[115]

Bacon was a major investor in both the Virginia Company and The Newfoundland Colonial Company and clearly saw the Americas as essential for scientific progress. And as Sarah Hogan suggests, his *New Atlantis*, published posthumously in 1626 as an addendum to *Sylva Sylvarum*, provides particularly relevant insights into his mindset with regard to the ways in which he invested the hope of utopia in the "New World." The island in the *New Atlantis* is called Bensalem, and Hogan argues that "it encodes within its imaginative forms a specifically imperial relationship of privilege that prioritizes the needs of Bensalem over those of the rest of the world."[116] She continues, "While Bensalem may not overtly model a violent, militarily aggressive empire of direct domination, it is certainly a fantasy of empire where natural knowledge becomes a vehicle for and a product of mercantile exploitation."[117] Bensalem attains a privileged status through the opposing ideas about the irrational, inferior, foreign society. This confirms Wynter's assessment that the earliest racial and national divides began upon contact, on the grounds of rationality and irrationality, and Christianity and the flesh. Bacon's utopian society depended upon "a denial of the cultures and peoples of the New World" and indeed outlines a "hierarchy of national bodies, defined by factors such as Christianity, culture, and other forms of 'civility,' which locates European so between the poles of the model Bensalem and an infantilized America."[118] For Bacon, natural history was a path toward the redemption of Man from the fall from grace and "the attendant loss of humanity's original dominion over creation."[119] He believed that mastery over nature across the globe would unify mankind. What emerges from that point of view, arguably, is the idea that the Indigenous peoples living in the "New World" were among the natural objects to be submitted to study and control.[120]

The next two chapters show how the Baconian framework shaped Jefferson's racial classifications by examining his collection and cataloging practices for books about Black and Indigenous peoples.

# 5
# The Racial Aesthetic of Jefferson's Library Catalog

> Ontology—once it is finally admitted as leaving existence by the wayside—does not permit us to understand the being of the black man. For not only must the black man be black; he must be black in relation to the white man.
>
> —FRANZ FANON, *BLACK SKIN WHITE MASKS:*

> *What does Aesthetics do?*
>
> —SYLVIA WYNTER, "RETHINKING AESTHETICS"

Jefferson's library catalogs were unique for the way that they delineated texts within categories and outlined academic disciplines. Not only did he develop chapters according to subjects, but within those chapters, one can discern the emergence of subcategories—for example, several books on slavery are grouped together within the fields of Ethics, under the broad category of Philosophy.[1] Although Jefferson did not name a subject category for "Slavery," the analytic order of the catalog makes it clear that he associated these books with the concept and considered them within the broader category of ethics in the discipline of philosophy. Jefferson did not refer to academic subjects as disciplines, but it is appropriate to say that one can witness their emergence with categories in Jefferson's catalog. I suggest that installing subject categories, even if they were not yet fully formed in this early library information system, was one mechanism by which racialized categories were made. The codification of a US federal library into law was instrumental to democratization and the universalizing discourses of the era. The classified catalog, which implemented subject categories and defined their relations, was part of this codification process. The evidence of the emergence of disciplinary control with the classification of his books into chapters aligns with the emergent academic disciplines in universities and research libraries in the United States. The formulation of academic subjects and ideas about the proper methods for studying a given object within a discipline keeps things in their place. "In many academic worlds," according to Katherine McKittrick, "categories are organizational tools; categories are often conceptualized as discrete from each other. . . . Academic disciplines make knowledge into categories and subcategories; methodology and method make discipline and knowledge about categories."[2] Jefferson's contributions to disciplinary constructs reflect his vision for early America.

Ideology partly explains the conditions that fueled racism and racialization in the eighteenth century, but practicality informed the utility of categories: "In addition to noting race's development as an organised narrative or doctrine, we need to observe it in operation, as a set of classificatory regimes that seek to order subject populations differentially in pursuit of particular historical agendas."[3] Two distinct aspects of Enlightenment discourse were merged in the construct of race in the late eighteenth century: "the great taxonomies of natural science with the political rhetoric of the rights of man."[4] Patrick Wolfe identifies this as a "Jeffersonian fusion of bourgeois political ideology with classificatory natural science, of power with knowledge" that "gave race its epistemic purchase on post-Enlightenment thought."[5] The Library of Congress's adoption of Jefferson's library classification was a key mechanism by which the relationship between power and knowledge has been secured. Jefferson's classed catalog enacted a "code of imperialism"—a structuring mechanism that organized books for a particular reading public and eventually informed a global standard.[6] The wide circulation of information has been made increasingly possible with the development of shared catalogs and standards, many of which (including the Library of Congress Classification) have been designed by the Library of Congress.

The categories that Jefferson devised to organize his books were derived from life, his politics, and the scientific methods of the day. His classification and catalog should be read alongside his other writings, the knowledge management and surveillance techniques that he used to organize the people he enslaved and their work, as well as the prevailing theories of natural and civil law that he used to justify his policy and practices. Jefferson's mastery of knowledge is intrinsic to and entangled with the mastery of human subjects. Studying Jefferson as a master of his plantation, a revolutionary who would be president, and a classificationist and reader brings a depth of understanding to the role of knowledge organization in master/slave relations and the mastery of the disciplines. Mary Louise Pratt draws a connection between classification, travel literature, and colonialism during the Enlightenment in her book *Imperial Eyes*. She writes, "For what were the slave trade and the plantation system if not massive experiments in social engineering and discipline, serial production, the systematization of human life, the standardizing of persons?"[7] Marisa Fuentes describes the relationship between the plantation ledger and historical memory: "The objectification of the enslaved allowed authorities to reduce them to valued objects to be bought and sold, used to produce profit and to retain and bequeath wealth. It also made the enslaved disposable when they could no longer labor for profit. This same objectification led to the violence in and of the archive."[8] This overlap of capitalism, social engineering, and the classification of persons is evident across Jefferson's various writings, but becomes particularly clear in his book catalogs, where all subjects are drawn together and organized in relation to one another. By looking closely and carefully at Jefferson's library catalog, we glean a sense of his disciplinary imagination.

For this chapter and Chapter 6 I am relying primarily on the 1815 version of Jefferson's catalog because that is the one that would ultimately be inscribed into American memory when he sold his collection to the Library of Congress.[9] In the present chapter I am interested in how aesthetics and politics informed his classification about Africa and African peoples. This catalog was written when Jefferson's collection was probably at its largest, after he had acquired books in France, and after several deliveries from booksellers in America and abroad, inheritances, and bookshop visits. He divided this catalog into forty-four chapters, each designating something akin to an academic discipline. Within those chapters he wrote the book information in an analytic order according to his own associations. Although he did not name subdivisions or topics within those chapters, a careful reading of the list of books across the chapters reveals his categorizing mind. Analyzing his book classification alongside his other writings may help to make sense of some of his own contradictory positions, particularly where we find ontological and "epistemological questions shade into sublime dramas."[10]

## "The Bottom of the Column"

Jefferson acquired books primarily for their utility, and he arranged them according to his worldview, as well as his information needs. His book catalog chapters on world history, moral philosophy, and literature reveal his point of view regarding the utility of books by and about Black people, which he repeatedly placed at the ends of sections—enough times to suggest a pattern from which to draw conclusions about the Jefferson's racial ordering principles. His classification techniques secured an imagined difference between white and Black peoples according to the faculties of Memory, Reason, and Imagination. Below I highlight several instances of his organization of books by or about Africa, Africans, people of African descent, and slavery to show how his order produced a universalization of whiteness by placing books about the Other at "the bottom of the column." This was an early instantiation of marginalization that laid the groundwork for future subcategories, such as "special topics" and "elements in the population" in the present-day classifications to which I pointed in the Introduction. The section below is divided in the three broad categories from the Baconian system that Jefferson used: Memory (History), Reason (Philosophy), and Imagination (Fine Arts). I describe them in reverse order, in part because I view this as a question of aesthetics, and the Fine Arts section demonstrates this most clearly.

## Imagination/Fine Arts

Written at the same time as the 1783 version of his book catalog, Jefferson's *Notes on the State of Virginia* provides evidence of the reasoning behind his analytic order. In Query fourteen of *Notes*, which he titled "Laws," for example, he begins by describing Virginia's legal code and then goes into a detailed discussion of race and slavery, with a detailed defense of his beliefs about the inferiority of Black people. Query fourteen is rather peculiar for the way that it states and explains laws in mostly simplified statements, and then expounds for pages about scientific explanations of racial difference based on physiognomy, behaviors, and literary output. Why would he spend so much time discussing racial difference in a chapter on the laws of Virginia?

Jefferson and his colleagues believed that civil law followed natural law, and that the laws of nature can be inscribed into information, policy, and daily life. Moral, political, and legal norms were believed to follow from laws derived from or supplied by nature. They sought to understand the workings of the natural world through empirical observation, and they believed that moral laws prescribed by God were discoverable and understandable through reason. Understanding natural law required knowing the order of things. As Foucault points out, the biological sciences as we now know them were just emerging in the eighteenth century, but they were still framed in terms of natural *history*, following Bacon and other classical scholars. Jefferson stands in the moment that Foucault describes as an "in-between"—a transition from the Renaissance-era spectacle of tournaments, bestiaries, and gardens to "the classifications of words, languages, roots, documents, records" and the formation of positivist natural science. Jefferson's house at Monticello with its elaborate gardens, majestic views, and the museum that he installed in his entryway all show that he appreciated the spectacular, but he was also at the forefront of writing and organizing history and other kinds of facts into statistical tables and lists. Foucault writes, "What came surreptitiously into being between the age of the theatre and that of the catalogue was not the desire for knowledge, but a new way of connecting things both to the eye and to discourse. A new way of making history."[11] In this world, if Jefferson arrives at what he believes to be evidence of natural law regarding racial difference, or if he can apply science and reason to demonstrate that Black people are not capable of self-mastery, then he can translate that into codes of ethics and rights, and policies for state formation. The order of the classification confirms this thesis and encodes it in his catalog. The texts that confounded mastery or unsettled his claims were effectively written off, by fully excluding or otherwise marginalizing Black and Indigenous voices that challenged his views.

Among other sources of evidence to support his claims, Jefferson used the works of Ignatius Sancho and Phillis Wheatley (Peters) to demonstrate what he believed to be an imaginative and intellectual defect of Black people.[12] Sancho's book, *Letters of the Late Ignatius Sancho,* was one of the earliest accounts of African slavery written in English by a formerly enslaved person. Among Sancho's correspondents was Laurence Sterne, abolitionist and author of *The Life and Times of Tristram Shandy*, and a white English author whom Jefferson held in high esteem.[13] Sterne kept Sancho's letters, and these were included in *Letters of the Late Ignatius Sancho.*[14]

The passages in *Notes on the State of Virginia* reveal his method, as well as the inherent limits to reason in his justification of his position. His defense of these views relies on observations which take the appearance of scientific methods applied to literature. This may best be described as a willful refusal to admit certain knowledges, which is "aggressively made and reproduced" in the guise of science and reason.[15] On Sancho Jefferson writes:

> Ignatius Sancho has approached nearer to the merit in composition; yet his letters do more honour to the heart than the head. . . . He is often happy in the turn of his compliments, and his stile is easy and familiar, except when he affects a Shandean fabrication of words. But his imagination is wild and extravagant, escapes incessantly from every restraint of reason and taste, and, in the course of its vagaries, leaves a tract of thought as incoherent and eccentric, as is the course of a meteor through the sky. . . . Upon the whole, though we admit him to the first place among those of his own colour who have presented

> themselves to the public judgment, yet when we compare him with the writers of the race among whom he lived, and particularly with the epistolary class, in which he has taken his own stand, *we are compelled to enroll him at the bottom of the column.*[16]

Jefferson is showing us that his cataloging decisions are intentional and reasoned. He was writing *Notes* alongside his cataloging project. And in fact, what he wrote in *Notes* was precisely the action that he took in his book classification, placing Sancho's letters at the bottom of the Epistolary chapter in the Fine Arts section of the 1783 catalog[17] (see Figure 12). Arguably, the disciplinary assignment itself is a dismissal, as the term epistolary generally refers to works of fiction. One could argue that Sancho's letters should, in fact, be placed in history, rather than fine arts. The book remained at the bottom of the epistolary column until 1815, when he sold the collection to the Library of Congress.

In his discussion of the merits and faults of Black authors, Jefferson compares Black people to whites in terms of his perceptions of their respective faculties of memory, reason, and imagination. Jefferson was using Bacon's scientific framework not only for a structuring technique for a library catalog, but also to frame a wider discourse about race, citizenship, and government in a document meant to convey information about Virginia to a French diplomat. He determined that they are equal in memory, but not in reason and imagination and used Phillis Wheatley (Peters), the first African American published poet, as an example. She was born in Africa, came to America via the Middle Passage, and was taught and freed by the Wheatley family in Boston. Her 1773 poem "On Imagination" seems to point to Baconian ideas about the faculty of imagination:

> Such is thy pow'r, nor are thine orders vain,
> O thou the leader of the mental train:
> In full perfection all thy works are wrought,
> And thine the sceptre o'er the realms of thought.
> Before thy throne the subject-passions bow,
> Of subject-passions sov'reign ruler thou;
> At thy command joy rushes on the heart,
> And through the glowing veins the spirits dart.

One might read it as ironic that it is on the basis of the faculty of imagination which Jefferson dismisses Wheatley's poetry:

> Misery is often the parent of the most affecting touches in poetry. – Among the blacks is misery enough, God knows, but no poetry. Love

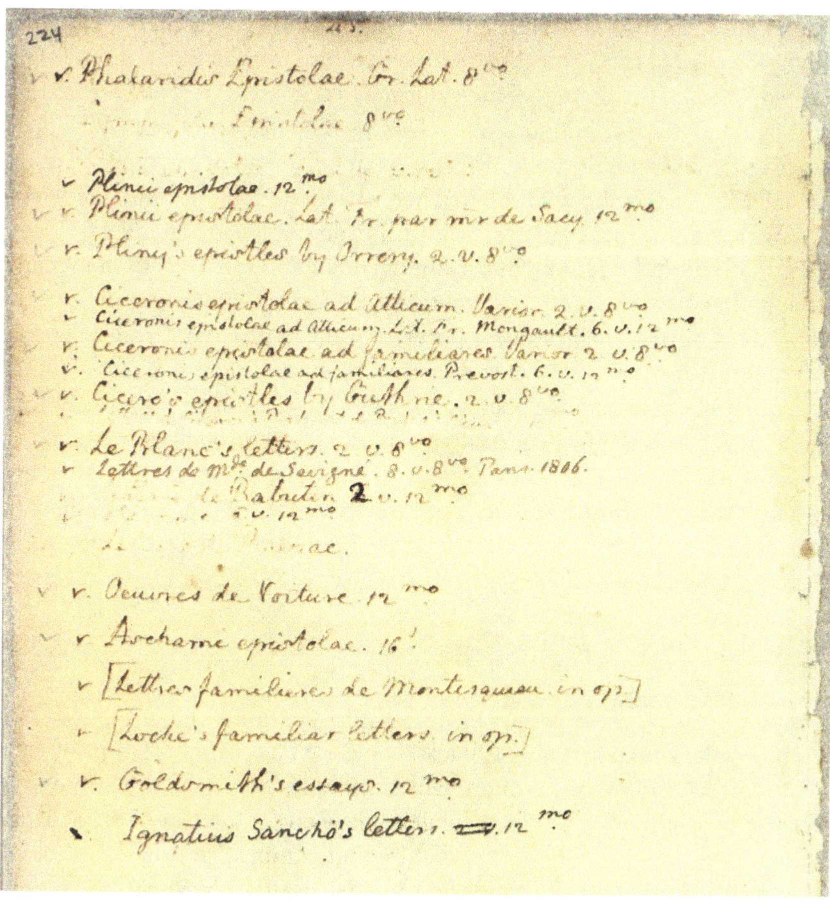
224

Phalaridis Epistolae. Gr. Lat. 8vo.

Plinii epistolae. 12mo

Plinii epistolae. Lat. Fr. par mr de Sacy. 12mo

Pliny's epistles by Orrery. 2. v. 8vo.

Ciceronis epistolae ad Atticum. Varior. 2. v. 8vo

Ciceronis epistolae ad Atticum. Lat. Fr. Mongault. 6. v. 12mo

Ciceronis epistolae ad familiares. Varior 2. v. 8vo

Ciceronis epistolae ad familiares. Prevost. 6. v. 12mo

Cicero's epistles by Guthrie. 2. v. 8vo.

Le Blanc's letters. 2. v. 8vo.

Lettres de Mde de Sevigne. 8. v. 8vo. Paris. 1806.

Rabutin 2. v. 12mo

Oeuvres de Voiture 12mo

Aschami epistolae. 16s.

[Lettres familieres de Montesquieu. in op.]

[Locke's familiar letters. in op.]

Goldsmith's essays. 12mo

Ignatius Sancho's letters. 12mo.

Figure 12. Ignatius Sancho's letters, at "the bottom of the column." Thomas Jefferson's 1783 Catalog of Books, page 224, [manuscript], [circa 1775–1812]. Original manuscript from the Coolidge Collection of Thomas Jefferson Manuscripts, Massachusetts Historical Society.

> is the peculiar oestrum of the poet. Their love is ardent, but it kindles the senses only, not the imagination. Religion indeed has produced a Phyllis Whately [*sic*]; but it could not produce a poet. The compositions published under her name are below the dignity of criticism.[18]

Jefferson's assessment of the formerly enslaved poet Phillis Wheatley (Peters) is stated in the negative: "no poetry," "not the imagination," "could not produce a poet," "below the dignity." Jefferson's opinion in fact diverged from that of many of his contemporaries, including George Washington, who viewed Wheatley's poetry to be evidence of her intellectual and creative talent.[19]

Reading his negation of Wheatley's intellect in *Notes on the State of Virginia* alongside his book classification, shows that his classificatory positioning of her work toward the bottom of the column is a statement in itself, a repetition of his narrative description of Wheatley's work. Jefferson placed Wheatley's poems in the "Pastorals, Odes, Elegies" chapter, ahead of ten other titles, in the 1783 catalog. At the time, he had not yet acquired the volume but placed a mark next to the title to indicate his wish to do so. By 1815, after it was added to his collection, he rethought the arrangement and moved it to the second from bottom of the column and transcribed the entry "Phyllis Whateley's poems." This would appear to be a purposeful move that reflects his views on Wheatley's volume in relation to the others, and one might speculate that for Jefferson, African American poetry ranks last in significance.[20] Simon Gikandi argues that this type of categorization was "achieved through a process of repression and denial in which those who didn't fit into the structures of feelings and institutional practices associated with taste were left out of its domain altogether." In marking a distinction between Sancho and Wheatley and white authors, Jefferson is "differentiating the subject of taste" from the savagery of racialized others.[21]

## Reason/Philosophy

Most of Jefferson's books about Black people are books about slavery and are classed in his Philosophy section, which includes books on ethics and law. Chapter 16 of Jefferson's 1815 book catalog is devoted to Ethics and is divided into "Moral Philosophy" and "Law of Nature and Nations," mirroring his commentary in *Notes on the State of Virginia*. The last third of Moral Philosophy features a list of books about ethical relations with the Other in Jefferson's world. There he classed books about women and family, religious tolerance, and slavery. The chapter begins with books by the ancient Greeks and Romans, followed by books by philosophers such as Spinoza, Bolingbroke, Hume, and Voltaire. Then there is a line break, followed by books that are almost entirely about ethical relations with gendered, racialized, and religious others. Of the 139 titles listed in Moral Philosophy, the thirteen works about slavery and Black culture are listed last of all the books in the chapter. They are transcribed below in the order in which they appear in Jefferson's catalog:

> Tracts in ethics, to wit, Swedenburg, Castiglione, Mably, Lites forenses, état primitive, slave trade, Benezet, &c on Slavery
> Stewarts's moral or intellectual Last will and testament
> Condorcet sur l'esclavage des Negroes

Ramsay on African slaves
Tracts on slavery, to wit. Teyroux, Mifflin, Nesbitt, Abolition, clavière
Tracts on slavery, French
Ray's horrors of slavery
Branagan on the oppression of the exiled sons of Africa
Branagan's Beautics of Philanthropy
Gregoire de la Litterature des Negres
Gregoire on the faculties and literature of the Negroes, by Warden
Clarkson's history of the abolition of the slave trade, in Gr. Br.
Caine's history of the convention of the Leeward Islands

These books are primarily about the ethics of slavery, written by white authors. Many of them expose the abuses of slavery and are explicitly abolitionist, and not all are only about the enslavement of Black people.[22] Ray's *Horrors of Slavery* narrates William Ray's "experience as a captive American sailor in North Africa during the Tripolitan War (1801–1805), the first military encounter of the United States with the Islamic world."[23] The two titles written by the Abbé Henri Jean-Baptiste Grégoire are the French and English editions of a powerful treatise on the intellectual and imaginative capabilities of people of African descent: *De la littérature des Nègres, ou, Recherches sur leurs facultés intellectuelles*, translated as *An Enquiry Concerning the Intellectual and Moral Faculties, and Literature of Negroes.*[24] The book was written in part as a response to Jefferson's explicitly racist commentary in his *Notes on the State of Virginia*. In this text, Grégoire provides a survey of Black literature and refutes Jefferson's assertions about the innate inferiority of Black intellect and imagination.

Joseph Eaton has shown that David Bailie Warden deliberately added and omitted material to please American readers in accordance with the political climate. Among the excisions were references to Jefferson's letter to Benjamin Banneker in which he softens his comments about the inferiority of Black people.[25] (This is discussed later in the chapter.) According to Eaton, the Warden translation should serve as a reminder that "Jefferson's reputation on the question of race was complex during his lifetime."[26] For example, Warden wrote, "the more respectful the authority of Jefferson is, the more important is it to combat his judgment, which seems too severe."[27] Grégoire sent Jefferson a manuscript copy of his 1808 work, to which Jefferson responded with a reply that seems to convey sympathy with the abolitionist cause:

> be assured that no person living wishes more sincerely than I do, to see a complete refutation of the doubts I have myself entertained and expressed on the grade of understanding allotted to them by nature, and to find that in this respect they are on a par with ourselves. . . . I pray

> you therefore to Accept my thanks for the many instances you have enabled me to observe of respectable intelligence in that race of men, which cannot fail to have effect in hastening the day of their relief, & to be assured of the Sentiments of high & just esteem & consideration which I tender to your self with all sincerity.[28]

In stark contrast, Jefferson reported to his friend Joel Barlow that Grégoire's method and defense of Black literature were flawed: "his credulity has made him gather up every story he could find of men of colour (without distinguishing whether black, or of what degree of mixture) however light the mention, or light the authority on which they are quoted."[29] Jefferson shows different faces in his letters to Barlow and Grégoire, but if his classification is indeed a blueprint of his mind, then his classification of Grégoire's book may reveal his true convictions. Rather than placing the book in the Fine Arts section, where it might have fit well within the chapter on criticism, Jefferson placed it in the chapter on Moral Philosophy, again, near the bottom of the column, with books on slavery. Placing it in this location makes two implicit statements: it refuses Grégoire's claim that Black literature is indeed art and that the Black imagination has value, and it places the work in the context of slavery, revealing that Jefferson's association of Black people with slavery, or perhaps his view of the implications of the book for the future of property and slavery in the republic. The inclusion of both the original French (1808) and Warden's 1810 translation into English is significant, though, as it signals Jefferson's choice to include work that was critical of his own. Both went to the Library of Congress in the sale of Jefferson's books.

## Memory/History

Jefferson's "History" section is composed of fifteen chapters, including ancient and modern histories, ecclesiastical history, agriculture, medicine, zoology, botany, and technical arts. According to the 1815 catalog, Jefferson owned and cataloged over four hundred history books. As books in the History (or Memory) section were regarded as established fact, some topics that twenty-first-century readers might think of as science were considered natural history in Jefferson's world. The histories of countries and peoples were considered civil history. The first chapter in History is "Ancient History," and chapter 2 is titled "Modern History. Foreign." First in that chapter are listed books about Italy, Rome, Florence, Naples, Venice, Spain, Portugal, and France. Then are books on Lapland, Russia, Poland, Hungary, Sweden, Denmark, Prussia, Germany, Flanders, United Netherlands, Switzerland, and

Geneva. And finally, Turkey, Asia, and Africa. British and American histories are arranged in chapters three and four of his catalog.

There are ten books under the subheading "Africa" in this world history chapter. They are all cataloged after books on the Ottoman Empire, Japan, China, and India. Listed last in the chapter is the entry, "Ludolphus' history of Ethiopia." Eight of the ten books in this section are about the countries often regarded as the "Barbary States" (the Ottoman Regencies of Algiers, Tunis, and Tripoli, along with independent Morocco), which were particularly relevant to US interests in Jefferson's time. Beginning in the 1780s, when Jefferson was in France, pirates from these North African countries seized American merchant ships in the Mediterranean, capturing and enslaving their crews and demanding ransom from the United States. This posed a particular threat to the United States' economic growth, and as the minister to France in the 1780s and then the US secretary of state in the 1790s, Jefferson played a significant role in negotiations and decisions regarding the conflict. Jefferson's early presidency was marked by the start of the Barbary Wars.[30] The First Barbary War, also known as the Tripolitan War, lasted from 1801 to 1805. As Jennifer Costello Brezina notes, this conflict should be understood in terms of late eighteenth- and early nineteenth-century American Orientalism, which became key to defining and narrating a shifting national identity "through conflicts with an Orientalized Other."[31] The "Barbary Captivity" narratives (like Ray's *Horrors of Slavery*) often told by former captives were widely produced because "the United States' reading public needed an Other to define themselves against—the more foreign the better."[32] Jefferson's actions were emblematic of, as Robin D. G. Kelley says, "this generation of enlightened European scholars," who "stripped all of Africa of any semblance of 'civilization,' using the printed page to eradicate African history and thus reduce a whole continent and its progeny to little more than beasts of burden or brutish heathens." In his forward to the rerelease of Cedric Robinson's *Black Marxism*, Kelley states that the "exorcising of the Black Mediterranean is about the fabrication of Europe as a discrete, racially pure entity solely responsible for modernity, on the one hand, and the fabrication of the Negro, on the other."[33]

This was a key moment in the history of American expansion and the accumulation of capital, international trade, and military dominance. Uniting Americans through narrative and political rhetoric was accomplished in part through anti-Islamist and racist ideology, which was also essential for gaining public and official support for the very expensive foreign military campaign. Jefferson's catalog reveals not only what he read in his research for his foreign policy and war efforts, but the order of the books also shows how he ranks African countries in relation to American national interest and compared to other countries. Jefferson's entries for books on histories of Africa are listed below:

> The revolt of Ali Bey, by S.L. Kosmopolitos
> Histoire des Etats Barbaresques, traduite de l'anglais
> L'Etat de l'empire de Maroc en 1694, par Pidou de S$^{t}$ Olon
> Révolutions de Maroc par Brathwaite, traduction
> Mémoire Sur le royaume de Tunis par S$^{t}$ Germais
> Ray's American Tars in Tripoli
> Etat de Tripoli, Tunis et Algers
> Histoire d'Algers, par Lauguer de Tassey
> Voyage dans les Etats Barbaresques
> Ludophus' history of Ethiopia

Jefferson shelved a smattering of other titles about Africa and African peoples in chapters on Religion and Natural History, but perhaps what is most striking is some of the absences across the section. We don't find sections for African politics or law or science, and plenty of important texts written by Black authors were never entered into his system at all. Autobiographies written by people who had been formerly enslaved were widely circulated, but Jefferson doesn't seem to have added one of the most significant titles to his catalog. Olaudah Equiano is among the most notable authors of the period in this genre. It is highly probable that Jefferson would have encountered Equiano's text, but whether he read it and what his impressions might have been we don't know.[34] Whereas British abolitionists like William Wilberforce, Granville Sharp, and Thomas Clarkson used Equiano's autobiography as evidence in the case for equality on the basis of intelligence and eloquence, I have not found a single reference to Equiano or his work in any of Jefferson's correspondence.[35]

Benjamin Banneker, a Black astronomer, mathematician, farmer, and surveyor, was a crucial member of Andrew Ellicott's team that surveyed the original borders of Washington D.C. He may be best known, however, for his Almanac, published from 1792 to 1802. Banneker sent Jefferson a manuscript copy of the first issue of the Almanac ahead of publication. This was the first such work created by a Black American, and along with the manuscript, he sent a letter refuting Jefferson's assertion about the intellectual inferiority of Black people and urging Jefferson to renounce slavery. He went as far as to hold Jefferson accountable for his contradictory actions:

> but Sir how pitiable is it to reflect, that altho you were so fully convinced of the benevolence of the Father of mankind, and of his equal and impartial distribution of those rights and privileges which he had

> conferred upon them, that you should at the Same time counteract his mercies, in detaining by fraud and violence so numerous a part of my brethren under groaning captivity and cruel oppression, that you should at the Same time be found guilty of that most criminal act, which you professedly detested in others, with respect to yourselves.[36]

Jefferson responded to Banneker politely, but as Annette Gordon-Reed writes:

> As one might expect, Jefferson's answer to Banneker was an artful dodge. He gave ground to Banneker, complimenting the astronomer on his achievements, taking care to let Banneker know that he was sending the Almanac to the secretary of the Academy of Sciences at Paris, the marquis de Condorcet. Wanting as ever to appear the good scientist, Jefferson presented himself as open to any evidence that his suspicions of black inferiority were incorrect. Yet he was careful not to meet the full force of Banneker's complaint.[37]

In the letter to Barlow in which he denounced Grégoire's volume, he also called Banneker's intelligence into question and suggested that his success was most likely attributable to Ellicott: "the whole do not amount in point of evidence, to what we know ourselves of Banneker. we know he had spherical trigonometry enough to make almanacs, but not without the suspicion of aid from Ellicott, who was his neighbor & friend, & never missed an opportunity of puffing him."[38]

Jefferson did not simply happen to overlook some authors. He clearly articulated his disavowal of these texts in letters and other writings. The absences tell us about what wasn't considered knowledge and may provide more information about the ways the classification reflected and upheld a particular point of view. Jefferson's system does not obviously provide spaces into which these works can fit. What is missing from the catalog is at least as important as what is there, and the sorting of works into a category of fiction instead of history and placing books by Black authors at the bottom of the column are collectively structuring events that do not simply reflect social conditions, nor do they only produce problems in private. These categorizations consolidate racializing discourses by repeating them in different contexts across disciplines.

## Jefferson's Racial Aesthetics

The arrangement and display of his books in his home asserted a particularly American Enlightenment aesthetic. As Henry Louis Gates and Andrew Curran write, "Jefferson remained unsure just what constituted the physical essence of blackness. Yet he shared the belief that the 'fixed nature' of black skin was undoubtedly rich with taxonomical and political significance. The debate had shifted from the cause of blackness to its effect."[39] The sections of his classification that I have just described should be regarded as an early classificatory exercise in the history of race science, and Jefferson's catalog should be regarded as an essential primary source in the history of library and information science.

Historicizing information in Western culture and cultural studies is a particularly useful method for the project that Paul Gilroy calls for in his *Black Atlantic*—"tracing the racial signs from which the discourse of cultural value was constructed and their conditions of existence in relation to European aesthetics and philosophy as well as European science."[40] As an intellectual who came of age in the late eighteenth century, Jefferson was personally and professionally affected by the philosophical conversations about beauty and the sublime. Most of the titles on the 1771 list of books that Jefferson sent to Skipwith fall under the categories of "Fine Arts" and "Criticism of Fine Arts." The list shows his young classifying mind, with the other categories being Politicks; Trade; Religion; Law; History. Antient; History. Modern; Natural Philosophy; Natural History, &c.; and Miscellaneous. Jefferson makes a clear distinction between the utility of the books activated by the faculties of memory and imagination, explaining to Skipwith that certain history books are certainly useful, but they lack the capacity to excite the "sympathetic emotion of virtue." The books written from the imagination contain lessons that "illustrate and carry home to the mind every moral rule of life." Of these books, the ones that fall into the category "Criticism of the Fine Arts" provide insights into the works that would have influenced his ideas about aesthetics. The three selections that are firmly about aesthetics are cataloged in Jefferson's hand as "Ld. Kaim's elements of criticism," "Burke on the sublime and the beautiful," and "Hogarth's analysis of beauty." Jefferson was writing among other early national landscape writers for whom "the fluid and dynamic forms of beauty discover in natural objects ideas of change, progress, and renewal, and those of sublimity express ideas of coercion, confusion, and crisis."[41]

My analysis of Jefferson's racial aesthetic is guided by Sylvia Wynter's assessment of what aesthetics *does*, which provides the ground from which to consider the effects of Jefferson's categories. For Wynter, a deciphering practice turns a critical lens toward the "discursive-cum-biochemical causality of our narratively instituted 'cultural Imaginaries,'" their "modes of the subject, and 'forms' or 'ways' of life." In other words, a cultural imaginary is produced in discourse, which encodes and naturalizes particular possibilities for living according to aesthetic principles:

> It is these "Imaginaries," and the modes of altruistic symbolic kin-relatedness they induce, that necessarily set the parameters of possibilities both for the stable replication of the pre-assigned places of the group-categories of our order . . . and for the fictional projection of these group-categories and their role-allocated places at the levels of representation, in terms which normatively legitimate the process of role-allocating hierarchies.[42]

Whereas the purposes of Jefferson's catalog were to inventory and organize his books, its order indexes not only the ownership and location of his books, but the worldview from which he read and his own intellectual terrain. Susan Manning writes in her analysis of *Notes on the State of Virginia*, "Classification, empirical observation and an aesthetics of response combine to suggest an image of America which is as much hopeful to prognosis as it is recorded fact."[43] Aesthetic concerns were particularly important to Jefferson, and he looked to philosophers' ideas about beauty and the sublime.

The codification of race in *Notes* relies on a racial aesthetic for which he seems to borrow heavily from Hogarth and Burke, perhaps even more than he does from the natural historians who advance early scientific theories about the biological and environmental explanations of race. The text is remarkable for the way that it combines the political, aesthetic, and scientific discourses of the day in a highly stylized document intended for diplomacy with France. Bearing in mind Edward Cahill's caution against limiting this type of analysis "to narrow discussions of aesthetic theory, invoking a reductively 'Burkean' aesthetics or focusing merely on a single aesthetic category (typically, the sublime)," I focus my attention here on the pervasive racial aesthetic that influenced Jefferson's cataloging practices.[44] Jefferson was writing in a genre of landscape writing that pointed toward grand narratives of political strength and progress. J. Hector St. John de Crèvecœur's *Letters from an American Farmer*, published in 1782 is the most exemplary of these writings about the American landscape. I do emphasize Edmund Burke's and William Hogarth's texts because Jefferson read, used, and recommended these works, and they have been examined by other scholars in the context of eighteenth-century racialization.[45] Burke's chapter titled "The Effects of Blackness" is especially relevant.

I provide several direct quotations below because the precision of language is so crucial to these passages. In these texts the association between beauty and morality authorized the aesthetic values by which to measure a person's virtue and goodness. As Nelson Maldonado-Torres writes, "Goodness, truth, and beauty make reference to the broader areas of ethics, epistemology, and aesthetics, which find expression in the formation of the modern nation-state."[46]

The formulation of race has been integral to these ideas, and as Gikandi so plainly states, "the search for an idea of the aesthetic constructed on notions of universality, the moral sense, and human rights, was simultaneously accompanied by a racist ideology."[47] In fact, the American Enlightenment aesthetic relied upon and propelled ideas about sexual, national, and racial difference. Andrea Wulf points out that, although the concept of the sublime was invented in Europe, "in America, buoyed by the continent's scale, it would become distinctively patriotic."[48] The prevailing discourses about beauty and the sublime were integral to the construction of a self-governing elite, a class whose identity and status was strengthened by discourses about order and difference. Members of the planter class imagined themselves to possess a disposition of a subject capable of aesthetic judgment. As Romana Byrne writes, "In its initial conception, the aesthetic had less to do with art than with social and political overhaul: its development within the Enlightenment hinged upon its potential to encourage social harmony and political order by instating a model of instinctive morality and a mode of subjectivity ideal for the 'material operations' of the bourgeoisie."[49] The subjectivity produced by the aesthetic was instrumental to self-fashioning.

This aesthetic also informed the creation of public institutions. Cahill notes that Adam Smith, following David Hume, said that objects are perceived as beautiful and produce feelings in the eye of the beholder "because we appreciate the abstract or potential value of their utility or fitness. One need not possess a fine property or a thriving settlement to admire the benefit it might provide to others."[50] Cahill cites Smith's "Theory of Moral Sentiments," which appeared in a 1790 issue of *Universal Asylum*, where Smith suggests that the "love of utility extends to 'those institutions which promote the public welfare' because we 'take pleasure in beholding the perfection of so beautiful and grand a system.'"[51] Cahill explains that in the landscape genre within which Jefferson was writing, movements from terror to pleasure were essential to visions of progress and national futurity. "In scenes of natural and moral sublimity," writes Cahill, "we see not only images of individual empowerment and imperial ascendance but also those of resistance, revolution, and chaos. In distinctions between elite and vulgar aesthetic subjects, we see disparate political interests contending for superior perspectives."[52]

Jefferson found sublimity and beauty in places one might expect, and nowhere was this so carefully narrated as with his experience of the Natural Bridge in Virginia (see Figure 13), "the most sublime of Nature's works":

> Though the sides of this bridge are provided in some parts with a parapet of fixed rocks, yet few men have resolution to walk to them

Figure 13. Frederic Edwin Church, *The Natural Bridge*, Virginia, 1852. Fralin Museum of Art, Wikimedia Commons.

> and look over into the abyss. You involuntarily fall on your hands and feet, creep to the parapet and peep over it. Looking down from this height about a minute, gave me a violent head ach. If the view from the top be painful and intolerable, that from below is delightful in an equal extreme. It is impossible for the emotions arising from the sublime, to be felt beyond what they are here: so beautiful an arch, so elevated, so light, and springing as it were up to heaven, the rapture of the spectator is really indescribable![53]

In Jefferson's above passage, the influence of eighteenth-century natural philosophy is obvious. See Burke on the sublime:

> The passion caused by the great and the sublime in nature, when those causes operate most powerfully, is Astonishment; and astonishment is that state of the soul, in which all its motions are suspended, with some degree of horror. In this case the mind is so entirely filled with its object, that it cannot entertain any other, nor by consequence reason on that object which employs it. Hence arises the great power of the sublime, that far from being produced by them, it anticipates our reasonings, and hurries us on by an irresistible force.[54]

Jefferson invokes the language of the sublime to describe the kind of object that escapes description and exceeds sensory experience, so much so that Jefferson first experienced a "violent head ach[e]" when he peered out over the abyss below, and then extreme pleasure, which arose in him when viewing from beneath and contemplating this rapturous arch that appears to reach heaven. Burke's sublime is terrifying because what appears in the visual field seems to threaten a person's bodily existence and may even incite physical pain.[55] When the terror subsides and the danger is removed, those feelings are replaced with ecstasy and fascination. The sublime precipitates a variety of responses, including a desire to control that which exceeds experience, or to explain what is happening. In other words, the sublime propels a drive toward mastery. According to Meg Armstrong, Burke's description of the different types of feelings one experiences when encountering the sublime is actually "preparatory to a classification of objects which produce these feelings."[56] Indeed, he lists categories of the sublime: obscurity, power, privation, vastness, infinity, difficulty, and magnificence. For each of these it is vision that provokes the experience, and very often Burke describes them in terms of darkness and light, or blackness and color.

For Burke the eye was the most "effective in conveying notions of the sublime," and was "therefore also the primary organ through which the aesthetic can regulate passionate excess associated with the power, magnitude, and obscurity of sublime visions."[57] Burke was most concerned with visual images presented in painting and nature, and textual material like poetry. Visuality and textuality are also featured heavily in Jefferson's imagination and scientific analysis. And like Burke, Jefferson was particularly preoccupied with color and blackness and used aesthetic standards to rationalize the exclusion of Black people from the universal human and human rights. First, Jefferson leans on theories of skin tone in his assessments of beauty:

> The first difference which strikes us is that of colour. Whether the black of the negro resides in the reticular membrane between the skin and scarf-skin, or in the scarf- skin itself; whether it proceeds from the colour of the blood, the colour of the bile, or from that of some other secretion, the difference is fixed in nature, and is as real as if its seat and cause were better known to us. And is this difference of no importance? Is it not the foundation of a greater or less share of beauty in the two races?

Here we see a blatant example of "epidermalization." As described by Franz Fanon, a "racial epidermal schema" has created the conditions in which, "in the white world the man of color encounters difficulties in the development of his bodily schema. Consciousness of the body is solely negating."[58] In other words, epidermalization is the process by which Fanon experienced himself becoming "an object in the midst of other objects."[59] In Jefferson's emergent categories we witness "the very institutionalized production and reproduction of our present hegemonic sociogenic code" in the making.[60] Wynter, expanding upon Fanon's descriptions, explains how the sociogenic principle operates at the level of cultural code: "although born as biological humans (as human *skins*), we can *experience ourselves as human* only through the mediation of the processes of socialization effected by the invented *tekhne* or cultural technology to which we give the name *culture*."[61] Jefferson borrowed the reference to "scarf-skin" from medical scientists and natural historians of the day who had begun to see the textures and layers of skin through the use of microscopes.[62] Some called the layer "scarf-skin," and others, like Hogarth, who brought the medical discourse into the realm of aesthetic judgment, called it the "cuticula." As Sara Crouch indicates, Hogarth's writing "hints at a familiarity with the seminal works for understanding skin from a medical perspective in the first half of the eighteenth century." Crouch continues, "Hogarth's casual borrowing from medical terminology clarifies the relationship between medicine and art that existed during the eighteenth century, revealing the ways in which artists (and novelists) imported available medical knowledge, and at times ignorance, into their works."[63] William Hogarth's description was meant to instruct readers about pigment and painting. That he draws from medical science to compare the pigmentation of skin with paint colors is remarkable on its own.

Jefferson repeats these ideas to inject both medical and artistic knowledge into politics and his explication of the natural history and civil laws of Virginia. Indeed, as Rana Hogarth writes, "This antiblackness is apparent in medical and scientific writings in the eighteenth century and beyond; it emerges as the textual and material subjugation of black people's bodies that occurred when physicians framed research questions around race, conducted experiments to learn more about race, and, in some cases, circulated ideas about racial difference based on their results."[64] The anatomization of Blackness provided scientific grounds for rationalizing the presumed superiority of whiteness and the ordering of society. The "black African's presumed natural alterity" served several agendas: "it allowed Europeans to produce new definitions of whiteness; it provided a coherent concept around which the first 'scientifically based' human classification schemes were organized; and, most infamously, it replaced theological and even economic justifications as the most compelling rationale for African chattel slavery."[65] This explains how a planter elite could see others as objects that could cause feelings of sympathy, inspiration, or terror in themselves.

William Hogarth's writings demonstrate the interlocking ideas from aesthetic theory and biology in advancing ideas about race: "These different coloured juices, together with the different *mashes* of the network, and the size of its threads in this or that part, causes the variety of complexions."[66] Here is Hogarth on the ways that a network of threads affects blushing: "Some persons have the network so equally wove over the whole body, face and all, that the greatest heat or cold will hardly make them change their colour; and these are seldom seen to blush, tho' ever so bashful, whilst the texture is so fine in some young women, that they redden, or turn pale, on the least occasion."[67] Hogarth's comparison of the persons who hardly blush, with the young women who change color with their emotions, resembles Jefferson's commentary: "Are not the fine mixtures of red and white, the expressions of every passion by greater or less suffusions of colour in the one, preferable to that eternal monotony, which reigns in the countenances, that immoveable veil of black which covers all the emotions of the other race?"[68] A veil is a reference to a textile, resonating with Hogarth's network of threads.

Jefferson's description seems to postulate a lack of shame among Black people, which is also one of the claims that Linnaeus made in his *Systema Naturae*. Indeed, Jefferson referenced Linnaeus's taxonomic project frequently in *Notes on the State of Virginia*, and in letters he noted his admiration for the Linnaean system. His commentary about the immoveable veil is addressing Linnaeus's notes in his taxonomy for human variety under the "Afer" class: "*Women* without shame . . . *Crafty*, indolent, negligent . . . *Governed* by caprice." As Greta LaFleur observes, "Linnaeus offers no evidence for his observation that women of the Afer class are 'without shame'; on the contrary, shamelessness here is itself evidence, glibly put forward to support his taxonomic division of the human species into different ethnic classes."[69] Linnaeus is widely cited by historians of race as progenitor of nineteenth-century scientific racism, and his outline of human variety was among the most important eighteenth-century classificatory projects. Consistent with the aesthetic theories of the day, he equated whiteness with light and beauty, and Blackness with the degradation of beauty. Linnaeus first wrote his taxonomical system two decades before Hogarth wrote his *Analysis of Beauty*. There is a likeness between the two, as demonstrated in another Hogarth passage, where beauty is ranked:

> But as white is nearest to light it may be said to be equal if not superior in value as to beauty, with class 4. therefore the classes 5, 6, 7, have also, almost equal beauty with it too, because what they lose of their brilliancy and permanency of colour, they gain from the white or light; whereas 3, 2, 1, absolutely lose their beauty by degrees as they approach nearer to black, the representative of darkness.[70]

Returning to Burke on the sublime, he cites the story of the English medical scientist William Cheselden, "who has given us a very curious story of a boy," who had been born blind but underwent a surgical operation at the age of around thirteen or fourteen. The sight of a Black woman "caused" horror along the lines of the sublime, but that feeling, according to Cheselden, was not followed by pleasure or fascination:

> He was then couched for a cataract, by which operation he received his sight. Among many remarkable particulars that attended his first perceptions and judgments on visual objects, it gave him great uneasiness; and that some time after, upon accidentally seeing a negro woman, he was struck with great horror at the sight. The horror, in this case, can scarcely be supposed to arise from any association. The boy appears by the account to have been particularly observing and sensible for one of his age; and therefore it is probable, if the great uneasiness he felt at the first sight of black had arisen from its connexion with any other disagreeable ideas, he would have observed and mentioned it.[71]

David Lloyd points to this passage of Burke's to highlight the significance in this story of a boy seeing a Black woman, particularly because she is a woman: "The feminine, the support of the beautiful that relaxes and dissolves the subject, comes into conjunction with the dark mark of the racialized body, thus bringing about the collapse of the carefully maintained distinction between the domains of self-preservation and or reproduction, of the sublime and the beautiful, of subject and object, of the barred 'Savage' and the civilized 'social.'"[72] One wonders also if the use of the boy as an example is meant to supply a sense of innocence lost, or vulnerability to a radically Other person. Or how this description justifies or supports the particular abuses suffered by Black women who were enslaved, and the sexualization and use of their bodies by white men. Indeed, these passages all combine to show that the discourses about sex, gender, race, and aesthetics were deeply intertwined, and how they sustained white supremacy. As Roderick Ferguson observes, the long history of regarding African American familial forms and gender relations as perversions has supported rationales for exclusion. Such projections have defined "African-American racial difference as a violation of the heteronormative demands that underlie liberal values."[73] Further, writes Ferguson, "As figures of nonheteronormative perversions, straight African Americans were reproductive rather than *productive*, heterosexual but never *heteronormative*. . . . This construction of African-American sexuality as wild, unstable, and undomesticated locates African-American sexuality within the irrational and therefore outside the bounds of the citizenship machinery."[74] These various types of portrayals of Black sexuality repeat frequently across early American archives and served to justify mastery and enslavement, but what I find so remarkable about Jefferson is the way that he simultaneously inscribed this sentiment into state and personal systems.

For Burke, whereas darkness is the absence of light in space, Blackness is an attribute of an object—one that does not reflect light. Burke wrote of the dark: "We have considered darkness as a cause of the sublime; and we have all along considered the sublime as depending on some modification of pain or terror."[75] This matches his description of the white boy seeing a Black woman. It is the experience of the surprise—white people seeing Black bodies where they didn't expect them to be—which was apparently shocking and horrifying. This is the other side of what Fanon describes—the white gaze, the white response to a Black body, which culminates in "*Maman*, look, a Negro; I'm scared!"—that informs his experience of what it is like to be Black. As Fanon describes, "Beneath the body schema I had created a historical-racial schema. The data I used were provided . . . by the Other, the white man, who had woven me out of a thousand details, anecdotes, and stories."[76] Fanon describes a scene that is likely to have described so many experiences of Blackness in the eighteenth century, and it would be the type of scene upon which the "the facts of blackness" would have been established by Jefferson and others.

To be clear—what Burke was describing is actually the inability of white people to manage their emotional responses to Black "objects," which included Black people, but he was casting the responsibility for white feelings onto Black objects—whether a person or an inanimate object—rather than considering his own investments in the truth of this belief. Perhaps Jefferson compared Black skin to a veil because he believed it hides a person's emotions and renders a person unknowable or unmasterable.[77] And perhaps Jefferson's inability to register their emotional lives, imagination, and talent inhibited his own capacity to imagine their humanity. His presentation of statements as facts or data are one way that biopower asserts itself—"not through top-down state-sanctioned policy but through the seemingly ad hoc ways that data are extracted from black people's bodies . . . to presumably explain a trend, solve a problem, or support a theory."[78] In an observation that speaks to the problem of thingification, Gikandi writes, "It is instructive that in key sections of his Enquiry, Burke would give 'the properties of things' precedence over the ideas or feelings that they generated, for as was true for the writings of many of his contemporaries in the crucial 1750s and 1760s, a turn to matters of taste was also an attempt to account for the meaning and nature of trade or the production of wealth."[79] In other words, Burke was concerned about the utilitarian measures of pain and pleasure derived from objects.

So often those theories were drawn from presumptions about the peculiarity of Blackness that upheld their alterity against a universalized whiteness. In other words, Jefferson's lengthy analysis-based racial aesthetics provided the basis on which he ordered his books, consistently placing books written by Black authors at the "bottom of the column." This practice operationalized aesthetic theory and universalizing discourses, and it is the same set of logics that has resulted in the location of Simone Browne's *Dark Matters* in the section on African Americans, near books about other "elements of the population." Although there may be utility in shelving this book with others on African American history, the separation of Browne's work from general books on surveillance is a statement that signals a long history of racial categories. On a related note, according to the current Library of Congress catalog, books of poetry by Phillis Wheatley (Peters) and most of Audre Lorde's writings are shelved with literature written in English alphabetically by last name according to the time period in which they lived. Books *about* their writings, however, are shelved in sections labeled "History of American Literature—Special topics, A-Z—Black people. African Americans" or

"History of American Literature—Special classes of authors—Other classes of authors, A-Z—Black people. African Americans." Relatedly, the French and English editions of Grégoire's *Enquiry Concerning the Intellectual and Moral Faculties, and Literature of Negroes* are presently shelved at the Library of Congress under HT1581, defined in the Social Sciences as "Communities. Classes. Races.—By Race—Black, Hamitic." This categorization seems to suggest a scientific basis for discrete racial groups. And Sancho's Letters are curiously classed in CT788 with books on "National biography—By region or country—Europe—Great Britain, England." It is likely that the shifts to Grégoire's and Sancho's placements occurred when the Library moved into the Jefferson Building and reclassed the books according to the current Library of Congress Classification, so I won't attribute these locations to current decision making processes. Rather, the point here is to point to the "informative potential of bibliographic classification systems," and the ways that they memorialize events, persons, and ideas.[80]

According to Cahill, landscape writings like *Notes on the State of Virginia* were used to "justify the otherwise interested rhetoric of conquest and cultivation by obscuring the racial, social, and economic contradictions that shaped western settlement."[81] Rich with metaphors associated with cultivation, discovery, and mastery, they contained models for national progress based in a vision of settlement and expansion across an imagined western frontier. The notion of "beautiful utility" is evident across Jefferson's writings. His catalog and the display of books on his shelves at Monticello demonstrate this function, and the "peculiar satisfaction" of viewing them derives from the classified order combined with the appreciation of the knowledge held within the books themselves, as well as his own awareness of the importance of these books to his own personal growth and the expansion of the American landscape. In Chapter 6 I turn to the ways that his imperial ambitions influenced his organization of books about Indigenous people.

# 6
# From Geography to History

> Standing where they do—almost never identifying as indigenous people themselves—scientists who study Native American migrations turn and look back over their shoulders with desire to know the "origins" of those who were first encountered when European settlers landed on the shores of these American continents.
>
> —KIM TALLBEAR, *NATIVE AMERICAN DNA*

> It is to be lamented then, very much to be lamented, that we have suffered so many of the Indian tribes already to extinguish, without our having previously collected and deposited in the records of literature, the general rudiments at least of the languages they spoke. Were vocabularies formed of all the languages spoken in North and South America, preserving their appellations of the most common objects in nature, of those which must be present to every nation barbarous or civilized, with the inflections of their nouns and verbs, their principles of regimen and concord, and these deposited in all the public libraries, it would furnish opportunities to those skilled in the languages of the old world to compare them with these, now, or at any future time, and hence to construct the best evidence of the derivation of this part of the human race.
>
> —THOMAS JEFFERSON, *NOTES ON THE STATE OF VIRGINIA*

On the one hand, Jefferson seemed to idealize Indigenous people and wrote extensively about their intellectual and moral capacity. He revered certain chiefs, particularly for their oratory and leadership skills. Always in relation to an ideal based on whiteness, he studied Indigenous languages and culture, and as he did with Black peoples, Jefferson made biological assessments that supported his and his peers' early racial science and patriotic vision, arguably setting the stage for future ethnographic and scientific research. Even the eventual genomic scientists' quest for biological origin stories through DNA in the present is tied to old narratives and assumptions inherited from people like Jefferson and his peers. Kim TallBear says as much of early scientific practices in the context of the history of anthropology:

> It is also important to look back at how Native American bodies have been treated historically, for knowledge-producing cultures and practices that shaped earlier research continue to influence the way science is done today. . . . Anthropological geneticists want to understand which human groups, or "populations," are related to which others, and who descended from whom. Where geographically did the ancestors of different human groups migrate from? What were their patterns of geographic migration, and when did such migrations occur? In the genomes of the living and the dead, scientists look for molecular sequences—the "genetic signatures" of ancient peoples whom they perceive as original continental populations: for example, Indo-Europeans, Africans, Asians, and Native Americans. Native American DNA, as a (threatened and vanishing) scientific object of study, can help answer what are, for these scientists, pressing human questions.[1]

Jefferson sought answers to these same questions, albeit in eighteenth-century terms—ones that did not include concepts like "molecular sequences" or "DNA," but nevertheless inquired into origins and inheritance. He was considering biological and environmental explanations for degeneracy and progress in human and nonhuman animal populations and used Indigenous people as documentary evidence to refute Buffon's claims about the inferiority of American land and climate. As Meredith Palmer explains, "He framed his counter-narrative as a moral imperative and historical destiny linked to reaching a white societal utopia. Yet beyond a mere racial counter-narrative, Jefferson aimed to pave the way for the US American nation's diffusion of power through calculable techniques rooted in his racial theorems."[2] Anthropology in North America "found its legs as a documentary project," and Jefferson's methods for gathering and archiving documentary evidence are important in the histories of information, ethnography, and geography.[3] Indeed, the notion of progress also implies its opposite—degeneration, the language of which was pervasive among natural historians with an eye toward the Americas. One way that Jefferson invented history was to forge a "fiction of kinship" between

Indigenous peoples and settlers. Holland registers this "genealogical nationalism" as "Jefferson's most troubling legacy," observing that, by drawing a link between Indigenous people and settlers, "the raced body becomes the foundation for citizenship itself."[4] It required a belief that Indigenous peoples would mix with white settlers, acquire the tools and techniques of "civilization," and fundamentally disappear. His library and classified catalog were integral to his research practice, including his anthropological science.

His second inaugural address offers insight into his cataloging method with regard to materials about Indigenous communities:

> The Aboriginal inhabitants of these countries I have regarded with the commiseration their history inspires. endowed with the faculties & the rights of men, breathing an ardent love of liberty and independance, & occupying a country which left them no desire but to be undisturbed, the stream of overflowing population from other regions directed itself on these shores. without power to divert, or habits to contend against it, they have been overwhelmed by the current, or driven before it. now reduced within limits too narrow for the hunter-state, humanity enjoins us to teach them agriculture & the domestic arts; to encourage them to that industry which alone can enable them to maintain their place in existence, & to prepare them in time for that state of society, which to bodily comforts adds the improvement of the mind & morals.[5]

Jefferson uses the occasion of his inaugural address to spread the word about his goals toward preparing Indigenous peoples for living in the American society that he envisioned. His emphasis on their faculties and rights indicates that he views them to be equal to white men, but in need of education, training, and supplies.

Scholars have drawn attention to the ways that popular eighteenth- and nineteenth-century novels like *The Last of the Mohicans* and *Robinson Crusoe* have narrativized the vanishing of Indigenous communities to place them in a romanticized past and support the dream of Euro-American settlement of an uninhabited, wild frontier. Centering the ways that such novels frequently relied on kinship narratives, Ezra F. Tawil argues that by "describing race in terms of kinship, domestic frontier fiction used one kind of classification to produce another."[6] Jefferson's personal catalog and the Library of Congress catalog, past and present, reveal the ways that Indigenous communities are continually depicted as existing before history and out of place in an American imaginary. Here I again draw connections between *Notes on the State of Virginia* and his catalog and turn to his catalog chapters on Geography and

History to ascertain his ordering principles for books on travel and accounts of Indigenous communities.

## Geography and Ethnography in Jefferson's Catalog

Jefferson's *Notes on the State of Virginia* include information on Indigenous communities in three sections—in Query 6, "Productions, Mineral, Vegetable, and Animal"; Query 11, "Aborigines"; and Query 14, "Laws." In Query 6, the chapter on Virginia's minerals, flora, and fauna, he describes the life and death of Chief Logan, to draw attention to an ideal Indigenous man with great intelligence and morality—one who could be civilized, assimilated, and rise to the level of whiteness, but whose murder stood as an example of the inevitable extermination of the Native population.[7] His descriptions of Indigenous people in the chapter on Laws appears in the same section in which Jefferson provides his analysis of Black people. His account of Indigenous peoples' potential for civilization through education stands in contrast to the descriptions I cited in Chapter 5, and Jefferson again uses aesthetic terms in his account: "[Indigenous people] astonish you with strokes of the most sublime oratory; such as prove their reason and sentiment strong, their imagination glowing and elevated."[8] In the chapter titled Aborigines, written in response to the query, "A description of the Indians established in that state?," Jefferson provides a statistical overview of the decline of the Indigenous populations, as well as a detailed description of his archaeological excavation of Monacan burial grounds. As Anthony Wallace explains, these descriptions, with their errors, omissions, and distortions, "had the practical function of further sanctioning the cause of white settlement in the New World."[9] These sections of *Notes on the State of Virginia* deploy different techniques of description and analysis for the purpose of statecraft. On the one hand, drawing attention to the superior oratory techniques of particular Indigenous individuals allowed Jefferson to claim that the American landscape is capable of supporting healthy and intelligent peoples, as opposed to the Comte de Buffon's assertions about the inferiority of the American climate. Jefferson also draws from aesthetic theory and natural history to produce an anthropological study of the Indigenous communities in Virginia, and then turns to statistical methods to show their declining numbers. In Jefferson's early ethnographic and archaeological practices, we see the emergence of "culture" in the context of nation-making and expansion. Jefferson's chapters contained difference "into neat, ethnically-defined territorial spaces that now needed to be made sense of, to be ordered, ranked, to be governed, to be possessed."[10] The separation of methodological techniques into different chapters in *Notes* aligns with his disciplinary arrangement in his book catalog, and together, these documents were also instruments of "governmental and disciplinary possession of bodies and territories, and in this were included existent forms of philosophy, history and social life that Empire sought to speak of and speak for."[11] Ethnographic inquiry into "different cultures" became a technique of control, introducing relations of power between a researcher who knows and a subject of study.

According to Audra Simpson, anthropological methods have "accorded with the imperatives of Empire," and specific technologies have long been deployed to acquire knowledge about peoples for the purpose of acquiring their land. Simpson writes, "Knowing and representing the 'voices' within those places required more than military might, it required the methods and modalities of knowing, in particular: categorisation, ethnological comparison, linguistic translation and ethnography."[12] The relationships between the science, classification, anthropology, geography, land, objectification, and disciplinary arrangements are complex, and Jefferson's analytical order in his book catalog does not simply reflect existing ideas and knowledge. The classifications in Jefferson's catalog and in *Notes on the State of Virginia* informed and produced knowledge, while giving it shape in relation to empire.

Kevin Hayes observes that a "library patron browsing the stacks in American history who notices that the volumes are generally arranged from North to South can see the books through Jefferson's eyes."[13] Hayes is drawing a lineage. This north-south arrangement appears not only in the American History section of the Library of Congress system and Jefferson's chapter 4, but also in Geography of America (Jefferson's chapter 29). Gilreath and Wilson point to the Geography chapter as being exemplary of his method: "his weaving of topics and titles, far from being obvious or straightforward, is artful and deft."[14] It is possible to find patterns and categories in Jefferson's catalog, even if he did not name subsections according to his analytical order. The books listed first in the American subsection of Jefferson's Geography chapter are maps and general texts on exploration of the Americas. They are followed by books on exploration, many of which are primarily about Indigenous peoples. Texts about specific areas of the Americas are listed in order from Northern Canada to South America, with a final section that includes a handful of books on the West Indies.

Libraries have inherited not only the north-south orientation, but fundamental organizational principles based on ideas about nature, race, gender, property, and peoples of the world in relation to early American national interests. Jefferson's chapter 4, titled "Modern history. American," is one of the few chapters that explicitly includes subdivisions, as well as an indication of the arrangement within each subsection: "Ante-Revolutionary.

General—Particular," "Post-Revolutionary. General—Particular." A precolonial history of America or history of Indigenous peoples are relatively absent in this chapter, even in the Ante-Revolutionary section. The few titles in his History chapters that can be said to be about Indigenous peoples are located in that section because they primarily relate to American interests in commerce, settlement, wars, and treaties. The titles suggest their purpose. For example, Cadwallader Colden's *History of the Five Indian Nations of Canada, which are dependent on the province of New-York in America, and are the barrier between the English and French in that part of the world* (circa 1747). Colden was a colonial administrator who was the first representative to the Haudenosaunee Confederacy and served as the governor of New York. The placement of this book in Jefferson's American History chapter may also provide support to the well-documented claim that the writers of America's founding documents, including the Articles of Confederation, the Declaration of Independence, and the US Constitution, were significantly informed by their relations with Indigenous communities, especially the Haudenosaunee (also known as Iroquois) Confederacy. As Ned Blackhawk has made clear, "Iroquois peoples responded to the cycles of colonialism and shaped the continent's historical development. They came to control many aspects of the economic, social, and political affairs in eastern America during the seventeenth and much of the eighteenth century."[15] The five nations that comprised the early confederacy—the Mohawk, Oneida, Onondaga, Cayuga, and Seneca—were united in a Great League of Peace in the precontact era and held and continue to carry common teachings and rituals. They also share "a system of clans and chieftainships, representative councils, and governing practices," which includes recitations of wampum belts that record their stories, events, and philosophies.[16] Still, to qualify as American History in Jefferson's catalog, a history of Indigenous peoples would need to be relevant to American nationalism and expansion. One entry near the end of the American History section is titled "Pamphlets historical." It is a bound assemblage of a variety of articles and pamphlets including Abiel Holmes's *Memoir of the Moheagan Indians* and his *History of Cambridge* [Massachusetts], which provided an account of Eliot's "Indian Bible."[17] Also in the bound volume is Hutchins's *Topographical Description of Virginia*, which includes an appendix that features a "correct List of the different Nations and Tribes of Indians."[18] Jefferson's interest in Native Americans seems to cross with the history of specific states in the union. Perhaps more significant, however, is the notion that the data about Indigenous languages and peoples recorded in these texts attain the status of history, or facts. They resemble the tables of information about Native American tribes in his *Notes on the State of Virginia*.

Most of the titles about Indigenous peoples, such as *Jone's Journal to the Indian Nations* and *Adair's History of the American Indians*, and other books that may not directly index the contents about Indigenous peoples in their titles, are located in the Geography chapter, one of the largest chapters in Jefferson's catalog. Whereas American History is chapter 4 in the broader section on History, Geography is chapter 29, which places the volumes therein at a significant distance from the History books. Geography falls in the Philosophy section, where science and the faculty of reason are the organizing principles. The books in this section are accounts of voyages and scientific expeditions. They are the kinds of books to which Mary Louise Pratt refers when she says that travel narratives of the period were "organized by the cumulative, observational enterprise of documenting geography, flora, and fauna. . . . The landscape is written as uninhabited, unpossessed, unhistoricized, unoccupied even by the travelers themselves."[19] These are books that document what natural philosophers and explorers saw and studied in their encounters; they are generally not about what the people being studied say about themselves. As Cahill observes, "In most travel narratives, the narrator is no mere perceiver but an active and intentional subject whose self-described curiosity leads him to seek out interesting objects."[20] Given this description it stands to reason that Geography is in the sciences. These books were regarded as texts that advanced knowledge about natural history through scientific methods. In Jefferson's library we discover the ways that he organized the book objects that contained stories of exploration and information about encounters with Others through the eyes of a scientist.

Jefferson's Geography chapter is one of the spaces into which he placed many of the interdisciplinary books that challenged his subject system. The irreducibility of the books to a single subject is related to the challenges of listing and classifying Native languages. He could not easily resolve "the complexity of the encounters that took place between Indian agents and indigenous peoples who were reducible neither to a political agenda nor to objects of inquiry."[21] Sarah Rivett argues that his efforts to record, preserve, classify, and standardize Indigenous languages in a unified system were thwarted by deliberate acts of resistance and refusal on the part of his Indigenous informants. It seems that the people whom Jefferson was studying were enacting a form of "ethnographic refusal"—a set of acts that protected their language and stories from capture, that resisted becoming objects of study, and refused to be written down.[22] Jefferson had hoped that he could transcribe tribal languages according to an English orthographic system, but this proved to be more challenging than he expected, as Indigenous communities and social organization confound any Euro-American classification system.

One possible reading of Jefferson's book catalog is that he was actively writing Indigenous people out of History by classing them in Geography. Scholars have concluded that eighteenth-century archaeological and ethnographic studies of Native Americans were knowledge-gathering projects that aimed to transform a past into opportunity for expansion and land acquisition. They were also meant to serve as evidence that Indigenous peoples were primitive savages, "thus paving the way for the justification of future policies of removal."[23] Expansion was an ongoing land speculation project, and classification was one of the mechanisms used to reconcile and control the competing claims to the land.[24] By classing Indigenous peoples as geographic subjects, they remain Other, of a land that is not (yet) American, outside of American History, and without justification for claims to the land within a colonial framework. The principles on which the arrangement is based align with Jefferson's chapter in *Notes on the State of Virginia* titled "Aboriginals" and the concomitant exclusion of statistical data on Indigenous peoples in the chapter titled "Population," which counts all "tithable people" living in Virginia.[25] Arguably, these are classificatory acts of removal from American History and land at the level of knowledge organization. "The stories of nations belong to the domain of modern history, while the stories of tribes and races belong more properly to the domain of ancient history (the tribes of Israel, the aboriginal races) or even natural history."[26] Claims to knowledge are tied to land claims, and the excision or omission of peoples from History is an essential mechanism in colonial expansion and Indian removal policies.

Another possible explanation is, as Gordon M. Sayre suggests, that Jefferson transferred his fascination with classical antiquities and architecture to the North American landscape, using Native American cultural artifacts and burial practices as evidence of a disappeared ancient civilization. He, along with other excavators like William Bartram, was able to manufacture a narrative that rejected Buffon's claim that North America's landscape and climate were inferior and inconducive to advanced civilization. In fact, Jefferson himself dug into Monacan burial mounds in Virginia, and like his peers, created stories that "became a fantastic reflection of images of the land's history and of the nation's future."[27] He found the bones of adult, children, and infant members of the Monacan community at Monasukapanough near his home and estimated that the mound was the burial site of as many as a thousand people. He described what he found in great detail over several pages in *Notes on the State of Virginia.* When Jefferson was a boy, he had observed Native Americans conducting a ceremony at the same site, but as an adult he wrote about Indigenous peoples as if they were near extinction and pursued ethnographic research in order to conduct a history of origins. As Sayre suggests, the narrative about the disappearance of Native populations fixed them in the past and hides the actual agent of their extinction, Euro-American expansionism. Jefferson admired Native oratory and customs, pursued a huge project toward archiving native languages, and excavated burial sites, but "he did not try to ask the Indians themselves for their history"—at least not directly. He did dispatch Lewis and Clark to gather information from Indigenous people on their mission, but their purpose was strategic.[28]

Query 11, titled "Aborigines," begins with a historical account of English settlement of Virginia, as well as a table and description of the Indigenous communities within the boundaries of the state of Virginia (see Figure 14). Jefferson explains that, in 1607, "the country from the sea-coast to the mountains, and from Patowmac to the most southern waters of James river, was occupied by upwards of forty different tribes of Indians. Of these," he wrote, "the *Powhatans*, the *Mannahoacs*, and *Monacans*, were the most powerful."[29] He describes the relations among the Indigenous nations, their practices of governance, and their histories as he understood them. Jefferson's table includes the names of the tribal bands within each nation, the part of Virginia in which they lived (in colonial American geographic terms), their "Chief Town" if known, and the number of warriors in each nation in the years 1607 and 1669 if that information was available. He then tells a history of the confederacy of the Six Nations (Haudenosaunee) before describing his excavation of the burial mounds. For instance, he indicated that the Monacans lived on the James River "above the falls," and their "chief town" was the "Fork of James R." This place is called Rassawek and is still regarded by the Monacan nation as their historical capital. It was documented by Captain John Smith in 1612 as "the chiefest town" in Monacan territory, which covered half of what is today Virginia. Monacans inhabited Rassawek for two hundred generations, beginning at least 4,730 years ago.[30]

Toward the end of the chapter, Jefferson explains his process of writing, tabulating, and sorting information about the Indigenous communities in other parts of the United States:

> I will now proceed to state the nations and numbers of the Aborigines which still exist in a respectable and independent form. And as their undefined boundaries would render it difficult to specify those only which may be within any certain limits, and it may not be unacceptable to present a more general view of them, I will *reduce with the form of a Catalogue all those within*, and circumjacent to, the United States, whose names and numbers have come to my notice.[31]

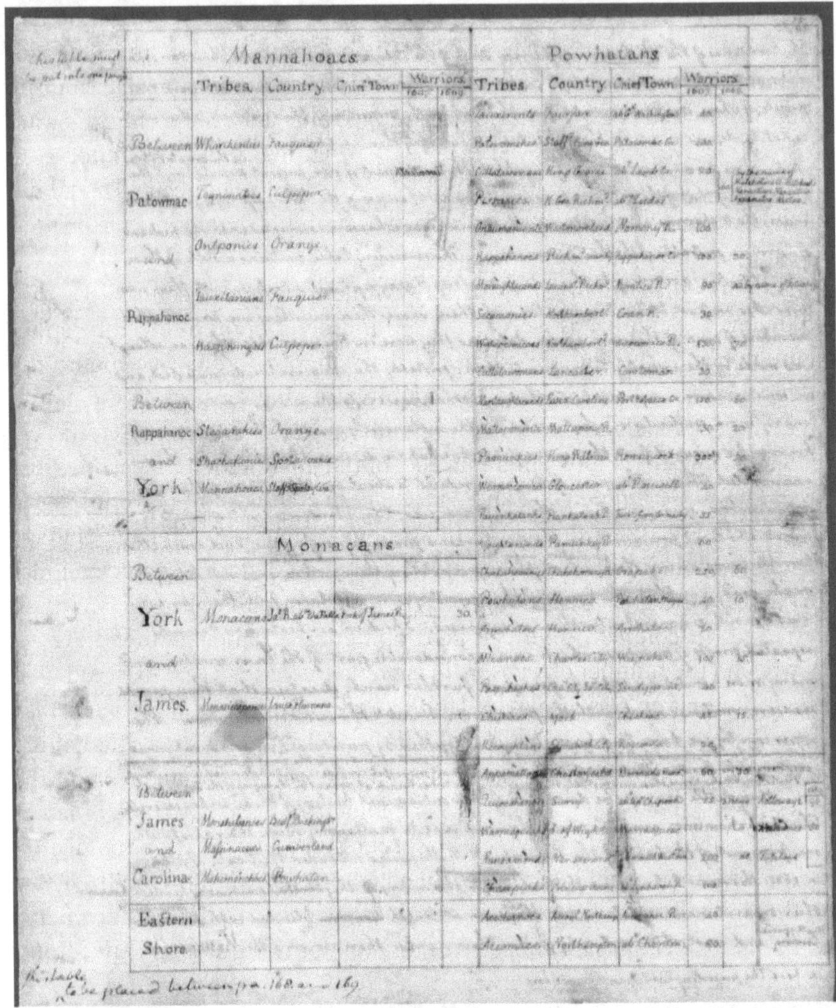


Figure 14. "Mannahoacs Powhatans (Table). . ." *Notes on the State of Virginia*, (Query 11), Manuscript page 55. Coolidge Collection of Thomas Jefferson Manuscripts, Massachusetts Historical Society.

The abstraction of Indigenous communities into tabular data is very closely associated with the reduction to subjects in the book catalog. As it was with his cataloging practices with regard to books about Africa and Black people, where Jefferson placed Ignatius Sancho's book at "the bottom of the column," *Notes on the State of Virginia* is perhaps best understood when viewed alongside his catalog, as well as his land policies and correspondence to and about Indigenous people.

His justification for the assimilation of Native Americans rested in part in his belief that white Americans and Indigenous people share a history of being of the same land. Clearly, white Americans were not indigenous to the land, but Jefferson participated in creating a mythology of the land belonging to white Americans. In this narrative he created a sense of kinship between them, with stories of a shared history and a common homeland. Upon his retirement, he addressed the chiefs of the Wiandot, Ottawa, Chippewa, Potawatomi, and Shawnee communities. In this speech we see how he put this message into discourse:

> I take you and your people by the hand and salute you as my Children; I consider all my red children as forming one family with the whites, born in the same land with them, and bound to live like brethren, in peace, friendship, & good neighborhood.[32]

Jefferson could imagine that Native Americans could become white over time by living and intermarrying with the settler population and adopting Euro-American customs. That mythology was articulated and repeated directly to the Indigenous communities with whom the terms of white expansion were negotiated. Insofar as Indigenous people were willing and able to transform their lives by adopting agricultural technologies, the English language, and American ideas, they were allowed to remain. Acts of resistance to the new American standards of living were punished through threats, starvation, or outright warfare.

For Jefferson, the history of Indigenous peoples was useful insofar as it could explain human origins or provide evidence of the fruitfulness of the American landscape. Any Indigenous person who resisted assimilation, however, was not fit for the republic as Jefferson imagined it. As Brenna Bhandar writes, "Those communities who lived as rational, productive economic actors, evidenced by particular forms of cultivation, were deemed to be proper subjects of law and history; those who did not were deemed to be in need of improvement as much as their waste lands were."[33] The Jeffersonian program for assimilation and extermination amounted to inducing Native Americans to sell their lands by deprivation and containment, bribery, and warfare. The presence of Native Americans in Jefferson's time was a barrier to expansion, which is partly why they could not be granted a history of their own—certainly not in the context of US history. At the same time, Indigenous peoples unsettled his ideas about the direct connection between natural and national harmony.

In Christopher Looby's view, Jefferson's organization of *Notes on the State of Virginia* reflected and contained the anxieties associated with the birth of the nation: "Whatever would falsify the classificatory system was regarded as dangerous. . . . [A] being that disrupts the ordered categories of nature is bound to make political trouble somewhere."[34] We see this difficulty playing out in his classificatory decisions regarding the books on Indigenous peoples in North America. By design, the future of Native Americans was meant to be nonexistent, and Jefferson projected that vision into the classifications. His system also served as a way to resolve this classificatory danger, which left unaddressed might threaten the very order on which colonialism and expansion relied. Jefferson's ordering principles functioned as disordering mechanisms imposed by colonialism that severed Indigenous communities from their histories. Jefferson's insistence on relying upon empirical evidence as the basis for science is itself called into question when it comes to his racial science. Robert Owens notes, "While an empiricist in so many facets of his life, when it came to Indian policy, and race relations generally, Thomas Jefferson carefully selected data that would not jar his predetermined conclusions. Regarding western lands, his thinking came from the Virginia plantation rather than a Parisian salon."[35] Jefferson is guilty of what scientists today call confirmation bias—collecting and analyzing data that supports one's already existing beliefs. But Jefferson's confirmation bias carried dire consequences, and his methodologies are designed with the specific purpose of justifying the acquisition of land. Using "scientific" methods to "prove" that Native Americans were inferior but could be improved by adopting civilizing techniques, Jefferson rationalized the brutality of expansion.

## "Indians of North America" in the Twenty-First-Century Library of Congress

The Library of Congress's redistribution of Jefferson's books around the library in its current classification illustrates the changes and continuities in the American disciplinary imagination. The Library of Congress began to replace the Jeffersonian system with its current classification divided into academic disciplines around 1900 (see Figure 15). Librarians have assigned his books new call numbers, so we can see how they shifted the books from his system to the present one, and how the newer classification makes different kinds of associations. Most of the books that Jefferson classed as Geography, including books on encounters with Indigenous peoples in the Americas, have been reassigned to history sections by the Library of Congress. A few of these books remain in the Geography section of the library.

Today, maps, atlases, and books on Anthropology and Geography all reside together in the G section of the Library of Congress Classification, retaining an association between scientific studies of peoples, geography, and foreign lands in ways that resemble Jefferson's plan. Indeed, when librarians reclassified the collection, they produced tables and lists that mapped Jefferson's chapters to the classification that organizes the Library of Congress today. Chapter 29 was to go into G, but in reality, only a few books from Jefferson's Geography chapter are currently shelved in the part of the G section designated for voyages and travels. Examples of books that have been located there are indeed about travel expeditions: *Delle navigazione e viaggi raccolte* (Navigation and Route Collection) by Giovanni Ramusio; *The principall nauigations, voiages, and discoueries of the English nation*, by Richard Hakluyt; and *Le voyageur françois, ou, La connoissance de l'ancien et du nouveau monde* (The French Traveler, or, Knowledge of the Old and New Worlds), by Joseph de Laporte.

The vast majority of Jefferson's books on "Indians of North America" and voyages and travel to the Americas are placed in E, the section designated for American History. At first glance, this seems to indicate an assertion that Indigenous people do have histories and are no longer viewed as ethnographic subjects—that they belong in the history of the Americas.

A 1901 Library of Congress document titled "America—History and Geography: Preliminary and Provision Scheme of Classification," which now comprise the E and F sections of the classification, reveals the original relocation of Jefferson's geography books into this section. Books continue to be added to the range reserved for "Indians of North America," which means that books from Jefferson's era are comingled with books published in the twenty-first century. Adair's The *History of the American Indians* is shelved in E78.S65, which is defined according to US political borders: "Indians of North America—By state, province, or region, A-Z—Southern States." Colden's *History of the Five Indian Nations of Canada* is shelved according to tribes at E99.I7: "Indians of North America—Tribes and cultures, A-Z—Iroquois." Between these two books is the 2014 *Red Skin, White Masks: Rejecting the Colonial Politics of Recognition*, by Glen S. Coulthard. This book is located at E92, which the Library of Congress defines as "Indians of North America—Government relations—Canada." Anthony Wallace's *Jefferson and the Indians* is shelved at E93, "Indians of North America—Government relations—United States."[36] Other interesting examples include the shelving of Robin Kimmerer's *Braiding Sweetgrass* in E98.P5, defined as "Indians of North America—Other topics—Philosophy." This classification effaces Kimmerer's purpose, which is to show how Potawatomi knowledge systems and relations with the natural world can inform Western biological sciences.

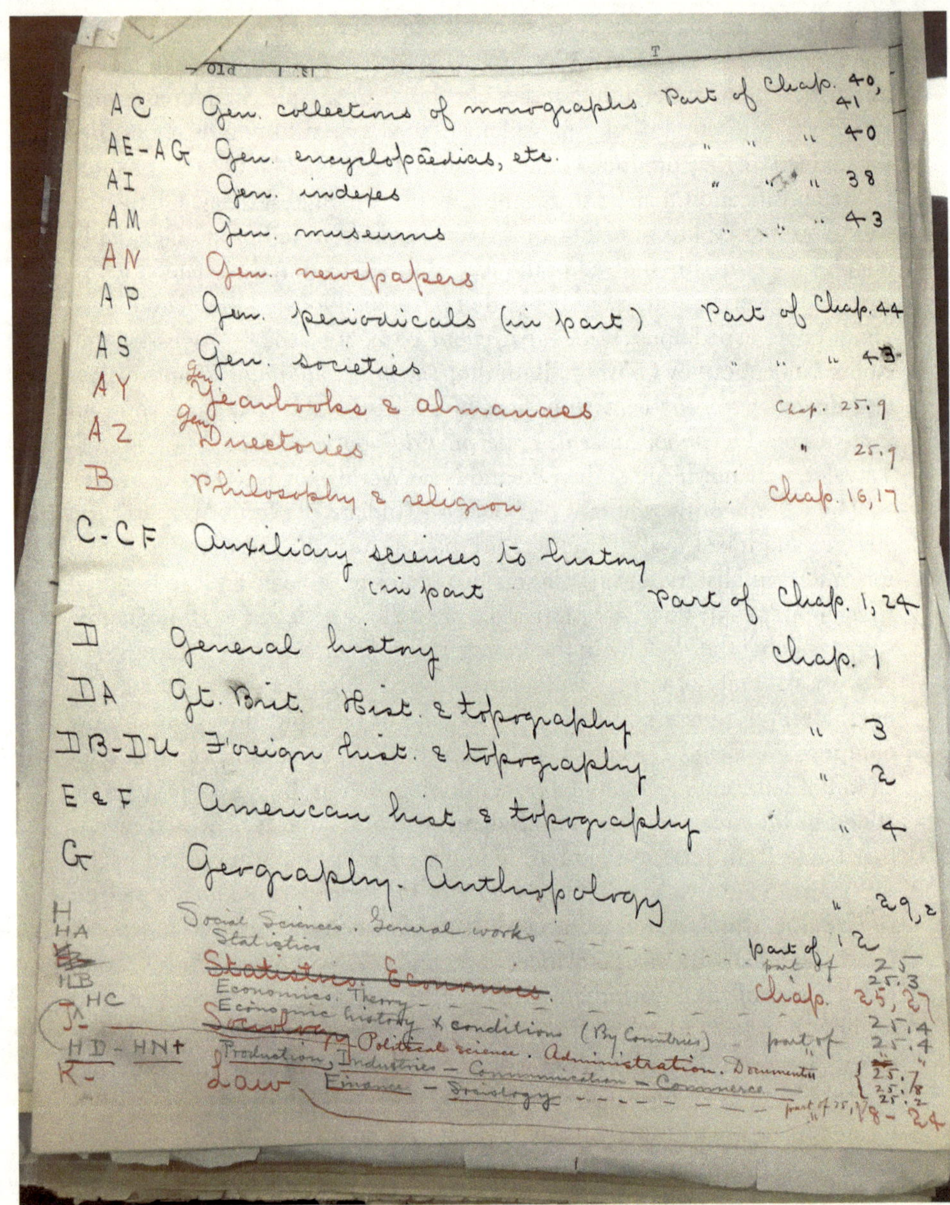

AC Gen. collections of monographs Part of Chap. 40, 41
AE-AG Gen. encyclopaedias, etc. " " " 40
AI Gen. indexes " " " 38
AM Gen. museums " " " 43
AN Gen. newspapers
AP Gen. periodicals (in part) Part of Chap. 44
AS Gen. societies " " " 43
AY Gen. Yearbooks & almanacs Chap. 25.9
AZ Gen. Directories " 25.9
B Philosophy & religion Chap. 16, 17
C-CF Auxiliary sciences to history (in part) Part of Chap. 1, 24
D General history Chap. 1
DA Gt. Brit. Hist. & topography " 3
DB-DU Foreign hist. & topography " 2
E & F American hist & topography " 4
G Geography. Anthropology " 29, 2
H Social Sciences. General works part of 12
HA Statistics part of 25
HB ~~Statistics. Economics~~ Economics. Theory 25.3
HC Economic history & condition (By Countries) Chap. 25, 27 25.4
HD-HN+ Production, Industries — Communication — Commerce — Finance — Sociology part of 25.4 25.7 25.8 25.2
J Political science. Administration. Documents
K Law part of 25, 18 - 24

Figure 15. Library of Congress. (c. 1900). List that maps the new LC classification to Jefferson's catalog chapters. Library of Congress Archives Collection, Manuscript Division.

To be clear, these specific classificatory decisions are made by librarians who categorize books according to the system's design. Many other choices could have been made, as there are classes for "Indians of North America—Tribes and cultures, A-Z—Potawatomi," or "Indians of North America—Other topics—Science," or "Indians of North America—Other topics—Biology. Ethnobiology." One could also place the book in the Biology section of the library, under QH. None of these are adequate, of course.

Librarians have shown that the arrangement of E section is problematic, particularly because it locates Indigenous peoples in pre-Columbian time and space in the hierarchy.[37] The relocation of books on Indigenous peoples provides evidence about the processes by which the organization of information ensures the durability of racialization and racism. Although the books have been removed from geography and anthropology, they are *dis*placed in another significant way in the history sections of the classification. They are hierarchically located in precolonial times, outside of the United States or North American present. In a 1971 response to recommendations for revising the classification to remedy this problem, Eugene Frosio, principal subject cataloger at the Library of Congress wrote:

> It is quite clear from the tables themselves that the intention of the creators of the classification was to treat the modern Indians as remnants of a vast group of peoples who once populated the entire New World long before the arrival of Europeans. This conceptualization of the Indians is still valid today, it seems to us.[38]

On the one hand this is a repetition of the Jeffersonian structure's inability to accommodate Indigenous communities and knowledges. Just as Indigenous languages could not be mapped to Jefferson's orthographic system, Indigenous peoples and geographies confound and resist the US library cataloging system. They do not ascribe to or fit within state and provincial boundaries, and so one way that the Library of Congress reconciles the problem is by placing books about Indigenous people in precolonial history. Below is the most recent iteration of the Library of Congress Classification for materials about American Indians and the United States.

| | |
|---|---|
| E31-49.2 | North America |
| E51-73 | Pre-Columbian America. The Indians. |
| E75-99 | Indians of North America |
| E81-83 | Indian wars |
| E99 | Indian tribes and cultures |
| E101-135 | Discovery of America and early explorations |

| | |
|---|---|
| E103-110 | Pre-Columbian period |
| E111-120 | Columbus |
| E121-135 | Post-Columbian period. El Dorado |
| E141-143 | Descriptive accounts of America. Earliest to 1810 |
| E151-889 | United States |
| E151-169.12 | General |
| E171-183.9 | History |
| E171-180 | General |
| E173 | Sources and documents |
| E175-175.7 | Historiography |
| E176-176.8 | Biography |
| E179.5 | Historical geography |
| E181 | Military history |
| E182 | Naval history |
| E183-183.3 | Political history |
| E183.7-183.9 | Diplomatic history. Foreign and general relations. |
| E183.8 | Relations with individual countries |
| E184-185.98 | Elements in the population |
| E184.5-185.98 | Afro-Americans[39] |

The outline above shows broad categories, but within the more granular version of the classification, the category "Indians of North America" is subdivided according to a variety of types. Subdivisions include "By state, province, or region, A-Z," categories such as education, which includes "Indian schools," "Indian wars," and a large range of special topics. At the end there is a subdivision for "Tribes and cultures," which extends for several pages and are listed alphabetically by name.[40]

This case exemplifies Kim Christen and Jane Anderson's observation—that "placing the past and present within a shared frame of modernity privileges non-Native sensibilities and protects the power structures that maintain settler colonial logics and violence."[41] Frosio appears to be acknowledging the incommensurability of these knowledge systems suggesting that it would have been a mistake to attempt to map communities to the boundaries of the United States.[42] He indicates that the intention was not to segregate knowledges, but rather, this arrangement is meant to contain books about "Indians of all of the Americas" together, and to "represent the fact that they were the first inhabitants of North America, that today they are still found in Canada as well as the United States, and that they possessed unique cultures of their own."[43] Frosio's use of the past tense gives him away, however. While his defense does address the irresolvable tension inherent in the classification, it inadequately acknowledges the existence of Indigenous peoples in the present.

On the shelves this means that books about Indigenous peoples are spatially separated from books about people in the United States and Canada.

And intellectually they are a certain kind of historical subject—seemingly not subjects whose history is continually in-the-making. This structure supports the ongoing perception of Indigenous peoples as being from another time, of not belonging to a place. The location in the text of the classification and the physical placement of books on the shelves visualize the fact that the "present is defined by the political projects of dispossession and settlement, and the difference that is Indigeneity is the maintenance of culture, treaty, history, and self within the historical and ongoing context of settlement."[44] The classification is a simplification and abstraction but serves to demonstrate the interdependence of the processes of knowledge claims and dispossession of land.

I suggest that this is connected to Jefferson's Geography chapter, where Indigenous peoples were regarded as objects of ethnological science. Placing books in a precolonial history is another form of separation, and this order is affirmed and solidified each time a volume is added to this section. This is one of the ways that separateness becomes systemic without our noticing. It is a reaffirmation in the present of the belief that Indigenous people are prior to history, uncivilized, and vanishing, but remain objects worth studying in service to settler scientific progress. It is a manifestation of what Anne McClintock refers to as *anachronistic space*. McClintock writes, "Since indigenous peoples are not supposed to be spatially there—for the lands are 'empty'—they are symbolically displaced. . . . According to this trope, colonized people . . . do not inhabit history proper but exist in a permanently anterior time within the geographic space of the modern empire as anachronistic humans, atavistic, irrational, bereft of human agency."[45] The catalog violates what Mark Rifkin calls *temporal sovereignty*, which recognizes the "importance of attending to Native conceptualizations, articulations and impressions of time" that cannot be reduced to or contained within settler norms and structures.[46] Emphasizing temporal sovereignty demands that we jettison notions of a "shared modernity or presentness of Natives and non-Natives" because it "implicitly casts Indigenous peoples as inhabiting the current moment and moving toward the future in ways that treat dominant non-Native geographies, intellectual and political categories, periodizations, and conceptions of causality as given—*as the background against which to register and assess Native being-in-time*."[47] Current efforts toward decolonizing libraries and archives confront the complexities and incommensurability of Indigenous and settler time. On the one hand, all archives "have built into them the instrumental, historical, and cultural meanings of whatever media they include," and any materials retrieved from an archive built from theft and plunder will carry the traces of the imperial archive with them.

One of the essential actions for reparative decolonial archival practice is to "operate through an understanding of *time immemorial* that belies the imperial creation of tradition marked along Western timelines." Ellen Cushman (Cherokee) insists that reconciling this problem requires "relocating meaning in the context of its unfolding."[48] Contrary to colonial ethnographic and archival practices of observation, data collection and analysis, classification, storage, and retrieval, decolonial archives "operate through the *co*-construction of knowledge based on interactions between storytellers and listeners that counter the imperial archive's insistence on expert codification of knowledge. And they operate through linguistic and cultural perseverance rather than the imperialist agenda of preservation of cultural tradition as hermetically sealed, contained, and unchanging."[49] This message is equally important for libraries that use the Library of Congress system to organize their shelves. Indeed, even new books that are published about Indigenous peoples in the present are shelved in this precolonial historical section if they follow the Library of Congress standard.

## Jefferson's Travels

Reading Jefferson's book classification alongside some of his other writings—especially his *Notes on the State of Virginia*, but also some of his own travel journals and letters—provides important context and depth of understanding into how he ordered his books. In *Notes* under "Laws," he compares Indigenous people to Black people, treating them as types to be studied and evaluated as points of contrast with white people. One of the most striking points of comparison is gender roles in family structures. We see in Jefferson's projects the emergence of racial categories based significantly on gender and sexuality. As Greta LaFleur argues in her *Natural History of Sexuality*, Jefferson's *Notes on the State of Virginia* exemplifies the eighteenth-century texts about racial difference, which "are embedded with quiet but proliferate narratives about the meaning of sexual behavior as well."[50] Studying Jefferson's works closely helps us to understand the emergence of race and sexuality in the context of identifying and managing populations to optimize empire expansion. And as Helena Holgersson-Shorter writes, "Since his discursive mastery in Notes parallels his rule as governor, the textual effort to discredit any prevailing concept of American degeneracy becomes intertwined with his own concerns about fulfilling a paternal legacy of mastery."[51]

In his travel journals, Jefferson described his observations of European and Indigenous gender roles. His analysis highlights the ways in which the racialization of Indigenous people was manufactured by reading Indigenous kinship structures and gender roles through Western eyes. In his travels across the northeastern French countryside, for example, Jefferson observed the expression of gender roles in comparison with what he believed was a woman's purpose:

> The women here, as in Germany, do all sorts of work. While one considers them as useful and rational companions, one cannot forget that they are also objects of our pleasures; nor can they ever forget it. While employed in dirt and drudgery, some tag of a ribbon, some ring, or bit of bracelet, earbob or necklace, or something of that kind, will show that the desire of pleasing is never suspended in them.

In other words, despite the fact that French women "do all sorts of work," they still attend to their appearance for the pleasure of their men. Jefferson suggests that, generally speaking, however, gender roles will fall into proper alignment when people are relatively at ease. A man will be able to turn his attention toward his female partner and conduct the labor required for a civilized people to thrive. In the following sentences, he explains his belief that Indigenous people in his home country were unable to meet this aim because they were always at war:

> every Indian man is a soldier or warrior, and the whole body of warriors constitute a standing army, always employed in war or hunting. To support that army, there remain no laborers but the women. There, then, is so heavy a military establishment, that the civil part of the nation is reduced to women only. But this is a *barbarous perversion* of the natural destination of the two sexes. Women are formed by nature for attentions, not for hard labor. A woman never forgets one of the numerous train of little offices which belong to her. A man forgets often.[52]

Again, we see Jefferson's "scientific" observations at work and how they furnish the material on which to intensify the mission to break existing Native kinship formation and enforce heteropatriarchal ones in the name of civilization. As Peter Onuf writes, "For Jefferson the familial forms that governed Indian diplomacy and made European sovereigns into 'fathers' of dependent native peoples represented another, more dangerous manifestation of the fundamental flaw of Indian societies, the tyranny of Indian men over their women."[53] I am struck especially by the line: "this is a barbarous perversion of the natural destination of the two sexes." The woman's role is fundamentally to please the man, and in order to do that, she cannot be engaging in any work that would remove her from her domestic duties, nor should "the civil part of the nation [be] reduced to women only." He misunderstands matrilineal and matriarchal culture, and he projects his own point of view while speaking so authoritatively on "natural destination" and "perversion." This passage shows just how integral gender and sexuality were to the racialization of Indigenous peoples. What's more, we can observe here an emergence of "sexuality" as "a colonial discourse produced through biopower," as well as confirmation that "the colonial hope is that the whiteness of the normative human can be extended to the very people who were premised as non-human, gender-deviant savages."[54] The imposition of European kinship forms and gender-based governance, as well as sexual violence, were among some of the most terrorizing methods of colonization.

Jefferson used *Notes on the State of Virginia* to refute Buffon's degeneracy theory, using Indigenous bodies and the size and quantity of wild animals as evidence. (He also famously shipped a moose to France to prove that animals grew large on the American landscape). Jefferson admitted that there may be intellectual and physiological differences among races, but he was skeptical of theories that advance the idea that difference is due to geographical location, or, as he wrote, "Whether nature has enlisted herself as a Cis or Trans-Atlantic partisan."[55] As LaFleur explains, "For Jefferson, then, it is not anything in the climate or air of North America that encourages degeneration among humans or other animals; rather, it is the lack of civilization in Native societies that renders women subordinate and men weak and dispassionate."[56] Throughout *Notes* Jefferson conveys "the environmental thinking that characterized the way the body was understood more generally" and shows how that "provided one of the strongest ideological frameworks through which people of that era explained sexual behavior."[57] He also stated that determining the mental and intellectual capacity of Indigenous people would require more study, but he does assert that it is likely that "we shall probably find that they are formed in mind as well as in body, on the same module with the 'Homo sapiens Europæus,'" according to Linnaeus's system.[58]

The enforcement of settler sexuality and gender roles did several things. As a racializing technique it produced an "Other" on the basis of deviations from presumed European norms for gender and sexuality. On that basis settlers justified genocidal policies and practices, insisting that it was in the interest of not only the colonizers but the Indigenous people, as well. Survival depended on assimilation, including family structures and gender hierarchies. Anyone who did not conform to such "civilizing" practices was regarded as disposable, and even those who did assimilate were subjected to violent removal from their homes and land. Additionally, the heterosexualization of women justified their conquest. As Chris Finley, member of the Colville Confederated Tribes, points out, the mythologized story of Pocahontas and John Smith has produced a narrative in which "Native women embody the reproductive position of receiver of the fertile white colonial heteropatriarchy and the mother of the U.S. nation."[59] The child of an Indigenous woman and a white man, under settler colonial rule, was considered to have become white because patriarchal inheritance is passed through the father. All of these elements of settler colonial myth-making were used to justify killing, removal, sexual violence, and coerced assimilation. In other words, as Kim TallBear writes, "Settler sexuality—this hetero- and increasingly homonormative compulsory monogamy society tied to settler-colonial ownership of property and Indigenous dispossession—is *a structure*."[60] We might also argue, following Scott Morgensen, that Indigenous people were effectively queered by settler rulers, as Jefferson's reference to the "barbarous perversion of the natural destination of the two sexes" makes clear. This was well before the invention of the words "homosexuality" and "heterosexuality," long before the concept of trans and nonbinary genders, and before Two-Spirit was a term and concept. Before these terms became part of the sexual science lexicon, attacks on gender and sexual expressions like polyamory, kinship-based governance, people who presented as masculine and feminine, or had sexual intercourse with people across genders, were used in processes of racialization. TallBear writes about the specific context of Dakota kinship structures:

> Before settler-imposed monogamy, marriage helped to forge important Dakota kinship alliances, but divorce for both men and women was possible. Women also owned household property. They were not tied to men economically in the harsh ways of settler marriage. More than two genders were recognized, and there was an element of flexibility in gender identification. People we might call "genderqueer" today also entered into "traditional" Dakota marriages with partners who might be what we today consider "cisgendered." In a world before settler colonialism—outside of the particular biosocial assemblages that now structure settler notions of "gender," "sex," and "sexuality," persons and the intimacies between them were no doubt worked quite differently.[61]

As Morgensen writes, the "imposition of colonial heteropatriarchy relegates Native people and all non-Native people of color to queered statuses as racialized populations amid colonial efforts to eliminate Native nationality and settle Native lands."[62] Rifkin affirms this view and adds that "U.S. imperialism against native peoples over the past two centuries can be understood as an effort to make them 'straight'—to insert indigenous peoples into Anglo-American conditions of family, home, desire, and political identity."[63] Marriage was seen to advance civilization in the sense of procreation and multiplication, especially insofar as it provided the evidence of an imagined nation fulfilled.

The removal and assimilation of Indigenous people depended on the tightly interwoven projects of destroying kinship and knowledge formations, treating people as objects of study, and collecting and organizing ethnographic and biological "knowledge" *about* them according to early scientific classifications. Across Jefferson's writings and cataloging techniques, we observe heteronormativity in the making—and come to some clarity about the "processes through which a particular configuration of *home* and *family* [was] naturalized and administratively implemented."[64] Jefferson relied on assumptions about binary gender, social structure, and labor built into this assessment, and did not acknowledge the effects of the ravages of settler colonialism on Indigenous families. But Jefferson's conclusions did support his political economic agenda and desire for the expansion of the American empire. Over and over again, Jefferson acquired, observed, cataloged, and objectified Indigenous peoples, their land, and their knowledges. The emergence of categories in his library catalog and *Notes on the State of Virginia* are best understood in the context of statecraft, expansion, and cultivating an empire. That marked racialized others to strengthen and center whiteness.

# PART 3

## *Museums*

# 7

# Jefferson's "Indian Hall" and the Doctrine of Discovery

A rising nation, spread over a wide and fruitful land, traversing all the seas with the rich productions of their industry, engaged in commerce with nations who feel power and forget right, advancing rapidly to destinies beyond the reach of a mortal eye; when I contemplate these transcendent objects, and see the honour, the happiness, and the hopes of this beloved country committed to the issue and the auspices of this day, I shrink from the contemplation & humble myself before the magnitude of the undertaking.

—THOMAS JEFFERSON'S FIRST INAUGURAL ADDRESS, 4 MARCH 1801

Meriwether Lewis' Diary 1805:
*The water of this river possesses*
*a peculiar whiteness, being about*
*the color of a cup of tea with milk*
*we called it milk river.*

A domesticated line—

each movement becomes thing,
each thing, already a word,
is etched in place.

A peculiar whiteness—

*The River that Shuns all Others*
becomes a cup of tea with milk.
Living water, distant ritual.

—FROM DAVID JANZEN, *CANOEING THE MILK RIVER: A THEORY OF LINES*

Standing at the foot of a map of loss is clarity.

—LEANNE BETASAMOSAKE SIMPSON, *AS WE HAVE ALWAYS DONE*

Let's return to the 1770 fire that took Jefferson's childhood home and books and papers—the one that he reported to John Page.

> These are gone, and "like the baseless fabric of a vision, Leave not a trace behind." The records also and other papers, which furnished me with states of the several cases, having shared the same fate, I have no foundation whereon to set out anew.[1]

In his letter, Jefferson quoted Shakespeare's *The Tempest* and compared his experience of loss with Prospero's passions.[2] To him, the memory contained within the books and papers had vanished like a mostly forgotten dream. And like Prospero, his books were more important to him than the temples and pageantry of aristocratic life.[3] Jefferson was just beginning to build his home on the top of the mountain at Monticello, a few miles away from Shadwell. The cases to which he referred would have included disputes about land claims, the litigation of which were formative for his career. In this chapter I examine the museum that he installed in the entryway to his home at Monticello to show how collecting and displaying objects of American natural history were integral to Jefferson's vision of statecraft. It sets the stage for Chapter 8 by showing how non-human animals and exploration were integral to processes of racialization and expansion.

The reference to *The Tempest* is even more telling than it might first appear, particularly when we recognize how Prospero's own literacy practices were so crucial to the entire plot of the play, and how they stood in direct contrast to Caliban's education. Sylvia Wynter's analysis of Shakespeare's play is helpful in this regard. Expanding on Édouard Glissant's writings about the Caribbean, she explains that colonial structures were put in place beginning with "Western Europe's first colonial act."[4] According to Wynter, Shakespeare's Caliban is a depiction of the first "native" whom the Europeans encountered, and the story demonstrates how "this originary putting in place" installed a "model of structuration based on the ontological axioms of the rational-nature/sensory-nature dichotomy that was to be as fundamental to the colonial (or Other) social formation."[5] This originary structuring event was repeated and reinstituted across the Americas, including Virginia. Jefferson grew up surrounded by Indigenous peoples, some of whom were regular visitors to his parents' home when he was a child. He was raised within the context of a colonial imaginary that simultaneously idealized and condemned the Native Americans around him.

As Wynter writes, "In the plot of *The Tempest*, the central opposition is represented as being between Prospero and Caliban; that is, between Higher Reason as expressed in the former, and irrational, sensual nature as embodied in the latter."[6] Jefferson was a great imitator of Prospero, especially in his implementation of a "master code of rational nature/irrational nature, together with the new 'idea of order.'"[7] Jefferson brought this set of principles into being as a means to achieve order in the young republic. Whether intended or not, these structures enacted and maintained divisions between the rational and the irrational, and they upheld and were supported by the belief that the politically rational man commanded "mastery over their own sensory, irrational nature—and, as well, of all those Human Other categories who," like Shakespeare's Caliban, remained enslaved to his.[8] Caliban stands for both the enslaved African (who Jefferson believed was not educatable) and the Indigenous "savage" (who could become civilized through education). Caliban is also "placed under the sign of 'the animal,' namely irrational and sexual intemperance." Zakiyyah Jackson argues that Caliban is not simply "animalized," but in fact, "figures like Caliban are constitutive to 'the animal' as a general term."[9] Caliban is an amalgamation of Man's "constitutive outside."[10] Jackson cites Laurie Shannon's "The Eight Animals in Shakespeare; or, Before the Human," to support her claim about Caliban as animal. Remarkably, Shannon observes that, although nonhuman creatures are ever-present throughout Shakespeare's oeuvre, "beast" appears 141 times and "creature" twenty-seven, Shakespeare only writes the word "animal" eight times in all of his plays. This pattern corresponds to the uses of these words in Shakespeare's era, and Shannon attributes the increase of the term "animal" to Descartes's division of the human from all other species. The utterance *cogito ergo sum* installed a split between rational and irrational animals. "It culled humans, who alone were equipped with a rational soul, from the entire spectrum of creatures, and the rest were then compressed within the mechanistic limits of purely instinctual behavior."[11] Shannon presses her point:

> To put it in the broadest terms: before the cogito, there was no such thing as "the animal." There were creatures. There were brutes, and there were beasts. There were fish and fowl. There were living things. There were humans, who participated in animal nature and who shared the same bodily material with animals. . . . These humans were measured as much in contradistinction to angels as to animal, taking

> their place in a larger cosmography, constitution, or even "world picture" than the more contracted post-Cartesian human/animal divide with which we customarily wrangle.[12]

Extending scholarship on the animalization of Black people in cultural discourse, Jackson thinks Caliban and other figures "demonstrate the necessity of the abjection and bestialization of black gender and sexuality for both the normative construction of 'the human' as rational, self-directed, and autonomous and as the reproduction of the scientific matrix of classification."[13] In Jackson's view, critiques of anthropocentricism and scholars who analyze the connection between animals and Blackness, fall short of subjecting "the very humanity they want to decenter and/or expand to sufficient interrogation. As a result, they authorize the violence of the state, one that protects, criminalizes, enforces, and prosecutes differentially based on race, class, gender, sexuality, national origin, religion, ability, and immigration status."[14] In other words, in efforts to expand rights among racialized communities or to grant personhood to nonhuman species, many scholars and activists fail to challenge the production of the liberal subject itself. Jackson offers a corrective to certain calls for greater inclusion: "what is commonly deemed dehumanization is, in the main, more accurately interpreted as the violence of humanization or the burden of inclusion into a racially hierarchized universal humanity."[15] What is needed is clarification of the processes by which the taxonomic projects of early modern and early American science and politics have contributed to the ontological primacy of Man.

Relatedly, Indigenous and non-Indigenous scholars and artists have shown that the cultural effects of the destruction of bison, fish, and other nonhuman animal populations and habitats can't be separated from the systematic elimination of Indigenous lives and communities and land theft.[16] As settler scholar and artist Michelle Wilson writes, "Settler-colonial ways of knowing attempt to decontextualize, quantify, and isolate beings into taxonomies. These ontological strategies have resulted in an exploitive relationship to the world because it frames humans as sentient masters surrounded by inert resources."[17] My analysis of Jefferson and his colleagues' collection, classification, and exhibition of animal specimens in the third section of this book provides an account of the ways that the mastery of nature included a thingification of life through a variety of documentary techniques, while the utilitarian concept of "resource" was applied to land, information, animals, and human labor. These assumptions and political agendas, as well as the scientific practices that authorized and advanced the rearrangement of relations with the human and more-than-human in North America, were put on display in the entryway to Jefferson's home at Monticello.

Returning to the Shadwell fire, it is reasonable to suggest that this early loss of books, papers, and home induced or strengthened an already existing archival impulse in Jefferson. The timing of the Shadwell fire is significant—in 1770 Jefferson was something of a Prospero figure, not shipwrecked on an island, but rather, bereft after the loss of his home and his possessions, on the cusp of building a new dream, and about to begin construction of his house at Monticello, on top of the "little mountain." He would eventually populate this mountain with enslaved laborers, his families—white and Black—as well as animal life for consumption, ornament, companionship, and labor. In each case, human and nonhuman animals were regarded as Jefferson's property.[18] From this vantage point we can consider the ways that his own theories about literacy, education, and information are tied to his vision for a future republic, as well as his later written rationalizations of the enslavement of Black people and the displacement and killing of Indigenous people in the name of progress. Jefferson's Caliban was anyone he regarded as incapable of self-government and destined for a life of servitude, but also someone upon whom Jefferson depended.

## The Museum at Monticello

Jefferson's archival, library, and museum practices each emerged as a threshold between his private and public worlds. As a collector of books, historical documents, and cultural artifacts, as well as a leader in scientific and political circles, Jefferson was uniquely positioned to connect other scientists, politicians, and publics to a wide range of scientific, humanist, and historical knowledges. His museum demonstrates what Tony Bennett has identified as a particular expression of Foucauldian disciplinary power. Jefferson's Indian Room signals the emergence of an "exhibitionary complex," which featured both the enclosure of objects and an opening to viewers.[19] Bennett identifies "the institutions comprising 'the exhibitionary complex'" as being "involved in the transfer of objects and bodies from the enclosed and private domains in which they had previously been displayed (but to a restricted public) into progressively more open and public arenas." Although European museums became institutionalized around the same time as the "carceral archipelago" came into formation, Bennett suggests that, rather than operating through a panoptic carceral power, museums put disciplinary knowledge on display to educate and inform citizenries and to magnify relations of power.[20] Hans Sloane's massive collection and its transition to the British Museum, which established a Linnaean classification of objects in the second half of the eighteenth century, is instructive as an example of the transition from cabinets of curiosity to ordered permanent collections that were meant to be viewed by the public.[21] "In an effort to distinguish itself from cabinets of curiosities and other nineteenth-century collections of novelties, the museum adamantly represented itself to the public as a 'classifying house,' emphasizing its scientific and instructional qualities."[22] Early American museums, including Jefferson's exhibition in the entryway to his house and Charles Willson Peale's Philadelphia Museum demonstrate some of the ways that "racial and colonial violence get[s] enfolded into an aesthetic that renders conquest natural, even righteous."[23]

Many museum historians locate the development of museums in the formation of the modern state in the nineteenth century, and many histories of American museums focus on the Smithsonian, which opened in 1846, or local historical societies like the Massachusetts Historical Society. When viewed along with the inception of the Library of Congress and early American archival practices, as well as the founding of the University of Virginia, Jefferson's "Indian Hall" and his participation in the American Philosophical Society and the Philadelphia Museum were important in the emergence of a network of institutions that displayed and distributed disciplinary power through education and information. What distinguished museums from other spaces, such as penitentiaries, schools, and factories was that they positioned museumgoers as both the beneficiary and subject of power—a relation "made manifest not in its ability to inflict pain but by its ability to organize and co-ordinate an order of things and to produce a place for the people in relation to that order."[24] And key to this mechanism of power was the marking of a "distinction between the subjects and the objects of power not within the national body but, as organized by the many rhetorics of imperialism."[25] Museums classified peoples as it classified nonhuman animals, plants, and minerals according to an imperial order and put specimens on display to establish and normalize distinctions between the body politic and others. Viewers were positioned in relation to this order, and their natural history education was infused with racial rhetoric and hierarchies.

Among the roles that Jefferson famously performed and the positions he held, the one about which he said was "the most flattering incident of my life" was the election to the presidency of the American Philosophical Society. He was made a member of the society in 1780 and remained until his death in 1826. He served as its president from 1797 to 1814, even while he was president of the United States.[26] In anticipation of receiving artifacts and specimens from the Lewis and Clark expedition, Jefferson began designing his "Indian Hall" in the entrance to Monticello in 1805. He filled this part of his house with objects from the Lewis and Clark expedition, as well as European paintings and artifacts, and he turned the entryway into something like a public museum. "Nowhere in the United States, at that time, would anyone have been able to see such a mingling of objects. In a country today known more than any other for its encyclopedic museums, one of the earliest was that created by Thomas Jefferson at Monticello."[27] The Indian Hall was in the same entrance space as his European art. "Ceracchi's and Houdon's busts, together with Old Master copies and a marble version of the classical Sleeping Ariadne, were shown alongside Native American art and artifacts, both ancient and contemporary, animal fossils, and other natural history specimens."[28]

His intention was to educate visitors to his home, especially about American flora and fauna and the Indigenous communities that Lewis and Clark encountered. We don't have a complete catalog of the items in Jefferson's museum, but there is correspondence that provides an indication of the types of materials he would have showcased. Meriwether Lewis sent several boxes of artifacts, two large trunks of skins and skeletons, and three cages with small live animals. In a letter to Charles Willson Peale, Jefferson wrote about his polygraph (described in Chapter 2), as well as his plans for his Indian Hall at Monticello. In this single communication we see the development of archival documentary technique alongside museum curation and natural history: "I arrived here two days ago, & found the articles which had been forwarded by capt Lewis. there is a box of minerals which he particularly desired should go to the Philosophical society. there are some articles which I shall keep for an Indian Hall I am forming at Monticello, e.g. horns, dressed skins, utensils &c."[29] The exchange of letters between Peale and Jefferson reveals their shared ideas about libraries, archives, museums, and nation-building. They agreed about the necessity of copying, preserving, keeping, and displaying writings and objects that informed the history of North America.

George Ticknor described Jefferson's exhibition space at Monticello in detail, noting a strangeness in the combination of disparate items:

> You enter, by a glass folding-door, into a hall which reminds you of Fielding's "Man of the Mountain," by the strange furniture of its walls. On one side hang the head and horns of an elk, a deer, and a buffalo; another is covered with curiosities which Lewis and Clarke found in their wild and perilous expedition. On the third, among many other striking matters, was the head of a mammoth, or, as Cuvier calls it, a mastodon, containing the only os frontis,[30] Mr. Jefferson tells me, that has yet been found. On the fourth side, in odd union with a fine painting of the Repentance of Saint Peter, is an Indian map on leather, of the southern waters of the Missouri, and an Indian representation of a bloody battle, handed down in their traditions. Through this hall—or rather museum—we passed to the dining-room.[31]

Barthélémy Sernin du Moulin, baron de Montlezun de Labarthette also referred to the room as a museum, and he seemed to be impressed with the same objects that Ticknor described:

> I went back inside with [Thomas Jefferson Randolph], who showed the museum in the entrance hall of the house to me. It contains both extremely rare items and others that you could find nowhere else, among them the upper jaw of a mammoth. It was discovered in Kentucky, and Mr. Peale used a *copy* of it to complete his mammoth at the Philadelphia Museum. The head is complete, but the lower jaw is not from the same individual. Two other infinitely curious pieces are: 1. An Indian painting representing a battle; it is on buffalo hide, about five feet square, and shows four lines of combatants. Each facing line has horses painted red and green and warriors armed and dressed in the manner of the savages. 2. A geographical map without the slightest flaw, also on buffalo hide and six feet square. It depicts a section of the Missouri River, and, although roughly drawn, is easy to understand.[32]

Montlezun went on to list several of the objects in Jefferson's museum, adding descriptions for some (see note for the list in full).[33] Among the items were two sculptures that belonged to an Indigenous community who had lived "on a high bluff on the north side of Cumberland River" in Tennessee. Jefferson obtained these in 1799 from Morgan Brown, who described the sculptures as "the largest which have ever been discovered in North America that were really made by the Original inhabitance—one is the likeness of a very old man from the waist upwards and the other a woman—they are about the size of children of eight or ten years old." The Mississippian stone figures were found by a farmer who was plowing the land. He seems to have damaged them with the plow, but this story reveals an even greater harm, which was the invasion of the burial mounds in which these sculptures were found. Standing side by side, they were buried about six inches under the earth's surface. Brown reported that "there were two large mounds a little to the West of them and a quantity of human bones under and near them." Brown offered to ship the sculptures to Jefferson, who was eager to accept, stating "such monuments of the state of the arts among the Indians are too singular not to be highly esteemed, and I shall preserve them as such with great care."[34]

This stands as a troubling example of the blatant theft of sacred objects from sacred land, the repurposing of those objects for material gain, exhibition, ownership, and cultural capital. Here we see the interrelatedness of processes rendering sacred objects into things that can be owned, land, and museums. In Brown's report and Jefferson's reply we see little evidence of regard for the people who created the burial grounds or for the dignity of the dead. Jefferson's archaeological and ethnographic projects established grounds for anthropology as a field. Benedict Anderson suggests that, to understand the proliferation of public museums "requires a consideration of the novel nineteenth-century colonial archaeology that made such museums possible," but through Jefferson's archive, we find that the timeline starts earlier, at least as early as the archaeological dig that he described in *Notes on the State of Virginia*.[35]

Today's visitors to Jefferson's house at Monticello (the entire house is a museum) enter through a re-creation of his original museum space, with many of the original objects on display, arranged as best as possible according to his descriptions. Jefferson called the entranceway-turned-exhibition space his "Indian Hall" because it included Indigenous materials brought back from expeditions, such as maps drawn on bison hides, the statues described above, and so on. Jefferson's museum and gardens, perhaps more uniquely than his other information techniques, demonstrates the connection between information and the dispossession of Indigenous people of their land, objects, and knowledges, as well as the geographical metaphors that have become fundamental to information storage, retrieval, and seeking. In Jefferson's world, political science and natural science were inextricably linked. For the rest of this chapter I rely on scholarship that examines Jefferson's land policies and practices in the context of the Doctrine of Discovery to show how Monticello functioned as a "center of calculation" from which Jefferson participated in westward expansion at a distance. Jefferson put various objects that provided evidence from expeditions, academies, and trade on display in the entryway of his house. Here mathematics, natural history, and mapmaking converged in the coherence of a collection in an exhibition space, as "part of a complex assemblage, networked into ever shifting sets of relations—people, spaces and other things, humans and non-human, that are holding together social and political relations."[36] The objects in Jefferson's Indian Hall and the seeds that he planted in his gardens were acquired from scientific and militaristic expeditions, which were instrumental to obtaining knowledge from distant lands and bringing them back.

Borrowing from Latour, who argues that mobility, stability, and combinability make "domination at a distance feasible," I view Jefferson's museum as a key participant in setting the stage for American natural history museum practices.[37] Gathering objects from a distance required systems of exchange and portability. Lewis and Clark were sent on their expedition equipped with several bundles that were to be used as items of exchange or gifts for the Indigenous community leaders from whom they intended to obtain information, objects, and eventually, land. They returned with canoes full of plant and animal specimens and Indigenous belongings. Latour explains that knowledge has to be understood in the context of a "whole cycle of accumulation: how to bring things back to a place for someone to see it for the first time so that others might be sent again to bring other things back."[38] Lewis and Clark were, among other things, sent to become "familiar with things, people and events, which are *distant*" so that the federal government could gain knowledge about the territories that it aspired to claim.[39] Practices of extraction, abstraction, and documentation are fundamental to the institutions in which relations of domination take form. Latour states that the "compromise between presence and absence is often called **information**. . . . When you hold a piece of information you have the *form* of something without the thing itself—a map, for example."[40] In other words, information about the things can be much more readily accumulated and combined in the centers and is essential for sharing, trade, contracts, and records-keeping. Information multiplies and accelerates the actions and relations of all the other elements of the networks. And as we have seen, "the forms of objects raise fundamental political questions about aesthetic response."[41]

Latour's expansion of his analysis of information as relation is essential for understanding what Jefferson and his colleagues were up to:

> One sees that information is not a "form" in the Platonic sense of the word, but rather a very practical and very material relationship between two places, where the first negotiates what must be collected from the second in order to observe and act on it from a distance. Depending on the progress of sciences, on the frequency of the voyages, on the faithfulness of the draftspersons, the breadth of the taxonomies, of the size of the collection, the wealth of the collectors, and the power of the instruments, one can more or less take samples and more or less further reliably load the vehicles of information.[42]

The display and use of materials acquired in the Lewis and Clark and other expeditions are best understood as expressions of the Doctrine of Discovery—one of the earliest examples of agreed upon "legal principles that apply to the conduct of nations vis-à-vis other nations."[43] Developed by Christian European countries to manage conflict regarding trade, exploration, and colonization of lands beyond Europe, the Doctrine fundamentally served European domination by rationalizing and justifying claims to lands held by non-Christian and non-European peoples. The Doctrine can be traced back to the Crusades, which Pope Innocent viewed as legitimate and "just" wars fought for the defense of Christians and what he believed to be their sovereign right to land occupied by non-Christians. This was a crucial moment in the formation of Man1 as described by Sylvia Wynter, establishing the basis on which distinctions between Christian and non-Christian and "civilized" and "savage" served as justifications for conquest. Palmer succinctly describes the Doctrine of Discovery's lasting relevance to Euro-American claims to land:

> Confirmed in a Papal Bull of 1493, the Doctrine of Discovery claimed that Christians could justly kill, and seize land from, any people who were not subjects of a Christian monarch. This form of Indigenous dispossession via racialized "just war" enabled in law by the Doctrine of Discovery was declared US policy by Thomas Jefferson in 1792 and was retroactively codified into federal law in the 1823 supreme court case Johnson v M'Intosh.[44]

The dispossession of Indigenous communities of their knowledges, including the theft, collection, study, and exhibition of every aspect of their cultural life, was also rationalized by the Doctrine of Discovery.[45] Professor and tribal judge Robert Miller has carefully demonstrated that Jefferson enacted policy according to the Doctrine of Discovery and understood that doctrine as an international code of law.[46] He was, according to Miller, the "architect of the removal policy," and he "exercised the government's sovereign Discovery authority over the Indian nations."[47] Presenting his case with an attorney's eye for detail, Miller writes, "The legal and factual evidence of American history proves that the expansion of the United States from the 13 original colonies, or states, in 1774 until 1855, when the Pacific Northwest was acquired by the United Sates, was rationalized on the basis of the Doctrine of Discovery."[48] All aspects of the Doctrine of Discovery pertain to Jefferson's land policies, including the notion of "first discovery," which meant that the first European country to "discover" new lands unknown to other European countries gained rights of preemption. Jefferson and his colleagues were continuing the European project of acquisition, collection, and science but now instead of an English colony it was a newly independent nation aspiring to empire.

Jefferson sent the explorers out to gather information, survey the terrain, and use technological instruments and mathematical techniques to encode early American ideas about land use, progress, and property in maps. "By coding every sighting of any land in longitude and latitude," writes Latour "and by sending this code back, the shape of the sighted lands may be redrawn by those who have not sighted them."[49] Jefferson never traveled west of the Blue Ridge Mountains, but he was an expert surveyor and geographer, and his maps, tables, and descriptive entries across his written work communicated the scientific information that Jefferson needed as president of the United States to enact policy toward growth and expansion. Meriwether Lewis's dispatch on 7 April 1805 conveys important context, as it immediately draws attention to the fact that all of the information that they gathered from Indigenous communities was passed to the secretary of war. The information was military intelligence, and the expedition was fundamentally a military and communication mission:

> I have transmitted to the Secretary at War, every information relative to the geography of the country which we possess, together with a view of the Indian nations, containing information relative to them, on those points with which, I conceived it important that the government should be informed.[50]

He explained that some of the boats loaded with skins and other goods would be dispatched from "the falls of the Missouri," and with their load lightened they would proceed at a quicker pace along the Missouri river. Lewis indicated that it would be impossible to be sure how long the remainder of the journey to the Columbia River would take given the difficulty of the terrain through the Rocky Mountains and the unpredictability of relations with Indigenous communities along the way. As Ned Blackhawk explains, "Native peoples controlled essential arteries, and thus access into the continent. Powerful allies, trading partners, and antagonists, Native villagers shaped the contours of the century's crucible of war."[51] The rivers were channels for communication, transportation, trade, and information. The materials that Lewis and Clark brought to Jefferson from Indigenous communities were obtained in acts of aggression. Additionally, as Tony Castanha writes, "The discovery principle that justified the taking of indigenous lands in the Americas also paved the way for the anthropological study of Native cultures, sacred sites, artifacts, and ancestral remains."[52] Jefferson's cataloging, excavation, study, and display of Indigenous artifacts, which were formative in American archaeological and anthropological and museum sciences, were driven in part by the drive toward empire.

## Jefferson's Natural History

Scholars have written in detail about Jefferson's Indian Hall, and so my purpose here is to contextualize it within this broader account of Jefferson's cataloging and classification practices and current conversations about decolonizing museums. As J. J. Ghaddar explains, one of the ongoing consequences of colonialism is "Indigenous people's lack of control over how their information, histories, and cultural knowledge are used and interpreted."[53]

Not only do "colonial processes undermine the ability of Indigenous peoples to generate and maintain their own records (broadly defined) of their cultures and histories," but the archives of colonizers and their governments also acquire, select, organize, and store vast amounts of Indigenous materials. Indeed, "the information, knowledge, and cultures of Indigenous peoples, like their territories, ancestral remains, and possessions, were stolen or coerced from them—not traded, discovered, or given freely."[54] Another consequence has to do with access. The information professions have been guided by a principle that values access to the most information for the most people, and there are long-held assumptions that all things of cultural value should be preserved for posterity and "equitable" access. This runs contrary to the traditions and values among Indigenous communities, who regard many objects as sacred or kin. As Daniel Heath Justice writes, "Not all things are meant for all people. There are boundaries to some forms of knowledge; to insist that all things should be available without limit to everyone is to exercise a particularly corrosive kind of universalizing colonialist privilege; claiming entitlement to all peoples' knowledge is, after all, just one of the many expropriating features of settler colonial violence."[55] The notion that museums are protectors of Indigenous materials because they have the resources to preserve and store them, or that because they are the present owners of the materials it follows that they have the right to determine the terms of access, are based in old settler colonial paternalism. Settler scholar Hannah Turner's observations are relevant here. Turner's research focuses on the Smithsonian, a later period in the history of American natural history museums. She observes the ways that nineteenth-century scholars used scientific methods to study Indigenous peoples and identifies natural history museums like the Smithsonian as essential to that science. Turner writes, "throughout the history of settler colonialism, administrative and bureaucratic structures would enable and solidify these interpretations, creating part of an infrastructure of oppression. Like the early catalogues and atlases from scientific pursuits, many museum catalogues resemble or grew out of attempts to categorize the natural world."[56]

What's more, as Kim TallBear explains, not only have materials of a community become appropriated, but so have people. Origin stories and ethnographic studies have treated Indigenous peoples as objects of research, and in Jefferson's Indian Hall, objects that stand as representations of peoples were displayed in the context of cultivating a national imaginary. For TallBear, these types of appropriation carry serious implications with regard to relations, which also "get appropriated if you will and made into 'things.'" In the process of being objectified, "relations then become resources for the settler state to measure, monitor, and exploit to in complex ways build settler knowledge and national identity."[57] In other words, people and their human and nonhuman relations become "resources" to be mined for research data. Jefferson and his colleagues set the stage for using scientific methods for studying and exhibiting animals and Indigenous artifacts, as well and Indigenous human remains, in the Americas.[58]

For many Indigenous communities, the very idea of treating the weavings, beadwork, clothing, and musical instruments that they make or parts of the natural world as "objects" at all is offensive. Robin Wall Kimmerer describes the differences between Potawatomi language and the English language, noting that in Potawatomi there are far more verbs and a greater capacity to talk about the aliveness of the natural world. She writes, "A bay is a noun only if water is *dead*. When *bay* is a noun, it is defined by humans, trapped between its shores and contained by the word. But the verb *wiikwegamaa*—to *be* a bay—releases the water from bondage and lets it live."[59] The English language objectifies much of the natural world, rendering it lifeless, whereas in Potawatomi, and many other Indigenous languages, water, land, rocks, fire, drums, stories, nonhuman animals, and plants are all alive. Language is "a mirror for seeing the animacy of the world, the life that pulses through all things."[60] She goes on to say that English just doesn't provide the tools for conveying the animacy and relations of all things; "In English, you are either a human or a thing," and when we make a living being into an object—an *it*—we absolve ourselves of responsibility toward that being. "Saying *it* makes a living land into 'natural resources.'"[61] Dylan Robinson, xwélmexw (Stó:lō/Skwah) artist, curator, and scholar, adds, "For Indigenous people, experiencing the objectifying system of display is often traumatic because that which is on display does not fit the category of object or artifact. Instead, such belongings hold life in various ways, whether that life is understood as a being, ancestor, or kin, or whether such life is understood as life untethered to a cohesive subjectivity."[62]

These points all become even more salient when we understand that settlers also regarded human beings as objects that could be enslaved or otherwise used or killed. Objectifying beings in language puts distance between, rather than cultivating kinship among. This marks a fundamental difference between settler and Indigenous ways of organizing the world and knowledges. Indeed, the impulse for appropriating Indigenous belongings and remains and bringing them back to a center where they will be studied and displayed as evidence of their demise "formed a double-act of colonialism."[63] Euro-Americans asserted their ownership of Indigenous materials while replacing Native knowledges and peoples with their own. Instead of investing in the constraining methods of cataloging and classifying and the chemical and physical practices inherent to preserving materials, museums can choose to honor the aliveness of objects, and accept that it may be best to allow things to decay and disintegrate according to their own life cycles and according to the ways in which the materials mattered to the communities in which they were situated.

The terms of museum and archival practice tend to sanitize their colonialist contexts. Acquisition is in fact capture, and storage and display are terms for incarceration, restrictions on privacy, and separations of kin. Robinson maintains that any anti-colonial efforts toward repatriation and repair must not only amplify Indigenous voices, labor, and presence, but need to "reconnect Indigenous life held by museums with kin."[64] He warns that many of the attempts at inclusion "can also re-entrench the values of the museum as a site of public education about Indigenous culture that does not firstly serve the needs of the Indigenous people and communities the museum centers in its collections and displays." He urges museum staff and curators to see that they "are not custodians of objects, but carers for life." Robinson offers tangible methods, guided by a set of questions regarding museums' treatment of Indigenous belongings. The cataloging practices and ethnographic field notes that have long been written in terms that foreground utility from a settler colonial perspective have the effect of foreclosing visits with kin: "Museum categorization systems often place Indigenous life together based on the type of object (masks, baskets) or nation/region. This system may also be understood as segregating kinship relations between ancestors from the same family."[65]

Another fundamental difference between colonial and Indigenous cultural practices resides in economies oriented around giving and receiving versus buying, stealing, and possessing. Jefferson and his colleagues understood that Native gift economies based in reciprocity were essential for relationship building, and they used this to attain their goals. It is certainly true that many Indigenous communities in the newly acquired territory were already participating in trade economies with British, French, and Spanish colonizers, and so it would be a mistake to suggest that Jefferson was imposing something dramatically new. Lewis and Clark were the first official representatives of the United States to do so in that part of the continent, and they presented themselves not as traders, but as people who opened the west to trade for early Americans. This required engaging in and enacting particular rituals, such as gift exchanges, feasting, using and exchanging symbolic items like wampum, pipes, and robes, and speaking in terms of kinship in addressing one another—words like "brother," "children," "brethren," and "father." It is safe to say that Jefferson's use of giving and receiving in the guise of benevolence and friendship was calculated. It does seem that he truly believed that forcing Native peoples to adopt modern agriculture, gender roles, and language was in their best interest—that becoming more "civilized" would improve their conditions, and that, in a sense, the acquisition of these skills and customs constituted a "gift of freedom." As Mimi Thi Nguyen writes, "the gift of freedom calls for the realignment of heterogeneous social forms of organization with abstract categories and properties, rendered natural, ineffable, and inalienable, but also *objectified, calculable,* and *exchangeable.*"[66] The gift of freedom incurs a debt of obligation. This has to also be understood as a self-serving rationale that supported empire expansion. Placing civilization and freedom within an exchange framework in which freedom is bestowed by those in power on Others who have been disenfranchised, displaced, and rendered dependent, is one of the techniques that underwrites US policy toward Indigenous peoples.

Jefferson understood the value of offering items in the guise of a "gift" to persuade or mislead tribal leaders into selling their lands.[67] In 1791, when he was secretary of state, he expressed his views about the political economy of westward expansion in the context of a dispute with federalists over the cost and efficacy of military force: "Constant murders committing by the Indians, and their combination threatens to be more and more extensive. I hope we shall give them a thorough drubbing this summer, and then change our tomahawk into a golden chain of friendship. The most economical as well as most humane conduct towards them is to bribe them into peace, and to retain Them in peace by eternal bribes."[68] Rather than being based on reciprocity and respect, the exchange of gifts was seen by Jefferson and his colleagues as a means to extract information and unite Indigenous peoples with settlers. Although Indigenous leaders certainly had agency in these offerings, the terms on which they made them were based in uneven relations of power and manipulation.

In Lewis's letter that accompanied an "invoice of certain articles" (see Figure 16) delivered to Jefferson from the expedition.[69] The invoice is copied in full below.

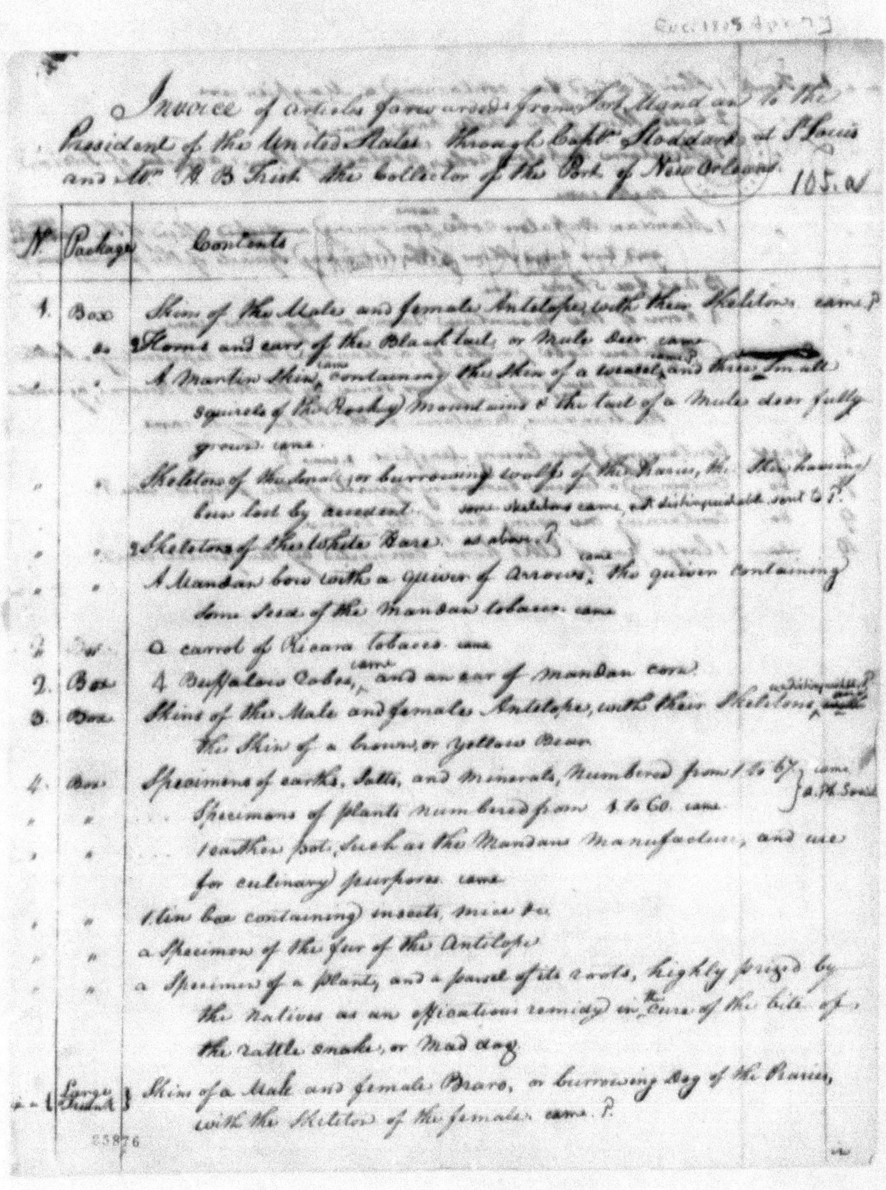

Invoice of articles forwarded from Fort Mandan to the President of the United States through Capt. Stoddard at St. Louis and Mr. H. B. Trist the Collector of the Port of New Orleans. 105.a

| No. | Package | Contents |
|---|---|---|
| 1. | Box | Skins of the Male and female Antelope, with their Skeletons. came |
| " | " | Horns and ears of the Black tail, or Mule deer. came |
| " | " | A Martin skin, containing the skin of a weasel, and three small squirrels of the Rocky Mountains & the tail of a Mule deer fully grown. came |
| " | " | Skeletons of the small, or burrowing wolf of the Prairies, the skin having been lost by accident. |
| " | " | Skeleton of the White Hare |
| " | " | A Mandan bow with a quiver of Arrows, the quiver containing some seed of the Mandan tobacco. came |
| " | " | a carrot of Ricara tobacco. came |
| 2. | Box | 4 Buffalow Robes, and an ear of Mandan corn |
| 3. | Box | Skins of the Male and female Antelope, with their Skeletons, and the Skin of a brown, or yellow Bear |
| 4. | Box | Specimens of earths, salts, and minerals, Numbered from 1 to 67. came |
| " | " | Specimens of plants numbered from 1 to 60. came |
| " | " | 1 earthen pot, such as the Mandans manufacture, and use for culinary purposes. came |
| " | " | 1 tin box containing insects, mice &c. |
| " | " | a Specimen of the fur of the Antelope |
| " | " | a Specimen of a plant, and a parcel of its roots, highly prized by the natives as an efficatious remedy in the cure of the bite of the rattle snake, or Mad dog. |
| 1 | Large Trunk | Skins of a Male and female Braro, or burrowing dog of the Prairies, with the Skeleton of the female. came |

Figure 16. Meriwether Lewis to Thomas Jefferson, 7 April 1805, with Invoice. Manuscript/Mixed Material. The Thomas Jefferson Papers at the Library of Congress. Series 1: General Correspondence. 1651–1827, Microfilm Reel: 033.

Invoice of articles forwarded from Fort Mandan to the President of the United States through Captn. Stoddard at St. Louis and Mr. H. B. Trist the Collector of the Port of New Orleans.

| No. | Package | Contents |
|---|---|---|
| 1. | Box | Skins of the Male and female Antelope, with their Skeletons. *came. P.* |
| | do | 2 Horns and ears, of the Blacktail, or Mule deer. *came* |
| | | A Martin skin *came* containing the Skin of a weasel *came. P.* and three Small squirels of the Rocky Mountains & the tail of a Mule deer fully grown. *came.* |
| | | Skeletons of the Small, or burrowing wolf of the Praries, the Skin having been lost by accedent. *some skeletons came, not distinguishable. sent to P.* |
| | | 2 Skeletons of the White Hare. *as above. P.* |
| | | A Mandan bow with a quiver of arrows *came* the quiver containing Some Seed of the Mandan tobacco. *came* |
| 2. | Box | A carrot of Ricara tobacco. *came* |
| 2. | Box | 4 Buffalow Robes, *came* and an ear of Mandan corn. |
| 3. | Box | Skins of the Male and female Antelope, with their Skeletons *undistinguishable.* and the Skin of a brown, or yellow Bear. |
| 4. | Box | Specimens of earths, Salts, and Minerals, numbered from 1. to 67. *came A. Ph. Society* |
| | | Specimens of plants numbered from 1. to 60. *came* |
| | | 1 earthen pot, Such as the Mandans manufacture, and use for culinary purposes. *came* |
| | | 1. tin box containing insects, mice &c. |
| | | a Specimen of the fur of the Antilope. |
| | | a Specimen of a plant, and a parsel of its roots, highly prized by the natives as an efficatious remidy in the cure of the bite of the rattle-snake, or mad dog. |
| in a | Large Trunk | Skins of Male and female Braro, or burrowing Dog of the Praries, with the Skeleton of the female. *came. P.* |
| in a | large Trunk | 1 Skin of a red fox containing a Magpie. *came.* |
| | | 2 Cases Skins of the white hare. *came. P.* |
| | | 1 Minetarre Buffalow robe, *came* containing some articles of Indian dress. *came.* |
| | | 1 Mandan Buffalow robe *came* containing a dressed Skin of the Lousiana *came* and two cased Skins of the burrowing Squirels of the praries. *came P.* |
| | | 13 red fox skins. *came* |
| | | 4 horns of the mountain ram, or *big* horn. *came.* |
| | | 1 Buffalow robe painted by a Mandan man representing a battle which was faught 8 years since, by the Sioux and Ricaras, against the Mandans, Minitarras and Ahwahharways. *came.* |
| 6 | Cage | Containing four liveing Magpies. *1. came P.* |
| 7 | do. | Containing a liveing burrowing Squirel of the praries. *came. P.* |
| 9 | do. | Containing one liveing hen of the Prarie. |
| 10 | — | 1 large par of Elk's horns connected by the frontal bone. |

Herewith inclosed you will receive an invoice of certain articles, which I have forwarded to you from this place. among other articles, you will observe by reference to the invoice, 67. specimens of earths,

> salts and minerals; and 60 specimens of plants: these are accompanyed by their rispective labels expressing the days on which obtained, places where found, and also their virtues and properties when known. by means of these labels, reference may be made to the Chart of the Missouri forwarded to the Secretary at War, on which, the encampment of each day has been carefully marked; thus the places at which these specimens have been obtained may be easily pointed out, or again found, should any of them prove valuable to the community on further investegation. these have been forwarded with a view of their being presented to the Philosophical society of Philadelphia, in order that they may under their direction be examined or analyzed. after examining these specimens yourself, I would thank you to have a copy of their labels made out, and retained untill my return. the other articles are intended particularly for yourself, to be retained, or disposed off as you may think proper.[70]

Eighteen months after the materials were sent from Fort Mandan, Jefferson instructed Meriwether Lewis to tell the Mandan chief that he would like for him to visit Monticello "and see in what manner I have arranged the tokens of friendship I have recieved from his country particularly as well as from other Indian friends: that I am in fact preparing a kind of Indian hall."[71] Expressions of friendship and Jefferson's Indian Hall must be examined in the context of the history of museums in the Americas, which have long been naturalizing and glorifying colonialism, "first, by taking land theft and the plundering of knowledge and artifacts as their material point of departure."[72] Conversations about decolonization and reconciliation often center around the repatriation of objects to the Indigenous communities to whom they belong and insisting on Indigenous language, description, and terms of access to materials.[73] Jefferson's collection of Indigenous materials, his anthropological methods for learning about Indigenous cultures and languages, including the violation of burial grounds, and his participation in promoting the collection of Indigenous materials for study by the American Philosophical Society and other organizations were, I suggest, instrumental in his plans for extermination and expansion. Studying the Indigenous communities who inhabited the lands that US officials aimed to obtain was among the various scientific objectives of the expeditions. As Latour explains, collections of items could be gathered from the extraction of materials from their place and their communities. Whereas the "shapes of the lands have to be coded and drawn in order to become mobile," plant and animal specimens, rocks, minerals, and fossils, artworks, and artifacts, could be taken away in these expeditions. Importantly, it was through this process of extraction and abstraction of local knowledge that materials became part of "universal histories," and by turning them into scientific objects that served as evidence, the Indigenous knowledges were made to appear to vanish.

## Information Metaphors

The relationship between empire and information becomes especially striking when we consider the extent to which metaphors for information storage and retrieval systems are based in land, geography, and property. The metaphors of knowledge organization call forth their colonial and imperial histories. For example, as Dani Stuchel points out, "The archives is necessarily a contact zone with politics of engagement and power. For instance, we do not expect archival things to access us, to engage with us as we engage with them. . . . The ubiquitous phrase 'information resources' is perhaps clear enough evidence that archival things are in the resource class: sought out, extractable, immanent, waiting to be subjected to human will."[74] Perhaps we should be asking, as Stuchel and others do, how the information professions can revise their relationship with the "vibrant matter" of the archive, and instead of thinking about material as resources for human use, how to think about the aliveness of archives.[75] Max Liboiron explains that to call something a resource is to define relations: "Resources refer to unidirectional relations where aspects of land are useful to particular (here, settler colonial) ends. In this unidirectional relation, value flows in one direction, from the Resource to the user, rather than being reciprocal."[76] The flattening of land relations into relations defined according to a thing's usefulness for colonial conquest and extraction emerged with information in modernity, which required information to be a thing that could be stored, counted, processed, and used.

Unangax̂ scholar Eve Tuck and K. Wayne Yang have thoroughly explained that "decolonization is not a metaphor." They write:

> When metaphor invades decolonization, it kills the very possibility of decolonization; it recenters, it resettles theory, it extends innocence to the settler, it entertains a settler future. Decolonize (a verb) and decolonization (a noun) cannot easily be grafted onto pre-existing discourses/frameworks, even if they are critical, even if they are anti-racist, even if they are justice frameworks. The easy absorption, adoption, and transposing of decolonization is yet another form of settler appropriation.[77]

Users of colonial information technologies *search* for information by *navigating* systems and *discover/master* knowledge across the *disciplines*, we organize that information into *domains*, we speak of *acquisitions* of *resources*. *Claims* to knowledge become the *property* of those who know, researchers can stake their claims on something they "discovered" in a library or archive. Many of us aspire to *mastery* over a *subject* in a *field* of inquiry. What does it mean to be a *subject* about whom someone else claims knowledge? What is the relationship between classifications divided into subjects and human lives? And to what extent does mastery depend on the reduction of something to a single subject? In what ways does this kind of categorization make universal systems possible? In what ways is it both a tool and consequence of domination?

Metaphors are important, not simply as rhetorical devices, but for their political power. They become entrenched as "master tropes" that guide and structure culture and thought, and in the context of information systems, the land-based metaphors undergird the structures that organize knowledge about race, gender, sexuality, and empire expansion into disciplines and statistical tables.[78] As T. L. Cowan and Jas Rault write in their introduction to a special issue on metaphors in technoscience, "Metaphor has the power to materialize and dematerialize." They consider what it means to work with metaphor, distinguishing between metaphors that "invade," that evacuate meaning, or "casually recenter and glorify whiteness, hetero-cis-ness, hyper-ablebodiedness and hyper-ablemindedness, natalist, masculinist, and monied-class dominant cultural norms and biases."[79] Metaphor is an information and communication technology that is embedded within the many technologies that carry the "worldviews, legacies, values, and problems of those who make them."[80] My hope, following Cowan and Rault, is that "grappling with the material histories and consequences of metaphors allow us not only to clap back against metaphors that oppress, but also to signal boost new metaphors, to performatively emancipate ourselves, taking on new epistemological shapes, or manifesting the knowledges that dominant epistemologies and sign systems have long undermined and attempted to destroy."[81] This resonates with Foucault's call in "Questions on Geography," to "decipher discourse through the use of spatial, strategic metaphors," which he believed could enable "one to grasp precisely the points at which discourses are transformed in, through and on the basis of relations of power."[82] Katherine McKittrick also invites a questioning of metaphors to see how they are "structured by and through the complex groundedness of black life—as extraliterary-storied-material-metaphoric-interdisciplinary-dynamic-curious-scientifically-creative (feeling)"—to "sit with metaphor," in order to consider the colonial histories upon which they are constructed and what they enact when they are invoked.[83] At the same time, Tapji Garba and Sara-Maria Sorentino's call to attend to slavery-as-metaphor as grounds for political ontology opens space for accounting "for the genesis and structure of modernity."[84] In this view, metaphor is an essential technique for addressing the ways that enslaved Black people were brought to a continent on which they could not make any former or present claims to land and on which they were other peoples' property. The placeness of Jefferson's information includes the overlapping built and natural spaces and places of the plantation, Indigenous lands, waters, settlements, the colonial Americas, the United States, and beyond. The geographies of information are directly tied to the metaphors through which we produce and consume information.

What do we do with the fact that land and colonial metaphors are so central to libraries, archives, museums, and universities? Situating the connections between the materials in the archive, their organization, and colonization might, as Walter Mignolo advocates, assist in efforts to "delink" knowledge from colonial systems. What is the relationship between information *resources* and natural resources? A "'resource' cannot exist without some intervening human agency which defines it."[85] There are only "possibilities of resources," which are "provided by nature in the context of a given society."[86] Labeling elements of ecosystems as resources is a culturally specific practice that locates them within a system of exchange.

Settler colonialist perceptions of "resources" were produced in a culture of commodification, and because European economies measured commodities in terms of currency and property, and because currency was an indicator and propagator of wealth and social status, their use of the land was based on abstraction, extraction, accumulation, utility, and growth, rather than relationality and sustainability. Thinking about information and natural resources together can bring clarity about the ongoing consequences of rendering of nature, documents, and cultural artifacts into commodifiable, useful things. It also serves as a point of departure for considering the techniques by which citizenries were defined and educated along lines of distinction. Laws of natural and national history were inscribed in museums, setting the stage for natural history museums today, many of which continue to hold and display Indigenous materials and animal specimens for the education and information of their visitors. Among the specimens sent by Lewis and Clark were antelope skins and bones. In Chapter 8, I connect Jefferson's antelope to current uses of the antelope in documentation theory to show how the print culture of museums (descriptions, advertisements, catalogs, correspondence, etc.) is tied to imperial expansion and natural history.

# 8
# How the American Antelope [*sic*] Became a Document

If I can mount one of the Antilopes to be decent, it will be a valuable addition to my Antilopes. I am very much obliged to Captn. Lewis for his endeavors to increase our knowledge of the Animals of that new acquired Teritory. . . . It is more important to have this Museum supplied with the American Animals than those of other Countryes, yet for a comparative view it ought to possess those of every part of the Globe!

—CHARLES WILLSON PEALE TO THOMAS JEFFERSON, 3 NOVEMBER 1805

No human contact, but relations of domination and submission which turn the colonizing man into a classroom monitor, an army sergeant, a prison guard, a slave driver, and the indigenous man into an instrument of production. My turn to state an equation: colonization = "thingification."

— AIMÉ CÉSAIRE, *DISCOURSE ON COLONIALISM*

In the Introduction to this book, I argued documents became monumental in part because of the architectures that organize them. There was also a concomitant *thingification* of information by way of memorialization and modern scientific methods. Information is not something that always already objectively exists in the world. An open question remains, does something have to be activated by humans and put to use to be regarded as information? Here I return to that question by using documentation theory to frame a discussion of Jefferson's scientific and museum practices.

For context, I refer to Suzanne Briet's treatise on documentation, first published in French in 1951, which has become canonical in the field of library and information studies. In that paper Briet uses the example of an antelope to explain how the human use of an animal renders it a document.[1]

> Let us admire the documentary fertility of a simple originary fact: for example, an antelope of a new kind has been encountered in Africa by an explorer who has succeeded in capturing an individual that is then brought back to Europe for our Botanical garden [*Jardin des Plantes*]. A press release makes the event known by newspaper, by radio, and by newsreels. The discovery becomes the topic of an announcement at the Academy of Sciences. A professor of the Museum discusses it in his courses. The living animal is placed in a cage and cataloged (zoological garden).
>
> Once it is dead, it will be stuffed and preserved (in the Museum). It is loaned to an Exposition. It is played on a soundtrack at the cinema. Its voice is recorded on a disk. The first monograph serves to establish part of a treatise with plates, then a special encyclopedia (zoological), then a general encyclopedia. The works are cataloged in a library, after having been announced at publication (publisher catalogues and Bibliography of France). The documents are recopied (drawings, watercolors, paintings, statues, photos, films, microfilms), then selected, analyzed, described, translated (documentary productions). The documents that relate to this event are the object of a scientific classifying (fauna) and of an ideologic [*idéologique*] classifying (classification).[2]

Briet's treatise signals the centrality of the document to the natural sciences, and it also indicates the ways that things of all types, including life forms, become resources for human use and mediums for understanding. As Ron Day explains, for Briet, "Entities are allegorized as signs of universal truth, emerging through processes of scientific revelation, led by ontological naming, whereby the entity gains its importance and value for truth by representing something other than its own particularity, a mode of generalized being that transcends particular entities and that appears through vigorous methods and techniques."[3] Entities become evidence by gaining the property of indexicality through primary and secondary documentary techniques. In the case of an antelope, the singular animal becomes representative of a type through naming and classificatory techniques. Secondarily, it is mounted in an exhibition hall, discussed, and written about in academic publications, which are cataloged in a library and copied and revised and re-cited. Rendering an animal into a type is important, because that type enters into "a documentary ontology" in which "beings are evidence of the existence of types and are proof of their factual emerge."[4] But, as Day calls to notice, "such truths are products of cultural techniques, foremost, documentation techniques."[5] Being informational and evidentiary requires *becoming* a document, a thing of utility. Pressing Briet further opens pathways to think about what the antelope points to—not just as a specimen that proves the existence of a type, but how it serves as an index to ideas about natural history and national identity in early America, disciplinary convention, and the "colonial entailments that cling" to information and documentation practices in the present.[6] Information became a particular kind of "thing" throughout the formation of the early United States, and its thingification depended upon and reified the concomitant commodification of nature and human life.

Bernd Frohmann complicates Briet's assessment by inviting us to consider the antelope as something that "becomes a document by virtue of its arrangements with other things," rather than as "a privileged form of those arrangements, such as their evidentiary functions." In Frohmann's view, Briet's message is that "in complex arrangements things exercise documentary agency, which is capable of being detected, understood, and engaged in many different ways, and by many different kinds of actors, both human, and nonhuman." Documentary agency, in Frohmann's view, does not require human contact, nor does its evidentiary status determine its existence. Rather, a thing's documentary agency, power, or force—what Frohmann refers to as "documentality"—is enacted by virtue of its situatedness in the world of other things. This perspective recognizes a thing, or a thingified being as having a capacity to "produce, afford, allow, encourage, permit, influence, render possible, block, or forbid the generation of marks, traces or inscriptions" in relation to others.[7] When we are talking about the lives that have been thingified through processes of datafication and documentation in different points in history, it is not enough to suggest that they are rendered docile subjects. They can resist or refuse, block or deceive, or strategically submit to documentary processes of sorting, naming, counting, and diagramming. One of the ways that information's own history has been obscured is by naturalizing processes of abstraction so that we see numbers, projections, and aliases in place of life and experience. We might attribute the obfuscation of processes of thingification in the discipline of information to "the dematerialization of an event's documentality." The reduction of documents to the function of communication, according to Frohmann, "avoids ethical and moral consequences of the erasure of the object or event that occasions attunement to it."[8] Frohmann also argues that information "exists only as an effect of the ontologically primary elements: documents and documentary practices. It has, therefore, only a secondary or derived ontological status; it is an effect of the relative stability of documentary practices. Once practices stabilize, information can emerge"[9] I think that's right on a certain level, as information requires a medium to be registered as such. But another point to be made is that the process of privileging informational aspects of a being always centers Man and a Euro-American way of seeing.

How is the actualization of a being's documentality—its agency—manifested in relationships to other things and the political, historical, and cultural time and space in which that thing exists? How do the terms of agency become institutionalized and universalized in assemblages of documentary power?

## "Why Look at Animals?"

Jefferson and his colleague Charles Willson Peale shared a vision for a museum in Philadelphia to inform and entertain a broad American public about natural history. Peale expressed that vision in a letter to Jefferson on 12 January 1802:

> I have long contemplated that by industry such a variety of interesting subjects of Nature might be collected in one view as would enlighten the minds of my countrymen, and, demonstrate the importance of diffusing a knowledge of the wonderful and various beauties of Nature, more powerful to *humanize the mind*, promote harmony, and aid virtue, than any other School yet immagened.[10]

Peale was a portrait painter, engraver, and natural historian who organized North American expeditions and established one of the first museums in the United States. Opened to the public in 1786, it was first called the Peale Museum and was also known as the Philadelphia Museum.[11] Peale appointed a "Committee of Visitors" in 1792, which included Alexander Hamilton, James Madison, David Rittenhouse, Benjamin Smith Barton, William Barton, and others. Thomas Jefferson was the first president of the committee. The board's very first recommendation was for the museum to produce a full catalog of the museum's contents.[12] The museum moved to the American Philosophical Society in 1794, and then was located in Independence Hall starting in 1802. By 1831, when Peale's son was at the helm, "the museum contained 250 quadrupeds, 1,310 birds, more than 4,000 insects, 8,000 minerals, 1,044 shells, several hundred fish, more than 200 snakes, lizards, turtles and tortoises and the major U.S. Collection of fossil bones; it had become the primary resource for American natural history."[13] Peale taught himself the methods for taxidermy, preservation of specimens, and mounting for display mostly by reading books and exchanging letters with European scientists.

Peale's hope was for his museum to be established someday as a national museum of natural history, with support and status as a US cultural and educational institution. That dream was not realized, and most of the materials that he collected were lost due to fire or were dispersed in auction. Jefferson, Peale, and many of their colleagues understood education to be essential to the growth of the early American republic. Peale's museum should be understood as a nationalist project in educating American citizens in natural history. Peale's museum was a statist natural history project that enacted divisions between those who know and those who are regarded as knowable, evidence-bearing *documents*.

My aim is to understand how the antelope has been animated as a document and recurs as a signifier for the field of library and information science. From letters exchanged between Jefferson and Peale, as well as the journals of the Lewis and Clark expedition, I will show how an animal was rendered into a thing, as well as how the animal resists its own objectification. This provides important context for the colonial history of museums but also speaks to the agency of information objects more generally.

■

In *The Animal That Therefore I Am*, Derrida considers the ways that people observe animals but don't often think about the animals looking back at them. He notes that, since the book of Genesis, and even more egregiously, since René Descartes, philosophers have been reiterating and revising a Man vs. animal divide. By creating the dividing line between "animal" in the singular and "Man" according to his own capacity to pronounce "I think," Descartes introduced a distinction that philosophers following him have repeated up to the present. The tired debate about whether or not animals have language arises over and over, consequentially serving as a justification for using animals without regard for their being.

Theodor Adorno describes this as warfare, which Derrida follows, along with the assertion that this is part of a long tradition of war against animals beginning with the book of Genesis: "And that war is not just one means of applying technoscience to the animal in the absence of another possible of foreseeable means; no, that violence or war has until now been constitutive of the project or of the very possibility of technoscientific knowledge within the process of humanization or of the appropriation of man by man."[14] In this worldview, empathy and compassion for animals has no place. There is no space for feeling and *being with* them as they get scripted into extractive and accumulative knowledge systems. The incredible increase in scientific knowledge in early America owes itself to the harvesting of animal and plant life from their habitats and submitting them to study. It also required the decimation of life forms from Indigenous communities, as well as the theft and foreclosure of Indigenous knowledges. For Derrida, the trace of scientists' and philosophers' signatures in the form of documentation, the ways in which those marks have endured over time in scientific discourse is important:

> In the first place there are texts signed by people who have no doubt seen, observed, analyzed, reflected on the animal, but who have never been *seen* by the animal. . . . They neither wanted nor had the capacity to draw any systematic consequence from the fact that an animal could, facing them, look at them, clothed or naked, and in a word, without a word, *address them*. They have taken no account of the fact that what they call "animal" could *look at* them, and *address* them from down there, from a wholly other origin.[15]

Those of us who work in the field of information bear a *response*-ability to all life forms. My hope is that by following the tracks of natural philosophers in documents, we can find our way to the animals and engage with them more fully and imagine ways of undoing the coloniality of documentation. As John Berger writes, "animals are always the observed. The fact that they can observe us has lost all significance. They are the objects of our ever-extending knowledge. What we know about them is an index of our power, and thus an index of what separates us from them. The more we know, the further away they are."[16] Indeed, treating animals as objects of inquiry is another way of saying that animals have become informational, which means that they are ontologically no longer beings in their own right, but documents that contain evidence for human use.

The journals of Meriwether Lewis and William Clark are full of accounts of sightings and killings of animals, close encounters, and data gathering. William Clark first wrote about his encounter with antelopes in an entry labeled "Missouri River, Vermilion to Teton" on 14 September 1804 (see Figure 17). He refers to the animal as a "Buck Goat" because he does not yet know what it is. He offers a detailed description:

> in my walk I Killed a Buck Goat of this Countrey, about the hight of the Grown Deer, its body Shorter the Horns which is not hard and forks 2/3 up one prong Short the other round & Sharp arched, and is imediately above its Eyes the Colour is a light gray with black behind

> its ears down its neck, and its face white round its neck, its Sides and its rump round its tail which is Short & white: Verry actively made, has only a pair of hoofs to each foot, his brains on the back of his head, his Norstrals large, his eyes like a Sheep he is more like the Antilope or Gazella of **Africa** than any other Species of Goat.[17]

Within a few days, Lewis was referring to this animal as an antelope in his own journal. He observes a great number of wolves, bison, elk, deer, and beavers, as well as the expansiveness of the landscape in this journal: "I do not think I exagerate when I estimate the number of Buffaloe which could be comprehended at one view to amount to 3000."[18] But his description of the antelope is particularly telling, as it begins, "my object was if possible to kill a female Antelope having already procured a male."[19] Already, Lewis is setting out to kill an animal so that it can be studied.

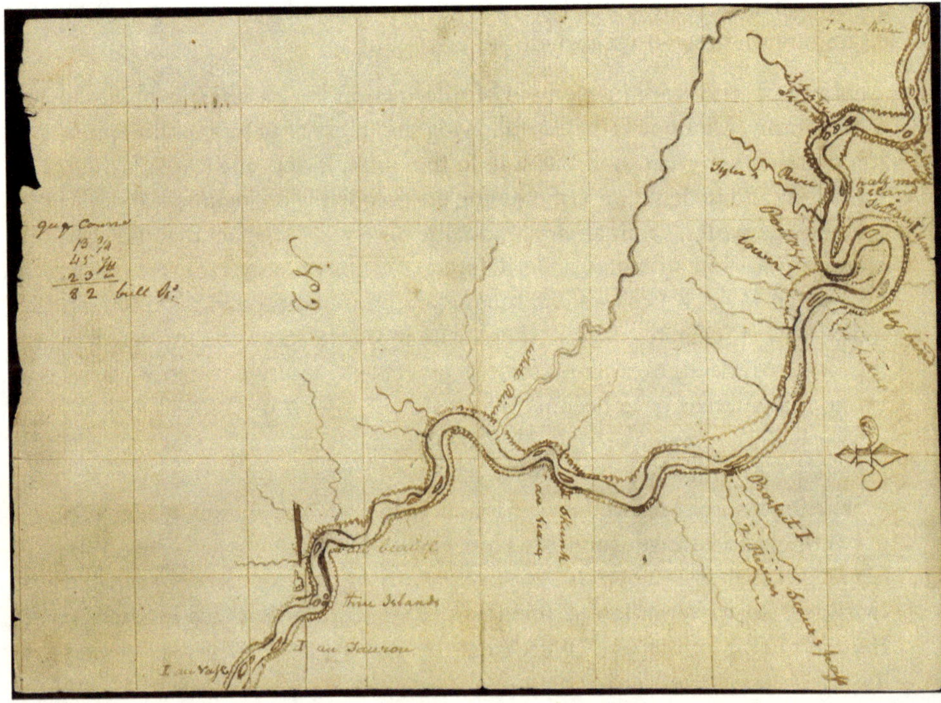

Figure 17. Map of the territory in which Lewis and Clark first captured their antelopes. In a later map drawn by the German prince, Maximilian of Wied, the area was labeled "Killed the first Antelope." Lewis and Clark Expedition maps and receipt, ca. 1803–1810, Beinecke Rare Book and Manuscript Library. See Moulton (1983), Map 29. Meriwether Lewis, 1774–1809. Evans's Map 2 (the Expedition's route about 10–23 September 1804). Box 1 | Folder 5. 1804. https://collections.library.yale.edu/catalog/2002446.

Figure 18. Titian Ramsey Peale. *American Antelope. Antilocapra americana.* 1799–1885. American Philosophical Society.

The details in this passage show in several instances just how elusive the animal is, and how difficult it is to capture:

> we had now after various windings in pursuit of several herds of antelopes which we had seen on our way made the distance of about eight miles from our camp. we found the Antelope extreemly shye and watchfull insomuch that we had been unable to get a shot at them; when at rest they generally seelect the most elivated point in the neighbourhood, and as they are watchfull and extremely quick of sight and their sense of smelling very accute it is almost impossible to approach them within gunshot; in short they will frequently discover and flee from you at the distance of three miles. I had this day an opportunity of witnessing the agility and the superior fleetness of this anamal which was to me really astonishing. . . . I got within about 200 paces of

> them when they smelt me and fled. . . . I beheld the rapidity of their flight along the ridge before me it appeared rather the rappid flight of birds than the motion of quadrupeds.[20]

Although some European explorers had encountered this animal, the Lewis and Clark expedition afforded the first scientific investigation.[21] In April of the following year, Lewis described "a most pleasing view of the country, particularly of the wide and fertile valleys formed by the Missouri and the Yellowstone Rivers. . . . The whole face of the country was covered with herds of buffalo, elk and antelope; deer are also abundant, but keep themselves more concealed in the woodland." He noted their curiosity, which was something that the antelope was particularly known for. Lewis wrote, "when we attract their attention, they frequently approach us more nearly to discover what we are, and in some instances pursue us a considerable distance apparently with that view."[22]

The antelope skins and skeletons were delivered to Jefferson's home in Washington. Six months later, on 6 October 1805, Jefferson sent two "skins of the male & female antelope with their skeletons," along with several other specimens and a living magpie and a living "burrowing squirrel" to Peale. In the letter accompanying the specimens, Jefferson expressed confusion about the antelope:

> I have some doubts whether Capt Lewis has not mistaken the Roe for the Antelope, because I have recieved from him a pair of horns which I am confident are of the Roe (tho' I never before supposed that animal to be in America) and no Antelope horns came. these you know are hollow, annulated, & single. those of the Roe are bony, solid, & branching. I hope you will have the skeletons well examined to settle this point. you will recieve them in great disorder as they came here, having been unpacked in several places on the road, & unpacked again here before I returned, so that they have probably got mixed.[23]

Just three days later, Jefferson realized he'd made an error and hurriedly sent a follow-up to Peale. He corrected himself, based on a more careful examination of the skins and skeletons (the documentary evidence), and stated "these sufficiently prove that the animal is of the Antilope family."[24] Upon the arrival of the specimens, Peale responded to Jefferson with both curiosity and frustration about the poor condition of the specimen. The antelope was itself perplexing in terms of type, and he wondered if it was a "singular Animal" in a class of its own, but they were in such "bad condition owing to the Moth &

Dermest having made great havock."[25] Peale describes this mess in detail, but remains hopeful:

> If I can mount one of the Antilopes to be decent, it will be a valuable addition to my Antilopes. I am very much obliged to Captn. Lewis for his endeavors to increase our knowledge of the Animals of that new acquired Teritory. I wish I could get one of the sheep that carry such large horns as those you have done me the favor of sending—It is more important to have this Museum supplied with the American Animals than those of other Countryes, yet for a comparative view it ought to possess those of every part of the Globe![26]

The conversation about the antelopes continued as Peale did manage to mount the antelope in April 1806. It was not perfect, but "being so interesting an Animal," he thought it better to display an imperfect specimen than no specimen at all.[27] He made a drawing of the animal and sent it to Jefferson. The drawing remains unlocated, but his son Titian Peale painted a watercolor from the mounting (see Figure 18). At the same time, he continued to be confounded by this animal and how it fits within the order of the animal kingdom. He compares all of its features to those of the common deer and elk. He examines and dissects, measures and calculates, and assesses the animal's scent, teeth, bones, hair, horns, skin, and so on: "I wish I could know more of this Animal, it may be a small Elk, as the rump is white—or a small species of Deer, having no Scar we cannot determine what the horns might have been, whether hollow or solid—Linneus gives to Deer and also to Antilopes the character of 8 front under teeth, but no mention of a difference in the size of them."[28] The ongoing discussion about this animal's position within an existing taxonomy demonstrates what Robert Montoya has observed. In his view Briet's commentary on the antelope is a bit misguided. "The truth is," writes Montoya, "that the type specimen is not related to the taxon concept as directly as we might think—and certainly not as neat and straightforward as Briet's exemplar." The function of type specimens is primarily "to anchor and regulate nomenclature" within scientific discourses.[29]

On 4 August 1806, Peale told Jefferson that he had presented the antelope drawing to the American Philosophical Society. At that meeting, "A member demanded of me, what name I gave it? to which, after a few moments reflection, I replyed *The forked Horned Antilope*. but Sir that is not a scientific name. It is not a Lattin Name but one most descriptive of the Animal, since we knew of no Antilope besides having forked Horns."[30] Peale invited Jefferson to offer a name, hoping that an Indigenous name for the animal might be applied.

The correspondence is fascinating for the way that Peale seems to find his colleagues to be pretentious for their insistence on a Latin name:

> As men pretending to a knowledge must be humoured with the high sounding names made from the dead Languages, I most humbly request of you my dear Sir, to give me a Name for this American Antilope, perhaps the Indian Name, if it could be had would be a proper one. however I leave it to your superior judgement, and shall only say that whatever you think proper to give it, will be placed in print on the Animal in the Museum, and given to the Society, as of your choise or not as you may please to direct.[31]

The name matters, and it seems that this confirms the idea that naming is entirely instrumental to the specimen entering into scientific society.[32] Peale expresses unease about naming, and although one can only speculate about his motivations in this case, it does seem likely that he felt inadequate to the task. He studied and organized animal, plant, and mineral specimens, but naming them was a responsibility that would have been outside of his wheelhouse. Jefferson seems not to have provided a name, and it was not until a decade later that it was given the name *Antilocapra americana*, which translates to "American antelope goat," by George Ord.[33] Clearly, this creature continued to confound, as the name reflects the fact that natural scientists could not determine whether it was a goat or an antelope. And with good reason.

This antelope, as it turns out, is not an antelope at all. This is in fact the pronghorn. Still, the animal continues to be referred to as the "American antelope." It is the only horned animal that sheds its horns. It is also North American in origin and habitat.

## From Antelope to Pronghorn (and Back Again)

Zoologists came closer to understanding how to position this animal in the following decades but continued to cling to the idea of the antelope. In 1866 the family name *Antilocapridae* ("goat-like antelopes") was established, and the pronghorn is the only species that belongs to that family. Scientists believe that there was a time when as many as a dozen species belonged to this family, and all except for the pronghorn have been extinct for thousands of years. It is not closely related to the African antelopes, as believed in Jefferson, Lewis, Clark, and Peale's day, and, in fact, it has no close relatives anywhere on earth.

The pronghorn is a prime example of the way that naming as a classificatory practice gets embedded in culture. To this day, the scientific name for the species is *Antilocapra americana*, and in common language it is often referred to as the pronghorn antelope. Some people continue to use "pronghorn" and "antelope" interchangeably. The pronghorn is the fastest animal in North America, and without guns, they are extraordinarily challenging to hunt. Long ago they were pursued by cheetahs, other big cats, and wolves, and are capable of running sixty miles per hour, "in bounds exceeding 20 feet."[34] They are remarkable creatures, standing three feet high, weighing 90–140 pounds, with astounding musculature. They have a large windpipe and lungs, and their heart is twice as large as other animals of the same size. Their eyes protrude so that they have a nearly 360-degree field of vision, and their eyesight is equal to a human's looking through 8× binoculars. But they did have habits and migration patterns that communities were attuned to. Pronghorn congregated in large herds and could very often be ambushed near water sources along migration routes. Another of their vulnerabilities is what people have described as their curiosity. Several stories describe the pronghorn as appearing to willingly come near people, as surprisingly tame, and even capable of domestication.

Scientists estimate that there were perhaps twenty to forty million pronghorns in western North America in 1800, before the arrival of Lewis and Clark. But the first European encounter with the species occurred in 1542, when, according to Russel Tanner, Juan de Torquemada described a hunt in western Hidalgo, Mexico: "The hunt took the form of a great drive of game by the Indians, during which 600 deer were killed, among which were large stags and those which they call *verrendo* [*sic*]," according to Torquemada.[35] The *berrendo* were what we now call pronghorns. The invention of repeating firearms during the Civil War, along with increased settlement of the western United States, led to the rampant slaughter not only of bison, but of smaller animals like the pronghorn.[36] By 1920 they were on the brink of extinction, with fewer than 15,000 pronghorns in the wild. The good news is that, due to conservation efforts of the twentieth century, the pronghorn population reached about a million by the 1980s.

Still, the increase in population, measured in numbers, does not account for the ecological loss or the loss of long-standing Indigenous relationships with the pronghorn. We have archaeological, ethnographic, documentary, and oral history evidence of the significance of the pronghorn to Indigenous life and culture. Archaeological sites in the north-central Great Basin, for example, contain hundreds of projectile points, which suggests that Indigenous communities have had elaborate communal pronghorn hunting practices for at least 4,000 to 5,000 years.[37] In the Northern Plains pronghorns were integral to the Blackfoot, Mandan, Crow, Arapaho, Arikara, Cheyenne, and Lakota communities. They used pronghorn hides for dresses, shirts, moccasin tops, and cover, hair for pillows, bones for pipes, and horns for headdresses. A Cheyenne creation story tells of a Great Race between the two-legged animals and the four-legged animals. They all ran around the Black Hills, "inside the natural enclosure formed by the sandstone rim that surrounds the interior mountain ranges." According to Linea Sundstrom, this event established a relationship in which people could hunt and consume the four-legged animals.[38] In most versions of this story, the place of the Great Race is Buffalo Gap—which matches a gap in the sandstone rim that served as the entrance to the enclosure described in the story.

Further south, pronghorns/antelopes were essential to Pueblo communities in what is now called New Mexico, and as Leslie Marmon Silko explains, their creation story is also intimately connected with the landscape. There was an eight-mile path from the natural springs to the sandstone hilltop at Laguna, which was marked with boulders, mesas, springs, and river crossings. Silko describes it as a ritual circuit that the Laguna people made as part of a way to both differentiate themselves from the other beings around them, and to honor the relationality of all beings. Silko gracefully describes how respect and appreciation for the antelope that gave its life was central to the ceremonial hunt:

> The ANTELOPE MERELY consents to return with the hunter. All phases of the hunt are conducted with love: the love the hunter and the people have for the Antelope People, and the love of the antelope who agree to give up their meat and blood so that human beings will not starve. Waste of meat or even the thoughtless handling of bones cooked bare will offend the antelope spirits. Next year the hunters will vainly search the dry plains for antelope. Thus, it is necessary to return carefully the bones and hair and the stalks and leaves to the earth, who first created them. The spirits remain close by. They do not leave us.[39]

## Taxonomic Resistance

The exchange of and correspondence about animal specimens between Jefferson and Peale is significant because they were both important players in the scientific community that believed in the efficacy of the Linnaean classification system. Recall from Chapter 4 that Jefferson regarded Linnaeus's taxonomy as both universal and useful, "because it is sufficient as a groundwork;

admits of supplementary insertions, as new productions are discovered, and mainly because it has got into so general use that it will not be easy to displace it."[40] Jefferson appreciated the flexibility of the system as it was a global system that could be modified according to local and disciplinary norms and expectations. He also recognized that it had already become so widely used that it was becoming a standard, and to try to reinvent a system would confuse matters so much as to slow scientific progress.

Greta LaFleur suggests that the Linnaean system is particularly relevant for historians of race and science because he included "humans in his taxonomy of the animal world and because he was one of the first naturalists to divide humans into regional taxa." Indeed, he organized humans according to four regions—Europaeus, Asiaticus, Americanus, and Afer, which explained and determined "'types' of humans according to phenotypic, cultural, and even characterological qualities."[41] Linnaeus revised his system over time, and eventually provided details regarding types of humans. One quickly notices the differences between his description of Indigenous (*Americanus*) and European humans:

> AMERICANUS a. reddish, choleric, erect.
> *Hair* black, straight, thick; Nostrils: wide; Face: harsh,
> *Beard* scanty.
> *Obstinate*, merry, free.
> *Paints* himself with fine red lines.
> *Regulated* by customs.
>
> EUROPAEUS b. white, sanguine, muscular.
> *Hair* flowing, long. Eyes blue.
> *Gentle*, acute, inventive.
> *Covered* with close vestments.
> *Governed* by laws.[42]

Peale was deeply invested in scientific classification for his museum of natural history and his museum was the first major museum to adopt the Linnaean classification.[43] Of course, the antelope was just one of many types of animals that were preserved, mounted, and displayed at Peale's museum. It belonged to the quadrupeds. Peale did produce a *Scientific and Descriptive Catalogue* in 1796, at the board of visitors' behest. He classified it according to Linnaeus's system, thereby placing primates as the first order of quadrupeds, which included Man, monkeys, lemurs, and bats. Based on existing criticisms of Linnaeus, he seems to anticipate resistance among his visitors and provides an explanation for how Man could be regarded as a relative of the bat: "Candid and enlightened men, however, who know that Linneaus did not attempt to form a natural system, but an artificial one, only in order to facilitate the study of this science, will perceive the injustice of their criticisms."[44] Here he leans on the ancient Greek maxim (which had been reinvoked by Linnaeus), seeming to suggest that the way that Man knows himself is by observing and measuring the animals:

> We have in this followed his example; but deeming it unnecessary to enter upon a particular description here, shall only subjoin with that celebrated naturalist, "MAN 'KNOW THYSELF.'"[45]

Peale included Indigenous remains in his museum, and classed them under "Quadrupeds, American Indian, *Homo Sapiens Americanus*, Lin." He put three Indigenous materials on display: "Skeletons of an Indian man and woman of the Wabash Nation," "Skin of the thigh, and part of the leg of an Indian," and "A piece of human skin, tanned with bark, in the common way," are in fact the first three entries in the catalog, which suggests that they may have been the among the first pieces that museum visitors would have seen.[46] It is abhorrent to us to consider the display of human remains in a national museum, and as much as I believe the catalog entry provides insights into the settler mindset, I will not reproduce it here. It is enough to know that natural historians used these remains to draw conclusions about anatomy, culture, and natural history, and then exhibited them to inform and educate the public for a fee.

Peale spent hours upon hours learning and applying the classification. Importantly, Lee Alan Dugatkin observes that, "Linnaeus's system appealed to Peale not only because of its power to organize, but because it was so in line with the Enlightenment ethos that things made sense—that complex totalities, be they political systems, cities (such as gridded Philadelphia), or the world of natural things, were interpretable and amenable to order and systematization."[47] This is key to our understanding of why such careful attention and deliberation was paid to the antelope. It was partly about the animal itself for its exceptional characteristics, but more than that, it confounded the system and challenged Peale and his colleagues in their efforts to place this animal in the order of the great chain of beings. Its refusal to be captured—both in the wild and in the totality of the system, are what made this animal such an "evocative object."[48]

The classificatory capture and the conversations, drawings, and writings in scientific circles all produced meaning about the so-called antelope. In the field of library and information studies, the antelope has become so iconic that the society called the Document Academy has made a logo in the animal's likeness. Importantly, the sign of the antelope, according to Day, "whether it be a common name, a Linnaean name, a picture of the antelope, etc.—circulates and flows in discursive networks that can't be characterized by controlled vocabulary or classification structures. Instead, these networks use the sign to point to the animal. *And the animal, and those who point, can push back on this identification*."[49]

Whereas the antelope and other life forms were intimately connected to many Indigenous communities in stories, hunting, and everyday life, the colonial universalizing classifications and their categories necessarily eliminate the complexity of knowledge associated with animals, plants, and minerals in various contexts.

Peale's attempts to put them back into context is remarkable for the way that it seems to signal the loss inflicted on the animal, but one sees that his approach is meant to entertain while it educates.[50] Rembrandt Peale, one of Peale's sons, recorded an elaborate description of the exhibit, which shows the extent to which Peale tried to recreate the natural environment. He made mounds of earth that were "covered with green turf" and trees. On that mound of earth, he exhibited birds that walk on the ground and "different kinds of wild animals—bear, deer, leopard, tiger, wild-cat, fox, raccoon, rabbit, squirrel, etc." There were snakes in a thicket, birds in the trees, and fish in an artificial pond. On a beach surrounding the pond, he mounted "an assortment of shells of different kinds, turtles, frogs, toads, lizards, water snakes, etc. In the pond was a collection of fish with their skins stuffed, water fowls, such as the different species of geese, ducks, cranes, herons, etc.; all having appearance of life, for their skins were admirably preserved."[51]

We have enough details about Peale's museum from the period in which it was located on the second floor of Independence Hall beginning in 1802 to envision its magnitude. The painting *The Long Room, Interior of Front Room in Peale's Museum* (see Figure 19) shows in detail how the exhibition was arranged. The long room was one hundred feet long and twelve feet high and featured over a thousand birds. Above them were portraits of scientists, explorers, and revolutionary figures—people such as Washington, Franklin, Rittenhouse, Lafayette, and so on. What we notice by looking at the painting of the long room is that these portraits are meant to convey order according the Linnaean system, with Man at the top. As Dugatkin explains, "Though initially the art had stood alone, separate from the other parts of the museum, soon Peale erased the physical boundary between the portraits and the natural history specimens, hanging the portraits over exhibits of the latter to capture 'the great chain of being,' from the lowly to the grand, with man atop it all."[52]

The quadrupeds were exhibited in a separate room, which was forty feet long. Peale mounted his specimens to make them look alive and in action.

Figure 19. Charles Willson Peale, Titian Ramsay Peale. *The Long Room, Interior of Front Room in Peale's Museum*, 1822. Detroit Institute of Arts.

The larger specimens were situated in natural-appearing settings, and the smaller ones were placed in glass cases, animated with painted landscape backgrounds. Very often, these paintings were of specific locations, sometimes depicting the precise spot from which the specimen was collected. These cases that featured realistic paintings of the animals' natural environments were "by all accounts, the first habitat dioramas in the United States as well as the entire world."[53] Each room, according to Robert Schofield, "contained a framed Linnaean catalogue of the genus and species of every object in it, keyed by number to the cases, and over each case, the Latin, English and French names of the objects when known."[54] Across the yard in Philosophical Hall were the mastodon, an antique room that featured archaeological and ethnological items, and a room with models of recent technological inventions.

## The Thingification of the Antelope

Let's return to Briet and the notion that "A document is a proof in support of a fact."[55] As Day writes, the professional culture of documentation has to be understood in the context in which Briet was working. The formulation of the definition of documentation, which would later be incorporated into

American information science to explain the concept of "information-as-thing" was figured into "the cultural destiny of documentation as science, which for Briet rides on the rails of earlier European colonialism, through the dominance of three European languages across the world." Indeed, the culture of documentation takes hold within "the metaphysical and political destiny of 'the West' as a culture, which in the postwar years is characterized as world development and progress."[56] It is particularly interesting that the animal she chose to exemplify a primary document and the processes of secondary documentation that grow from it is an African antelope. French colonialism in Africa, while perhaps not explicitly evident in Briet's account, resembles the documentary practices over a hundred years earlier in the United States. In his analysis of John Wesley Powell's policymaking at the helm of the late nineteenth-century Bureau of American Ethnology, Montoya suggests that "the collection of knowledge was less about the epistemic expansion of knowledge and more about the collection of knowledge-as-resource that was quickly dissipating because of the damaging US policies that were to eventually (nearly) eradicate the widespread existence of native knowledge."[57] Briet's discussion of removing an antelope from the African wild and placing it in a zoo or a museum is akin to the removal of animals from the American wild. In both cases, the capture of the antelope simultaneously advances knowledge of the colonial power.

The pronghorn in the wild is not a document. The processes by which an pronghorn becomes a document (and an antelope) are submission by force, killing, mounting, and naming. We see the relationship between naming, classification, and colonialism in this process of objectifying animals for the sake of science. And we see that epistemic violence is not just a metaphor, but that there is a series of violent acts that produces the docile subject and renders it into a document. The message that I want to drive home is twofold: genocide and colonial expansion depend on epistemological and ontological control and violence; and the recurrence of the antelope as a document to signal the concept of "information as thing" continues to participate in cartesian dichotomy that severs human/other-than-human relations and upholds the "overrepresentation of Man." The same is certainly true of the processes and practices by which human beings were rendered as informational. The stories of the mammoth and Jefferson's moose have taken on mythical proportions, and we know that they were important for several reasons, including the refutation of Buffon's claims that the American climate and landscape were inferior and would only support degenerate life. These stories engaged in conversations about climate and extinction and scientific classification.

These stories are also important in documentation theory because of the ways in which documents carry the quality of indexicality. They contain evidence. They are meant to be used. This is where the use of the antelope as an example gets particularly interesting. Buckland points to the term "evidence," which "implies passiveness." He writes, "Evidence, like information-as-thing, does not do anything actively. Human beings do things with it or to it. They examine it, describe it, and categorize it."[58] Once something becomes informational, it becomes passive. This runs counter to the Latourian notion that objects have agency, and whether or not it is an accurate characterization, Buckland's assessment is worth pursuing. He points out that "document" is derived from the Latin *docére,* which means "to teach." And he talks about evidence as being passive. But we can take this connection even further, noting that *docére* is also the root of "docile." Even Foucault (as far as I know), does not seem to notice this Latin root common to *le document* and *docile* in the connections he draws between docile subjects, documentation, and discipline.

The *Oxford English Dictionary*'s definition of docile is fascinating for the way that it indicates teaching and teachability, submission, and that this can be "*transferred* of things."

1) a) apt to be taught; ready and willing to receive instruction; teachable
   b) Submissive to training; tractable, manageable
2) *transferred* of things: Yielding readily to treatment; easily managed or dealt with; tractable[59]

The antelope—or rather, the pronghorn—strikes me as anything but docile. Indeed, the documentary evidence surrounding the pronghorn shows the extent to which natural historians struggled to name this animal, and tried to force it into categories, until it became clear that it occupies its own. It evades description, confounds taxonomy, exceeds its own name, just as it so often escaped capture in the wild. In fact, upon closer analysis, we find that the *OED* offers obsolete definitions of "document" as a noun, which parallel the concept of information-as-action described in Chapter 1 (document is also used as a verb, even today, with similar meanings): "Teaching, instruction, warning"; "An instruction, a piece of instruction, a lesson; an admonition, a warning." Both of these definitions for document as noun were in use through the eighteenth century. Another application persisted through the first half of the nineteenth century: "That which serves to show, point out, or prove something; evidence, proof"—or what we might call its indexicality.[60] Joacim Hansson argues that "the passivity of a document in Briet and Buckland's understanding is not self evident." Rather, there exists "a source of activity, or at least potential activity within the document that governs or at least has the ability to influence the social and institutional usage of it." This source, according to Hansson, "is its indexicality."[61]

The classification and documentation of animals is directly connected to the dispossession and removal of Indigenous communities from their land, knowledge, and essential sustenance. Chickasaw scholar Jodi Byrd, Alyosha Goldstein, Jodi Melamed, and Chandan Reddy, in the introduction to a special issue on dispossession, articulate the condition of making the natural world into property, and invite us to imagine otherwise:

> By decentering the human, such theories require us to consider further how colonialism has already inflected our understanding of nature, memory, and history through the production of archives and certain kinds of knowledge production that favor hegemonic white possession. . . . What would it mean to consider the land itself as a site of an agentive fungibility that has been conscripted into the proprietary spatialities of colonial possessiveness and constrained into geographies of exploitation that no longer serve the relationalities of presence and care that have for so long been its domain as a common for all? The loss of land is not just a loss of property, territoriality, power, nation, or sovereignty; it is the loss of those philosophies that derive from the relationships the land itself activates, fosters, and nourishes.[62]

The information professions and their practices are affected by the legacy of taking animals from the wild for the purposes of acquiring settler colonial knowledge, which included the cruelty and morbidity of removing animals and plants from their habitat and transporting them to a museum space in which their original habitat is re-created and the preserved remains of the dead animals are set up for display. As Danielle Taschereau Mamers writes, "To move from this multispecies site of colonization to multispecies practices of decolonization requires the withdrawal of those forms of epistemological violence that animate policies of dispossession and elimination. Specifically, such a withdrawal requires ceasing material violence: unfencing land, releasing animal-bodies from the biopolitical thrall of classification and enumeration."[63] Leanne Betasamosake Simpson insists that rather than extracting from lifeworlds to gain certain forms of knowledge that support settler colonial goals, we stay close to the land and find meaning there: "Meaning then is derived not through content or data, or even theory in a western context, which by nature is decontextualized knowledge, but through a compassionate web of interdependent relationships that are different and valuable because of that difference."[64] Removing the animal from its habitat and from the Indigenous communities that have had long-standing relationships with the pronghorn and so many other species resulted in ecological, communal, and cultural loss, not to mention the loss of pronghorns' lives and the lifeways and worlds in which these animals flourished. Still, the lives that have been thingified through processes of informationalization and documentation in different points in history have resisted and refused, blocked and deceived, or strategically submitted to documentary processes of sorting, naming, counting, and diagramming.

What the example of the pronghorn/antelope conveys is that documents are informational things that act. The infrastructures that organize and circulate information in archives, libraries, and museums are also active agents in communities, histories, and politics. What I hope has become apparent over the course of this book is the ways that Jefferson's classificatory actions shaped the early American republic and continue to affect our daily interactions with information in our human and more-than-human worlds. In a framework that understands information as revolutionary action, we understand that informative things have powers that derive from their condition of being both particular and members of a group or type. As such Day assures us that, "entities give evidence of themselves as powerful particulars (commonly called agents or actors) through their expressions, and so they are informative to others. They affect others and their future selves through these expressions. They are ontologically evident partly because of their powers."[65] This means that we individually and collectively have the power to resist taxonomic capture, and we have the capacity to commit to working toward the aims of a more equitable and just society in our libraries, archives, and museums.

# Coda

## *Afterlife of Information*

Two of Jefferson's white granddaughters, Ellen Randolph Coolidge and her sister Cornelia Randolph, visited Monticello when they heard of his passing. They missed the funeral but paid their respects independently by spending time at the house. Years later Ellen recounted how it felt to return to Monticello after Jefferson's death: "He was gone. His place was empty. I visited his grave, but the whole house at Monticello, with it's large apartments and lofty ceilings, appeared to me *one vast monument*." Still, his presence seemed to remain. "I could not always feel that I should see him no more. I wandered about the vacant rooms as if I were looking for him. Had I not seen him there all the best years of my life?" Ellen "passed hours in his chamber" and library, which she recalled in detail:

> It was just as he had left it. There was the bed on which he had slept for so many years—the chair in which, when I entered the room, I had always found him sitting—articles of dress still in their places—his clock by which he had told so many useful hours—In the cabinet adjoining were his books, the beloved companions of his leisure—his writing table from which I gathered some small relics, memoranda and scraps of paper which I still preserve. All seemed as if he had just quitted the rooms and there were moments when I felt as if I expected his return. . . . An invisible presence seemed every where to preside![1]

Ellen's description is particularly poignant for her expressed attachment to Jefferson's objects—most of all, his books. A year after visiting Monticello, in 1827, Cornelia visited his books at the congressional library, which resulted in a dramatic and emotional scene:

> I made haste to renew my acquaintance with my old friends the books particularly the annals Les beaux arts which I looked over and wished I had my pencil and paper that I might sketch the outlines of some of my favorite figures just for old acquaintance sake. the library seems to me to be a convenient room though not strikingly handsome. nevertheless I staid & stood & thought of the time when the books were ours & looked out . . . of the windows & felt so strangely as the recollections of six years old came to my mind & gradually I recognised things long long forgotten; the past returned like a dim dream & I thought whose granddaughter I was & that his fame would make the eyes of every body in the room turn on me if they knew who I was & I shrank away & hid myself in a nitch with some of the books & felt so strangely & such mixed sensations that I began to feel sick. & then I thought what a strange uproar it would make if I were to faint or have the hystericks among those strange people & then it would get out that Mr Jeffersons granddaughter had fallen into a fit at the sight of her grandfathers books & how some few persons would pity her & think it very natural & amiable & showed much feeling & how some would exclaim against the abominable affectation of the thing.[2]

That Jefferson's books could elicit such powerful emotional responses in his granddaughters is perhaps not terribly surprising, especially knowing what we do about his own *bibliomanie* realized in his book purchases and catalogs. He invested tremendous emotional labor in developing his collections, and in his moments of greatest anguish, turned to cataloging as an act of mourning. We know that as a father and grandfather, he provided instructions about books and reading, and that some of the most intimate family moments centered on shared readings.

Books as objects also carried memories of people lost and places traveled. He even kept the epitaph that he had written for his boyhood friend Dabney Carr in the book that mentioned Carr's achievements—Philip Mazzei's *Recherches historiques et politiques sur les États-Unis de l'Amérique Septentrionale*. A series of letters between Carr's son (also named Dabney) and Jefferson reveals this intimate connection between books and memorialization. Mazzei had included an account of Carr's role in proposing the establishment of a Committee of Correspondence in the Virginia National Assembly. In 1815, more than four decades after Carr's passing in 1773, his son mentioned the epitaph in a letter, prompting Jefferson to reply with a fond recollection of the elder Dabney:

> I well remember the pleasure expressed in the countenance & conversation of [the] members generally on this debut of mr Carr, &

> the hopes they conceived as well from the talents as the patriotism it manifested. but he died within two months after; & in him we lost a powerful fellow laborer. his character was of a high order.

In the same letter Jefferson asked of the younger Dabney, "You mention that I shewed you an inscription I had proposed for the tombstone of your father. did I leave it in your hands to be copied? I ask the question, not that I have any such recollection, bu[t] that I find it no longer in the place of it's deposit, and think I never took it out but on that occasion."[3] To which the younger Dabney replied:

> You ask me whether you left in my hands, the inscription you had proposed for my father's tombstone? I am very certain that you did not—I have a pretty distinct recollection, of seeing you, when about to close Mazzei's book, (from which you had read, the notice he takes of my father) put the paper, containing the inscription, (which was a small one), into the book, & shut it; & I think it very probable, that the paper is now in the book in Washington.[4]

When Jefferson realized he had left the paper with the epitaph inside one of the books that had been transferred to the Library of Congress, he asked Librarian of Congress George Watterston to retrieve it. Jefferson recalled the exact location within the classification scheme and used this to direct the librarian's search: "this work is Ch. 24. N° 246. if there, will you be so good as to inclose it to me?"[5] Indeed, Watterston found the book and the slip of paper within and promptly returned it to Jefferson.[6]

Today the Library of Congress stands as a monument to Jefferson and his legacy, as well as the foundational principles that unite knowledge and republicanism together in the liberal democratic government of the United States. A subset of the collection—indeed the original books from which the Library of Congress was formed—stand in a special exhibition room on the second floor of the Thomas Jefferson Building of the congressional library. Thousands of daily visitors view Jefferson's original collection, comprised of the books that he had at Monticello, shelved in the order in which he cataloged them. The collection stands as a testament to the durability of the connection between the United States and knowledge, and in particular, to the Library's deep connection to Jefferson the man, as well as his ideas, including the possibilities of universality and liberty.

Of the installation of Jefferson's reconstructed library in 2008, the fourteenth Librarian of Congress Carla Hayden remarks that the project changed peoples' views of Jefferson, the man. "We were certain of our understanding of

Jefferson—we knew him as a political thinker, as a president, and as a Virginia planter," writes Hayden. "Now, more than two decades later, we understand that 'knowing' Jefferson is hard work indeed. But over the years, as we have pondered the more than six thousand titles that make up his library, we have come to understand the man through his books and his correspondence. An inordinately complex Jefferson emerges—determined, expansive, deliberate, conflicted, engaged, modern, inquisitive, open, and adamant. The legacy of Jefferson, in all its complexity, is to be found in his books."[7] Jefferson's book classification is a source in which we observe a clear and direct link between library classification and democratization. His belief in public education and the notion that the best reading would inform and empower the people of the young republic may have contributed to this drive to standardize the organization of collections according to his ideal.

## Monuments, Revisited

A return to monuments brings us to thinking conceptually about documents, information, collective and national memory, and repression. In particular, we can think about the afterlife of information, and how the monumentalization of documents in the revolutionary moment continues to affect our own encounters with information in public spaces like libraries, archives, and museums. I turn here to epitaphs and gravestones to show the ways that Jefferson inscribed the lives of his white family in history, compared with his omissions and denials of Indigenous and Black burial practices and memory. There are two graveyards at Monticello—one for his white family and close friends, complete with markers that convey names of the deceased, and one for members of the Black enslaved community, the identities of whom are unknown. Today the graveyard that contains Jefferson's remains is owned and maintained by the Monticello Association, membership in which is restricted to descendants of Thomas and Martha Wayles Skelton Jefferson. Burial plots are available for "direct, lineal descendants of Thomas Jefferson, through his daughters Martha and Maria."[8]

Dabney Carr, described above, was Jefferson's closest childhood friend and became his brother-in-law by his marriage to Jefferson's sister Martha. His story is essential to the history of the graveyard at Monticello. When Carr and Jefferson were young, they went to the mountain on which Jefferson would build his home to read together beneath the shade of an oak tree. They made a promise to each other that whoever died first would be buried at the foot of this tree. Sarah N. Randolph described their friendship in *The Domestic Life of Thomas Jefferson*:

> Of the many friends by whom Jefferson was surrounded in his college days Dabney Carr was his favorite: his friendship for him was strengthened by the ties of family connection, on his becoming his brother-in-law as the husband of his sister Martha. As boys they had loved each other; and when studying together it was their habit to go with their books to the well-wooded sides of Monticello, and there pursue their studies beneath the shade of a favorite oak. So much attached did the friends become to this tree, that it became the subject of a mutual promise, that the one who survived should see that the body of the other was buried at its foot.[9]

Carr married Jefferson's sister Martha in 1765 and died at the age of thirty in 1773. According to family lore, Carr was originally buried at Shadwell while Jefferson was away, but upon his return Jefferson arranged for Carr to be reinterred at Monticello at the spot that had been promised. Here Jefferson then established his family cemetery, which would include his own burial plot. On the same paper that included the instructions for Carr's epitaph, Jefferson noted that "two hands grubbed the grave yard" of eighty square feet and calculated the amount of time required to lay out the cemetery with a fencing chain. "80. f. sq. = 1/7 of an acre in 3 ½ hours, so that one would have done it in 7. Hours, and would grub and acre in 49. Hours = 4 days."

It was of course enslaved laborers that made the graveyard at Monticello and dug the ground for the burial of Jefferson's friends and white family members.

Jefferson also planned to have an engraved copper plate "to be nailed on the tree at the foot of [Carr's] grave," with lines borrowed from Alexander Pope's "Elegy to the Memory of an Unfortunate Lady":

> Still shall thy grave with rising flow'rs be dress'd
> And the green turf lie lightly on thy breast:
> There shall the morn her earliest tears bestow,
> There the first roses of the year shall blow:
> While angels with their silver wings o'ershade
> The ground now sacred by thy reliques made.

Jefferson loved Alexander Pope's poetry. His *Iliad* is on the 1771 list of books that he'd sent to Skipwith, and this passage, as well as many other excerpts from Pope's works, are included in the "Literary Commonplace Book" that Jefferson made between the ages of fifteen and thirty and his Garden Book.[10]

Writing epitaphs was for Jefferson a very particular form of writing, and he frequently drew lines from poets that would have signaled the bond between himself and the person he had lost to death. For his wife Martha's epitaph, he transcribed lines from Homer's *Iliad* in Greek that convey the lament for Patroclus spoken by Achilles after his triumph over Hector: "Though the dead forget their dead in the House of Death, I will remember, even there, my dear companion." Before he died, Jefferson wrote his own epitaph, along with instructions for the composition of his tombstone, reflecting first, could the dead feel any interest in Monuments or other remembrances of them, when, as:

Anacreon says Ολιγη δε κειςομεςθα
Κονις, οστεων λυθεντων

[We shall lie down as a small amount of dust, our bones being dissolved.]

His epitaph was to include the achievements for which he wanted to be most remembered.

'Here was buried
Thomas Jefferson
Author of the Declaration of American Independence
of the Statute of Virginia for religious freedom
& of the University of Virginia.'

He added that the obelisk should be made of the same "course stone" as the columns of his house so that people would not try to destroy the obelisk for the value of the stone. As much as Jefferson tried to control how he would be remembered—through his archival practices, political actions, architectural designs, and his own gravestone—he and the people in his milieu left enough traces for other impressions of the man to be exposed. Although he took care not to leave a paper trail that identified Sally Hemings's children as his own, "to shield his white family from further notoriety," the inclusion of the manumission of his enslaved sons and Sally's brother John in his will "reveal something of the Black family network as it then existed, and never again would, at Monticello."[11] And he could not have imagined that "the words of Black Americans would be as carefully analyzed as his own and that their representations of him as a paradoxical patriarch would largely shape the current and popular consensus."[12]

There is a stark contrast between the burial grounds for his white and Black families, and the distance between the two set by their locations at opposite sides of the mountain underscores the intentionality of the division between white and Black. The omission of names and markers, the fact that the Burial Ground for Enslaved People at Monticello only contains the remains of forty people—a small fraction of the over four hundred people who lived and labored at Monticello in Jefferson's lifetime (over six hundred across his properties)—and that it follows that we do not know where the other enslaved bodies rest, stands as an important set of statements regarding the production of knowledge in collective memory. Despite Jefferson's reputation as a meticulous bookkeeper, to my knowledge, we have no documentation in his hand of any burial grounds or funerals for the people he enslaved. The burial ground for the people who were enslaved at Monticello is located about two thousand feet south of the main house, near what is now the visitor parking lot. Monticello archaeologists identified the graveyard in 2001, and in that year, a commemorative ceremony was given, with remarks from Julian Bond, president of the NAACP and Daniel P. Jordan, president of the Thomas Jefferson Foundation. The Burial Ground for Enslaved People was rededicated in a private ceremony attended by descendants from all over the country in 2022, following completion of the project led by guidance from the Getting Word advisory committee, a "group of descendants representing the interests of multiple families enslaved on this plantation." Now the space includes "more accessible pathways, new plantings, dedicated parking for descendants, additional seating, and new signage."[13] Some of the graves have uninscribed fieldstones at the head or foot, but most have no surviving markers, and none are labeled to give any indication who is buried there. We do not know where Sally Hemings is buried.

As for Indigenous communities in Virginia, we have already observed the ways that Jefferson dug into Monacan burial mounds to study them, as well as his lists, classifications, and ethnographic descriptions of Indigenous peoples. One of the Comte de Marbois's queries requested information about the Indigenous communities in Virginia: "A description of the Indians established in the state before the European settlements and those who are still remaining. An indication of the Indian *monuments* in that state."[14] In his description of the Monacan burial grounds that he had excavated, Jefferson replied using Marbois's terminology: "I know of no such thing existing as an Indian monument: for I would not honour with that name arrow points, stone hatchets, stone pipes, and half-shapen images." To his mind, the mounds did not rise to the status of monuments, nor did the implements and possibly ceremonial objects that remained with the bones of the dead. He recalled witnessing people visiting the site thirty years earlier and discerned that this was a place in which people had been buried, and he concluded that some form of ritual had taken place there:

> But on whatever occasion they may have been made, they are of considerable notoriety among the Indians: for a party passing, about thirty years ago, through the part of the country where this barrow is, went through the woods directly to it, without any instructions or enquiry, and having staid about it some time, with expressions which were construed to be those of sorrow, they returned to the high road, which they had left about half a dozen miles to pay this visit, and pursued their journey.[15]

Jefferson provided extensive details about his archaeological methods and findings, but neglected to include an account of the laborers who would have performed the manual work of excavating this site. Jeffrey Hantman calls this to attention, noting that the "scale of the excavation he reports would have required the use of additional labor, almost certainly enslaved laborers, either from his Monticello plantation or from the plantation of the property owner." They dug a trench through the center of the mound, "wide enough for a man to walk through and examine its sides." Jefferson estimated that a thousand bodies were buried in this mound.[16] What he seems unable to appreciate were the Monacans' memorializing practices as such. In Jonathan Elmer's assessment, "Everything about this native archive seems ambiguous and unreliable," including the acts of mourning. "In this aboriginal archive, both affect and event seem bound to each other by relations only uncertainly graspable by Jefferson." Elmer concludes, "This is a monument which is not really recognized as such: no longer nature but not yet culture."[17] It is the inscrutability of the mounds according to his own worldview that leads Jefferson to determine that they cannot be considered monuments. This illegibility also fueled his curiosity and the rendering of the sacred site into an object of study, rather than a place worthy of preservation and safety from harm.

In fact, the mound was the result of dozens of acts of secondary burials. This location was meant to be the final resting place in a process that included an initial burial, decomposition, and a secondary burial within five to seven years. Each secondary burial included approximately twenty-five people, and roughly fourteen of these secondary burials, totaling around 350 individuals, would have taken place per century. The ritual secondary burial at the mound is estimated to have been carried out for at least three hundred years. Each addition added to the height of the mound, until it reached at least twelve feet, and forty feet in diameter. "Furthermore," Hantman writes, "knowing from Jefferson's account that Indian people visited the

Rivanna Mound even after it was no longer the site of bone deposition, the life of the mounds as burial sites and cemeteries should almost certainly be measured in centuries." This "conveys a regional picture with permanence of place and territory, and one not forgotten when the adjacent kings' house or town was left. The bones of the ancestors placed into a living, sacred earthwork defined the Monacan landscape."[10] The fact that Jefferson could not see these sites as monuments in the sense in which he described other burial markers, documents, and edifices is a reflection of his limited vision. This point of view may well have derived from and certainly seemed to have been used as justification for the conviction that Indigenous people did not possess histories of their own and that their knowledge systems and rituals were proper material for Western scientific study. Whereas Jefferson recorded data that he collected about Indigenous communities, languages, and burial practices in documents like *Notes on the State of Virginia* and other scholarly communications for the purpose of advancing science and nation, we might also view this as documentary evidence of destruction and genocide as it was happening. That Jefferson was documenting his own actions and the consequences thereof, many of which are ongoing, leaves us with a complicated set of problems that are perhaps impossible to reconcile.

Indeed, Monticello itself has become a museum. One of the strengths of Monticello as a museum and tourist destination is its ongoing reclamation of the stories of the enslaved people that lived there. Visitors can view and learn about Mulberry Row, where enslaved laborers made nails, textiles, furniture, and building materials. They can see Jefferson's elaborate gardens, with the cultivars that he grew and studied, as well as restored slave quarters and the cemeteries for Jefferson's white family and members of the enslaved community. The house itself has been restored according to his design for his library, study, bedrooms, dining room, and so on. Underneath the main house, visitors learn about the cellar, where food and wine were stored and prepared and where enslaved people conducted the work of Jefferson's domestic life, out of view. Upon entering the main house, visitors are welcomed by a room filled with scientific gadgets, paintings, art objects, and artifacts collected from natural history expeditions. Historians, archaeologists, and museum workers have consulted Jefferson's documents and regathered the objects that he once exhibited in his museum in the entryway to his house, which he referred to as to his "Indian Hall." From my visits to Monticello, I have gleaned that this room arouses great interest in visitors, eliciting questions about the objects and how they arrived in Jefferson's hands. Although there are acknowledgments, there isn't a great emphasis on the Monacans who inhabited the land on which the house stands or the imperialist aims of the Lewis and Clark mission that resulted in Jefferson's ownership of objects that came from several Indigenous tribes that would soon be removed from their lands, as well as animals and plants that arrived both dead and alive for study and cultivation. Fundamentally, the entryway to Jefferson's house is staged to educate and inform visitors about Jefferson the collector and scientist.

## Angels of History

Where does this awareness of the mechanisms of racialization in information leave us? Are we living amid the afterlife of Jefferson's information and classificatory techniques? Some might say that, with the massive rise in artificial intelligence, information has taken on a life of its own. We are certainly experiencing a moment in which information and the public institutions that facilitate access to information with the aim of supporting democratic processes, as well as the government, are under the threat of increasing privatization, underfunding, distrust, disinformation, and President Trump's antidemocratic, anti-diversity agenda.

Let's again consider the angels of history. In his first inaugural address, Jefferson stated:

> Sometimes it is said that man cannot be trusted with the government of himself. Can he then be trusted with the government of others? Or have we found angels, in the form of kings, to govern him? Let history answer this question.

Walter Benjamin provides a response: "Where we perceive a chain of events, he sees one single catastrophe which keeps piling wreckage upon wreckage and hurls it in front of his feet. The angel would like to stay, awaken the dead, and make whole what has been smashed."

The 250th anniversary of the signing of the Declaration of Independence—the Fourth of July in 2026—provides us with a "revolutionary now-time" to think about how to redeem our public institutions, without further deferring the urgent task of reassembling the social worlds of information. Might we put information to work toward an intentionally reparative, more democratic future?

As I hope this book has demonstrated, Jefferson's ideas about freedom and equality continue to shape our own institutions, including the limits to his vision and the contradictions of his stated and enacted positions. What we are witnessing in this moment is a perverse inversion of that vision—one that aims to increase wealth and power for a select few and deny freedoms and rights for others and is predicated on white supremacy and heteropatriarchal rule.

At the same time, this administration is attacking precisely the institutions that are meant to uphold freedom. They know that access to information and spaces for gaining knowledge and gathering are sources of democratic participation. Many of us have chosen the information professions because we believe that they have transformative potential. I have witnessed some of the most heroic acts of leadership and daily interactions in the types of public institutions described here. When Trump was first elected, for instance, a bilingual public library branch that I had frequented invited lawyers to offer a Spanish and English language information session for immigrants in the city. The room was overflowing with families worried about their rights. This is a branch that provides Spanish language collections, a fully bilingual staff, after school homework help (with snacks), and extraordinary programming and workshops for youth. This is just one of thousands and thousands of stories of community-centered work that happens in local libraries, archives, and museums.

I am putting the final touches on this coda on 13 May 2025—by the time this book is in your hands the events of this moment will have unfolded in ways that I can't possibly predict. President Trump has just unceremoniously "fired" Carla Hayden, the first African American Librarian of Congress and the first woman Librarian of Congress. Appointed by President Barack Obama, Carla Hayden highlighted and advanced the library's efforts toward diversity, inclusion, and equity, along with advanced extraordinary technologies, and local, national, and global conversations about reading and information. Staff and members of Congress are pushing back on the attempt to appoint the deputy attorney general and Trump's personal attorney to the post. Two days ago, the Trump administration also terminated Shira Perlmutter, the director of the US Copyright Office, where questions concerning authorship and intellectual property are being challenged by advances in AI. Hayden appointed Perlmutter to lead the Copyright Office in 2020. Earlier in his term Trump also dismissed Colleen Shogan, the head of the National Archives and Records Administration—the agency that recovered fifteen boxes of classified materials from Trump's Mar-a-Lago estate in 2022. And the Institute of Museums and Library Services (IMLS) has been hijacked and defunded, meaning that essential research, programming, and services have been halted.

In this moment in which many of us worry about the future of democracy at the hands of corporate interests, the acceleration of propaganda, and the annihilation of institutions, I believe that one of the most significant things we can do is to guard the core principles upon which public institutions were founded and to honor the aspiration toward freedom and equality. By responding to the findings put forth in this book through repair, revision, and reinvention of organizing principles, the task of unsettling the coloniality and heteropatriarchal assumptions that are built into the systems that organize information is as urgent as ever, and differently challenging under President Trump. I will admit that writing this closing chapter has been a daunting exercise in hope. Critical Race Theory, Ethnic Studies, and Queer and Trans Studies are among the fields of inquiry under fire. Library workers are being criminalized and their jobs terminated, while collections are eviscerated, and the cultural institutions described here are being defunded and dismantled. History is being rewritten according to a radical right vision for white supremacy masked as a "colorblind," "merit-based" society.

My sense is that this moment is presenting an urgent call to come together in various communities and locales to reassemble information so that it acts in accord with an equitable vision for a diversity of information users, needs, and desires. Perhaps this moment is best regarded as a messianic one, akin to the moment predicted by Walter Benjamin. Andy McLaverty-Robinson provides a useful explanation of the concept, particularly with regard to objects:

> The messianic moment also ruptures things from their particular locations in an order of things. Objects, ruins, ideas and language become rearticulable, or can be "redeemed" (something Benjamin also relegates to allegories, collecting, and nonstandard uses). An old factory is "redeemed" as a squat, a community is "redeemed" as meaningful to a collector, a word is "redeemed" by being used allegorically. A date such as Mayday, or November 17th in Greece, can capture a range of historical precedents and "redeem" them in present revolt, ignoring the time-lapses in between.[19]

This means standing up for the expansion of accessibility, the inclusion of diverse books and programming, support for the workers on the front lines, and actively engaging in these places to realize their potential as spaces of appearance and political participation. It also means sustaining and forming partnerships with community archives, libraries, and museums, as well as perpetual consultation with community members and expanding the possibilities for local and international interventions in organizing information. There are many efforts along these lines, but a few stand in my mind as excellent models for those aims.[20] I highlight them here, in part because they are the products of communities whose stories and histories the far right is trying to erase. The Getting Word African American Oral History Project, for example, collects the oral histories of Monticello's enslaved families and their descendants. Getting Word was initiated in 1993 by Lucia Stanton and Dianne Swann-Wright, with consultation from Beverly Gray. Today over two hundred stories have been told and archived, in addition to family photographs, newspaper articles, and private and public papers. What is so often overlooked in Jefferson's legacy is the fact that his own death left Black families at the mercy of his white family, who auctioned the enslaved people over the course of five days on the Monticello lawn to avoid their own financial ruin.[21] He left a debt of $107,000—nearly 3.5 million in today's dollars.[22] This meant that several families were separated, with some enslaved people being sold to enslavers in states in the Deep South to labor on large-scale cotton plantations.[23] It also means that the storytellers were redistributed to many locations, making it even more difficult to trace family ties. By foregrounding the histories of the Black families who lived and labored at Jefferson's plantations, talking to their descendants, and gathering them together for events at Monticello and beyond, the Thomas Jefferson Foundation is recasting the narrative, forming "an archive of freedom." Public Relations and Community Engagement Officer at Monticello Gayle Jessup White, a descendant of the Hemingses and Thomas Jefferson, has described the significance of oral history in her own family:

> Like most African Americans, oral history is my primary source for deep family roots. There are not birth certificates, marriage licenses or census records. Our great-great grandmothers, great-great grandfathers, aunts, uncles and cousins were items on manifests, bills of sale and plantation ledgers. Sometimes, our forefathers or their families owned our foremothers.

It was via these oral histories, along with painstaking historical research with Lucia Stanton and others including the Getting Word project, that Jessup White learned the truth of her story.[24] Along with this ongoing project is also the exhibit that tells Sally Hemings's story in what is believed to have been her living quarters at Monticello, the tours that focus on the stories of the enslaved community, the archaeological studies of their dwellings across the plantation, and the renovation of their burial grounds.

Other projects center on classification systems for communities for which global systems like the Library of Congress Classification and Subject Headings have been found to be limited in precision, scope, or naming conventions. The *Homosaurus* is a lovely example of a community-based vocabulary for queer and trans materials in libraries, archives, and museums. Initially begun as a Dutch thesaurus by Jack van der Wel in 1982, the vocabulary was expanded over the following decades and translated into English in 1997. Nearly a decade later K. J. Rawson applied the vocabulary to the emerging Digital Transgender Archive, and by 2015 the *Homosaurus* was converted into a linked data vocabulary. The *Homosaurus* is not only an exceptionally useful tool, but it is a politically urgent project, as rights for 2SLGBTQIA+ people are increasingly under the threat of violence and censorship. Its extraordinarily expansive vocabulary has been created with wide consultation and uses terms that members of the 2SLGBTQIA+ community are likely to prefer.

For Indigenous materials, the Xwi7xwa (pronounced "whei wha") library at the University of British Columbia has developed a variant of the Brian Deer Classification System, developed by Kahnawake librarian Brian Deer in the 1970s for the National Indian Brotherhood (now the Assembly of First Nations). The only Indigenous branch of an academic library in Canada, the X̱wi7x̱wa library also uses First Nations House of Learning subject headings developed at the University of British Columbia to better reflect Indigenous peoples' knowledges, histories, and identities. Terms from the *Homosaurus* and the First Nations House of Learning Subject Headings can be written into catalog records of libraries of all types, along with Library of Congress Subject Headings, and they can also be used to organize and facilitate access to archival, museum, and digital collections.[25] These initiatives demonstrate ways that community archives and community-based researchers can partner with institutions that possess the technical infrastructure, funding, and staff to sustainably support them.[26]

■

The American War of Independence arose out of collective action toward a common cause. As Arendt attests, "the specifically American experience had taught the men of the Revolution that action . . . can be accomplished only by some joint effort in which the motivation of single individuals" are given over to the collective.[27] The Declaration of Independence was a revolutionary event in writing, and after the war was won, the main task for the revolutionaries was "not how to limit power but how to establish it, not how to limit government but how to found a new one." If, writes Arendt, "one keeps in mind that the end of rebellion is liberation, while the end of revolution is the foundation of freedom . . . the Constitution of the United States [is] the true culmination of this revolutionary process."[28] The drafting and ratification of the US Constitution was another documentary event that ushered in a new form of government that would check the powers of the country's leaders. The establishments of libraries, museums, public squares, and archives, as sites adjacent to agencies of government, were also constitutive events. Public cultural institutions were essential to constituting a government by and for the people, and the political reason by which these agencies collected, organized, and circulated information for the instruction of the citizens is directly tied to the establishment of laws and order of the newly formed United States. The body politic, government, memory and educational institutions, and information were co-constitutive in the revolutionary moment in which the United States was formed. The fact that they are the target of fascist, right-wing vitriol is a sign that they are seen to be strongholds of democracy.

Imperfect as they may be, I believe strongly that democracy requires us to defend our public libraries, archives, and museums. I believe that they are monuments to a vision for the expansion of democracy, and even when (or perhaps especially when) their core values of protecting privacy, public ownership, collective and shared use, and equity of access are threatened or undermined, they stand as a testament to the ongoing and necessarily incomplete project toward freedom.

# Acknowledgments

This book would not be possible were it not for library, archives, and museum workers and the institutions they serve. I extend gratitude to Endrina Tay and Anna Berkes at the Jefferson Library at the Robert Smith International Center for Jefferson Studies (ICJS) for their constant research support, as well as Megan Brett, who started working there just before my final research trip in Charlottesville. Thanks to the ICJS for the two short-term residential fellowships, and everything that they entailed, including the housing on Tufton Farm. Of course, I must also thank the library and archives staff at the Library of Congress, especially Cheryl Fox. Many thanks to the archives staff at the University of Virginia's Small Library, the Beinecke Library at Yale University, the American Philosophical Society Library, and the Warburg Institute Library. Thanks also to the librarians and collections at Western University Libraries, the Faculty of Information & Media Studies Graduate Library, Huron University Library, and London Public Library in London, Ontario. I also want to acknowledge the tremendous work of the archivists who have digitized the founders' papers in *Founders Online*, an extraordinary resource that allowed me to conduct most of my research from home.

Thanks to Andrew O'Shaughnessy for welcoming me to the ICJS while he was director and providing essential support during my two fellowships there. Andrew was also my undergraduate history professor at the University of Wisconsin-Oshkosh, and along with Jeanie Grant Moore, led a life-changing semester abroad in Cambridge, England. I especially want to thank Jeanie for encouraging me to embark upon that journey, which has put me on a path of study. Thanks also to Andrew Davenport, John Ragosta, Whitney Pippin, and archaeologists Fraser Neiman and Derek Wheeler at the ICJS. And to Patrick Spero, Adrianna Link, and Brian Carpenter for their invitation to discuss my work in progress and their research support at the American Philosophical Society.

I must thank my friends, some of whom read chapters in addition to providing sustenance, conversation, inspiration, and warmth: David Nemer, David Janzen, Kate Lawless, Ron Day, Luke Stark, Chris Koottatep, Joanna Redden, Basil Chiasson, Carol Mason, Rachel Elliott, Dorit Osher, Tom Streeter, Jo Rivas, and Paul Meadows. Special thanks to Gail Atkinson-Ireland and the community at Elements Yoga. Thanks to a few current and former graduate students who provided brilliant research and editorial support: Jack Kausch, Karolina Kayco, and Marnie James. And to the many graduate students at Western who have enriched my thinking: Alec Mullender, Gigi Wong, Mackenzie Jessop, Leslie Shi, Jasmine Proctor, Revna Altiok, Eden Hoffer, Hillary Anderson, Selena Gignac, D. Saint Amour, and Amber Matthews. Thanks also to Michelle Wilson.

Thanks to Western University and FIMS for the generous funding and for being a place at which I love to work. It's a special honor to teach in a program that insists on "the L" in Library and Information Studies, as well as community, critique, creating, and doing. Thanks to Lisa Henderson, Isola Aserjifuke, and Karen Kueneman for the research support, as well as the Social Science and Humanities Research Council, which supported the research on the museum chapters. Much gratitude to Tom Glynn, Nathan Snaza, and an anonymous reviewer for their careful review of the manuscript. Nathan, I especially appreciate our ongoing conversations. Thanks to James Crimmins, Endrina Tay, and Andrew O'Shaughnessy for reading a chapter back when I thought this was only going to be an article. Thanks also to Paul Edwards for reading an earlier rendition of this work.

Thanks to some of the most extraordinary librarians I have had the pleasure to know: Emily Drabinski, Baharak Yousefi, Hazel Jane Plante, Courtney Waugh, Kristen Hoffmann, Greg Nightingale, and so many others of course. Thanks to all of the aspiring librarians and archivists who have come through the MLIS program at Western.

To Richard Morrison at Fordham I am so grateful for your friendship and faith in this ongoing library research project. Thanks to Lis Pearson for your eagle eye. A special thanks to Kem Crimmins and team for your patience and fortitude. Thanks to Cathy Hannabach and Rachel Fudge at Ideas on Fire for reviewing two chapters.

Thanks to Penn State, Florida Libraries, and Rachel Ivy Clarke at Syracuse University. Thanks to Julia Bullard and Hannah Turner for invitations to present an early version of Chapter 8. I have presented parts of this work at several association meetings, including the International Communication

Association, the American Studies Association, the American Library Association, 4S, and the Document Academy. An earlier version of Chapter 8 appeared in the *Canadian Journal of Information and Library Science*. Thanks to Greg Nightingale for allowing me to reuse a small portion of our co-authored *Proceedings of the Document Academy* paper in Chapter 7. Thanks to Greg also for suggesting Benjamin's line, "glass before its time, premature iron," in relation to AI. For the record, I did not use AI tools like ChatGPT or Grammarly in any phase of writing, editing, or indexing. Any errors in this text are my own.

I am a settler—European by descent, American by birth, and Canadian by choice and circumstance. I grew up in Green Bay, Wisconsin (home of the Packers). The city of Green Bay occupies the ancestral home of the Menominee Tribe of Wisconsin and the Ho-Chunk Nation, who have resided in Northeast Wisconsin for over 10,000 years. Today, Green Bay has a rich urban Indigenous community, and the state of Wisconsin is home to twelve First Nations communities including the Menominee Tribe of Wisconsin, the Ho-Chunk Nation, Oneida Nation of Wisconsin, Forest County Potawatomi, Ojibwe Nation communities, Stockbridge-Munsee Community Band of Mohican Indians, and the Brothertown Indian Nation.

My grandmother was a public librarian in Marshfield, Wisconsin, and she and my dad instilled in me an appreciation for libraries from early childhood. I originally wanted to work in a public library, too, but the job I got right out of library school was in an academic library in a small Catholic university run by the Sisters of Saint Agnes in Fond du Lac. After four years, I decided to return to school and signed up to do a PhD at the University of Wisconsin-Madison. Beginning in 2013 I worked as an assistant professor at the University of Kentucky, on lands inhabited for millennia by the ancestors of the Shawnee, Cherokee, Chickasaw, and other Nations. In 2017 I moved to London, Ontario, on land connected with the London Township and Sombra Treaties of 1796 and the Dish with One Spoon Covenant Wampum and through which the river Deshkan Ziibi (Antler River, now referred to as the Thames) flows. This land is the traditional territory of the Anishinaabek, Haudenosaunee, Lūnaapéewak, and Chonnonton Nations, and today the Chippewas of the Thames First Nation, Oneida Nation of the Thames, and Munsee-Delaware Nation are downriver from London.

# Notes

## Prologue

1. Hayes, *Road to Monticello*, 563.

2. The Copyright Act was enacted into law in 1790, when Jefferson was secretary of state. He administered the law and also signed the 1793 Patent Act. The Copyright Act of 1870 resulted in the centralization of copyright in the Library of Congress and required the submission of two copies of copyrighted works.

3. Quoted in Smith, "Copyright at 125."

4. Thomas Jefferson (hereafter TJ) to George Watterston, 7 May 1815, *Founders Online*, National Archives, https://founders.archives.gov/documents/Jefferson/03-08-02-0376. (emphasis added).

5. See Tennis and Jacob, "Toward a Theory of Structure": "A statement is an assertion of a relationship between a resource of interest, an attribute that can be ascribed to that resource, and the value of the attribute as it applies to the subject resource. As such, a statement is a representation of a resource that conforms to the subject-predicate-object format of a simple clause." They continue by saying that classifications are statements about the topics and intellectual content of information resources.

6. Library of Congress, Classification, E: History, 43.

7. I am using the Library of Congress Classification schedules available via the Library of Congress website. They were revised in 2024. https://www.loc.gov/aba/publications/FreeLCC/freelcc.html.

8. Library of Congress Classification, E 185.62–E 185.86: "United States—Elements in the population—African Americans—Special topics," transcribed from the 2024 edition. https://www.loc.gov/aba/publications/FreeLCC/freelcc.html.

9. Browne, *Dark Matters*, 9.

10. Library of Congress, Classification, J: Political Science, 33.

11. Library of Congress, Classification, H: Social Science, 596.
12. Foucault, *Discipline and Punish*, 143.
13. David J. Hudson writes that whiteness is "the production of shared norms underwritten by physical and epistemological violence, a violence invisibilized as a condition of governance." Hudson, "Whiteness of Practicality," 214.
14. Butler, "Endangered/Endangering," 16.
15. Beauchamp, *Going Stealth*, 20.
16. Fanon, *Black Skin White Masks*, 82.
17. Foucault, *History of Sexuality*, 11.
18. Davenport, "Mourning at Monticello," 44–45. Davenport's post as vice president was announced in early 2025 and before that he was director of the Getting Word African American Oral History Project at Monticello.
19. Arendt, *The Human Condition*, 50.
20. Arendt, *The Human Condition*, 52.
21. Honig, *Public Things*, 4.
22. Arendt, *The Human Condition*, 52–53.
23. Butler, *Notes Toward a Performative Theory of Assembly*, 127.
24. Klinenberg, *Palaces for the People*, 5.
25. Drabinski, "The Library is a Commons."
26. Hardt and Negri, *Assembly*, 292.
27. Hardt and Negri, *Assembly*, xvi.

## Note on Language, Spelling, Naming, and Citationality

1. Liboiron, *Pollution is Colonialism*, 3n10.
2. McKittrick, *Dear Science and Other Stories*, 27–28. I feel compelled to note that "Books and Papers Scattered about on the Floor," is a reference to Nella Larsen's *Quicksand*, 13. McKittrick provides the citation in a footnote but doesn't explain. *Quicksand* is widely regarded as a semi-autobiographical novel. Larsen's mother was a white immigrant to the United States from Denmark, and her father was a Black immigrant from the Danish West Indies. Larsen was a part of the Harlem Renaissance, and a librarian at The New York Public Library. She fell into obscurity after racially charged accusations of plagiarism. See Godfrey, "Rewriting White, Rewriting Black"; and Hochman, "Love and Theft."
3. Liboiron, *Pollution is Colonialism*, 3n10.

## Introduction: "These Precious Monuments of Our Property and Our History"

1. The resurgence of the organization in Charlottesville had begun well before the statues were erected. The *Daily Progress* reported on 1 November 1916, that in the midst of a Halloween parade, "a gay battalion of Ku Klux Klan came thundering down from the heights of the Midway, recalling other days." The KKK was first

formed after the Civil War, and was revived in around 1915, following the release of the film *Birth of a Nation*. Von Daacke and Schmidt, "UVA and the History of Race."

2. This and the previous quote are from "Ku Klux Klan Organized Here."

3. Court Square Park was originally named Jackson Park and has also been named Justice Park.

4. "Jackson Statue is Unveiled," 3.

5. Edgar Shannon was president of the University of Virginia, 1959–1974.

6. Alderman, "Address of Acceptance."

7. LeFevre, "Presentation Address," 1.

8. Thomas Jefferson (hereafter TJ) to George Rogers Clark, 19 April 1780, *Founders Online*, National Archives, https://founders.archives.gov/documents/Jefferson/01-03-02-0427.

9. Jefferson formerly owned the land at Montalto.

10. "Cross Burned on Patterson Mountain."

11. Originally, the county estate "Belmont" was owned by John M. Carr, the nephew of Dabney Carr, Thomas Jefferson's boyhood friend. It was later owned by Slaughter Ficklin, who used the land as a horse-breeding farm. It was converted into a subdivision in the 1890s and was a majority white working-class and poor neighborhood in the early twentieth century. Now it is regarded as a trendy neighborhood in Charlottesville.

12. The park was originally named Lee Park, was renamed Emancipation Park in June 2017, and renamed again to Market Street Park in July 2018. The Vinegar Hill neighborhood—homes, businesses, and cultural and religious spaces—was entirely demolished by the city of Charlottesville in 1965, as part of an "urban renewal" initiative. In 2011 the City Council issued an apology. See Saunders and Shackleford, *Urban Renewal and the End of Black Culture in Charlottesville, Virginia*; Moomaw, "Charlottesville Officially Apologizes"; Montalvo, "Vinegar Hill Remembered."

13. Rothman, "When Bigotry Paraded through the Streets."

14. "Virginia Health Bulletin." It wasn't until 1967 that the Racial Integrity Act was overturned by the US Supreme Court in the *Loving vs. Virginia* case.

15. Rothman, "When Bigotry Paraded through the Streets."

16. Mitchell, "Monuments, Memorials, and the Politics of Memory," 443.

17. "Ku Klux Klan," 3.

18. Von Daacke and Schmidt, "UVA and the History of Race." Baker, *Charlottesville*.

19. Pearce, "Chanting 'Blood and Soil.'"

20. Laughland, "White Nationalist Richard Spencer," para. 9.

21. Southern Poverty Law Center, "Hate Groups Reach Record High."

22. Nelson, "Why We Voted for Donald Trump."

23. See Bodroghkozy, *Making #Charlottesville* for a comparison of the Unite the Right rally with the Civil Rights era.

24. Armus and Natanson, “Charlottesville Takes Down Two More Statues.” The University of Virginia continues to refer to its campus as “Grounds,” a legacy of Jefferson’s original designs for the “academical village.”

25. Armus and Green, “Charlottesville’s Lee Statue Meets Its End.”

26. “Swords Into Plowshares,” https://sipcville.com/?itid=lk_inline_enhanced-template.

27. McCanse, “Rector Reaffirms,” para. 4.

28. It is actually a replica of a larger statue in Louisville, Kentucky, erected in 1901. Ezekiel designed both.

29. Thomas Soh, “Slavery in Charlottesville.”

30. For a framing of the Charlottesville riots in terms of free speech, see P. E. Moskowitz, *The Case Against Free Speech: The First Amendment, Fascism, and the Future of Dissent* (New York: Bold Type Books, 2019), chapter 1.

31. TJ to John Dickinson, 6 March 1801, *Founders Online,* National Archives, https://founders.archives.gov/documents/Jefferson/01-33-02-0156.

32. TJ to James Madison, 6 September 1789, *Founders Online,* National Archives, https://founders.archives.gov/documents/Jefferson/01-15-02-0375-0003.

33. TJ to William Stephens Smith, 13 November 1787, *Founders Online,* National Archives, https://founders.archives.gov/documents/Jefferson/01-12-02-0348.

34. I am borrowing “thingification” from Césaire, *Discourse on Colonialism.*

35. See Day, *The Modern Invention of Information.*

36. It is generally agreed upon that “After 1400, we see rulers across Europe shifting their record keeping from strongboxes full of charters to writing offices that managed archives filled with letters, reports, and deliberations. These archives became an important new site for producing information of value to rulers,” Head, “Records, Secretaries, and the European Information State, circa 1400–1700,” 139. See also Friedrich, *The Birth of the Archive,* for a comprehensive history of archives and archival practice.

37. Foucault, *Archaeology of Knowledge,* 7.

38. Ketelaar identifies an emerging “paradigm of patrimony” in the Netherlands in the seventeenth and eighteenth centuries, “Muniments and Monuments.”

39. Jefferson did not work alone in this regard. James Madison and John Adams were among the colleagues who understood the importance of archival preservation in controlling their personal and national legacies.

40. Drake, “Graveyards of Exclusion,” para. 14.

41. Foucault, *Order of Things,* 6.

42. Foucault, *Order of Things,* 345 (emphasis added).

43. Ferguson, *Reorder of Things,* 30, 31.

44. Foucault, *Order of Things,* 221.

45. Spahn, *Thomas Jefferson, Time, and History,* 2.

46. Spahn, *Thomas Jefferson, Time, and History,* 4–5.

47. Spahn, *Thomas Jefferson, Time, and History.* 4–7.

48. Nora, “Between Memory and History.”

49. Shelley, "Ebenezer Hazard: America's First Historical Editor."

50. TJ to Ebenezer Hazard, 18 February 1791, *Founders Online*, National Archives, https://founders.archives.gov/documents/Jefferson/01-19-02-0059.

51. TJ to George Wythe, 16 January 1796, *Founders Online*, National Archives, https://founders.archives.gov/documents/Jefferson/01-28-02-0454.

52. TJ to Isaiah Thomas, 14 October 1820, *Founders Online*, National Archives, https://founders.archives.gov/documents/Jefferson/03-16-02-0277.

53. See Nora, "Between Memory and History."

54. Schaefer, "The Things of Order," 2.

55. Schaefer, "The Things of Order," 3.

56. Foucault, *Power/Knowledge*, 194.

57. Schaefer, "The Things of Order," 24.

58. Weheliye, *Habeus Viscus*, 3.

59. Weheliye, *Habeus Viscus*, 3.

60. Butler, *Bodies that Matter*, 8.

61. Agamben, *The Open*, 26.

62. Agamben, *The Open*, 26.

63. Agamben, *The Open*, 80.

64. Agamben, *The Open*, 13, 37.

65. Coulthard, *Red Skin White Masks*, 7.

66. Butler, *Bodies that Matter*, 8

67. Weheliye, *Habeus Viscus*, 7.

68. Weheliye, *Habeus Viscus*, 13.

69. Woolford argues, "The rigid separation in genocide law between the physical, biological, and cultural is allowed to stand as is. But this modern typological contrivance reflects a distinctly European cosmology, protecting mostly those groups willing to divide their world as such. What is lost in the categorical separation between the physical, biological, and cultural is their deep intersections within Indigenous ontologies," Woolford, "Ontological Redress," 272–73. For clarity about definitions of cultural genocide see Bachman's Introduction to the edited volume, *Cultural Genocide*.

70. Davidson, *Cultural Genocide*, 1.

71. The concept of a "literary situation" is borrowed from Snaza, who defines it as "a situation where intrahuman politics of race, gender, sexuality, and geography shape the conditions of emergence for literacy events that animate subjects and the political relations with which they are entangled," Snaza, *Animate Literacies*, 4.

72. Benjamin, "Introduction," 4.

73. TallBear, *Native American DNA*, 11.

74. Woolford, "Ontological Redress," 273.

75. Woolford, "Ontological Redress," 273.

76. Harney and Moten, "Refusing Completion."

77. Foucault, *Power/Knowledge*, 143.

78. Pawley, "Information Literacy," 428.
79. Foucault, *Order of Things*, 221.
80. Wynter, "Unsettling the Coloniality of Being/Power/Truth/Freedom," 260.
81. Spivak, "Can the Subaltern Speak?," 27–28.
82. Gordon-Reed, *The Hemingses of Monticello*.
83. Luhmann, *Theories of Distinction*, 125.
84. Luhmann, *Theories of Distinction*, 125.
85. Barad, *Meeting the Universe Halfway*, 185.
86. Luhmann, *Theories of Distinction*, 127.
87. Luhmann, *Theories of Distinction*, 143.
88. Luhmann, *Theories of Distinction*, 111.
89. Haspo, "Teamwork at Its Best."
90. See Collins, *Library of Walls*.
91. The Library of Congress was enacted in law when Jefferson was vice president in 1800, and the first books arrived when he was president in 1801.
92. For literature on the Library of Congress and standardization, see Adler, *Cruising the Library*; Miksa, "The Development of Classification at the Library of Congress"; Olson, "Difference, Culture and Change"; Svenonius, "LCSH: Semantics, Syntax and Specificity."
93. Day, *Modern Invention of Information*, 4.
94. Bivens-Tatum, *Libraries and the Enlightenment*.
95. See Bowker and Star, *Sorting Things Out*, an essential text on classification systems and relations of power.
96. Sharpe, *Ordinary Notes*, 36.
97. Bergdoll, "Books, Buildings, and the Spaces of Democracy," 72.
98. Nora, "Between Memory and History."
99. Steedman, *Dust*, 9.
100. Mitchell, "Monuments, Memorials, and the Politics of Memory." 443.
101. Getting Word, https://gettingword.monticello.org/about/.
102. To name a few: Berman, *Prejudices and Antipathies*; Bowker and Star, *Sorting Things Out*; Bullard, Watson, and Purdome, "Misrepresentation in the Surrogate"; Harris, *Ghosts of Archive*; Olson, "The Power to Name"; Snow and Dunbar, "Advancing the Relationship Between Critical Cataloging and Critical Race Theory"; Turner, *Cataloging Culture*. Also see my book, *Cruising the Library*, where I articulate a claim that with every addition of an information resource to the catalog, we affirm and add strength to the Library of Congress's classifications.
103. See Drabinski, "Queering the Catalog," for an argument for integrating lessons about the politics of cataloging into information literacy education.

## 1. Information as Revolutionary Action

1. Shelley, "Ebenezer Hazard: America's First Historical Editor"; Thomas Jefferson (hereafter TJ) to Ebenezer Hazard, 30 April 1775, *Founders Online*. https://founders.archives.gov/documents/Jefferson/01-01-02-0102.

2. Remarkably, the *Oxford English Dictionary* cites a letter from TJ to John Melish as an example of this usage of "information," which is now rare. "information, n.," *OED Online*.

3. Elmborg, "Critical Information Literacy," 83.

4. Buckland, "Information as Thing," 352.

5. TJ to Ebenezer Hazard, 18 February 1791, *Founders Online*, National Archives, https://founders.archives.gov/documents/Jefferson/01-19-02-0059.

6. TJ, "Summary View," 105 (emphasis added).

7. TJ, "Summary View," 108 (emphasis added).

8. TJ, "Summary View," 105.

9. TJ, "Autobiography," 19.

10. Arendt, *On Revolution*, 130.

11. TJ, *Notes on the State of Virginia*, 274.

12. TJ, *Notes on the State of Virginia*, 192.

13. TJ, *Notes on the State of Virginia*, 192.

14. TJ, "Summary View." Over his lifetime Jefferson enslaved over six hundred people.

15. Jefferson wrote the initial draft of the Declaration of Independence. It was revised by a committee comprised of John Adams, Benjamin Franklin, Robert R. Livingston, Roger Sherman, and Jefferson. TJ, "original Rough draught" of the Declaration of Independence, 11 June–4 July 1776, *Founders Online*, National Archives, https://founders.archives.gov/documents/Jefferson/01-01-02-0176-0004.

16. US National Archives and Records Administration, *Declaration of Independence: A Transcription* (24 July 2020), https://www.archives.gov/founding-docs/declaration-transcript.

17. Head, "Records, Secretaries, and the European Information State, circa 1400–1700," 159.

18. Head, "Records, Secretaries, and the European Information State, circa 1400–1700," 159.

19. Head, "Records, Secretaries, and the European Information State, circa 1400–1700," 160.

20. Nunberg, "Farewell to the Information Age," 113.

21. Marklund and Skouvig, "Introduction," 8. Buckland is useful here again. "Data," as the plural form of the Latin word "datum," means "things that have been given." It is, therefore, an apt term for the sort of information-as-thing that has been processed in some way for use. Commonly "data" denotes whatever records are stored in a computer. Buckland, "Information as Thing," 353. Further to this point, see Ron Day on the transformation of persons into users in modern information systems, Day, *Indexing It All*, 42–49.

22. Nunberg, "Farewell to the Information Age," 112–13.

23. Pawley, "Information Literacy," 430.

24. Blair, *Too Much to Know*, 13.

25. Berlant, *Anatomy of National Fantasy*, 5.

26. Brown, "Mapping a Slave Revolt," 134.

27. Ferguson, *The Reorder of Things*, 15.
28. Honig, *Public Things*, 91.
29. Baharak Yousefi refers to community libraries that resist or serve as alternatives to public institutions as "parallel libraries" in her dissertation (in progress at Simon Fraser University).
30. Latour, "From Realpolitik to Dingpolitik."
31. Kosciejew, "Disciplinary Documentation in Apartheid South Africa," 99.
32. Latour, "From Realpolitik to Dingpolitik."
33. Honig, *Public Things*, 11.
34. Benjamin, "On Language as Such," 64–65.
35. Steyerl, "The Language of Things," (emphasis added).
36. Honig, *Public Things*, 5.
37. McKinney, *Information Activism*, 10.
38. Cheney-Lippold, *We Are Data*.
39. Zook et al., "Ten Simple Rules for Responsible Big Data Research."
40. Berlant, *Anatomy of National Fantasy*.
41. Dal Lago, "Patriarchs and Republicans," 508.
42. Dal Lago, "Patriarchs and Republicans," 503.
43. Foucault, *Technologies of the Self*, 27.
44. Berlant, *Anatomy of National Fantasy*, 20.
45. Foucault, *Archaeology of Knowledge*, 6.
46. I've borrowed this phrasing from Ron Day's essential work, *The Modern Invention of Information*.
47. Man2 refers to production of Man according to Charles Darwin's theoretical interventions on the evolution of species. It is beyond the scope of this project, so I refer readers to Wynter's "Unsettling the Coloniality of Being/Power/Truth/Freedom."
48. da Silva, "Before Man," 99.
49. Brown, *Undoing the Demos*, 116.
50. Lloyd, *Under Representation*, 2.
51. Butler, *Notes Toward a Performative Theory of Assembly*, 3.
52. Butler, *Notes Toward a Performative Theory of Assembly*, 5.
53. Brown, *Undoing the Demos*, 18.
54. Honig, *Public Things*, 16.
55. Barad, *Meeting the Universe Halfway*, 184.
56. For instance, Cait McKinney's book, aptly titled *Information Activism*, provides an account of lesbian archival activities that not only preserved and organized the documentary and media history of lesbian life and communities, but did so in ways that used queer and feminist archival techniques to facilitate connection and care.
57. Brown, *Undoing the Demos*, 205–6.
58. Brown, *Undoing the Demos*, 206.

59. Indeed, it should be noted that Jefferson's encouragement of dissent was within the context of an imagined unity among a homogeneous, white population, and herein lies one root of our present problems.

60. Eco, *How to Spot a Fascist*, 20.

61. Mattern, *Code + Clay . . . Data + Dirt*, xxvi.

62. Bassett, "Plantation Roads," 50–51.

63. Star and Ruhleder, "Steps Toward an Ecology of Infrastructure," 112.

64. Star and Ruhleder, "Steps Toward an Ecology of Infrastructure," 112.

65. Star and Ruhleder, "Steps Toward an Ecology of Infrastructure," 113.

66. Star, "Ethnography of Infrastructure," 381.

67. Edwards, "Infrastructure and Modernity," 185–86. Also see Star, "Ethnography of Infrastructure."

68. Mattern, "Library as Infrastructure."

69. Wolfe, *Traces of History*, 10.

70. Wolfe, "Settler Colonialism and the Elimination of the Native," 388.

71. Wolfe, "Settler Colonialism and the Elimination of the Native," 388 (emphasis added).

72. Kauanui, "A Structure, Not an Event," para. 9.

73. Englert, "Settlers, Workers, and the Logic of Accumulation by Dispossession," 1650.

74. Snaza, *Animate Literacies*, 102.

75. Snaza, "Why This?," 266–67. Snaza is signaling Lauren Berlant and Alfred North Whitehead in a description of the situation and the event.

76. Snaza, "Why This?," 267.

77. Snaza, "Why This?," 268.

78. Snaza, "Why This?," 270.

79. Snaza, "Why This?," 265.

80. Foucault, "What is Enlightenment?," 313.

81. Foucault, "What is Enlightenment?," 315.

82. Berlant, *On the Inconvenience of Other People*, 28.

83. Day, "Community as Event," 409. Also see Day, *Indexing It All*; and Day, *Documentarity*.

84. Day, "Community as Event," 409.

85. Derrida, "Declarations of Independence," 10.

86. Day, "Community as Event," 420.

87. Day, "Community as Event," 423.

88. Small, "Re-Enchantment of Humanism," 136.

89. See, for examples, Montenegro, "Subverting the Universality of Metadata Standards"; and Carroll, Rodriguez-Lonebear, and Martinez, "Indigenous Data Governance."

90. Sally's given name was likely Sarah.

91. Hartman, "Venus in Two Acts."

92. Ferguson, *Reorder of Things*, 232.

## 2. Archives and the Making of American History

1. Page's letters to Jefferson provide some of the most thorough reporting of the battles and other events of the early Revolutionary War in eastern Virginia as well as dispatches from the other colonies. At the time he was serving as president of the governor's council and after the revolution, he'd become governor. Page was descended from one of the wealthiest families in Virginia and resided at Rosewell Plantation, on the York River in Gloucester County, just across from Williamsburg. Rosewell was constructed on Powhatan land in 1725. Jefferson stayed at Rosewell often, and it is speculated that he wrote "A Summary View of the Rights of British America" or a draft of the Declaration of Independence there, although there is scant historical evidence to support this.

2. Césaire, *Discourse on Colonialism*, 42–43. Césaire was a Martinican poet, playwright, and politician, who cofounded the Negritude movement.

3. Thomas Jefferson (hereafter TJ) to John Page, 5 August 1776, *Founders Online*, National Archives, https://founders.archives.gov/documents/Jefferson/01-01-02-0202 (emphasis added). The Haudenosaunee ("people of the longhouse") Confederacy is also known in English as Six Nations, as well as the French name Iroquois. The Indigenous nations that originally comprised the confederacy are the Oneida, Mohawk, Cayuga, Seneca, and Onondaga. These nations lived in an area that included what are now called Canada and the United States, from the Genesee River in what is now New York State on the west, through the Finger Lakes regions, to the Hudson River on the east. In 1722 the Tuscarora moved from Virginia and North Carolina to join the confederacy. They each speak different languages and all live according to a matrilineal clan system. Ned Blackhawk (Western Shoshone), in *The Rediscovery of America*, provides a compelling account of the role of the Haudenosaunee Confederacy in French and British colonial relations and conflict.

4. It is worth noting that four of the first five US presidents were from Virginia.

5. Chief Logan's father was Oneida, and Logan became a leader among the Mingo people, who are ancestors of today's Seneca-Cayuga Nation. There has been some disagreement about Logan's name, but it may have been Tachnedorus. Elmer provides an overview of the events that Logan described.

6. Jefferson, *Notes on the State of Virginia*, 188.

7. TJ to John Henry, 31 December 1797, *Founders Online*, National Archives, https://founders.archives.gov/documents/Jefferson/01-29-02-0484.

8. Elmer, "Inclusion and Exclusion of the Indian in the Early American Archive," 65.

9. Sowerby, *Catalogue of the Library of Thomas Jefferson*, v. 5, vii.

10. Ellis, *American Sphinx*.

11. Foucault, *Power/Knowledge*, 62.

12. Commager, "Thomas Jefferson and the Character of America," 33.

13. "There is no new thing under the sun" is from Ecclesiastics 1:9 and is cited in Bacon's *Advancement of Learning*, 164; TJ to Joseph Priestley, 21 March 1801, *Founders Online*, National Archives, https://founders.archives.gov/documents/Jefferson/01-33-02-0336 (emphasis added).

14. Spahn, *Thomas Jefferson, Time, and History*, 7.

15. The National Archives in the United States was not formally established until 1935, but before that, archival documents and artifacts pertaining to the nation were kept in places such as the Library of Congress, university libraries, state offices, and the Smithsonian Institution.

16. Shelley, "Ebenezer Hazard," 44.

17. Quoted in Shelley, "Ebenezer Hazard," 48.

18. Importantly, Jefferson supplied a similar but much expanded catalog of the primary historical materials he had collected at the end of *Notes on the State of Virginia* in Query 23.

19. TJ to Ebenezer Hazard, 30 April 1775, *Founders Online*, National Archives, https://founders.archives.gov/documents/Jefferson/01-01-02-0102.

20. Samuel Huntington to TJ, 27 April 1781, enclosing a Letter from Ebenezer Hazard, 7 April 1781, *Founders Online*, National Archives, https://founders.archives.gov/documents/Jefferson/01-05-02-0691.

21. Shelley, "Ebenezer Hazard," 58.

22. Apparently, Washington was misinformed and had believed that Hazard opposed the ratification of the Constitution. Cogliano, *Thomas Jefferson*, 31.

23. TJ to Ebenezer Hazard, 18 February 1791, *Founders Online*, National Archives, https://founders.archives.gov/documents/Jefferson/01-19-02-0059.

24. De Tocqueville, *Democracy in America*, 420–21

25. TJ to George Wythe, 16 January 1796, *Founders Online*, National Archives, https://founders.archives.gov/documents/Jefferson/01-28-02-0454.

26. Editor's note in TJ to George Wythe, 16 January 1796, *Founders Online*, National Archives, https://founders.archives.gov/documents/Jefferson/01-28-02-0454.

27. Boyd, "These Precious Monuments," 176.

28. Goff, "Freedom of Challenge," 14.

29. Shelley, "Ebenezer Hazard," 63.

30. Shelley, "Ebenezer Hazard," 63.

31. Head, "Records, Secretaries, and the European Information State, circa 1400–1700," 146.

32. Eisenstein, *Printing Press as an Agent of Change*, 72.

33. Eisenstein, *Printing Press as an Agent of Change*, 88.

34. Eisenstein, *Printing Press as an Agent of Change*, 113.

35. Cogliano, *Thomas Jefferson*, 21.

36. TJ to George Wythe, 16 January 1796, *Founders Online*, National Archives, https://founders.archives.gov/documents/Jefferson/01-28-02-0454.

37. TJ to John Page, 21 February 1770, *Founders Online*, National Archives, https://founders.archives.gov/documents/Jefferson/01-01-02-0023. Some of the letters

in this passage were illegible. I have reproduced the text as given by the editors of *The Papers of Thomas Jefferson* but left out the brackets that indicate these are edits to the original.

38. Brannon, "Thomas Jefferson," 320.

39. O'Shaughnessy, *Illimitable Freedom*, 88.

40. Butterfield, "Papers of Thomas Jefferson," 132.

41. Betts, *Thomas Jefferson's Farm Book*, vii.

42. Cogliano, *Thomas Jefferson*, 75.

43. Butterfield, "Papers of Thomas Jefferson," 132.

44. Butterfield, "Papers of Thomas Jefferson," 132–33.

45. TJ to Hugh Paul Taylor, 4 October 1823, *Founders Online*, National Archives, https://founders.archives.gov/documents/Jefferson/98-01-02-3789.

46. TJ to Hugh Paul Taylor, 4 October 1823, *Founders Online*, National Archives, https://founders.archives.gov/documents/Jefferson/98-01-02-3789.

47. TJ to Hugh Paul Taylor, 4 October 1823, *Founders Online*, National Archives, https://founders.archives.gov/documents/Jefferson/98-01-02-3789.

48. Derrida, "Archive Fever," 11.

49. Elmer, "The Archive, the Native American, and Jefferson's Convulsions," 12.

50. Diane Ehrenpreis and Endrina Tay's study of Jefferson's home office demonstrates in great detail the lengths to which Jefferson designed and enhanced techniques to optimize efficiency and space. Ehrenpreis and Tay, "Enlightened Networks."

51. Rogers, "Thomas Jefferson's Office Copier."

52. TJ to James Madison, with a List of Books, 1 September 1785, *Founders Online*, National Archives, https://founders.archives.gov/documents/Jefferson/01-08-02-0360.

53. TJ to James Bowdoin, 10 July 1806, *Founders Online*, National Archives, https://founders.archives.gov/documents/Jefferson/99-01-02-3997.

54. TJ to James Bowdoin, 10 July 1806, *Founders Online*, National Archives, https://founders.archives.gov/documents/Jefferson/99-01-02-3997.

55. TJ to Charles Willson Peale, 6 October 1805, *Founders Online*, National Archives, https://founders.archives.gov/documents/Jefferson/99-01-02-2444.

56. Post, "Continuing Saga."

57. TJ to Isaac McPherson, 13 August 1813, *Founders Online*, National Archives, https://founders.archives.gov/documents/Jefferson/03-06-02-0322.

58. Locke, *Life of John Locke*, cited in Hughes, "Copyright and Incomplete Historiographies," 1012.

59. Following the ratification of the Constitution, the first Congress enacted national copyright and patent laws in 1790, making the provisions more precise. Titled "An Act for the Encouragement of Learning, by securing the Copies of Maps, Charts, and Books, to the Authors and Proprietors of such Copies, during the Times therein mentioned," the law entitled authors to "the sole right and liberty of

printing, reprinting, publishing, and vending" their works for fourteen years with the possibility of one renewal.

60. Vaidhyanathan, *Copyrights and Copywrongs*, 22.

61. TJ to James Madison, 28 August 1789, *Founders Online*, National Archives, https://founders.archives.gov/documents/Jefferson/01-15-02-0354.

62. Hughes, "Copyright and Incomplete Historiographies," 1031.

63. Gordon, "An Inquiry into the Merits of Copyright," 1364–65.

64. Gordon, "An Inquiry into the Merits of Copyright," 1379.

65. Vaidhyanathan, *Copyrights and Copywrongs*, 24.

66. TJ to James Madison, 6 September 1789, *Founders Online*, National Archives, https://founders.archives.gov/documents/Jefferson/01-15-02-0375-0003.

67. Ragosta, Onuf, and O'Shaughnessy, *Founding of Thomas Jefferson's University*, 1–2.

68. TJ to James Madison, 6 September 1789, *Founders Online*, National Archives, https://founders.archives.gov/documents/Jefferson/01-15-02-0375-0003.

69. TJ to George Wythe, 16 January 1796, *Founders Online*, National Archives, https://founders.archives.gov/documents/Jefferson/01-28-02-0454.

70. Hazard, *Historical Collections*, iii–iv.

71. Small, "Re-Enchantment of Humanism," 198.

72. Justice, *Why Indigenous Literatures Matter*, 19.

73. Samuel Huntington to TJ, 27 April 1781, enclosing a Letter from Ebenezer Hazard, 7 April 1781, *Founders Online*, National Archives, https://founders.archives.gov/documents/Jefferson/01-05-02-0691.

74. The papers in the packet are the following: (1) Alex. Cameron to Chiefs of Cherokees, 16 Jan. 1775; (2) Lord Dunmore's talk to Little Carpenter and other Cherokee Chiefs, 23 Mch. 1775; (3) instructions of the King to governors concerning Indian territory, signed by John Stuart, 4 July 1763; (4) Alex. Cameron, speech to Cherokees, 7 July 1774; (5) speech by an unidentified person to Cherokees, 3 June 1773; (6) abstract of treaty of cession to the King by Creeks and Cherokees, Augusta, 1 June 1773; (7) Alex. Cameron, speech to Cherokees, 30 Mch. 1773; (8) Alex. Cameron, warrant of protection for "the Great Warrior of Chote," 1 Mch. 1771; (9) Alex. Cameron, speech [to Cherokees] 5 Feb. 1772; (10) John Stuart to the Cherokees, 14 Jan. 1764; (11) Edw. Wilkinson to "the Great Warrior Onconnistota," 5 July 1778; (12) Wm. Preston to the Cherokee chiefs, 12 Apr. 1775; (13) David Taitt to Oconastota, 24 Jan. 1777; (14) John Stuart to "OuKonnestotah," n.d.; (15) map of "the New Province" at the junction of Scioto and Ohio Rivers, n.d.; (16) John Stuart, speech of "Oucconnastot," 6 Feb. 1777; (17) St. Andrews Club, Charles Town, S.C., membership card for "Oucconnastotah," signed by John Stuart, President, 30 Nov. 1773; (18) Patrick Henry to "Ouconostotah," 3 Mch. and Nov. 1777; (19) Patrick Henry to "Ouconostotah," n.d.; (20) John Stuart to the Cherokees, 30 June 1763; (22) treaty between state of Virginia and the Cherokee nation, Fort Henry, 20 July 1777." Editor's note, TJ to McKean, 20 December 1781, *Founders Online*, National Archives, https://founders.archives.gov/documents/Jefferson/01-06-02-0138.

75. TJ to Samuel Huntington, 17 February 1781, *Founders Online*, National Archives, https://founders.archives.gov/documents/Jefferson/01-04-02-0811.

76. Hartman, "Venus in Two Acts," 2.

77. Ghaddar, "Spectre in the Archive," 23.

78. TJ to José Corrêia da Serra, 26 April 1816, *Founders Online*, National Archives, https://founders.archives.gov/documents/Jefferson/03-09-02-0474.

79. Boyd, "These Precious Monuments," 177.

80. TJ, *Notes on the State of Virginia*, 221.

81. O'Brien, *Firsting and Lasting*, 107.

82. Elmer, "Inclusion and Exclusion of the Indian in the Early American Archive," 56.

## 3. Haunted Ontologies

1. Caswell, "Inventing New Archival Imaginaries," 49.

2. Benjamin, "Theses," 256.

3. Allen, *The End of Progress*, 169, 204.

4. Adorno, quoted in Allen, *The End of Progress*, 174.

5. Allen, *The End of Progress*, 204.

6. Allen, *The End of Progress*, 205.

7. Bastian, "Reading Colonial Records."

8. Caswell, "'The Archive' is Not an Archives."

9. Friedrich, *The Birth of the Archive*, 7.

10. See for example, Caswell, "Inventing New Archival Imaginaries"; Bastian and Alexander, eds. *Community Archives*.

11. Derrida, "Archive Fever," 9.

12. Derrida, "Archive Fever," 9.

13. "archive, n.," *OED Online*, December 2021.

14. "architect, n.," *OED Online*, December 2021.

15. "mastery, n.," *OED Online*, December 2024.

16. "archaeology, n.," *OED Online*, December 2021.

17. Arendt, *On Revolution*, 206.

18. Holland, *Body Politic*, xxi.

19. Thomas Jefferson (hereafter TJ) to Roger Chew Weightman, 24 June 1826, *Founders Online*, National Archives, https://founders.archives.gov/documents/Jefferson/98-01-02-6179.

20. Quoted in Cometti and Gennaro-Lerda, "The Presidential Tour of Carlo Vidua with Letters on Virginia," 398.

21. Johnson, *Architects of Memory*.

22. Caswell, *Urgent Archives*, 26.

23. Nyong'o, *Amalgamation Waltz*, 163.

24. Caswell, *Urgent Archives*, 32.

25. Caswell, *Urgent Archives*, 32.

26. TallBear, "Feminist, Queer, and Indigenous Thinking," 496.

27. Mattern, *Code + Clay . . . Data + Dirt*, xxvii–xxx.

28. Bowker, *Memory Practices in the Sciences*, 21.

29. Bowker, *Memory Practices in the Sciences*, 12.

30. Ragosta, *Religious Freedom*.

31. Jefferson, *Notes on the State of Virginia*, 289.

32. Benjamin, "Theses," 254.

33. Jefferson referred to the British as "these unfeeling brethren" in a draft of the Declaration of Independence.

34. Benjamin, "Theses," 257.

35. Benjamin, *Arcades Project*, 456–88.

36. Trouillot, *Silencing the Past*, 148.

37. Benjamin, "Theses," 257–58.

38. Holland, *Body Politic*, 2.

39. Luhmann, *Theories of Distinction*, 109.

40. For a description of several people's positions on slavery, including John Jay, the Marquis de Condorcet, Benjamin Rush, and Benjamin Franklin—all of whom advocated for gradual emancipation, see Dierksheide, *Amelioration and Empire*, 102.

41. TJ to Edward Bancroft, 26 January 1789, *Founders Online*, National Archives, https://founders.archives.gov/documents/Jefferson/01-14-02-0266.

42. Spahn, *Thomas Jefferson, Time, and History*, 62.

43. Dierksheide, *Amelioration and Empire*, 20.

44. Dierksheide, *Amelioration and Empire*, 29.

45. Stanton, *Those Who Labor for My Happiness*.

46. Dierksheide, *Amelioration and Empire*, 13, 20.

47. TJ to John Wayles Eppes, 30 June 1820, *Founders Online*, National Archives, https://founders.archives.gov/documents/Jefferson/03-16-02-0052.

48. Dierksheide, *Amelioration and Empire*, 53.

49. TJ to James Monroe, 24 November 1801, *Founders Online*, National Archives, https://founders.archives.gov/documents/Jefferson/01-35-02-0550.

50. TJ, *Notes on the State of Virginia*, 288.

51. Césaire, *Discourse on Colonialism*, 35–36.

52. Nyong'o, *Amalgamation Waltz*, 10.

53. Harney and Moten, *The Undercommons*, 26.

54. Foucault, *History of Sexuality*, 23.

55. Galison, "Blacked-out Spaces," 238.

56. Derrida, "Archive Fever," 43.

57. Derrida, "Archive Fever," 44.

58. Bowker and Star, *Sorting Things Out*.

59. Reinhardt, "Vision's Unseen," para 8.

60. Rose, "Femininity and Its Discontents," 16.

61. Galison, "Blacked-out Spaces," 237.

62. Hartman, "Venus in Two Acts," 10.

63. McInnis, "Liberty and Tyranny of Jefferson's Academical Village," 129.

64. McInnis, "Liberty and Tyranny of Jefferson's Academical Village," 132.

65. Bestor, *Three Presidents and Their Books*, 6.

66. Derrida, "Archive Fever," 63.

67. Gordon-Reed and Onuf, *"Most Blessed of the Patriarchs,"* 12–13.

68. TJ to John Page, 23 January 1764, *Founders Online*, National Archives, https://founders.archives.gov/documents/Jefferson/01-01-02-0008; See my forthcoming book, *Surveillance and Security in the "Empire of Liberty"* for a description of TJ and Page's encrypted correspondence.

69. Gilliland and Caswell, "Records and Their Imaginaries," 56.

70. Saidiya Hartman's method of critical fabulation can help us to imagine our way into these questions. See *Wayward Lives, Beautiful Experiments* and "Venus in Two Acts." Fiction is extremely useful, as well. Recently published works based on Monticello help to think our way into the lives that inhabited Jefferson's home and lands. See, for example, Ta-Nehisi Coates, *The Water Dancer*, and *My Monticello*, by Jocelyn Nicole Johnson.

71. Gordon-Reed and Onuf, *"Most Blessed of the Patriarchs,"* 313.

72. I am signaling TJ's famous "Head and Heart" letter to Maria Cosway. TJ to Maria Cosway, 12 October 1786, *Founders Online*, National Archives, https://founders.archives.gov/documents/Jefferson/01-10-02-0309.

73. Harris, "Insistering," 8.

74. Harris, "Insistering," 9.

75. Derrida, "Freud and the Scene of Writing," 196.

76. Ruiz, "Freud and Derrida," 98.

77. Derrida, "Freud and the Scene of Writing," 211.

78. LaMontagne, *American Library Classifications*, 152.

79. Derrida, "Archive Fever," 51.

80. Derrida, "Archive Fever," 51.

81. Ferguson, *Reorder of Things*, 19.

82. Wynter, "Ceremony Found," 210.

83. Wynter, "On How We Mistook the Map for the Territory," 114.

84. Luhmann, *Theories of Distinction*, 139.

85 Wolfe, *What is Posthumanism?*, xxiv.

86 Cambridge Union, *James Baldwin Debates William F. Buckley*.

87. Wolfe, *What is Posthumanism?*, xxv.

88. I would also like to note that this critique of Jefferson's techniques may be implicated. Katherine McKittrick's use of autopoiesis demonstrates the repetition of conceptualizations and constructions, even when they are presenting biological theories of race as false, "the biocentric system of knowledge remains powerful and empowered and loops around, again, to naturalize racial-sexual differentiation." McKittrick, *Dear Science*, 134–35.

89. Wynter, "On How We Mistook the Map for the Territory," 117.

90. Wynter, "On How We Mistook the Map for the Territory," 128–29.

91. Halberstam, *Wild Things*, 89.
92. Halberstam, *Wild Things*, 90.
93. Derrida, *Specters of Marx*, 9.
94. Stuchel, "Material Provocations in the Archives," 20.
95. Gordon, *Ghostly Matters*, 8.
96. Derrida, *Specters of Marx*, 9.
97. Brodie, *Thomas Jefferson*, 174.
98. Gruber, "Translation Approach," 199.
99. Cheney-Lippold, "New Algorithmic Identity," 174.
100. McKittrick, "Plantation Futures," 3.
101. Gikandi, *Slavery and the Culture of Taste*, xii-xiii.
102. Gordon, *Ghostly Matters*, 8.
103. Harris, "Insistering Derrida."
104. Gordon, *Ghostly Matters*, 22.
105. Gordon, *Ghostly Matters*, 178.
106. Walcott, *Long Emancipation*, 46.
107. McKittrick, "Mathematics Black Life," 16.
108. Shuffleton, "Binding Ties," 28.
109. Best, *None Like Us*, 21.
110. Best, *None Like Us*, 7.
111. Best, *None Like Us*, 22.
112. Tuck and Yang, "Decolonization is Not a Metaphor," 2.
113. Gikandi, *Slavery and the Culture of Taste*, 109.
114. Gikandi, *Slavery and the Culture of Taste*, xii.
115. McInnis, "Black Women's Geographies."
116. Snaza, *Animate Literacies*, 21.
117. Snaza, *Animate Literacies*, 21.
118. Derrida, *Specters of Marx*, xviii.
119. Derrida, *Specters of Marx*, xvii–xviii.

## 4. "A Blueprint of His Own Mind": Jefferson's Libraries

1. Bestor, *Three Presidents and Their Books*, 6.
2. Lorde, "Age, Race, Class, and Sex," 123.
3. Smith-Cruz, "Referencing Audre Lorde."
4. Gilmore, *Abolition Geographies*, 79.
5. McKittrick, "Mathematics Black Life."
6. Lorde, "Age, Race, Class, and Sex," 123 (emphasis added).
7. Cogliano, *Thomas Jefferson*, 20.
8. Adams, *Three Americanists*, 95.
9. See Glynn, *Reading Publics*.
10. Brown, *Strength of the People*, 45.

11. Benjamin Franklin, "Address to Proprietors," quoted in Brown, *Strength of the People*, 45.

12. Wilson, *Jefferson's Literary Commonplace Book*, 3.

13. Wilson, *Jefferson's Literary Commonplace Book*, 4.

14. Wilson analyzed Jefferson's handwriting to assess the chronological order in which the entries were written. When Jefferson had the notebook bound, he reordered the entries according to type. "Thomas Jefferson's Early Notebooks"

15. For example, see Lockridge, *On the Sources of Patriarchal Rage*.

16. Thomas Jefferson (hereafter TJ) to Robert Skipwith, with a List of Books for a Private Library, 3 August 1771, *Founders Online*, National Archives, https://founders.archives.gov/documents/Jefferson/01-01-02-0056.

17. TJ to Robert Skipwith, with a List of Books for a Private Library, 3 August 1771, *Founders Online*, National Archives, https://founders.archives.gov/documents/Jefferson/01-01-02-0056.

18. Tarc, *Literacy of the Other*, 15.

19. TJ to John Page, 21 February 1770, *Founders Online*, National Archives, https://founders.archives.gov/documents/Jefferson/01-01-02-0023.

20. It might be noted that the theme of *The Tempest* aligns with TJ's repeated references to storms.

21. On Jefferson's designs for education see O'Shaughnessy, *Illimitable Freedom*; Taylor, *Thomas Jefferson's Education*.

22. Bill for Establishing a Public Library, 18 June 1779, *Founders Online*, National Archives, https://founders.archives.gov/documents/Jefferson/01-02-02-0132-0004-0081.

23. See Wilson, "Evolution of Jefferson's 'Notes.'" *Notes on the State of Virginia* is a fascinating document, written in response to a set of queries from the French legation in Philadelphia, François Marbois. Jefferson submitted his responses to Marbois in 1781 but significantly revised the manuscript before submitting it to printers in 1785. He continued to make adjustments to the text after that.

24. Although he provides the date 6 March 1783 when he tallied up the number of books in his collection at 2,640, he actually started compiling that catalog earlier. There has not yet been agreement on the date, however, and my own speculation is that he may have started the catalog between 1775 and 1778, but he may have classed it using the Baconian system after he acquired the Diderot and D'Alembert volumes while he was the governor of Virginia in 1781.

25. Gish and Klinghard, *Thomas Jefferson and the Science of Republican Government*, 87–93.

26. TJ to John Trumbull, 15 February 1789. *Founders Online*, National Archives, https://founders.archives.gov/documents/Jefferson/01-14-02-0321.

27. D'Alembert, *Preliminary Discourse*, xxxii.

28. D'Alembert, *Preliminary Discourse*, 29 (emphasis added).

29. D'Alembert, *Preliminary Discourse*, 47.

30. TJ to George Watterston, 7 May 1815, *Founders Online*, National Archives, https://founders.archives.gov/documents/Jefferson/03-08-02-0376 (emphasis added).

31. Bacon, *Gesta Grayorum*, 34–35.

32. Wood, *Friends Divided*, 10.

33. TJ to D'Anmours, 30 November 1780, *Founders Online*, National Archives, https://founders.archives.gov/documents/Jefferson/01-04-02-0198.

34. Amable and Alexander Lory to TJ, 16 December 1780, *Founders Online*, National Archives, https://founders.archives.gov/documents/Jefferson/01-04-02-0261.

35. TJ to David S. Franks, [March or April 1783], *Founders Online*, National Archives, https://founders.archives.gov/documents/Jefferson/01-06-02-0238.

36. Watts, "Thomas Jefferson," 319. Marbois was a significant figure in Jefferson's professional life. He negotiated the Louisiana Purchase Treaty in 1803 and was elected to the American Philosophical Society in 1780 (the same year that Jefferson was elected to the society).

37. Manning, "Naming of Parts," 348.

38. See Manning, "Naming of Parts," 349, for a comparison of Marbois's queries and Jefferson's chapters.

39. Elmer, "The Archive, the Native American, and Jefferson's Convulsions," 10.

40. This type of questionnaire was derived from earlier Spanish information-gathering techniques, exemplified by the *Relaciones Topográficas* (Topographical Accounts) after 1574, which featured questions that sought "information about physical features, animals and plants, recent history, religious life, and Indigenous languages," Head, "Records, Secretaries, and the European Information State, circa 1400–1700," 152.

41. Wilson, "Evolution of Jefferson's 'Notes,'" 103. Douglas Wilson has traced the confusing publication history of *Notes on the State of Virginia*. It was first published in England in 1785, and then in France in 1787, but Jefferson continued to revise it after its publication. Jefferson's quote is from his Autobiography, 1743–1790.

42. Brodie, *Thomas Jefferson*, 174.

43. Hayes, *Road to Monticello*, 259.

44. Manning, "Naming of Parts," 359.

45. TJ to Elizabeth Wayles Eppes, [3? October 1782], *Founders Online*, National Archives, https://founders.archives.gov/documents/Jefferson/01-06-02-0188.

46. Wilson, "Evolution of Jefferson's 'Notes,'" 112.

47. James Madison, "Notes on Debates," 23 January 1783. *Founders Online*, National Archives, http://founders.archives.gov/documents/Madison/01-06-02-0032.

48. James Madison, "Report on Books for Congress," [23 January] 1783, *Founders Online*, National Archives, https://founders.archives.gov/documents/Madison/01-06-02-0031. Hugh Williamson (NC) and Thomas Mifflin (DE) were the other committee members.

49. Madison's proposal for a library for Congress was rejected, and in 1790, a congressional committee again compiled a catalog of books for the reference use of government officers. The committee recommended the expenditure of $1,000 during the first year and an annual expenditure of $500 thereafter. According to

the editors of the Thomas Jefferson Papers, "The nature of the report, its timing, the inclusion of books on trade and parliamentary procedure, and TJ's desperate need of books on standards of weights and measures—to say nothing of Madison's desire for information on trade at the very time this report was made—would make it very surprising indeed if the two men had not had a hand in this proposal and in compiling the list in 1790 as they had done in 1782." "Editorial Note: Report on Weights and Measures," *Founders Online,* National Archives, https://founders.archives.gov/documents/Jefferson/01-16-02-0359-0001.

50. "A Bill to Promote the Progress of the Useful Arts, [1 December 1791]," *Founders Online,* National Archives, https://founders.archives.gov/documents/Jefferson/01-22-02-0322.

51. TJ, "Enclosure: List of Books for the Library of Congress," 14 April 1802, *Founders Online,* National Archives, https://founders.archives.gov/documents/Jefferson/01-37-02-0195-0002.

52. The first printed catalog was published by William Duane in April 1802. Library of Congress and Lessing J. Rosenwald Collection. *Catalogue of Books, Maps, and Charts, Belonging to the Library of the Two Houses of Congress: April.* Washington City: Printed by William Duane, 1802. https://www.loc.gov/item/81180057/.

53. Some scholars have suggested that this scheme was based on the Library Company's catalog, but closer inspection reveals that it all likely began with Jefferson. The Library Company organized its books by size until 1788, at which point Zachariah Poulson revised the catalog and organized it according to Bacon's scheme. James Green, librarian at the Library Company of Philadelphia suggests that, although there is no documented evidence, it seems quite likely that Jefferson would have shown Franklin his catalog, and that Franklin subsequently described it to Poulson. (Personal correspondence, 16 July 2018). Kevin Hayes also describes Jefferson and Franklin's common interest in books and reading, noting that Franklin had expanded his personal catalog significantly while in Paris (*Road to Monticello,* 281). If it is the case that the LoC adopted the Library Company's scheme, then it seems likely that they were actually adopting a Jeffersonian one, even if there are differences between Jefferson's and the Library Company's with regard to the placement of subjects in the broad categories of History, Philosophy, and Fine Arts. It is also worth noting that the *Catalogus Bibliothecæ Loganianæ* (Philadelphia, 1760) was organized by subject (not according to the Baconian method). This was the catalog for the Loganian Library, which became part of the Library Company in 1792. Thanks to Endrina Tay for suggesting the inclusion of this information.

54. TJ to Samuel H. Smith, 21 September 1814, *Founders Online,* National Archives, https://founders.archives.gov/documents/Jefferson/03-07-02-0484-0003. Here Jefferson is using the word "public" to refer to an institution of government for use on behalf of the people, as in a "public office," rather than as a public library in today's terms—one that is funded by tax dollars for the direct use of the people.

55. Johnston, *History of the Library of Congress*, 86.

56. TJ to Lucy Ludwell Paradise, 1 June 1789, *Founders Online*, National Archives, https://founders.archives.gov/documents/Jefferson/01-15-02-0166.

57. Dimunation, "Whole of Recorded Knowledge," 27.

58. Hayes, *Road to Monticello*, 283.

59. TJ to Samuel H. Smith, 21 September 1814, *Founders Online*, National Archives, https://founders.archives.gov/documents/Jefferson/03-07-02-0484-0003.

60. TJ to Samuel H. Smith, 21 September 1814, *Founders Online*, National Archives, https://founders.archives.gov/documents/Jefferson/03-07-02-0484-0003.

61. Tay, "Unquestionably the Choicest Collection of Books in the U.S.," para. 10.

62. Hayes, *Road to Monticello*, 551.

63. Dimunation, "Whole of Recorded Knowledge," 28.

64. Dimunation, "Whole of Recorded Knowledge," 28.

65. Quoted in Johnston, *History of the Library of Congress*, 146.

66. Ehrenpreis and Tay, "Enlightened Networks," 200.

67. Rosenberg, *The Nation's Great Library*.

68. In practice, what this means is that the examples described in the Introduction are repeated across libraries because they share catalog records through consortia and apply the standards established, maintained, and governed by international organizations. Local libraries can edit their catalog records, but the vast majority of libraries adhere to the rules that govern editorial decisions. Most likely, your library catalog's records for *Dark Matters* and *Going Stealth* closely resemble the Library of Congress's.

69. The Library of Congress posts "Monthly Lists" of proposed changes to be discussed. The changes described here were posted on 13 February 2025, with very little time for public comment. Library of Congress Subject Headings, Tentative Monthly List, https://classweb.org/tentative-subjects/2412a.html. For the newly authorized headings see, McKinley, Mount (Alaska): https://lccn.loc.gov/sh85082617; America, Gulf of: https://lccn.loc.gov/sh85084621.

70. TJ to Samuel H. Smith, 21 September 1814, *Founders Online*, National Archives, https://founders.archives.gov/documents/Jefferson/03-07-02-0484-0003.

71. TJ to George Watterston, 2 March 1816, *Founders Online*, National Archives, https://founders.archives.gov/documents/Jefferson/03-09-02-0366.

72. Quoted in Tay, "Forming the Body of a Library Based on the 'Illimitable Freedom,'" 215.

73. O'Shaughnessy, *Illimitable Freedom of the Human Mind*, 129.

74. O'Shaughnessy, *Illimitable Freedom of the Human Mind*, 257.

75. Quoted in O'Shaughnessy, *Illimitable Freedom of the Human Mind*, 251.

76. Thomas Jefferson to John Wyche, 19 May 1809," *Founders Online*, National Archives, https://founders.archives.gov/documents/Jefferson/03-01-02-0170.

77. TJ to John Wyche, 19 May 1809, *Founders Online*, National Archives, https://founders.archives.gov/documents/Jefferson/03-01-02-0170.

78. Glynn, *Reading Publics*, 18.

79. TJ, "A Bill for the More General Diffusion of Knowledge," 365.

80. Boston Public Library, founded in 1848 and officially opened to the public in 1854, is more commonly regarded as the first public library.

81. John Wyche to TJ, 19 March 1809, *Founders Online*, National Archives, https://founders.archives.gov/documents/Jefferson/03-01-02-0051.

82. John Wyche to TJ, 19 March 1809, *Founders Online*, National Archives, https://founders.archives.gov/documents/Jefferson/03-01-02-0051.

83. TJ to Frederick Winslow Hatch, 22 April 1823, *Founders Online*, National Archives, https://founders.archives.gov/documents/Jefferson/98-01-02-3473.

84. Memorandum Books, 1823, *Founders Online*, National Archives, https://founders.archives.gov/documents/Jefferson/02-02-02-0033.

85. Jackson Park (now Court Square Park) was established in Court Square, as well. A confederate monument called "At Ready" was removed in 2020.

86. O'Hare, "What Will Happen to Charlottesville's Auction Block Site."

87. I have not found a list of subscribers or committee members.

88. Virginia Assembly, "An Act Incorporating the Albemarle Library Society," 74–75.

89. Hubbard, "Libraries in Charlottesville," 7.

90. Hubbard, "Libraries in Charlottesville," 7.

91. Ditzion, *Arsenals of a Democratic Culture*, 52.

92. Popowich, *Confronting the Democratic Discourse of Librarianship*, 4.

93. Inklebarger, "Ferguson's Safe Haven."

94. Klinenberg, *Palaces for the People*, 32.

95. Klinenberg, *Palaces for the People*, 37.

96. Library of Congress, *Alphabetical Catalogue*, 3.

97. TJ to George Watterston, 7 May 1815, *Founders Online*, National Archives, https://founders.archives.gov/documents/Jefferson/03-08-02-0376.

98. See Eastman, *The Strange Genius of Mr. O*, for a thorough biography of James Ogilvie, an early American orator.

99. TJ to James Ogilvie, 31 January 1806, *Founders Online*, National Archives, https://founders.archives.gov/documents/Jefferson/99-01-02-3156.

100. TJ, 1783 *Catalog of Books*.

101. Yeo, "Reading Encyclopedias," 25–26.

102. Haraway, "Situated Knowledges," 48.

103. TJ to John Manners, 22 February 1814, *Founders Online*, National Archives, https://founders.archives.gov/documents/Jefferson/03-07-02-0132.

104. TJ to Augustus Elias Brevoort Woodward, 24 March 1824, *Founders Online*, National Archives, https://founders.archives.gov/documents/Jefferson/98-01-02-4139.

105. TJ to Augustus Elias Brevoort Woodward, 24 March 1824, *Founders Online*, National Archives, https://founders.archives.gov/documents/Jefferson/98-01-02-4139).

106. The twists and turns of the social and political lives of Diderot and D'Alembert, especially with regard to the *Encyclopédie* are tangential to this study. They had run-ins with various entities, including the Jesuits and other opponents. The project was outlawed and its circulation prohibited more than once. Diderot had a painful falling out with Jean Jacques Rousseau. For a full account see Curran, *Diderot and the Art of Thinking Freely*.

107. Darnton, *Great Cat Massacre*, 200.

108. D'Alembert, *Preliminary Discourse*, 128.

109. D'Alembert, *Preliminary Discourse*, 128.

110. Darnton, *Great Cat Massacre*, 209.

111. Vartija, *Color of Equality*, 88.

112. Vartija, *Color of Equality*, 89.

113. Vartija, *Color of Equality*, 139, 108.

114. Bacon, quoted in Irving, "In a Pure Soil," 249.

115. Irving, "In a Pure Soil," 253.

116. Hogan, "Of Islands and Bridges," 39.

117. Hogan, "Of Islands and Bridges," 40.

118. Hogan, "Of Islands and Bridges," 43.

119. Welburn, "Empire and Utopia," 161.

120. Much more can be said about Bacon's, D'Alembert's, and Diderot's points of view and place in history. This is beyond the scope of this research, but I refer readers to Curran's *Diderot and the Art of Thinking Freely* and Darnton's *Great Cat Massacre* for more about Diderot, and Hogan's "Of Islands and Bridges," Irving's "In a Pure Soil," and Welburn's "Empire and Utopia" for compelling analyses of the connections between Bacon's epistemology and colonialism.

## 5. The Racial Aesthetic of Jefferson's Library Catalog

1. The number of chapters varied across iterations of his catalogs.

2. McKittrick, *Dear Science*, 35.

3. Wolfe, *Traces of History*, 9–10.

4. Wolfe, *Traces of History*, 9.

5. Wolfe, *Traces of History*, 8–9

6. Smith, *Decolonizing Methodologies*, 28.

7. Pratt, *Imperial Eyes*, 36.

8. Fuentes, *Dispossessed Lives*, 5.

9. Gilreath and Wilson, *Thomas Jefferson's Library*. See note 20 below.

10. Elmer, "The Archive, the Native American, and Jefferson's Convulsions," 12.

11. Foucault, *Order of Things*, 131.

12. Wheatley was named for the ship, *Phillis*, which carried her as a small child from West Africa to her enslavement in North America. After marriage to John Peters in 1778, she signed her written texts as Phillis Peters.

13. Jefferson frequently recommended Sterne's books and cited his work in examples of how novels can be instructive.

14. According to Sowerby, v. 5, Jefferson had a third edition of Sancho's letters: *Letters of the Late Ignatius Sancho: An African, to Which are Prefixed, Memoirs of His Life* (Dublin: Brett Smith for Richard Moncrieff, 1784). For scholarship on Sancho see Carretta and Gould, *Genius in Bondage*, and for work on Wheatley see Carretta, *Phillis Wheatley*. Also see Bynum, Fielder, and Smith, "Special Issue Introduction." Sancho questioned the motives of white elites who celebrated her poetry, including the people who enslaved her and taught her to write. Sancho, "Letters," 175–76.

15. Vimalassery, Pegues, and Goldstein, "Introduction: On Colonial Unknowing," para.1

16. Thomas Jefferson (hereafter TJ), *Notes on the State of Virginia*, 267 (emphasis added).

17. It is important to note that this passage about Sancho was added later as an attachment to *Notes*. Massachusetts Historical Society has digitized the various iterations of *Notes on the State of Virginia*, with tabs that show the revisions over time. "When Jefferson was in Paris in 1785 representing the United States as a diplomat, he paid to have 200 copies of *Notes* printed for private distribution. Prior to publication, Jefferson reworked an earlier version of his manuscript by using sealing wax to attach corrections and changes written on small additional pieces of paper to full handwritten pages. He also expanded the text by inserting additional full pages. . . . This website allows the reader to interact directly with Jefferson's complex manuscript by reading the original manuscript and by following all the changes that he made to the text before it was first published." Thomas Jefferson Papers: An Electronic Archive. https://www.masshist.org/thomasjeffersonpapers/notes/.

18. TJ, *Notes on the State of Virginia*, 267.

19. Hannah Spahn offers a comparison of Wheatley's "Enlightenment of principle" with Jefferson's "Enlightenment of feeling" and discusses Wheatley's influence, beginning with her call for a universal "love of freedom." Spahn, *Black Reason, White Feeling*.

20. In 1814, just before selling the collection, he acquired Judy Lomax's volume of poetry and added it to the catalog, beneath the Wheatley entry. Via email correspondence Endrina Tay has provided me with a more detailed explanation for what may have happened: "Jefferson created a fair copy of his 1783 Catalog in 1812. It is this 1812 Catalog that is sent to Congress together with the books and ended up with the Librarian of Congress, George Watterston, and is today lost. So, when Jefferson created his 1812 Catalog, he placed Wheatley at the bottom of the chapter . . . such that when he acquired Lomax in 1814, he proceeded to add the later acquisition after Wheatley. The other possibility is that the quality of Lomax's work was in fact judged by Jefferson to warrant a position behind Wheatley. I posit this as the Trist Catalogue (i.e., the 1815 Catalog later transcribed and published by Gilreath & Wilson in 1989), which was a recreation of Jefferson's 1812 Catalog as it stood at the time of the library sale by Nicholas P. Trist at the direction of Jefferson in 1823. Jefferson was getting ready to build the library for the University of Virginia and wanted his 1812 Catalog to

be utilized as a reference source. He had an opportunity then to re-position Wheatley behind Lomax, but clearly chose not to do so at that point. It could well be that Lomax was listed last in the chapter in the Trist Catalogue simply because it was the latest work to be acquired by Jefferson at the time of library sale."

21. Gikandi, *Slavery and the Culture of Taste*, 23–24.

22. William Ray's *Horrors of Slavery* may be a duplicate listing, as the alternative title for the same work, *The American Tars in Tripoli*, appears in the history chapter, with books on the Barbary States.

23. Ray, *Horrors of Slavery*, ix.

24. Henri Grégoire, *De la littérature des Nègres, ou, Recherches sur leurs facultés intellectuelles, leurs qualités morales et leur littérature.* Paris: Chez Maradan, 1808. Citation drawn from Library of Congress catalog, which provides bibliographic information about Jefferson's personal copy.

25. Eaton, "Lost in Translation," 230.

26. Eaton, "Lost in Translation," 237.

27. Quoted in Eaton, "Lost in Translation," 234.

28. TJ to Henri Grégoire, 25 February 1809, *Founders Online*, National Archives, https://founders.archives.gov/documents/Jefferson/99-01-02-9893.

29. TJ to Joel Barlow, 8 October 1809, *Founders Online*, National Archives, https://founders.archives.gov/documents/Jefferson/03-01-02-0461.

30. This is an exceedingly complicated conflict that has recently been taken up by some historians as a point of comparison to America's "War on Terror." To my mind, this conflict is important in understanding the relationship between early American capitalism, global trade, and anti-Islamism. Jefferson's own position in this war is beyond the scope of this work. See Cogliano, *Emperor of Liberty*; Lambert, *The Barbary Wars*; Kilmeade and Yaeger, *Thomas Jefferson and the Tripoli Pirates*; Wheelan, *Jefferson's War*.

31. Brezina, "Nation in Chains," 217.

32. Brezina, "Nation in Chains," 206.

33. Kelley, "Foreword," xiii-xiv. *Black Marxism* was first published in 1983.

34. Equiano was known as Gustavus Vassa for most of his life. I searched TJ's corpus for this name, too, with no results.

35. See Lowe, *Intimacies of Four Continents*, 49, for a description of the use of Equiano's autobiography in abolitionist efforts.

36. Benjamin Banneker to TJ, 19 August 1791, *Founders Online*, National Archives, https://founders.archives.gov/documents/Jefferson/01-22-02-0049.

37. Gordon-Reed, "Engaging Jefferson," 173.

38. TJ to Joel Barlow, 8 October 1809, *Founders Online*, National Archives, https://founders.archives.gov/documents/Jefferson/03-01-02-0461.

39. Gates and Curran, "Inventing the Science of Race."

40. Gilroy, *Black Atlantic*, 8.

41. Cahill, *Liberty of the Imagination*, 105.

42. Wynter, "Rethinking 'Aesthetics,'" 260–61.

43. Manning, "Naming of Parts," 354.

44. Cahill, *Liberty of the Imagination*, 103–4.

45. To be sure, this is a specific reading that will diverge in some respects from certain histories of aesthetics. While the influence of natural historians on Jefferson's thinking cannot be underestimated, it seems most useful to consider the thinkers that Jefferson wrote about and engaged with the most. This includes Buffon, Chastellux, Condorcet, Raynal, and Humboldt. For more complete historical accounts see, for example, Bedini, *Thomas Jefferson*; Curran, *Anatomy of Blackness*; Lloyd, *Under Representation*; Hayes, *Road to Monticello*; Wulf, *Invention of Nature*. Jack Andersen, "Knowledge Organization as a Cultural Form," calls for greater attention to the aesthetic in knowledge organization. Following Lev Manovich, who highlights databases and new media that "aestheticize" information processing, Andersen suggests that seeing knowledge organization aesthetically "provides ground for an understanding of knowledge organization as a specific cultural practice; a specific way of handling the products of human culture and human activity." Jefferson did own Charles de Villers's eight-volume translation of Kant, but I have not found any direct references by Jefferson to the text in Jefferson's writings. Surely, though, the pervasiveness of a Kantian framework during the Enlightenment would have influenced Jefferson's thinking. Henry Louis Gates, Jr. and Andrew Curran explain how Kant's anthropological writing included several assertions about cognitive potential, capacity for reason, and morality, which supported the conclusion that Africans were incapable of reaching a level of civilization. In his 1777 essay, "Of the Different Human Races," Kant "provided the first philosophically rigorous definition of race, one that not only asserted the biological permanence of racial categories—'(1) the race of the Whites, (2) the Negro race, (3) the Hunnish (Kalmuck or Mongolian) race, (4) the Hindu or Hindustani race'—but positioned the African race as seemingly less than fully human." Gates and Curran regard this as a key moment – "the first light of scientifically rigorous racism: an era when naturalists and taxonomists divided the world's peoples into discrete subspecies, when skin color and category became synonymous with racial destiny." Kant's categories resemble those of other natural philosophers of the eighteenth century.

46. Maldonado-Torres, "Notes on Modernity and Extractivism," 150.

47. Gikandi, "Race and the Idea of the Aesthetic," 329.

48. Wulf, *Founding Gardeners*, 166.

49. Byrne, *Aesthetic Sexuality*, 12.

50. Cahill, *Liberty of the Imagination*, 110.

51. Smith, quoted in Cahill, *Liberty of the Imagination*, 110.

52. Cahill, *Liberty of the Imagination*, 115.

53. TJ, *Notes on the State of Virginia*, 148. Jefferson purchased the Natural Bridge in 1774; he received a patent for a 157-acre tract of land on which it was situated.

54. Burke, *Philosophical Enquiry*, 57.

55. Armstrong, "The Effects of Blackness."

56. Armstrong, "The Effects of Blackness," 217.

57. Armstrong, "The Effects of Blackness," 217.

58. Fanon, *Black Skin, White Masks*, 84, 83.

59. Fanon, *Black Skin, White Masks*, 82.

60. Wynter, "On How We Mistook the Map for the Territory," 118.

61. Wynter, "Towards the Sociogenic Principle," 53.

62. The works of William Cowper and Daniel Turner, respectively entitled *The Anatomy of Humane Bodies* (1698) and *De Morbis Cutaneis* (1714), were regarded as the authoritative texts on skin in the early eighteenth century.

63. Crouch, "Surface Tensions," 10–11.

64. Hogarth, "Of Black Skin and Biopower," 838.

65. Curran, *Anatomy of Blackness*, 168.

66. Hogarth, *Analysis of Beauty*, 114.

67. Hogarth, *Analysis of Beauty*, 116.

68. TJ, *Notes on the State of Virginia*, 264–65.

69. LaFleur, *Natural History of Sexuality*, 4.

70. Hogarth, *Analysis of Beauty*, 116.

71. William Cheselden, 1729, "Account of Some Observations Made by a Young Gentleman, Who was Born Blind, or Lost His Sight So Early, that He Had No Remembrance of Ever Having Seen, and Was Couch'd between 13 and 14 Years of Age," *Philosophical Transactions of the Royal Society* 35: 447–50, quoted in Burke, *Philosophical Enquiry*, 144.

72. Lloyd, *Under Representation*, 65.

73. Ferguson, *Aberrations in Black*, 86–87.

74. Ferguson, *Aberrations in Black*, 87.

75. Burke, *Philosophical Enquiry*, 143.

76. Fanon, *Black Skin, White Masks*, 91.

77. Burke launches into his discussion of the "effects of blackness" with a refutation of Locke, who argued that we fear the darkness because we associate it with stories of ghosts and goblins and scary events. A distinction is made between darkness and blackness, with the specific issue concerning darkness being the unknowable. Contra Locke, Burke believes that darkness is dangerous by nature. He regards the thought that "an idea so universally terrible in all times, and in all countries, as darkness" could not simply be the result of stories and representations, but that it harbours the unknown: for in utter darkness it is impossible to know in what degree of safety we stand; we are ignorant of the objects that surround us; we may every moment strike against some dangerous obstruction; we may fall down a precipice the first step we take; and if an enemy approach, we know not in what quarter to defend ourselves; in such a case strength is no sure protection; wisdom can only act by guess; the boldest are staggered, and he, who would pray for nothing else towards his defence, is forced to pray for light."

78. Hogarth, "Of Black Skin and Biopower," 845.

79. Gikandi, *Slavery and the Culture of Taste*, 16.

80. Hansson, "*Informative Potential of Bibliographic Classification Systems*."

81. Cahill, *Liberty of the Imagination*, 105. Cahill provides descriptions of Jefferson's *Notes on the State of Virginia* and Crèvecoeur's *Letters from an American Farmer*. It is important to note that these texts were published, translated, and revised

at around the same time, and they share stylistic and thematic tendencies. Jefferson owned three editions of Crèvecoeur's *Letters*, one of which was sent directly from the author to Jefferson, and he consulted Crèvecoeur on revisions. See Sowerby, *Catalogue of Thomas Jefferson's Library*, v. 4, 199–200.

### 6. From Geography to History

1. TallBear, *Native American DNA*, 3.
2. Palmer, "Rendering Settler Sovereign Landscapes," 797.
3. Simpson, "Settlement's Secret," 208.
4. Holland, *Body Politic*, 20.
5. Thomas Jefferson (hereafter TJ), Second Inaugural Address, 4 March 1805, *Founders Online*, National Archives, https://founders.archives.gov/documents/Jefferson/01-45-02-0637-0014.
6. Tawil, "Domestic Frontier Romance," 101.
7. Wallace, *Jefferson and the Indians*, 1–20.
8. TJ, *Notes on the State of Virginia*, 266.
9. Wallace, *Jefferson and the Indians*, 76.
10. Simpson, "On Ethnographic Refusal," 67.
11. Simpson, "On Ethnographic Refusal," 67.
12. Simpson, "On Ethnographic Refusal," 67.
13. Hayes, *Road to Monticello*, 563.
14. Gilreath and Wilson, *Thomas Jefferson's Library*, 8.
15. Blackhawk, *Rediscovery of America*, 74.
16. Blackhawk, *Rediscovery of America*, 75.
17. Sowerby, *Catalogue of the Library of Thomas Jefferson*, v. 2, 260.
18. Sowerby, *Catalogue of the Library of Thomas Jefferson*, v. 2, 259.
19. Pratt, *Imperial Eyes*, 51.
20. Cahill, *Liberty of the Imagination*, 110.
21. Rivett, "Unruly Empiricisms," 651.
22. Simpson's articulation of "ethnographic refusal" is referencing the responsibility of anthropologists, which "involves a calculus ethnography of what you need to know and what I refuse to write in." It seems appropriate to consider the ways that people who are being studied can refuse to participate in Jefferson's research, as well.
23. Rivett, "Unruly Empiricisms," 673.
24. For an account of Jefferson's own interest and involvement in land companies see Wallace, *Jefferson and the Indians*, 21–49.
25. In Jefferson's tables in *Notes on the State of Virginia*, "tithable persons" included "free men" and "slaves" but not white male minors or women. Indigenous peoples are counted in the chapter on Aboriginal peoples. See Dikant, "Settler Colonial Statistics."
26. Maddox, *Removals*, 9.

27. Sayre, "Mound Builders," 226.
28. Sayre, "Mound Builders," 245.
29. TJ, *Notes on the State of Virginia*, 219.
30. For a full account of the Monacan Nation's relationship to Rassawek, see Cultural Heritage Partners, on behalf of the Monacan Indian Nation. Comments from the Monacan Indian Nation. In 2022 they won a lawsuit, resulting in the "selection of an alternative route for the construction of the James River Water Authority (JRWA) water withdrawal and pipeline, which will avoid destroying the Monacan historic capital of Rassawek." "Rassawek Saved." Settlers named this place "Point of Fork," and during the American Revolution, it was used as a storage space for ammunition.
31. TJ, *Notes on the State of Virginia*, 228 (emphasis added).
32. TJ to Indian Nations, 10 January 1809, *Founders Online*, National Archives, https://founders.archives.gov/documents/Jefferson/99-01-02-9516.
33. Bhandar, *Colonial Lives of Property*, 8.
34. Looby, "Constitution of Nature," 269.
35. Owens, *Mr. Jefferson's Hammer*.
36. Each of these shelf locations was found in the Library of Congress catalog, 18 April 2019, https://catalog.loc.gov; the classification captions are from the Library of Congress Classification, E-F. Some of Jefferson's books are placed in other locations, including the F section designated for local history, where books on the Lewis and Clark expedition are shelved.
37. Webster and Doyle, "Don't Class Me in Antiquities!," 191.
38. Frosio, "Comments on the Thomas Yen-Ran Yeh Proposals," 129.
39. E31-185. "Indians of North America" is classed in "Pre-Columbian America" in the Library of Congress Classification, 2024 edition, https://www.loc.gov/aba/publications/FreeLCC/LCC_E-F2024OUT.pdf.
40. Library of Congress Classification E-F.
41. Christen and Anderson, "Toward Slow Archives," 90.
42. The incommensurability of settler colonial and Indigenous systems are obvious, but manifestations of incommensurability arise among different efforts that aim toward social justice. An "ethic of incommensurability" can also be grounds for solidarity among decolonial, transnational, anti-racist, and abolitionist movements. Tuck and Yang, "Decolonization is Not a Metaphor," 28.
43. Frosio, "Comments on the Thomas Yen-Ran Yeh Proposals," 129.
44. Simpson, "Settlement's Secret," 208.
45. McClintock, *Imperial Leather*, 30.
46. Rifkin, *Beyond Settler Time*, 4.
47. Rifkin, *Beyond Settler Time*, viii (emphasis added).
48. Cushman, "Wampum, Sequoyan, and Story," 116.
49. Cushman, "Wampum, Sequoyan, and Story," 117.
50. LaFleur, *Natural History of Sexuality*, 33.
51. Holgersson-Shorter, "Authority's Shadowy Double," 53.

52. TJ, "Memorandums on a Tour from Paris to Amsterdam, Strasburg, and Back to Paris," 651 (emphasis added).

53. Onuf, *Jefferson's Empire*, 34.

54. Driskill, Finley, Gilley, and Morgensen, *Queer Indigenous Studies*, 16; la paperson, *A Third University is Possible*.

55. TJ, *Notes on the State of Virginia*, 189.

56. LaFleur, *Natural History of Sexuality*, 57.

57. LaFleur, *Natural History of Sexuality*, 33.

58. TJ, *Notes on the State of Virginia*, 187.

59. Finley, "Decolonizing the Queer Native Body," 35.

60. TallBear, "Yes, Your Pleasure!"

61. TallBear, "Yes, Your Pleasure!"

62. Morgensen, *Spaces Between Us*, 1.

63. Rifkin, *When Did Indians Become Straight?*, 8.

64. Rifkin, *When Did Indians Become Straight?*, 7.

## 7. Jefferson's "Indian Hall" and the Doctrine of Discovery

1. Thomas Jefferson (hereafter TJ) to John Page, 21 February 1770, *Founders Online*, National Archives, https://founders.archives.gov/documents/Jefferson/01-01-02-0023.

2. The lines from *The Tempest* appear toward the end of the play, when Prospero appears to have gone mad. After this scene he resolves to punish Caliban for plotting to kill him. He addresses Ferdinand:

> You do look, my son, in a mov'd sort,
> As if you were dismay'd; be cheerful, sir.
> Our revels now are ended. These our actors
> (As I foretold you) were all spirits, and
> Are melted into air, into thin air,
> And like the baseless fabric of this this vision,
> The clowd-capp'd tow'rs, the gorgeous palaces,
> The solemn temples, the great globe itself,
> Yea, all which it inherit, shall dissolve,
> And like this insubstantial pageant faded
> Leave not a rack behind.

3. Some of the text in the introductory pages of this chapter are revised from Adler and Nightingale, "Books and Imaginary Being(s)." I extend gratitude to Greg Nightingale for so many thrilling conversations and for granting permission to reproduce some of the material here.

4. Wynter, "Beyond the Word of Man," 644.

5. Wynter, "Beyond the Word of Man," 644.

6. Wynter, "Unsettling the Coloniality of Being," 289.

7. Wynter, "Unsettling the Coloniality of Being," 289.
8. Wynter, "Unsettling the Coloniality of Being," 290.
9. Jackson, *Becoming Human*, 13.
10. Butler, *Bodies that Matter*, 8.
11. Shannon, "Eight Animals of Shakespeare," 474.
12. Shannon, "Eight Animals of Shakespeare," 474.
13. Jackson, *Becoming Human*, 13.
14. Jackson, *Becoming Human*, 15.
15. Jackson, *Becoming Human*, 18.
16. For examples from Canadian artists and scholars: Wilson (settler/uninvited guest), "Remnants. Outlaws, and Wallows"; Bachman, *Cultural Genocide*; Hubbard (Peepeekisis First Nation in Treaty Four Territory), "Buffalo Genocide in Nineteenth-Century North America"; Taschereau Mamers (settler scholar, raised in Amiskwaciwâskahikan on Treaty 6 territory), "Human-Bison Relations"; Todd (Red River Métis), "Fish Pluralities." Kent Monkman (Fisher River Cree Nation in Treaty 5 Territory) has conveyed this throughout his written and visual art work, especially in the exhibition *The Rise and Fall of Civilization*. Also see Monkman and Cordon (settler), *The Memoirs of Miss Chief Eagle Testickle*, vols. 1 and 2. Michi Saagiig Nishnaabeg scholar Leanne Betasamosake Simpson's novels, poetry, essays, and videos are essential. See, for example, *A Short History of the Blockade* and "Land as Pedagogy."
17. Wilson, "Remnants, Outlaws, and Wallows," xiii.
18. In Chapter 8 of this book, where I demonstrate the processes by which the pronghorn became a document, I discuss the ways in which the idea of information as resource is connected to the classification and thingification of life.
19. Bennett, *Museums, Power, Knowledge*, 23.
20. Bennett, *Museums, Power, Knowledge*, 25.
21. Delbourgo, *Collecting the World*.
22. Lee, *Decolonize Museums*, 100.
23. Lee, *Decolonize Museums*, 97. On museums as "classifying houses" see Whitehead, "Museums in the History of Zoology." Whitehead divides museum history into several eras, and regards 1750–1850 as the "Linnaean Period."
24. Bennett, *Museums, Power, Knowledge*, 31.
25. Bennett, *Birth of the Museum*, 67.
26. On 14 May 1743, Benjamin Franklin wrote *A Proposal for Promoting Useful Knowledge*, *Founders Online*, National Archives, https://founders.archives.gov/documents/Franklin/01-02-02-0092. For more complete histories of the society see Orosz, *Curators and Culture* and Spero, "The Other Presidency."
27. Salomon, "A Mirror of the World," 90.
28. Salomon, "A Mirror of the World," 89.
29. TJ to Charles Willson Peale, 6 October 1805, *Founders Online*, National Archives, https://founders.archives.gov/documents/Jefferson/99-01-02-2444.
30. *os frontis* means frontal bone.

31. We don't have a complete catalog of the museum, but there are a few descriptions from which historians have been able to arrive at a fairly accurate account of its contents and arrangement: George Ticknor's Account of a Visit to Monticello, [4–7 February 1815], *Founders Online*, National Archives, https://founders.archives.gov/documents/Jefferson/03-08-02-0190. George Ticknor would become one of the founders of Boston Public Library. Jefferson drafted a "Catalogue of Paintings &c. at Monticello," probably sometime after 1809, which includes locations of paintings and objects in the house. The full catalog is Jefferson's Catalogue of Paintings &c., Accession #2958-b, The Thomas Jefferson Papers, Special Collections, University of Virginia Library. It was transcribed by Seymour Howard, "Thomas Jefferson's Art Gallery for Monticello," *The Art Bulletin* 59, no. 4 (1977): 597–600. Transcription available at https://www.monticello.org/research-education/thomas-jefferson-encyclopedia/catalogue-paintings/#fn-src-1.

32. "Montlezun's Account of a Visit to Monticello, 20 September 1816," *Founders Online*, National Archives, https://founders.archives.gov/documents/Jefferson/03-10-02-0285.

33. "Montlezun's Account of a Visit to Monticello, 20 September 1816," (editors' translation), *Founders Online*, National Archives, https://founders.archives.gov/documents/Jefferson/03-10-02-0285.

> One also sees there a tusk from a mammoth and one from an elephant, with a tooth from the latter animal to show how different it is from those of the former, which are conical and designed for a carnivorous animal, whereas the others have flat and scratched crowns, as is characteristic of a frugivore.
>
> A head of a gigantic ram; one supposes that it is from the primitive breed that used to live in North America.
>
> Mr. Randolph next showed me the pictures and portraits that decorate the different rooms.
>
> The portraits of Washington, Lafayette, Adams, Franklin, Walter Raleigh, Amerigo Vespucci, Columbus, Bacon, Locke, Newton, etc., etc.
>
> Pictures: a dead man emerging from the tomb to tell his story;
>
> The surrender of Cornwallis in October 1781 at Yorktown, Virginia;
>
> Diogenes looking for a man;
>
> Alexander and Diogenes;
>
> Democritus and Heracleitus, etc., etc., etc.
>
> I also saw:
>
> A bear's claw from Missouri. This species is larger and much more ferocious than the others;
>
> A mammoth's tusk;
>
> Several teeth from the same animal;
>
> The thighbone of the same.

The mammoth's head is constituted, as I said before, of a perfect upper jaw and two lower half-jaws from different animals; one of the latter is much larger than the other.

A European coat of mail used by those who fought the Indians early on. With it, they were in no danger of being wounded by their arrows.

Antlers of the American elk and other animals of that sort. Those of the elk are considerable; these animals, as well as the buffalo and several others, have been killed off in the parts of Virginia where the population is densest. One may find them in the Ohio territory, to which the large number of hunters have relegated them.

Two stone busts sculpted by the savages, one representing a man and the other a woman. The faces are hideous and quite coarsely made. They were no doubt used for worship and have a lot in common with the Egyptian and oriental divinities, whose images are engraved in most of the books that deal with those peoples.

A small Indian hatchet made from a kind of polished porphyry, with the top in the shape of a pipe;

A figure of an animal in the same type of stone;

Various petrifactions.

Bows, arrows, spears, and lots of objects made by the savages;

A life-size marble statue similar to that of Cleopatra. She is lying down, and a snake encircles her left arm. This is a copy from the ancients. Mr. Jefferson believes that she represents Ariadne.

An elephant's tooth, which, being from an herbivorous animal, is totally different from those of the mammoth. Nevertheless, it is generally thought that the latter is just a kind of elephant.

34. TJ to Morgan Brown, 16 January 1800, *Founders Online*, National Archives, https://founders.archives.gov/documents/Jefferson/01-31-02-0266. Ronan, "Kicked About."

35. Anderson, *Imagined Communities*, 178.

36. Weizman et al., "Forensic Architecture," 62.

37. Latour, *Science in Action*, 223.

38. Latour, *Science in Action*, 220.

39. Latour, *Science in Action*, 220.

40. Latour, *Science in Action*, 243.

41. Cahill, *Liberty of the Imagination*, 105.

42. Latour, "The Networks That Reason Ignores."

43. Miller, *Native America*, 12.

44. Palmer, "Rendering Settler Sovereign Landscapes," 799.

45. Recently the Catholic Church repudiated the Doctrine of Discovery. The Vatican's Dicastery for Promoting Integral Human Development, headed by Canadian Cardinal Michael Czerny, and the Dicastery for Culture and Education issued a joint statement on 30 March 2023, indicating that the Doctrine of Discovery

is not part of the teachings of the Catholic Church. "At the same time, the church acknowledges that these papal bulls did not adequately reflect the equal dignity and rights of Indigenous peoples. The church is also aware that the contents of these documents were manipulated for political purposes by competing colonial powers in order to justify immoral acts against Indigenous peoples," Reguly, "Vatican Formally Rejects Doctrine of Discovery."

46. Miller is an enrolled citizen of the Eastern Shawnee Tribe and Interim Chief Justice for the Pascua Yaqui Tribe Court of Appeals. He is the Willard H. Pedrick Distinguished Research Scholar at Arizona State University and the Faculty Director of the Rosette LLP American Indian Economic Development Program at ASU.

47. Miller, *Native America*, 59.

48. Miller, *Native America*, 2.

49. Latour, *Science in Action*, 224.

50. Meriwether Lewis to TJ, 7 April 1805, *Founders Online*, National Archives, https://founders.archives.gov/documents/Jefferson/01-46-02-0170-0001.

51. Blackhawk, *Rediscovery of America*, 109.

52. Castanha, "Doctrine of Discovery," 51.

53. Ghaddar, "Spectre in the Archive," 22.

54. Ghaddar, "Spectre in the Archive," 23.

55. Justice, *Why Indigenous Literatures Matter*, 25.

56. Turner, *Cataloging Culture*, 29.

57. TallBear, "Yes, Your Pleasure!"

58. Martin Nord has considered the implications of Briet's theory for "human documents" by examining the case of Ishi, a living Yahi man who was studied, documented, and displayed by anthropologists in the early twentieth century. See his "Ishi, Briet's Antelope, and the Documentality of Human Documents."

59. Kimmerer, *Braiding Sweetgrass*, 55.

60. Kimmerer, *Braiding Sweetgrass*, 55.

61. Kimmerer, *Braiding Sweetgrass*, 56–57.

62. Robinson, "Shxwelí li te shxwelítemelh xíts' etáwtxw," 238.

63. O'Brien, *Firsting and Lasting*, 94.

64. Robinson, "Shxwelí li te shxwelítemelh xíts' etáwtxw," 237.

65. Robinson, "Shxwelí li te shxwelítemelh xíts' etáwtxw," 242.

66. Nguyen, *Gift of Freedom*, 13.

67. For a book-length discussion of Western and Indigenous views of gifts, see Kuokkanen (Deatnu River, Ohcejohka/Utsjoki), *Reshaping the University*.

68. TJ to Charles Carroll, 15 April 1791, *Founders Online*, National Archives, https://founders.archives.gov/documents/Jefferson/01-20-02-0046.

69. Meriwether Lewis to TJ, 7 April 1805, *Founders Online*, National Archives, https://founders.archives.gov/documents/Jefferson/01-46-02-0170-0001.

70. Meriwether Lewis to TJ, 7 April 1805, *Founders Online*, National Archives, https://founders.archives.gov/documents/Jefferson/01-46-02-0170-0001.

71. TJ to Meriwether Lewis, 26 October 1806, *Founders Online*, National Archives, https://founders.archives.gov/documents/Jefferson/99-01-02-4473.

72. Maldonado-Torres, "Notes on Modernity and Extractivism," 150.

73. The United Nations Declaration on the Rights of Indigenous Peoples (UNDRIP) was adopted by the UN General Assembly on Thursday, 13 September 2007, by a majority of 144 states in favor, four votes against (including the United States) and several abstentions. The United States has since agreed to support the declaration, but it is not legally binding. The United Nations Human Rights Council (UNHRC) introduced a resolution in 2019 to provide a framework "to facilitate the international repatriation of indigenous peoples' sacred items and human remains through the continued engagement of the United Nations Educational, Scientific and Cultural Organization (UNESCO), the World Intellectual Property Organization, the Expert Mechanism, the Special Rapporteur on the rights of indigenous peoples, the Permanent Forum on Indigenous Issues, States, indigenous peoples and all other relevant parties in accordance with their mandates" (United Nations Human Rights Council, "Repatriation of Ceremonial Objects," 2). For sources on repatriation see, for example, Atalay, "Braiding Strands of Wellness"; Breske, "Politics of Repatriation"; Fforde, McKeown, and Keeler (Cherokee), *Routledge Companion to Indigenous Repatriation*; Turnbull and Pickering, *The Long Way Home*; Deloria (Yankton Dakota), "The New World of the Indigenous Museum"; Tsosie (Yaqui), "Native Nations and Museums."

74. Stuchel, "Material Provocations in the Archives," 8.

75. This phrasing is borrowed from Bennett, *Vibrant Matter*.

76. Liboiron, *Pollution is Colonialism*, 62.

77. Tuck and Yang, "Decolonization is not a Metaphor," 3.

78. See Lakoff and Johnson, *Metaphors We Live By*.

79. Cowan and Rault, "Introduction," 3.

80. Cowan and Rault, "Introduction," 8.

81. Cowan and Rault, "Introduction," 9.

82. Foucault, *Power/Knowledge*, 70.

83. McKittrick, *Dear Science*, 10.

84. Garba and Sorentino, "Slavery is a Metaphor."

85. Cronon, *Changes in the Land*, 165.

86. Godelier, "The Object and Method," quoted in Cronon, *Changes in the Land*, 165.

## 8. How the American Antelope [*sic*] Became a Document

1. Briet was a librarian at the French Bibliothèque Nationale and is often regarded as a founder of French documentation.

2. Briet, *What is Documentation?*, 10.

3. Day, *Documentarity*, 64. Ron Day co-translated Briet's work after Michael Buckland presented her theories in his papers on documentation.

4. Day, *Documentarity*, 62.

5. Day, *Documentarity*, 62.

6. Stoler, *Duress*, 25.
7. Frohmann, "Documentality of Mme Briet's Antelope," 175.
8. Frohmann, "Documentality of Mme Briet's Antelope," 177.
9. Frohmann, *Deflating Information*, 18.
10. Charles Willson Peale to Thomas Jefferson (hereafter TJ), 12 January 1802, *Founders Online*, National Archives, https://founders.archives.gov/documents/Jefferson/01-36-02-0215-0001 (emphasis added).
11. The first museum in Philadelphia was opened in 1782 by the Swiss collector Pierre Eugène Du Simitière, but it closed within a few years. Peale's is remarkable for its size and influence.
12. Dugatkin, *Behind the Crimson Curtain*, 78; Schofield, "Science Education of an Enlightened Entrepreneur," 35. For an account of the perfection of Linnaeus's system for Peale's museum, as well as the printed volumes consulted for identification, taxidermy, and natural history see Schofield.
13. Schofield, "Science Education of an Enlightened Entrepreneur," 21.
14. Derrida, *The Animal That Therefore I Am*, 101.
15. Derrida, *The Animal That Therefore I Am*, 13.
16. Berger, "Why Look at Animals?," 16.
17. Lewis and Clark, *Original Journals of the Lewis and Clark Expedition*, 147
18. Lewis and Clark, *Original Journals of the Lewis and Clark Expedition*, 153.
19. Lewis and Clark, *Original Journals of the Lewis and Clark Expedition*, 153.
20. Lewis and Clark, *Original Journals of the Lewis and Clark Expedition*, 153–54.
21. Peale, *Selected Papers*, 945 n.
22. Lewis and Clark, *Original Journals of the Lewis and Clark Expedition*.
23. Peale, *Selected Papers*, 894–95.
24. TJ to Charles Willson Peale, 9 October 1805, *Founders Online*, National Archives, https://founders.archives.gov/documents/Jefferson/99-01-02-2448.
25. Peale, *Selected Papers*, 908.
26. Peale, *Selected Papers*, 908–9.
27. Peale, *Selected Papers*, 951.
28. Peale, *Selected Papers*, 952.
29. Montoya, *Power of Position*, 103.
30. Charles Willson Peale to TJ, 4 August 1806, *Founders Online*, National Archives, https://founders.archives.gov/documents/Jefferson/99-01-02-4127.
31. Charles Willson Peale to TJ, 4 August 1806, *Founders Online*, National Archives, https://founders.archives.gov/documents/Jefferson/99-01-02-4127.
32. Peale withdrew the paper for publication on 17 June 1807 because he found out that Lewis planned to publish a description of the pronghorn in his book about the expedition. Drawing and article are both unlocated. There is no evidence that TJ responded with a name, *Selected Papers*, 974 n.
33. Ord, *A Reprint of the North American Zoology*.
34. McCabe, Reeves, and O'Gara. *Prairie Ghost*, xv.

35. Tanner, "Ethnohistorical Consideration of the Role of *Antilocapra americana*," 133.

36. Tanner, "Ethnohistorical Consideration of the Role of *Antilocapra americana*," 136.

37. Hockett and Murphy, "Antiquity of Communal Pronghorn Hunting," 708.

38. Sundstrom, "Cheyenne Pronghorn Procurement and Ceremony."

39. Silko, "Interior and Exterior Landscapes," 210.

40. TJ to John Manners, 22 February 1814, *Founders Online*, National Archives, https://founders.archives.gov/documents/Jefferson/03-07-02-0132.

41. LaFleur, *Natural History of Sexuality*, 2.

42. Quoted in LaFleur, *Natural History of Sexuality*, 3.

43. Dugatkin, *Behind the Crimson Curtain*, 75.

44. Peale and Palisot de Beauvois, *Scientific and Descriptive Catalogue of Peale's Museum*, 2.

45. Peale and de Beauvois, *Scientific and Descriptive Catalogue of Peale's Museum*, 2.

46. Peale and de Beauvois, *Scientific and Descriptive Catalogue of Peale's Museum*, 3–4.

47. Dugatkin, *Behind the Crimson Curtain*, 76.

48. Turkle, *Evocative Objects*.

49. Day, "Documentation to Documentality," 610.

50. Visitors to the Smithsonian's National Museum of Natural History today will see very similar displays, with animals mounted in ways that animate them in live-action scenes—sometimes as the hunter, sometimes the hunted. Painted scenery, artificial turf and trees, and video footage of the wild are placed across the animal exhibits there. See Hannah Turner's *Cataloguing Culture* (2020) for a fascinating history of the museum's documentation practices.

51. Rogers, Shreckengast, and Dorfman, "Origins and Contemporary Status of Habitat Dioramas in the United States," 27–28.

52. Dugatkin, *Behind the Crimson Curtain*, 67.

53. Rogers, Shreckengast, and Dorfman, "Origins and Contemporary Status of Habitat Dioramas in the United States," 13.

54. Schofield, "The Science Education of an Enlightened Entrepreneur," 31.

55. Briet, "What is Documentation?," 7.

56. Day, *Documentarity*, 63.

57. Montoya, *Power of Position*, 200.

58. Buckland, "Information as Thing," 353.

59. Oxford English Dictionary, "docile (adj.)," September 2024, https://doi.org/10.1093/OED/3955216339.

60. Also see Despret, *What Would Animals Say if We Asked the Right Questions?*

61. Hansson, "The Informative Potential of Bibliographic Classification Systems," 634.

62. Byrd, Goldstein, Melamed, and Reddy, "Predatory Value," 14.

63. Taschereau Mamers, "Human-Bison Relations," 32.
64. Simpson, "Land as Pedagogy," 11.
65. Day, "Documentation to Documentality," 608.

## Coda: Afterlife of Information

1. Ellen Wayles Randolph Coolidge to Henry S. Randall, 16 May 1857, University of Virginia, Ellen Wayles Randolph Coolidge Correspondence (emphasis added); Letterbook, Published in "Jefferson Quotes & Family Letters," Thomas Jefferson Foundation, Inc., https://tjrs.monticello.org/letter/466#X3184701.

2. Cornelia J. Randolph to Virginia J. Randolph Trist, 13 September 1827, University of North Carolina, Chapel Hill, Southern Historical Collection, Nicholas Philip Trist Papers, Published in "Jefferson Quotes & Family Letters," Thomas Jefferson Foundation, Inc., https://tjrs.monticello.org/letter/1103.

3. Thomas Jefferson (hereafter TJ) to Dabney Carr, 19 January 1816, *Founders Online*, National Archives, https://founders.archives.gov/documents/Jefferson/03-09-02-0238.

4. Dabney Carr to TJ, 29 January 1816, *Founders Online*, National Archives, https://founders.archives.gov/documents/Jefferson/03-09-02-0264.

5. TJ to George Watterston, 2 March 1816, *Founders Online*, National Archives, https://founders.archives.gov/documents/Jefferson/03-09-02-0366.

6. George Watterston to TJ, 8 March 1816, *Founders Online*, National Archives, https://founders.archives.gov/documents/Jefferson/03-09-02-0378. Jefferson contributed content to Mazzei's book. In the text, Mazzei described Carr as an "homme recommandable par les qualités les plus rares" ("commendable man with the rarest of qualities"). Editor's note, Dabney Carr to TJ, 1 December 1815, *Founders Online*, National Archives, https://founders.archives.gov/documents/Jefferson/03-09-02-0143.

7. Hayden, "The Choicest Collection of Books," 46.

8. Monticello Association, "Eligibility for Membership," http://www.monticello-assoc.org/eligibility-for-membership.html.

9. Randolph, *Domestic Life of Thomas Jefferson*, 45.

10. It should also be noted that, on the verso of this paper, Jefferson also wrote a seemingly unrelated dedication to John Page. I remain perplexed by this inscription:

> Joanni Page Opusculum hoc Amicitiae Pignus Dat, Donatque
> T. Jefferson. 17—

11. Davenport, "Mourning at Monticello," 36.

12. Davenport, "Mourning at Monticello," 41.

13. "Burial Ground for Enslaved People," https://www.monticello.org/exhibits-events/livestreams-videos-and-podcasts/burial-ground-for-enslaved-people/.

14. Hantman, *Monacan Millenium* (emphasis added).

15. Jefferson, *Notes on the State of Virginia*, 225-226.

16. Jeffrey Hantman has conducted extensive research with the Monacan Nation in recent years and has come to understand the significance of these mounds in the Monacan community. See *Monacan Millenium* for a thorough historical account.

17. Elmer, "The Archive, the Native American, and Jefferson's Convulsions," 8.

18. Hantman, *Monacan Millenium*, 69. Whereas he did not regard the Monacan burial mounds as monuments, Jefferson did write in a letter to surgeon and Indian Agent of the New Orleans Territory John Sibley, that he had "long considered [Indigenous] languages as the only remaining monument of a connection with other nations or of the want of it, to which we can now have access." Here again, he used the term "monument" to signal archival concepts of memory, preservation, and access, invoking "we" to include the settler statesmen; TJ to John Sibley, 27 May 1805, *Founders Online*, National Archives, https://founders.archives.gov/documents/Jefferson/01-46-02-0459.

19. McLaverty-Robinson, "Walter Benjamin."

20. For a rich account of the development of the *Chicano Thesaurus*, *A Women's Thesaurus*, and the *Homosaurus*, see Belantara and Drabinski, *Ways of Knowing*.

21. Another auction took place two years later at the courthouse. See Davenport, "Mourning at Monticello."

22. Jessup White, *Reclamation*, 207.

23. See Jessup White, *Reclamation* and Davenport, "Mourning at Monticello" for accounts of their common ancestors, Edmund Robinson and Sally Hemings Robinson.

24. Jessup White, *Reclamation*, 172.

25. Doyle, Lawson, and Dupont, "Indigenization of Knowledge Organization at the Xwi7xwa Library," 121.

26. See Sheffield, *Documenting Rebellions* for an account of the benefits and tensions that derive from these partnerships in some lesbian and gay archives.

27. Arendt, *On Revolution*, 174.

28. Arendt, *On Revolution*, 148, 142.

# Bibliography


Adams, Randolph G. *Three Americanists*. Philadelphia: University of Pennsylvania Press, 1939.

Adler, Melissa. *Cruising the Library: Perversities in the Organization of Knowledge*. New York: Fordham University Press, 2017.

Adler, Melissa, and Greg Nightingale. "Books and Imaginary Being(s): The Monstrosity of Library Classifications." *Proceedings from the Document Academy* 7, no. 1 (2020).

Agamben, Giorgio. *The Open: Man and Animal*. Translated by Kevin Attell. Stanford, CA: Stanford University Press, 2004.

Alderman, Edwin. "Address of Acceptance." In *The George Rogers Clark Statue: The Unveiling of the Monument to George Rogers Clark* by Robert Aitken, Charlottesville, VA, 3 November 1921. Special Collections. Alderman Library, University of Virginia.

Allen, Amy. *The End of Progress: Decolonizing the Normative Foundations of Critical Theory*. New York: Columbia University Press, 2017.

Andersen, Jack. "Knowledge Organization as a Cultural Form." *Culture and Identity in Knowledge Organization*, Proceedings of the Tenth International ISKO Conference. Montréal (2008): 269–74.

Anderson, Benedict. *Imagined Communities: Reflections on the Origin and Spread of Nationalism*. London: Verso, 2006.

Arendt, Hannah. *The Human Condition*. Chicago: University of Chicago Press, 1958.

Arendt, Hannah. *On Revolution*. New York: Viking Press, 1963.

Armstrong, Meg. "'The Effects of Blackness': Gender, Race, and the Sublime in Aesthetic Theories of Burke and Kant." *The Journal of Aesthetics and Art Criticism* 54, no. 3 (1996): 213–36.

Armus, Ted, and Hadley Green. "Charlottesville's Robert E. Lee Statue Meets Its End, in a 2,250-Degree Furnace." *Washington Post* (26 October 2023).

Armus, Ted, and Hannah Natanson. "Charlottesville Takes Down Two More Statues, Deemed Offensive to Native Americans, in Weekend of Removals." *Washington Post* (11 July 2021).

Atalay, Sonya. "Braiding Strands of Wellness: How Repatriation Contributes to Healing through Embodied Practice and Storywork." *The Public Historian* 41, no. 1 (2019): 78–89.

Bachman, Jeffrey S. *Cultural Genocide*. London: Routledge, 2019.

Bacon, Francis. *Of the Advancement of Learning*. London: J.M. Dent & Sons, 1915 (1605).

Bacon, Francis. *Gesta Grayorum, or, The History of the High and Mighty Prince, Henry, Prince of Purpoole. . . .* London: W. Canning, at his shop in the Temple Cloysters, 1688. https://archive.org/details/gestagrayorumorhoocann/page/n7/mode/2up.

Baker, Deborah. *Charlottesville: An American Story*. Minneapolis, MN: Graywolf Press, 2025.

Barad, Karen. *Meeting the Universe Halfway: Quantum Physics and the Entanglement of Matter and Meaning*. Durham, NC: Duke University Press, 2007.

Bassett, Hayden F. "Plantation Roads and the Impositions of Infrastructure: An Archaeology of Movement at Good Hope Estate, Jamaica." *Journal of African Diaspora Archaeology and Heritage* 11, no. 1 (2022): 48–73. DOI: 10.1080/21619441.2020.1840834.

Bastian, Jeannette Allis. "Reading Colonial Records through an Archival Lens: The Provenance of Place, Space and Creation." *Archival Science* 6, no. 3–4 (2006): 267–84.

Bastian, Jeannette A., and Ben Alexander, eds. *Community Archives: The Shaping of Memory*. London: Facet Publishing, 2009.

Beauchamp, Toby. *Going Stealth: Transgender Politics and U.S. Surveillance Practice*. Durham, NC: Duke University Press, 2019.

Bedini, Silvio A. *Thomas Jefferson: Statesman of Science*. New York: Macmillan, 1990.

Belantara, Amanda, and Emily Drabinski. *Ways of Knowing: Oral Histories on the Worlds Words Create*. Sacramento, CA: Library Juice Press, 2025.

Benjamin, Ruha. "Introduction: Discriminatory Design, Liberating Imagination." In *Captivating Technology: Race, Carceral Technoscience, and Liberatory Imagination in Everyday Life*, edited by Ruha Benjamin, 1–22. Durham, NC: Duke University Press, 2019.

Benjamin, Walter. "Theses on the Philosophy of History." In *Illuminations*, edited by Hannah Arendt, 253–64. Translated by Harry Zohn. New York: Schocken Books, 1968.

Benjamin, Walter. "On Language as Such and on the Language of Man." In *Selected Writings, Volume 1, 1913–1936*, edited by Marcus Bullock and Michael W. Jennings, 62–74. Cambridge, MA: Belknap Press, 1996.

Benjamin, Walter. *The Arcades Project*. Translated by Howard Eiland and Kevin McLaughlin. Cambridge, MA: Harvard University Press, 2002.

Bennett, Jane. *Vibrant Matter: A Political Ecology of Things*. Durham, NC: Duke University Press, 2010.
Bennett, Tony. *Birth of the Museum: History, Theory, Politics*. London: Routledge, 2013.
Bennett, Tony. *Museums, Power, Knowledge: Selected Essays*. London: Routledge, 2017.
Bergdoll, Barry. "Books, Buildings, and the Spaces of Democracy: Jefferson's Library from Paris to Washington." In *Thomas Jefferson Architect: Palladian Models, Democratic Principles, and the Conflict of Ideas*, edited by Lloyd De Witt and Corey Piper, 65–79. New Haven, CT: Yale University Press, 2019.
Berger, John. "Why Look at Animals?" In *About Looking*, v.1, 3–28. New York: Pantheon, 1980.
Berlant, Lauren. *The Anatomy of National Fantasy: Hawthorne, Utopia, and Everyday Life*. Chicago: University of Chicago Press, 1991.
Berlant, Lauren. *On the Inconvenience of Other People*. Durham, NC: Duke University Press, 2022.
Berman, Sanford. *Prejudices and Antipathies: A Tract on the LC Subject Heads Concerning People*. Metuchen, NJ: Scarecrow Press, 1971.
Best, Stephen M. *None Like Us: Blackness, Belonging, Aesthetic Life*. Durham, NC: Duke University Press, 2018.
Bestor, Arthur E. *Three Presidents and Their Books*. Urbana: University of Illinois Press, 1955.
Betts, Edwin Morris. *Thomas Jefferson's Farm Book with Commentary and Relevant Extracts from Other Writings*. Charlottesville: University of Virginia Press, 1953.
Bhandar, Brenna. *Colonial Lives of Property: Law, Land, and Racial Regimes of Ownership*. Durham, NC: Duke University Press, 2018.
Bivens-Tatum, Wayne. *Libraries and the Enlightenment*. Los Angeles, CA: Library Juice Press, 2012.
Blackhawk, Ned. *The Rediscovery of America: Native Peoples and the Unmaking of U.S. History*. New Haven, CT: Yale University Press, 2023.
Blair, Ann. *Too Much to Know: Managing Scholarly Information before the Modern Age*. New Haven, CT: Yale University Press, 2010.
Bodroghkozy, Aniko. *Making #Charlottesville: Media from Civil Rights to Unite the Right*. Charlottesville: University of Virginia Press, 2023.
Bowker, Geoffrey. *Memory Practices in the Sciences*. Cambridge, MA: MIT Press, 2006.
Bowker, Geoffrey C., and Susan Leigh Star. *Sorting Things Out: Classification and Its Consequences*. Cambridge, MA: MIT Press, 1999.
Boyd, Julian. "These Precious Monuments of . . . Our History." *The American Archivist* 22, no. 2 (1959): 147–80. https://doi.org/10.17723/aarc.22.2.b074277p07m43685.
Brannon, Rebecca. "Thomas Jefferson and the Quest for Legacy." *The Spirit of Inquiry in the Age of Jefferson, Transactions of the American Philosophical Society* 110, pt. 2 (2022): 313–27.

Breske, Ashleigh. "Politics of Repatriation: Formalizing Indigenous Repatriation Policy." *International Journal of Cultural Property* 25, no. 3 (2018): 347–73.

Brezina, Jennifer Costello. "A Nation in Chains: Barbary Captives and American Identity." In *Captivating Subjects: Writing Confinement, Citizenship, and Nationhood in the Nineteenth Century*, edited by Jason Haslam and Julia M. Wright, 201–19. Toronto: University of Toronto Press, 2005.

Briet, Suzanne. *What is Documentation?* Edited and translated by Ronald E. Day, Laurent Martinet, and Hermina G. B. Anghelescu. Lanham, MD: Scarecrow Press, 2006.

Brodie, Fawn. *Thomas Jefferson: An Intimate History*. New York: W.W. Norton, 2010.

Brown, Richard D. *The Strength of a People: The Idea of an Informed Citizenry in America, 1650–1870*. Chapel Hill: University of North Carolina Press, 1997.

Brown, Vincent. "Mapping a Slave Revolt: Visualizing Spatial History through the Archives of Slavery." *Social Text* 33, no. 4 (2015): 134–41.

Brown, Wendy. *Undoing the Demos: Neoliberalism's Stealth Revolution*. New York: Zone Books, 2015.

Browne, Simone. *Dark Matters: On the Surveillance of Blackness*. Durham, NC: Duke University Press, 2015.

Buckland, Michael K. "Information as Thing." *Journal of the American Society for Information Science* 42, no. 5 (1991): 351–60.

Bullard, Julia, Brian Watson, and Caitlin Purdome. "Misrepresentation in the Surrogate: Author Critiques of 'Indians of North America' Subject Headings." *Cataloging & Classification Quarterly* 60, no. 6–7 (2022): 599–619.

Burke, Edmund. *A Philosophical Enquiry into the Origin of Our Ideas of the Sublime and Beautiful*. Edited by James T. Boulton. Notre Dame, IN: University of Notre Dame Press, 1968.

Butler, Judith. "Endangered/Endangering: Schematic Racism and White Paranoia." In *Reading Rodney King/Reading Urban Uprising*, edited by Robert Gooding-Williams, 15–22. New York: Routledge, 1993.

Butler, Judith. *Bodies That Matter: On the Discursive Limits of Sex*. New York: Routledge, 2011.

Butler, Judith. *Notes Toward a Performative Theory of Assembly*. Cambridge, MA: Harvard University Press, 2015.

Butterfield, Lyman H. "The Papers of Thomas Jefferson: Progress and Procedures in the Enterprise at Princeton." *American Archivist* 12, no. 2 (1949): 131–45.

Bynum, Tara A., Brigitte Fielder, and Cassander L. Smith. "Special Issue Introduction: 'Dear Sister: Phillis Wheatley's Futures.'" *Early American Literature* 57, no. 3 (2022): 663–79.

Byrd, Jodi A., Alyosha Goldstein, Jodi Melamed, and Chandan Reddy. "Predatory Value." *Social Text* 36, no. 2 (2018): 1–18.

Byrne, Romana. *Aesthetic Sexuality: A Literary History of Sadomasochism*. London: Bloomsbury, 2013.

Cahill, Edward. *Liberty of the Imagination: Aesthetic Theory, Literary Form, and Politics in the Early United States*. Philadelphia: University of Pennsylvania Press, 2012.

Cambridge Union. *James Baldwin Debates William F. Buckley* (The Cambridge Union, 1965).

Carretta, Vincent. *Phillis Wheatley: Biography of a Genius in Bondage*. Athens: University of Georgia Press, 2011.

Carretta, Vincent, and Philip Gould. *Genius in Bondage: Literature of the Early Black Atlantic*. Lexington: University Press of Kentucky, 2001.

Carroll, Stephanie Russo, Desi Rodriguez-Lonebear, and Andrew Martinez. "Indigenous Data Governance: Strategies from United States Native Nations." *Data Science Journal* 18 no. 31 (2019): 1–15.

Castanha, Tony. "The Doctrine of Discovery: The Legacy and Continuing Impact of Christian 'Discovery' on American Indian Populations." *American Indian Culture and Research Journal* 39, no. 3 (2015): 41–63.

Caswell, Michelle. *Urgent Archives: Enacting Liberatory Memory Work*. London: Routledge, 2021.

Caswell, Michelle L. "Inventing New Archival Imaginaries: Theoretical Foundations for Identity-Based Community Archives." In *Identity Palimpsests: Archiving Ethnicity in the U.S. and Canada*, edited by Dominique Daniel and Amalia S. Levi, 35–58. Sacramento, CA: Litwin Books, 2014.

Caswell, Michelle L. "'The Archive' Is Not an Archives: On Acknowledging the Intellectual Contributions of Archival Studies." *reconstruction* 16, no. 1 (2016). https://escholarship.org/uc/item/7bn4v1fk.

Césaire, Aimé. *Discourse on Colonialism*. Translated by Joan Pinkham. New York: Monthly Review Press, 2000.

Cheney-Lippold, John. "A New Algorithmic Identity: Soft Biopolitics and the Modulation of Control." *Theory, Culture & Society* 28, no. 6 (2011): 164–81.

Cheney-Lippold, John. *We Are Data: Algorithms and the Making of Our Digital Selves*. New York: New York University Press, 2017.

Christen, Kimberly, and Jane Anderson. "Toward Slow Archives." *Archival Science* 19, no. 2 (2019): 87–116.

Coates, Ta-Nehisi. *The Water Dancer*. New York: One World, 2019.

Cogliano, Francis D. *Thomas Jefferson: Reputation and Legacy*. Edinburgh: Edinburgh University Press, 2006.

Cogliano, Francis D. *Emperor of Liberty: Thomas Jefferson's Foreign Policy*. New Haven: Yale University Press, 2014.

Collins, Samuel Gerald. *Library of Walls: The Library of Congress and the Contradictions of Information Society*. Sacramento, CA: Litwin Books, 2009.

Cometti, Elizabeth, and Valeria Gennaro-Lerda. "The Presidential Tour of Carlo Vidua with Letters on Virginia." *The Virginia Magazine of History and Biography* 77, no. 4 (1969): 387–406.

Commager, Henry Steele. "Thomas Jefferson and the Character of America." In *The Garden and Farm Books of Thomas Jefferson*, edited by Robert C. Baron, 8–37. Golden, CO: Fulcrum, 1987.

Coulthard, Glen Sean. *Red Skin White Masks: Rejecting the Colonial Politics of Recognition*. Minneapolis: University of Minnesota Press, 2014.

Cowan, T. L., and Jas Rault. "Introduction: Metaphors as Meaning and Method in Technoculture." *Catalyst: Feminism, Theory, Technoscience* 8, no. 2 (2022).

Cronon, William. *Changes in the Land: Indians, Colonists, and the Ecology of New England*. New York: Hill and Wang, 2003.

"Cross Burned on Patterson Mountain." *Daily Progress* (17 May 1924), p. 1. https://search.lib.virginia.edu/sources/uva_library/items/uva-lib:2590109.

Crouch, Sara Dominique. "Surface Tensions: Representations of Skin in the Long Eighteenth Century." PhD dissertation. University of Sydney, 2018.

Cultural Heritage Partners, on behalf of the Monacan Indian Nation. Comments from the Monacan Indian Nation. 7 June 2020. https://culturalheritagepartners.com/wp-content/uploads/2020/06/FINALCOMMENTS_MIN_withappendices_6_7_2020-1.pdf.

Curran, Andrew S. *The Anatomy of Blackness: Science & Slavery in an Age of Enlightenment*. Baltimore, MD: Johns Hopkins University Press, 2011.

Curran, Andrew S. *Diderot and the Art of Thinking Freely*. New York: Other Press, 2019.

Cushman, Ellen. "Wampum, Sequoyan, and Story: Decolonizing the Digital Archive." *College English* 76, no. 2 (2013): 115–35.

D'Alembert, Jean Le Rond. *Preliminary Discourse to the Encyclopedia of Diderot*. Translated by Richard N. Schwab. Indianapolis, IN: Bobbs-Merrill Company, 1963.

da Silva, Denise Ferreira. "Before Man: Sylvia Wynter's Rewriting of the Modern Episteme." In *Sylvia Wynter: On Being Human as Praxis*, edited by Katherine McKittrick, 90–105. Durham, NC: Duke University Press, 2015.

Dal Lago, Enrico. "Patriarchs and Republicans: Eighteenth-Century Virginian Planters and Classical Politics." *Historical Research*, 76 (2003): 492–511.

Darnton, Robert. *The Great Cat Massacre, And Other Episodes in French Cultural History*. New York: Basic Books, 1984.

Davenport, Andrew. "Mourning at Monticello." In *Mourning the Presidents: Loss and Legacy in American Culture*, edited by Lindsay M. Chervinsky and Matthew R. Costello, 33–55. Charlottesville: University of Virginia Press, 2023.

Davidson, Lawrence. *Cultural Genocide*. New Brunswick, NJ: Rutgers University Press, 2012.

Day, Ronald E. *The Modern Invention of Information: Discourse, History, and Power*. Carbondale: Southern Illinois University Press, 2001.

Day, Ronald E. "Community as Event." *Library Trends* 52, no. 3 (2004): 408–26.

Day, Ronald E. *Indexing It All: The Subject in the Age of Documentation, Information, and Data*. Cambridge, MA: MIT Press, 2014.

Day, Ronald E. *Documentarity: Evidence, Ontology, and Inscription*. Cambridge, MA: MIT Press, 2019.

Day, Ronald E. "Documentation to Docmentality in the works of Michael Buckland." *Journal of Documentation* 80, no. 3 (2024): 606–17.

Delbourgo, James. *Collecting the World: The Life and Curiosity of Hans Sloane*. London: Penguin, 2017.

De Tocqueville, Alexis. *Democracy in America*, Vol. 2, 3rd edition. Translated by Henry Reeve and Francis Bowen. Cambridge, MA: Sever and Francis, 1863.

Deloria, Philip J. "The New World of the Indigenous Museum." *Daedalus* 147, no. 2 (2018): 106–15.

Derrida, Jacques. "Freud and the Scene of Writing." In *Writing and Difference*. Translated by Alan Bass, 196–231. Chicago: University of Chicago Press, 1978.

Derrida, Jacques. "Declarations of Independence." *New Political Science* 7, no. 1 (1986): 7–15.

Derrida, Jacques. "Archive Fever: A Freudian Impression." *Diacritics* 25, no. 2 (1995): 9–63.

Derrida, Jacques. *Specters of Marx: The State of the Debt, the Work of Mourning and the New International*. London: Routledge, 2006.

Derrida, Jacques. *The Animal That Therefore I Am*. Edited by Marie-Louise Mallet. Translated by David Wills. New York: Fordham University Press, 2008.

Despret, Vinciane. *What Would Animals Say if We Asked the Right Questions?* Translated by Brett Buchanan. Minneapolis: University of Minnesota Press, 2016.

Dierksheide, Christa. *Amelioration and Empire: Progress and Slavery in the Plantation Americas*. Charlottesville: University of Virginia Press, 2014.

Dikant, Thomas. "Settler Colonial Statistics: Jefferson, Biopolitics, and Notes on the State of Virginia." *Early American Literature* 54, no. 1 (2019): 69–96.

Dimunation, Mark. "'The Whole of Recorded Knowledge': Jefferson as Collector and Reader." In *The Libraries, Leadership, & Legacy of John Adams and Thomas Jefferson*, edited by Robert C. Baron and Conrad Edick Wright, 21–40. Golden, CO: Fulcrum Publishing, 2010.

Ditzion, Sidney H. *Arsenals of a Democratic Culture: A Social History of the American Public Library Movement in New England and the Middle States from 1850 to 1900*. Chicago: American Library Association, 1947.

Doyle, Ann M., Kimberley Lawson, and Sarah Dupont. "Indigenization of Knowledge Organization at the X̲wi7x̲wa Library." *Journal of Library and Information Studies* 13, no. 2 (December 2015): 107–34.

Drabinski, Emily. "Queering the Catalog: Queer Theory and the Politics of Correction." *The Library Quarterly* 83, no. 2 (2013): 94–111.

Drabinski, Emily. "The Library is a Commons." *In These Times* (15 July 2024).

Drake, Jarrett M. "'Graveyards of Exclusion': Archives, Prisons, and the Bounds of Belonging." *Medium* (24 March 2019). https://medium.com/community-archives/graveyards-of-exclusion-archives-prisons-and-the-bounds-of-belonging-c40c85ff1663.

Driskill, Qwo-Li, Chris Finley, Brian Joseph Gilley, and Scott Lauria Morgensen, eds. *Queer Indigenous Studies: Critical Interventions in Theory, Politics, and Literature*. Tucson: University of Arizona Press, 2011.

Dugatkin, Lee Alan. *Behind the Crimson Curtain: The Rise and Fall of Peale's Museum*. Louisville, KY: Butler Books, 2019.

Eastman, Carolyn. *The Strange Genius of Mr. O: The World of the United States' First Forgotten Celebrity*. Chapel Hill: University of North Carolina Press, 2021.

Eaton, Joseph. "Lost in Translation: David Bailie Warden, the Abbé Grégoire's *De la littérature des Negres*, and the Limits to Franco Jeffersonian Cultural Exchange." *The Spirit of Inquiry in the Age of Jefferson, Transactions of the American Philosophical Society* 110, pt. 2 (2022): 219–40.

Eco, Umberto. *How to Spot a Fascist*. New York: Random House, 2020.

Edwards, Paul. "Infrastructure and Modernity: Force, Time, and Social Organization in the History of Sociotechnical Systems." In *Modernity and Technology*, edited by Thomas J. Misa, Philip Brey, and Andrew Feenberg, 185–226. Cambridge, MA: MIT Press, 2003.

Ehrenpreis, Diane, and Endrina Tay. "Enlightened Networks: Thomas Jefferson's System for Working from Home." *The Spirit of Inquiry in the Age of Jefferson, Transactions of the American Philosophical Society* 110, pt. 2 (2021): 197–218.

Eisenstein, Elizabeth L. *The Printing Press as an Agent of Change: Communications and Cultural Transformations in Early Modern Europe*. Cambridge: Cambridge University Press, 1980.

Ellis, Joseph J. *American Sphinx: The Character of Thomas Jefferson*. New York: Knopf, 1996.

Elmborg, James. "Critical Information: Definitions and Challenges." In *Transforming Information Literacy Programs: Intersecting Frontiers of Self, Library Culture, and Campus Community*, edited by Carroll Wetzel Wilkinson and Courtney Bruch, 75–96. Chicago: Association of College and Research Libraries, 2012.

Elmer, Jonathan. "The Archive, the Native American, and Jefferson's Convulsions." *Diacritics* 28, no. 4 (1998): 5–24.

Elmer, Jonathan. "Inclusion and Exclusion of the Indian in the Early American Archive." *Soziale Systeme* 8, no.1 (2002): 54–68.

Englert, Sai. "Settlers, Workers, and the Logic of Accumulation by Dispossession." *Antipode* 52, no. 6 (2020): 1647–66.

Fanon, Franz. *Black Skin White Masks*. Translated by Charles Lam Markmann. London: Pluto Press, 2008.

Ferguson, Roderick. *Aberrations in Black: Toward a Queer of Color Critique*. Minneapolis: University of Minnesota Press, 2004.

Ferguson, Roderick. *The Reorder of Things: The University and its Pedagogies of Minority Difference*. Minneapolis: University of Minnesota Press, 2012.

Fforde, Cressida, C. Timothy McKeown, and Honor Keeler. *The Routledge Companion to Indigenous Repatriation*. London: Routledge, 2020.

Finley, Chris. "Decolonizing the Queer Native Body (and Recovering the Native Bull-Dyke): Bringing 'Sexy Back' and Out of Native Studies' Closet." In *Queer Indigenous Studies: Critical Interventions in Theory, Politics, and Literature*, edited by Qwo-Li Driskill, Chris Finley, Brian Joseph Gilley, and Scott Lauria Morgensen, 31–42. Tucson: University of Arizona Press, 2011.

Foucault, Michel. *The Order of Things: An Archaeology of the Human Sciences*. New York: Vintage Books, 1973.

Foucault, Michel. *Power/Knowledge: Selected Interviews & Other Writing 1972–1977*. Edited by Colin Gordon. New York: Harvester Press, 1980.

Foucault, Michel. "What is Enlightenment?" In *The Foucault Reader*, edited by Paul Rabinow, 32–50. New York: Pantheon Books, 1984.

Foucault, Michel. *Technologies of the Self: A Seminar with Michel Foucault*. Edited by Luther H. Martin, Huck Gutman, and Patrick H. Hutton. Amherst: University of Massachusetts Press, 1988.

Foucault, Michel. *History of Sexuality, Volume 1: An Introduction*. Translated by Robert Hurley. New York: Vintage, 1990.

Foucault, Michel. *The Archaeology of Knowledge and the Discourse on Language*. Translated by A. M. Sheridan Smith. New York: Vintage, 1992.

Foucault, Michel. *Discipline and Punish: The Birth of the Prison*. Translated by Alan Sheridan. New York: Vintage, 1995.

Freud, Sigmund. "A Note Upon the Mystic Writing Pad." In *The Standard Edition of the Complete Psychological Works of Sigmund Freud*, vol. 19 (1923–1925), edited by James Strachey, 227–32. London: Hogarth Press, 1961.

Friedrich, Markus. *The Birth of the Archive: A History of Knowledge*. Ann Arbor: University of Michigan Press, 2018.

Frohmann, Bernd. *Deflating Information: From Science Studies to Documentation*. Toronto: University of Toronto Press, 2004.

Frohmann, Bernd. "The Documentality of Mme Briet's Antelope." In *Communication Matters: Materialist Approaches to Media, Mobility and Networks*, edited by J. Packer & S. B. Crofts Wiley, 173–82. New York: Routledge, 2012.

Frosio, Eugene T. "Comments on the Thomas Yen-Ran Yeh Proposals." *Library Resources & Technical Services* 15, no. 2 (1971): 129.

Fuentes, Marisa J. *Dispossessed Lives: Enslaved Women, Violence, and the Archive*. Philadelphia: University of Pennsylvania Press, 2016.

Galison, Peter. "Blacked-Out Spaces: Freud, Censorship and the Re-Territorialization of Mind." *The British Journal for the History of Science* 45, no. 2 (June 2012): 235–66.

Garba, Tapji, and Sara-Maria Sorentino. "Slavery is a Metaphor: A Critical Commentary on Eve Tuck and K. Wayne Yang's 'Decolonization is Not a Metaphor'." *Antipode* 52, no. 3 (2020): 764-782.

Gates, Henry Louis, Jr., and Andrew S. Curran. "Inventing the Science of Race." *New York Review of Books* (16 December 2021). https://www.nybooks.com/articles/2021/12/16/inventing-the-science-of-race/.

Ghaddar, J. J. "The Spectre in the Archive: Truth, Reconciliation, and Indigenous Archival Memory." *Archivaria* 82 (Fall 2016): 3–26.

Gikandi, Simon. "Race and the Idea of the Aesthetic." *Michigan Quarterly Review* 40, no. 2 (Spring 2001): 318–50. http://hdl.handle.net/2027/spo.act2080.0040.208.

Gikandi, Simon. *Slavery and the Culture of Taste*. Princeton, NJ: Princeton University Press, 2011.

Gilliland, Anne J, and Michelle Caswell. "Records and Their Imaginaries: Imagining the Impossible, Making Possible the Imagined." *Archival Science* 16, no. 1 (2015): 53–75.

Gilmore, Ruth Wilson. *Abolition Geographies: Essays Towards Liberation*. London: Verso, 2022.

Gilreath, James, and Douglas L. Wilson, eds. *Thomas Jefferson's Library: A Catalog with the Entries in His Own Order*. Washington, D.C.: Library of Congress, 1989.

Gilroy, Paul. *Black Atlantic: Modernity and Double Consciousness*. Cambridge, MA: Harvard University Press, 1993.

Gish, Dustin, and Daniel Klinghard. *Thomas Jefferson and the Science of Republican Government: A Political Biography of Notes on the State of Virginia*. Cambridge: Cambridge University Press, 2017.

Glynn, Tom. *Reading Publics: New York City's Public Libraries, 1754–1911*. New York: Fordham University Press, 2015.

Godelier, Maurice. "The Object and Method of Economic Anthropology." In *Relations of Production*, edited by David Seddon, 49–126. Translated by Helen Lackner. London: Frank Cass and Company, 1978.

Godfrey, Molley. "Rewriting White, Rewriting Black: Authentic Humanity and Authentic Blackness in Nella Larsen's 'Sanctuary.'" *MELUS* 38, no. 4 (December 2013): 122–45.

Goff, Frederick. "Freedom of Challenge: The (Great) Library of Thomas Jefferson." In *Thomas Jefferson and the World of Books: A Symposium Held at the Library of Congress, September 21, 1976*, 9–18. Washington, D.C.: Library of Congress, 1977.

Gordon, Avery F. *Ghostly Matters: Haunting and the Sociological Imagination*. Minneapolis: University of Minnesota Press, 2008.

Gordon, Wendy J. "An Inquiry into the Merits of Copyright: The Challenges of Consistency, Consent, and Encouragement Theory." *Stanford Law Review* 41 (1988): 1343–1469.

Gordon-Reed, Annette. "Engaging Jefferson: Blacks and the Founding Father." *The William and Mary Quarterly* 57, no. 1 (2000): 171–82.

Gordon-Reed, Annette. *The Hemingses of Monticello: An American Family*. New York: W.W. Norton, 2008.

Gordon-Reed, Annette, and Peter S. Onuf."*Most Blessed of the Patriarchs*": *Thomas Jefferson and the Empire of the Imagination*. New York: W.W. Norton, 2016.

Grégoire, Henri. *An Enquiry Concerning the Intellectual and Moral Faculties, and Literature of Negroes: Followed with an Account of the Life and Works of*

*Fifteen Negroes & Mulattoes, Distinguished in Science, Literature and the Arts.* Translated by D. B. Warden. Brooklyn, NY: Thomas Kirk, 1810.

Gruber, Thomas R. "A Translation Approach to Portable Ontology Specifications." *Knowledge Acquisition* 5, no. 2 (1993): 199–220.

Halberstam, Jack. *Wild Things: The Disorder of Desire.* Durham, NC: Duke University Press, 2020.

Hansson, Joacim. "The Informative Potential of Bibliographic Classification Systems: Reflections on a Discussion in the French Documentation Movement." *Journal of Documentation* 80, no. 3 (2024): 632–48.

Hantman, Jeffrey L. *Monacan Millennium: A Collaborative Archaeology and History of a Virginia Indian People.* Charlottesville: University of Virginia Press, 2018.

Haraway, Donna J. "Situated Knowledges: The Science Question in Feminism and the Privilege of Partial Perspective." *Feminist Studies* 14, no. 3 (1988): 575–99.

Harney, Stefano, and Fred Moten. *The Undercommons: Fugitive Planning & Black Study.* Brooklyn: Minor Compositions, 2013.

Harney, Stefano, Fred Moten, and Stephen Shukaitis. "Refusing Completion." *e-flux Journal* 116 (March 2021). https://www.e-flux.com/journal/116/379446/refusing-completion-a-conversation/.

Harris, Verne. "Insistering Derrida: Cixous, Deconstruction, and the Work of Archive." In "Critical Archival Studies," edited by Michelle Caswell, Ricardo Punzalan, and T-Kay Sangwand. Special Issue, *Journal of Critical Library and Information Studies* 1, no. 2 (2017): 1–19.

Harris, Verne S. *Ghosts of Archive: Deconstructive Intersectionality and Praxis.* Abingdon, Oxon: Routledge, 2021.

Hardt, Michael, and Antonio Negri. *Assembly.* Oxford: Oxford University Press, 2017.

Hartman, Saidiya. "Venus in Two Acts." *Small Axe* 12, no. 2 (2008): 1–14.

Hartman, Saidiya. *Wayward Lives, Beautiful Experiments.* New York: W.W. Norton, 2019.

Haspo, Beatriz. "Teamwork at Its Best: The Stack Numbering Project." *Guardians of Memory* (24 March 2022). https://blogs.loc.gov/preservation/2022/03/stack-numbering-project/.

Hayden, Carla. "'The Choicest Collection of Books.'" In *Thomas Jefferson at Monticello,* edited by Leslie Greene Bowman and Charlotte Moss, 45–50. New York: Rizzoli, 2022.

Hayes, Kevin J. *The Road to Monticello: The Life and Mind of Thomas Jefferson.* Oxford: Oxford University Press, 2008.

Hazard, Ebenezer. *Historical Collections: Consisting of State Papers, and Other Authentic Documents, Intended as Materials for an History of the United States of America,* Volume 1. Philadelphia: T. Dobson for the author, 1792.

Head, Randolph C. "Records, Secretaries, and the European Information State, circa 1400–1700." In *Information: A Short History,* edited by Ann Blair, Paul Duguid, Anja-Silvia Goeing, and Anthony Grafton, 136–67. Princeton, NJ: Princeton University Press, 2024.

Hochman, Barbara. "Love and Theft: Plagiarism, Blackface, and Nella Larsen's 'Sanctuary.'" *American Literature* 88, no. 3 (2016): 509–40.
Hockett, Bryan, and Timothy W. Murphy. "Antiquity of Communal Pronghorn Hunting in the North-Central Great Basin." *American Antiquity* 74, no. 4 (2009): 708–34.
Hogan, Sarah. "Of Islands and Bridges: Figures of Uneven Development in Bacon's *New Atlantis*." *Journal for Early Modern Cultural Studies* 12, no. 3 (2012): 28–59.
Hogarth, Rana. "Of Black Skin and Biopower: Lessons from the Eighteenth Century." *American Quarterly* 71, no. 3 (2019): 837–47.
Hogarth, William. *The Analysis of Beauty: Written with a View of Fixing the Fluctuating Ideas of Taste*. London: Printed by J. Reeves for the author. 2016 (1753). Project Gutenberg. https://www.gutenberg.org/files/51459/51459-h/51459-h.htm.
Holgersson-Shorter, Helena. "Authority's Shadowy Double: Thomas Jefferson and the Architecture of Illegitimacy." In *The Masters and the Slaves: Plantation Relations and Mestizaje in American Imaginaries*, edited by Alexandra Isfahani-Hammond, 51–66. New York: Palgrave Macmillan, 2005.
Holland, Catherine A. *The Body Politic Foundings, Citizenship, and Difference in the American Political Imagination*. New York: Routledge, 2001.
Honig, Bonnie. *Public Things: Democracy in Disrepair*. New York: Fordham University Press, 2017.
Hubbard, Robert M. "Libraries in Charlottesville and Albemarle: A Brief History." *The Magazine of Albemarle County History* 37/38 (1979–1980): 7–17.
Hubbard, Tasha. "Buffalo Genocide in Nineteenth-Century North America: 'Kill, Skin, and Sell.'" In *Colonial Genocide in Indigenous North America, edited* by Andrew Woolford, Jeff Benvenuto, and Alexander Laban Hinton. Durham, NC: Duke University Press, 2014.
Hudson, David James. "The Whiteness of Practicality." In *Topographies of Whiteness: Mapping Whiteness in Library and Information Studies*, edited by Gina Schlesselman-Tarango, 203–34. Sacramento, CA: Library Juice Press, 2017.
Hughes, Justin. "Copyright and Incomplete Historiographies: Of Piracy, Propertization, and Thomas Jefferson." *Southern California Law Review* 79 (2005): 993–1084.
Inklebarger, Timothy. "Ferguson's Safe Haven: Library becomes Refuge during Unrest." *American Libraries* (10 November 2014). https://americanlibrariesmagazine.org/2014/11/10/fergusons-safe-haven.
Irving, Sarah. "'In a Pure Soil': Colonial Anxieties in the Work of Francis Bacon." *History of European Ideas* 32, no. 3 (2006): 249–62.
Jackson, Zakiyyah Iman. *Becoming Human: Matter and Meaning in an Antiblack World*. New York: New York University Press, 2020.
Janzen, David. "Canoeing the Milk River: A Theory of Lines." *Canada and Beyond: A Journal of Canadian Literary and Cultural Studies* 12 (2023): 169–72.
"Jackson Statue is Unveiled," *The Daily Progress* (Charlottesville) (19 October 1921).
Jefferson, Thomas. "A Summary View of the Rights of British America." In *Writings*, edited by Merrill D. Peterson, 103–22. New York: Library of America, 1984 (1774).

Jefferson, Thomas. 1783 *Catalog of Books*, [circa 1775–1812]. Original manuscript from the Coolidge Collection of Thomas Jefferson Manuscripts, Massachusetts Historical Society.

Jefferson, Thomas. "A Bill for the More General Diffusion of Knowledge." In *Writings*, edited by Merrill D. Peterson, 365–73. New York: Library of America, 1984 (1778).

Jefferson, Thomas. *Notes on the State of Virginia*. In *Writings*, edited by Merrill D. Peterson, 123–325. New York: Library of America, 1984 (1787).

Jefferson, Thomas. "Memorandums on a Tour from Paris to Amsterdam, Strasburg, and back to Paris." In *Writings*, edited by Merrill D. Peterson, 629–58. New York: Library of America, 1984 (1788).

Jefferson, Thomas. "Autobiography." In *Writings*, edited by Merrill D. Peterson, 1–101. New York: Library of America, 1984 (1821).

Jessup White, Gayle. *Reclamation: Sally Hemings, Thomas Jefferson, and a Descendant's Search for Her Family's Lasting Legacy*. New York: Harper Collins, 2022.

Johnson, Jocelyn Nicole. *My Monticello*. New York: Henry Holt & Company, 2021.

Johnson, Nathan R. *Architects of Memory: Information and Rhetoric in a Networked Archival Age*. Tuscaloosa: University of Alabama Press, 2020.

Johnston, William Dawson. *History of the Library of Congress, Volume 1, 1800–1864*. Washington, D.C.: Government Printing Office, 1904.

Justice, Daniel Heath. *Why Indigenous Literatures Matter*. Waterloo, Ontario: Wilfred Laurier University Press, 2018.

Kauanui, J. Kēhaulani. "'A Structure, Not an Event': Settler Colonialism and Enduring Indigeneity," *Lateral* 5, no. 1 (2016).

Kelley, Robin D. G. "Foreword." In *Black Marxism: The Making of the Black Radical Tradition*, by Cedric J. Robinson, 3rd edition. Chapel Hill: University of North Carolina Press, 2020

Ketelaar, Eric. "Muniments and Monuments: The Dawn of Archives as Cultural Patrimony." *Archival Science* 7, no. 4 (2007): 343–57.

Kilmeade, Brian, and Don Yaeger. *Thomas Jefferson and the Tripoli Pirates: The Forgotten War that Changed American History*. New York: Penguin, 2017.

Kimmerer, Robin Wall. *Braiding Sweetgrass: Indigenous Wisdom, Scientific Knowledge, and the Teachings of Plants*. Minneapolis: Milkweed Editions, 2014.

Klinenberg, Eric. *Palaces for the People: How Social Infrastructure Can Help Fight Inequality, Polarization, and the Decline of Civic Life*. New York: Crown, 2018.

Kosciejew, Marc Richard Hugh. "Disciplinary Documentation in Apartheid South Africa: A Conceptual Framework of Documents, Associated Practices, and Their Effects." *Journal of Documentation* 71, no. 1 (2015): 96–115.

"Ku Klux Klan Organized Here." *The Daily Progress* (Charlottesville, VA) (28 June 1921).

"Ku Klux Klan: Grand Dragon of the State Visits Charlottesville." *The Daily Progress* (23 August 1922).

Kuokkanen, Rauna. *Reshaping the University: Responsibility, Indigenous Epistemes, and the Logic of the Gift*. Vancouver: University of British Columbia Press, 2011.

LaFleur, Greta. *The Natural History of Sexuality in Early America*. Baltimore, MD: Johns Hopkins University Press, 2018.

Lakoff, George, and Mark Johnson. *Metaphors We Live By*. Chicago: University of Chicago Press, 2003.

Lambert, Frank. *The Barbary Wars: American Independence in the Atlantic World*. New York: Hill and Wang, 2007.

LaMontagne, Leo E. *American Library Classifications with Special Reference to the Library of Congress*. Hamden, CT: Shoe String Press, 1961.

Larsen, Nella. *Quicksand*. New York: Penguin, 1928.

Latour, Bruno. *Science in Action: How to Follow Scientists and Engineers through Society*. Milton Keynes: Open University Press, 1987.

Latour, Bruno. "The Networks that Reason Ignores: Laboratories, Libraries, Collections." Translated by Ron Day. [Original: Latour, B. (1996). Ces réseaux que la raison ignore - laboratoires, bibliothèques, collections. Le pouvoir des bibliothèques. La mémoire des livres dans la culture occidentale.] Paris: Albin Michel, 23–46.

Latour, Bruno. "From Realpolitik to Dingpolitik or How to Make Things Public." *Pavilion Magazine* 15 (2010). https://www.pavilionmagazine.org/bruno-latour-from-realpolitik-to-dingpolitik-or-how-to-make-things-public/.

Laughland, Oliver. "White Nationalist Richard Spencer at Rally over Confederate Statue's Removal." *The Guardian* (14 May 2017). https://www.theguardian.com/world/2017/may/14/richard-spencer-white-nationalist-virginia-confederate-statue.

Lee, Shimrit. *Decolonize Museums*. New York: OR Books, 2022.

LeFevre, Albert. "Presentation Address." In *The George Rogers Clark Statue: The Unveiling of the Monument to George Rogers Clark* by Robert Aitken. Charlottesville, VA, 3 November 1921, Special Collections, Alderman Library, University of Virginia.

Lewis, Meriwether, and William Clark. *Original Journals of the Lewis and Clark Expedition, 1804–1806*, vol. 1. Edited by Ruben Gold Thwaites. New York: Arno Press, 1969.

Liboiron, Max. *Pollution is Colonialism*. Durham, NC: Duke University Press, 2021.

Library of Congress. *Alphabetical Catalogue of the Library of Congress*. Washington, D.C.: Government Printing Office, 1864.

Library of Congress. Classification. *E: History: America*. Washington, D.C.: Library of Congress, 2024.

Library of Congress. Classification. *H: Social Sciences*. Washington, D.C.: Library of Congress, 2024.

Library of Congress. Classification. *J: Political Science*. Washington, D.C.: Library of Congress, 2024.

Library of Congress. *A Century of Lawmaking for a New Nation: U.S. Congressional Documents and Debates, 1774 –1875*. Statutes at Large, 7th Congress, 1st Session. https://www.loc.gov/collections/century-of-lawmaking/about-this-collection/.

Littletree, Sandra, Miranda Belarde-Lewis, and Marisa Duarte. "Centering Relationality: A Conceptual Model to Advance Indigenous Knowledge Organization Practices." *Knowledge Organization* 47, no. 5 (2020): 410–26.

Lloyd, David. *Under Representation: The Racial Regime of Aesthetics*. New York: Fordham University Press, 2019.

Lockridge, Kenneth A. *On the Sources of Patriarchal Rage: The Commonplace Books of William Byrd II and Thomas Jefferson and the Gendering of Power in the Eighteenth Century*. New York: New York University Press, 1994.

Looby, Christopher. "The Constitution of Nature: Taxonomy as Politics in Jefferson, Peale, and Bartram." *Early American Literature* 22, no. 3 (1987): 252–73.

Lorde, Audre. "Age, Race, Class, and Sex." In *Sister Outsider: Essays & Speeches by Audre Lorde*, 114–23. New York: Crossing Feminist Press, 2007.

Lowe, Lisa. *The Intimacies of Four Continents*. Durham, NC: Duke University Press, 2015.

Luhmann, Niklas. *Theories of Distinction: Redescribing the Descriptions of Modernity*. Edited by William Rasch. Stanford, CA: Stanford University Press, 2002.

Maddox, Lucy. *Removals: Nineteenth-Century American Literature and the Politics of Indian Affairs*. New York: Oxford University Press, 1991.

Maldonado-Torres, Nelson. "Notes on Modernity and Extractivism in Dialogue with Strike ~~MoMA~~!" *Strike ~~MoMA~~ Reader* (2021): 150–55.

Manning, Susan. "Naming of Parts; Or, the Comforts of Classification: Thomas Jefferson's Construction of America as Fact and Myth." *Journal of American Studies* 30, no. 3 (1996): 345–64.

Marklund, Andreas, and Laura Skouvig. "Introduction." In *Histories of Surveillance from Antiquity to the Digital Era*, edited by Andreas Marklund and Laura Skouvig, 1–19. Abingdon: Routledge, 2022.

Mattern, Shannon. "Library as Infrastructure." *Places Journal* (June 2014). https://doi.org/10.22269/140609.

Mattern, Shannon. *Code + Clay . . . Data + Dirt: Five Thousand Years of Urban Media*. Minneapolis: University of Minnesota Press, 2017.

McCabe, Richard E, Bart W O'Gara, and Henry M Reeves. *Prairie Ghost: Pronghorn and Human Interaction in Early America*. Boulder: University Press of Colorado, 2004.

McClintock, Anne. *Imperial Leather: Race, Gender and Sexuality in the Colonial Contest*. New York: Routledge, 1995.

McCanse, McGregor. "Rector Reaffirms UVA's Institutional Connection to Thomas Jefferson." *UVAToday* (16 September 2022). https://news.virginia.edu/content/rector-reaffirms-uvas-institutional-connection-thomas-jefferson.

McInnis, Jarvis C. "Black Women's Geographies and the Afterlives of the Sugar Plantation." *American Literary History* 31, no. 4 (2019): 741–74.

McInnis, Maurie D. "The Liberty and Tyranny of the Academical Village." In *The Founding of Thomas Jefferson's University*, edited by John A. Ragosta, Peter S. Onuf, and Andrew J. O'Shaughnessy, 126–40. Charlottesville: University of Virginia Press, 2019.

McKinney, Cait. *Information Activism: A Queer History of Lesbian Media Technologies*. Durham, NC: Duke University Press, 2020.

McKittrick, Katherine. "Plantation Futures." *Small Axe* 42 (November 2013): 1–15.

McKittrick, Katherine. "Mathematics Black Life." *The Black Scholar* 44, no. 2 (2014): 16–28.

McKittrick, Katherine. *Dear Science and Other Stories.* Durham, NC: Duke University Press, 2021.

McLaverty-Robinson, Andy. "Walter Benjamin: Messianism and Revolution—Theses on History, An A to Z of Theory." *Ceasefire* (15 November 2013). https://ceasefiremagazine.co.uk/walter-benjamin-messianism-revolution-theses-history/.

Miksa, Francis. "The Development of Classification at the Library of Congress." Occasional Papers, Number 164. Urbana-Champaign: University of Illinois, 1984.

Miller, Robert. *Native America, Discovered and Conquered: Thomas Jefferson, Lewis & Clark, and Manifest Destiny*. Westport, CT: Praeger, 2006.

Mitchell, Katharyne. "Monuments, Memorials, and the Politics of Memory." *Urban Geography* 24, no. 5 (2003): 442–59.

Monkman, Kent. *The Rise and Fall of Civilization.* Toronto: Gardiner Museum, 2015.

Monkman, Kent, and Gisèle Gordon. *The Memoirs of Miss Chief Eagle Testickle: A True and Exact Accounting of the History of Turtle Island*, vols. 1 and 2. Toronto: McClelland and Stewart, 2023.

Montalvo, Sonia. "Vinegar Hill Remembered: Eminent Domain, Urban Removal, and The Demolition of a People's Soul." *Vinegar Hill Magazine* (2 March 2024). https://vinegarhillmagazine.com/vinegar-hill-remembered-eminent-domainurban-removal-and-the-demolition-of-a-peoples-soul/.

Montenegro, María. "Subverting the Universality of Metadata Standards: The TK Labels as a Tool to Promote Indigenous Data Sovereignty." *Journal of Documentation* 75, no. 4 (2019): 731–49.

Montoya, Robert D. *Power of Position: Classification and the Biodiversity Sciences.* Cambridge, MA: MIT Press, 2022.

Moomaw, Graham. "Charlottesville Officially Apologizes for Razing Vinegar Hill." *The Daily Progress* (7 November 2011). https://dailyprogress.com/news/charlottesville-officially-apologizes-for-razing-vinegar-hill/article_83b8aed4-2f4a-5ee2-baaa-2e7c9d43c2b0.html.

Morgensen, Scott. *Spaces Between Us: Queer Settler Colonialism and Indigenous Decolonization.* Minneapolis: University of Minnesota Press, 2011.

Moskowitz, P. E. *The Case Against Free Speech: The First Amendment, Fascism, and the Future of Dissent*. New York: Bold Type Books, 2019.

Nelson, Libby. "'Why We Voted for Donald Trump': David Duke Explains the White supremacist Charlottesville Protests." *Vox* (12 August 2017). https://www.vox.com/2017/8/12/16138358/charlottesville-protests-david-duke-kkk.

Nguyen, Mimi Thi. *The Gift of Freedom: War, Debt, and Other Refugee Passages.* Durham, NC: Duke University Press, 2012.

Nora, Pierre. "Between Memory and History: *Les lieux de mémoire.*" *representations* 26 (1989): 7–24.

Nord, Martin I. "Ishi, Briet's Antelope, and the Documentality of Human Documents." *Proceedings from the Document Academy* 7, no. 1 (2020): Article 8.

Nunberg, Geoffrey. "Farewell to the Information Age." In *The Future of the Book*, edited by Geoffrey Nunberg, 103–38. Los Angeles: University of California Press, 1996.

Nyong'o, Tavia. *The Amalgamation Waltz: Race, Performance, and the Ruses of Memory*. Minneapolis: University of Minnesota Press, 2009.

O'Brien, Jean M. *Firsting and Lasting: Writing Indians Out of Existence in New England*. Minneapolis: University of Minnesota Press, 2010.

O'Hare, Erin. "What Will Happen to Charlottesville's Auction Block Site on Which Humans Were Bought and Sold? That Building is Now for Sale." *Charlottesville Tomorrow* (21 September 2021). https://www.cvilletomorrow.org/this-historic-building-now-for-sale-in-court-square-was-once-the-site-of-charlottesvilles-slave-auction-block-the-listing-does-not-include-that-fact/.

O'Shaughnessy, Andrew J. *The Illimitable Freedom of the Human Mind: Thomas Jefferson's Idea of a University*. Charlottesville: University of Virginia Press, 2021.

Olson, Hope. "The Power to Name: Representation in Library Catalogs." *Signs: Journal of Women in Culture and Society* 26, no. 3 (2001): 639–68.

Olson, Hope A. "Difference, Culture and Change: The Untapped Potential of LCSH." In *The LCSH Century*, edited by Alva T. Stone, 53–71. New York: Routledge, 2014.

Onuf, Peter S. *Jefferson's Empire: The Language of American Nationhood*. Charlottesville: University of Virginia Press, 2000.

Ord, George, Samuel N. Rhoads, and William Guthrie. *A Reprint of the North American Zoology, by George Ord: Being an Exact Reproduction of the Part Originally Compiled by Mr. Ord for Johnson & Warner, and First Published by Them in Their Second American Edition of Guthrie's Geography in 1815: Taken from Mr. Ord's Private, Annotated Copy, to Which Is Added an Appendix on the More Important Scientific and Historic Questions Involved*. Haddonfield, NJ: Published by the editor, 1894.

Orosz, Joel J. *Curators and Culture: The Museum Movement in America, 1740–1870*. Tuscaloosa: University of Alabama Press, 1990.

Owens, Robert M. *Mr. Jefferson's Hammer: William Henry Harrison and the Origins of American Indian Policy*. Norman: University of Oklahoma Press, 2007.

Palmer, Meredith Alberta. "Rendering Settler Sovereign Landscapes: Race and Property in the Empire State." *Environment and Planning D: Society and Space* 38, no. 5 (2020): 793–810.

paperson, la. *A Third University is Possible*. Minneapolis: University of Minnesota Press, 2017.

Pawley, Christine. "Information Literacy: A Contradictory Coupling." *The Library Quarterly* 73, no. 4 (2003): 422–52.

Peale, Charles Willson, Palisot de Beauvois, and Ambrose-Marie-Francois-Joseph. *Scientific and Descriptive Catalogue of Peale's Museum*. Philadelphia: Samuel H. Smith, printer. American Philosophical Society. Pam. v. 294, no.7 (1796).

Peale, Charles Willson. *The Selected Papers of Charles Willson Peale and His Family*. Edited by Lillian B. Miller. New Haven, CT: Published for the National Portrait Gallery, Smithsonian Institution, by Yale University Press, 1983.

Pearce, Matt. "Chanting 'Blood and Soil!' White Nationalists with Torches March on University of Virginia." *Los Angeles Times* (11 August 2017). https://www.latimes.com/nation/la-na-white-virginia-rally-20170811-story.html.

Popowich, Sam. *Confronting the Democratic Discourse of Librarianship: A Marxist Approach*. Sacramento, CA: Library Juice Press, 2019.

Post, David G. "The Continuing Saga of Thomas Jefferson and the Internet." Talk Delivered at The David Library Lecture Series on "The Unfinished Constitution." Washington Crossing, PA, 2011.

Pratt, Mary Louise. *Imperial Eyes: Travel Writing and Transculturation*. New York: Routledge, 1992.

Ragosta, John A. *Religious Freedom: Jefferson's Legacy, America's Creed*. Charlottesville: University of Virginia Press, 2013.

Ragosta, John A, Peter S. Onuf, and Andrew J. O'Shaughnessy. "Introduction." In *The Founding of Thomas Jefferson's University*, edited by John A. Ragosta, Peter S. Onuf, and Andrew J. O'Shaughnessy. Charlottesville: University of Virginia Press, 2019.

Randolph, Sarah N. *The Domestic Life of Thomas Jefferson: Compiled from Family Letters and Reminiscences*. New York: Harper and Brothers, 1871.

"Rassawek Saved from Destruction: After Four Year Battle, Water Authority Agrees to Alternate Route." *Cultural Heritage Partners* (16 March 2022). https://www.culturalheritagepartners.com/saverassawek/.

Ray, William. *Horrors of Slavery, or The American Tars in Tripoli*. Edited by Hester Blum. New Brunswick, NJ: Rutgers University Press, 2008.

Reguly, Eric. "Vatican Formally Rejects Doctrine of Discovery that Allowed Colonial-Era Seizure of Indigenous Lands." *Globe and Mail* (30 March 2023). https://www.theglobeandmail.com/world/article-doctrine-discovery-vatican-city/.

Reinhardt, Mark. "Vision's Unseen: On Sovereignty, Race, and the Optical Unconscious." *Theory & Event* 18, no. 4 (2015): n.p.

Rifkin, Mark. *When Did Indians Become Straight?: Kinship, the History of Sexuality, and Native Sovereignty*. Oxford: Oxford University Press, 2011.

Rifkin, Mark. *Beyond Settler Time: Temporal Sovereignty and Indigenous Self-Determination*. Durham, NC: Duke University Press, 2017.

Rivett, Sarah. "Unruly Empiricisms and Linguistic Sovereignty in Thomas Jefferson's Indian Vocabulary Project." *American Literature* 87, no. 4 (2015): 645–80.

Robinson, Dylan. "Shxwelí li te shxwelítemelh xíts' etáwtxw: The Museum's Confinement of Indigenous Kin." *American Anthropologist* 126, no. 2 (2024): 233–47.

Rogers, James T. "Thomas Jefferson's Office Copier." *Invention & Technology*. 17, no. 2 (2001). https://www.inventionandtech.com/content/thomas-jefferson%E2%80%99s-office-copier-1.

Rogers, Stephen, Rebecca Shreckengast, and Eric Dorfman. "Origins and Contemporary Status of Habitat Dioramas in the United States." In *Natural History Dioramas—Traditional Exhibits for Current Educational Themes*, edited by Annette Scheersoi and Sue Dale Tunnicliffe, 11–40. Cham, Switzerland: Springer, 2019.

Ronan, Kristine. "'Kicked About': Native Culture at Thomas Jefferson's Monticello." *Panorama: Journal of the Association of Historians of American Art* 3, no. 2 (Fall 2017). https://journalpanorama.org/article/native-culture-at-monticello/

Rose, Jacqueline. "Femininity and Its Discontents." *Feminist Review* 14 (Summer 1983): 5–21.

Rosenberg, Jane A. *The Nation's Great Library: Herbert Putnam and the Library of Congress, 1899–1939*. Urbana: University of Illinois Press, 1993.

Rothman, Joshua D. "When Bigotry Paraded Through the Streets." *The Atlantic* (4 December 2016). https://www.theatlantic.com/politics/archive/2016/12/second-klan/509468/.

Ruiz, Rosaura Martínez. "Freud and Derrida: Writing and Speculation (or When the Future Irrupts in the Present). *Filozofski vestnick* 36, no. 3 (2015): 93–112.

Salomon, Xavier F. "A Mirror of the World." In *Thomas Jefferson at Monticello*, edited by Leslie Greene Bowman and Charlotte Moss, 81–91. New York: Rizzoli, 2022.

Sancho, Ignatius. *Letters of the Late Ignatius Sancho: An African, to Which are Prefixed, Memoirs of his Life*, 2nd ed. London: J. Nichols and D. Dilly, in the Poultry, 1783.

Saunders, James R., and Renae Nadine Shackleford, *Urban Renewal and the End of Black Culture in Charlottesville: An Oral History of Vinegar Hill*. Jefferson, NC: McFarland, 2005.

Sayre, Gordon M. "The Mound Builders and the Imagination of American Antiquity in Jefferson, Bartram, and Chateaubriand." *Early American Literature* 33, no. 3 (1998): 225–49.

Schaefer, Donovan O. "The Things of Order: Affect, Material Culture, *Dispositif*." *Cultural Critique* 124 (2024): 1–30.

Schofield, Robert E. "The Science Education of an Enlightened Entrepreneur: Charles Willson Peale and his Philadelphia Museum, 1784–1827." *American Studies* 30, no. 2 (1989): 21–40.

Shakespeare, William. *The Tempest*. In *The Riverside Shakespeare*, 2nd ed. Edited by G. Blakemore Evans. Boston: Houghton Mifflin Co., 1997.

Shannon, Laurie. "The Eight Animals in Shakespeare; Or, before the Human." *PMLA: Publications of the Modern Language Association of America* 124, no. 2 (2009.): 472–79.

Sharpe, Christina. *Ordinary Notes*. Toronto: Knopf, 2023.

Sheffield, Rebecka Taves. *Documenting Rebellions: A Study of Four Gay and Lesbian Archives in Queer Times*. Sacramento, CA: Litwin Books, 2020.

Shelley, Fred. "Ebenezer Hazard: America's First Historical Editor." *The William and Mary Quarterly* 12, no. 1 (1955): 44–73.

Shuffleton, Frank. "Binding Ties: The Public and Domestic Spheres in Jefferson's Letters to his Family." In *Thomas Jefferson and the Education of a Citizen*, edited by James Gilreath, 28–47. Washington, D.C.: Library of Congress, 1999.

Silko, Leslie Marmon. "Interior and Exterior Landscapes: The Pueblo Migration Stories." In *Yellow Woman and a Beauty of the Spirit: Essays on Native American Life Today*, 25–47. New York: Simon & Schuster, 1996.

Simpson, Audra. "On Ethnographic Refusal: Indigeneity, 'Voice' and Colonial Citizenship." *Junctures: The Journal for Thematic Dialogue* 9 (December 2007): 67–80.

Simpson, Audra. "Settlement's Secret." *Cultural Anthropology* 26, no. 2 (2011): 205–17.

Simpson, Leanne Betasamosake. "Land as Pedagogy: Nishnaabeg Intelligence and Rebellious Transformation." *Decolonization: Indigeneity, Education & Society* 3, no. 3 (2014): 1–25.

Simpson, Leanne Betasamosake. *A Short History of the Blockade : Giant Beavers, Diplomacy, and Regeneration in Nishnaabewin*. Edmonton: University of Alberta Press, 2021.

Small, David. "The Re-Enchantment of Humanism: An Interview with Sylvia Wynter." *Small Axe* 8 (September 2000): 119–207.

Smith, Jeanne. "Copyright at 125: 1870 Law Important to Building LC's Collections." *Library of Congress Information Bulletin* (4 September 1995). https://www.loc.gov/loc/lcib/9516/copyright.html.

Smith, Linda Tuhiwai. *Decolonizing Methodologies: Research and Indigenous Peoples*, 2nd edition. London: Zed Books, 2012.

Smith-Cruz, Shawn(ta). Referencing Audre Lorde. In *Reference Librarianship and Justice*, edited by Liam Adler, Ian Beilin, and Eamon Tewell, 279–91. Sacramento, CA: Library Juice Press, 2018.

Snaza, Nathan. *Animate Literacies: Literature, Affect, and the Politics of Humanism*. Durham, NC: Duke University Press, 2019.

Snaza, Nathan. "Why This?: Affective Pedagogy in the Wake." In *The Affect Theory Reader 2: Worldings, Tensions, Futures*, edited by Gregory J. Seigworth and Carolyn Pedwell, 255–72. Durham, NC: Duke University Press, 2023.

Snow, Karen, and Anthony W. Dunbar. "Advancing the Relationship between Critical Cataloging and Critical Race Theory." *Cataloging & Classification Quarterly* 60, no. 6–7 (2022): 646–74.

Soh, Thomas. "Slavery in Charlottesville" (2021). https://storymaps.arcgis.com/stories/add16e32230741fabfeefd18a8d777ed

Southern Poverty Law Center, "Hate Groups Reach Record High" (19 February 2019). https://www.splcenter.org/news/2019/02/19/hate-groups-reach-record-high.

Sowerby, Millicent E. *Catalogue of the Library of Thomas Jefferson*, 5 vols. Washington, D.C.: Library of Congress, 1952–1959.

Spahn, Hannah. *Thomas Jefferson, Time, and History*. Charlottesville: University of Virginia Press, 2011.

Spahn, Hannah. *Black Reason, White Feeling: The Jeffersonian Enlightenment in the African American Tradition*. Charlottesville: University of Virginia Press, 2024.

Spero, Patrick. "The Other Presidency: Thomas Jefferson and the American Philosophical Society." *Proceedings of the American Philosophical Society* 162, no. 4 (2018): 321–60.

Spivak, Gayatri Chakravorty. "Can the Subaltern Speak?" In *Can the Subaltern Speak?: Reflections on the History of an Idea*, edited by Rosalind C. Morris, 21–79. New York: Columbia University Press, 2010.

Stanton, Lucia. *"Those Who Labor for My Happiness": Slavery at Thomas Jefferson's Monticello*. Charlottesville: University of Virginia Press, 2012.

Star, Susan Leigh. "The Ethnography of Infrastructure." *American Behavioural Scientist* 43, no. 3 (1999): 377–91.

Star, Susan Leigh, and Karen Ruhleder. "Steps Toward an Ecology of Infrastructure: Design and Access for Large Information Spaces." *Information Systems Research* 7, no. 1 (1996): 111–34.

Steedman, Carolyn. *Dust: The Archive and Cultural History*. New Brunswick, NJ: Rutgers University Press, 2002.

Steyerl, Hito. "The Language of Things." *Transversal* (June 2006). https://transversal.at/transversal/0606/steyerl/en.

Stoler, Ann Laura. *Duress: Imperial Durabilities in Our Times*. Durham, NC: Duke University Press, 2016.

Stuchel, Dani. "Material Provocations in the Archives." *Journal of Critical Library and Information Studies*. Special Issue: "Libraries and Archives in the Anthropocene" 3, no. 1 (2020). Edited by Eira Tansey and Robert Montoya. https://doi.org/10.24242/jclis.v3i1.103.

Sundstrom, Linea. "Cheyenne Pronghorn Procurement and Ceremony." *Plains Anthropologist* 45, no. 174 (2000): 119–32.

Svenonius, Elaine. "LCSH: Semantics, Syntax and Specificity." *Cataloging & Classification Quarterly* 29, no. 1–2 (2000): 17–30.

TallBear, Kim. *Native American DNA: Tribal Belonging and the False Promise of Genetic Science*. Minneapolis: University of Minnesota Press, 2013.

TallBear, Kim. "Yes, Your Pleasure! Yes, Self-Love! And Don't Forget, Settler Sexuality is a Structure." *The Critical Polyamorist* (22 April 2018). http://www.criticalpolyamorist.com/homeblog/yes-your-pleasure-yes-self-love-and-dont-forget-settler-sex-is-a-structure.

TallBear, Kim. "Feminist, Queer, and Indigenous Thinking as an Antidote to Masculinist Objectivity and Binary Thinking in Biological Anthropology." *American Anthropologist* 121, no. 2 (2019): 494–96.

Tarc, Aparna Mishra. *Literacy of the Other: Renarrating Humanity*. Albany: SUNY Press, 2016.

Taschereau Mamers, Danielle. "Human-Bison Relations as Sites of Settler Colonial Violence and Decolonial Resurgence." *Humanimalia* 10, no. 2 (2019): 10–41.

Tanner, Russel L. "An Ethnohistorical Consideration of the Role of *Antilocapra americana* in the Lives of Indigenous Peoples and American Pioneers." *Plains Anthropologist* 45, no. 174 (2000): 134–39.

Tawil, Ezra F. "Domestic Frontier Romance, or, How the Sentimental Heroine Became White." *Novel: A Forum on Fiction* 32, no. 1 (Autumn 1998): 99–124.

Tay, Endrina. "'Unquestionably the Choicest Collection of Books in the U.S.': The 1815 Sale of Thomas Jefferson's Library to the Nation." *Common-place.org* 16, no. 4 (2016).

Tay, Endrina. "Forming the Body of a Library Based on the 'Illimitable Freedom of the Human Mind.'" In *The Founding of Thomas Jefferson's University*, edited by John A. Ragosta, Peter S. Onuf, and Andrew J. O'Shaughenessy, 208–23. Charlottesville: University of Virginia Press, 2019.

Taylor, Alan. *Thomas Jefferson's Education*. New York: W.W. Norton, 2019.

Tennis, Joseph T., and Elin Jacob. "Toward a Theory of Structure in Information Organization Frameworks." Culture and Identity in Knowledge Organization, *Proceedings of the Tenth International ISKO Conference, August 5–8, 2008, Montréal, Canada. Advances in Knowledge Organization* 11 (2008): 262–68.

Thomas, Isaiah, *The History of Printing in America: With a Biography of Printers, and an Account of Newspapers. To which is Prefixed a Concise View of the Discovery and Progress of the Art in Other Parts of the World*, v.1, 2nd ed. New York: Burt Franklin, 1874.

Todd, Zoe. "Fish Pluralities: Human-animal Relations and Sites of Engagement in Paulatuuq, Arctic Canada." *Études/inuit/studies* 38, no. 1 (2014): 217–38.

Todd, Zoe. "An Indigenous Feminist's Take on the Ontological Turn: 'Ontology' is Just Another Word for Colonialism." *Journal of Historical Sociology* 29, no. 1 (2016): 4–22.

Trouillot, Michel-Rolph. *Silencing the Past: Power and the Production of History*. Boston: Beacon Press, 1995.

Tsosie, Rebecca. "Native Nations and Museums: Developing an Institutional Framework for Cultural Sovereignty." *Tulsa Law Review* 45, no. 1 (2009): 3–23.

Tuck, Eve, and K. Wayne Yang. "Decolonization is Not a Metaphor." *Decolonization: Indigeneity, Education & Society* 1, no. 1 (2012): 1–40.

Turkle, Sherry. *Evocative Objects: Things We Think With*. Cambridge, MA: MIT Press, 2011.

Turnbull, Paul, and Michael Pickering, eds. *The Long Way Home: The Meaning and Values of Repatriation*. New York: Berghahn Books, 2022.

Turner, Hannah. *Cataloguing Culture: Legacies of Colonialism in Museum Documentation*. Vancouver: UBC Press, 2020.

United Nations Human Rights Council. *Repatriation of Ceremonial Objects, Human Remains and Intangible Cultural Heritage under the United Nations Declaration on the Rights of Indigenous Peoples: Report of the Expert Mechanism on the Rights of Indigenous Peoples*. 45th session, 2020.

Vaidhyanathan, Siva. *Copyrights and Copywrongs: The Rise of Intellectual Property and How It Threatens Creativity*. New York: New York University Press, 2001.
Vartija, Devin J. *The Color of Equality: Race and Common Humanity in Enlightenment Thought*. Philadelphia: University of Pennsylvania Press, 2021.
Vimalassery, Manu, Juliana Hu Pegues, and Alyosha Goldstein. "Introduction: On Colonial Unknowing." *Theory & Event* 19, no. 4 (2016).
Virginia Assembly, Chapter 65. "An Act Incorporating the Albemarle Library Society." In Acts and Joint Resolutions (amending the Constitution) of the General Assembly of the State of Virginia, 74–75. Richmond: Commonwealth of Virginia, 1824.
"Virginia Health Bulletin: The New Virginia Law To Preserve Racial Integrity, March 1924." *Document Bank of Virginia*. https://edu.lva.virginia.gov/dbva/items/show/226.
Von Daacke, Kirt and Ashley Schmidt. "UVA and the History of Race: When the KKK Flourished in Charlottesville." *UVAToday* (25 September 2019). https://news.virginia.edu/content/uva-and-history-race-when-kkk-flourished-charlottesville.
Walcott, Rinaldo. *The Long Emancipation: Toward Black Freedom*. Durham, NC: Duke University Press, 2021.
Wallace, Anthony F. C. *Jefferson and the Indians: The Tragic Fate of the First Americans*. Cambridge, MA: Harvard University Press, 1999.
Watts, George B. "Thomas Jefferson, the 'Encylopédie' and the 'Encyclopédie Méthodique.'" *The French Review* 38, no. 3 (1965): 318–25.
Webster, Kelly, and Ann Doyle. "Don't Class Me in Antiquities! Giving Voice to Native American Materials." In *Radical Cataloging: Essays at the Front*, edited by K. R. Roberto, 189–97. Jefferson, NC: McFarland, 2008.
Weheliye, Alexander G. *Habeas Viscus: Racializing Assemblages, Biopolitics, and Black Feminist Theories of the Human*. Durham, NC: Duke University Press, 2014.
Welburn, Jude. "Empire and Utopia: Images of the New World in Francis Bacon's Works." *English Literary Renaissance* 48, no. 2 (2018): 160–90.
Weizman, Eyal, Paulo Tavares, Susan Schuppli, and Situ Studio. "Forensic Architecture." *Architectural Design* 80, no. 5 (2010): 58–63.
Wheatley Peters, Phillis. "On Imagination." *Poems on Various Subjects Religious and Moral* (1773). https://www.poetryfoundation.org/poems/52632/on-imagination.
Wheelan, Joseph. *Jefferson's War: America's First War on Terror 1801–1805*. New York: PublicAffairs, 2004.
Whitehead, P. J. P. "Museums in the History of Zoology," part II. *Museums Journal* 70, no. 4 (1971): 155–60.
Wilson, Douglas L. "Thomas Jefferson's Early Notebooks." *The William and Mary Quarterly* 42, no. 4 (1985): 433–52.
Wilson, Douglas L., ed. *Jefferson's Literary Commonplace Book*. Princeton: Princeton University Press, 1989.

Wilson, Douglas L. "The Evolution of Jefferson's 'Notes on the State of Virginia,'" *Virginia Magazine of History and Biography* 112, no. 2 (2004): 98–133.
Wilson, Michelle Margaret. "Remnants, Outlaws, and Wallows: Practices for Understanding Bison." Order No. 29308347. The University of Western Ontario (Canada), 2022.
Wolfe, Cary. *What Is Posthumanism?* Minneapolis: University of Minnesota Press, 2010.
Wolfe, Patrick. "Settler Colonialism and the Elimination of the Native." *Journal of Genocide Research* 8, no. 4 (2006): 387–409.
Wolfe, Patrick. *Traces of History: Elementary Structures of Race*. London: Verso, 2016.
Wood, Gordon S. *Friends Divided: John Adams and Thomas Jefferson*. New York: Penguin Press, 2017.
Woolford, Andrew. "Ontological Redress: The Natural and the Material in Transformative Justice for 'Cultural' Genocide." In *Cultural Genocide*, edited by Jeffrey S Bachman, 269–84. London: Routledge, 2019.
Wulf, Andrea. *Founding Gardeners: The Revolutionary Generation, Nature, and the Shaping of the American Nation*. New York: Alfred A. Knopf, 2011.
Wulf, Andrea. *The Invention of Nature: Alexander von Humboldt's New World*. New York: Vintage, 2015.
Wynter, Sylvia. "Beyond the Word of Man: Glissant and the New Discourse of the Antilles." *World Literature Today* 63, no. 4 (1989): 637–48.
Wynter, Sylvia. "Rethinking 'Aesthetics': Notes Towards a Deciphering Practice." In *Ex-iles: Essays on Caribbean Cinema*, edited by Mbye Cham, 237–79. Trenton, NJ: Africa World Press, 1992.
Wynter, Sylvia. "Towards the Sociogenic Principle: Fanon, Identity, the Puzzle of Conscious Experience." In *National Identities and Sociopolitical Changes in Latin America*, edited by Mercedes F. Durán-Cogan and Antonio Gómez-Moriana, 30–66. New York: Routledge, 2001.
Wynter, Sylvia. "Unsettling the Coloniality of Being / Power / Truth / Freedom: Towards the Human, After Man, Its Overrepresentation—An Argument." *Centennial Review* 3, no. 3 (2003): 257–337.
Wynter, Sylvia. "The Ceremony Found: Towards the Autopoetic Turn/Overturn, Its Autonomy of Human Agency and Extraterritoriality of (Self-) Cognition." In *Black Knowledges/Black Struggles*, edited by Jason R Ambroise and Sabine Broeck, 184–245. Liverpool: Liverpool University Press, 2015.
Wynter, Sylvia, "On How We Mistook the Map for the Territory, and Reimprisoned Ourselves in Our Unbearable Wrongness of Being, of Desêtre: Black Studies Toward the Human Project." In *Not Only the Master's Tools: African-American Studies in Theory and Practice*, edited by Lewis R. Gordon and Jane Anna Gordon, 107–69. Oxford: Blackwell Publishing, 2016.
Yeo, Richard. "Reading Encyclopedias: Science and the Organization of Knowledge in British Dictionaries of Arts and Sciences, 1730–1850." *Isis* 82, no. 1 (1991): 24–49.
Zook, Matthew, Solon Barocas, Danah Boyd et al. "Ten Simple Rules for Responsible Big Data Research." *PLoS Computational Biology* 13, no. 3 (2017): e1005399.

# Index

Let it be known that I have derived a *peculiar satisfaction* from cataloging the contents of this book to make topics findable via an index. It was a daunting exercise to decide what to include, how to name concepts, and how to organize subtopics within broader terms. I hope that this index is useful, but I admit that my terms and their order should be contested.


Adair, James: *History of the American Indians*, 179, 185
Adams, John, 61, 264n39, 267n15, 292n33
Adams, Richard, 118
Adorno, Theodor, 84, 224
Agamben, Giorgio, 17
Alderman, Edwin, 1
Albemarle Library Society, 137, 138
Allen, Amy, 84
American Philosophical Society, 202, 215, 223, 229, 279n36, 291n26
animals: classification of, xxi, 17, 22, 79, 143, 174, 176, 199–200, 202, 224, 229–30, 232–33, 237–39; as documents, 221–22, 237, 239; as evidence, 192, 210, 221, 225; Indigenous relations with, 210, 239–40; Lewis and Clark expedition, 203, 206, 215, 225–26; in museums, 202, 220, 223, 229–30, 235, 236, 292n33, 297n50; as property, 201, 239; and racialization, 200, 239; in Shakespeare plays, 199
Andersen, Jack, 286n45
Anderson, Benedict, 205
Anderson, Jane, 188
antelope. *See* pronghorn
archival imaginary: Caswell on, 83
Arendt, Hannah, xvii–xviii, 33, 86, 254
Armstrong, Meg, 166
Bacon, Francis, 23, 42, 147–48; *Advancement of Learning*, 126, 271n13; *New Atlantis*, 148; organization of knowledge, xx, 121, 125–26, 129, 142, 152, 154, 278n24, 280n53, 283n120, 292n33
Baldwin, Abraham, 130
Baldwin, James, 105
Ball, Kirstie: *Routledge Handbook of Surveillance Studies*, xiii
Banneker, Benjamin, 157, 160–61
Barad, Karen, 21
Barbary Wars, 159, 285n22
Barbé-Marbois, François, 127–29, 247, 278n23, 279n36, 279n38
Barlow, Joel, 158, 161
Barton, Benjamin, 79, 223
Bartram, William, 180
Beauchamp, Toby, xiv; *Going Stealth: Transgender Politics and U.S. Surveillance Practices*, xiii–xiv
Beckley, John J. (Librarian of Congress), 130
Benjamin, Walter: on documents, 84; on messianic time, 89–90, 252; "Theses on the Philosophy of History," 56, 89, 250; on things, 38
Bennett, Tony, 201

Bentham, Jeremy, 98
Bergdoll, Barry, 26
Berger, John, 225
Berlant, Lauren, 40, 42, 50, 269n75
Best, Stephen, 110–111
Bhandar, Brenna, 183
Billington, James (Librarian of Congress), x
Black Lives Matter, 4, 6
Blackhawk, Ned, 178, 208, 270n3
Bond, Julian, 247
Bowker, Geoffrey, 89, 96; *Sorting Things Out*, 266n95
Boyd, Julian, xx, 65, 79–80
Brezina, Jennifer Costello, 159
Brian Deer Classification, 254
Briet, Suzanne, 221–22, 229, 237, 294n58, 295nn1–3
British Museum, 201
Brodie, Fawn, 107, 108, 128
Brown, Michael, 140
Brown, Morgan, 204
Brown, Richard, 118
Brown, Vincent, 36
Brown, Wendy, 44, 45
Browne, Simone: *Dark Matters: On the Surveillance of Blackness*, xii–xiv, 171
Bryant, Zyahna, 5
Buckland, Michael 32, 238, 267n21
Buffon, 42, 128, 144, 146–47, 174, 176, 180, 192, 237, 285n45
Burke, Edmund, xx, 42, 127, 162, 163, 166–67, 169–71, 287n77
Burwell, Rebecca, 99
Butler, Judith, xviii, 44
Butterfield, Lyman, 68
Byrd, Jodi, 239
Byrd, William, 69
Byrne, Romana, 164

Cahill, Edward, 163, 164, 172, 179, 287–88n81
Caliban, 198–201, 290n2
Carr, Dabney, 242, 244–45, 263n11, 298n6
Carr, Martha Jefferson (TJ's sister), 245
Castanha, Tony, 208
Caswell, Michelle, 83, 85, 88, 100
Césaire, Aimé, 56, 93–94, 220, 264n34
Charlottesville, Virginia: Belmont, 3, 263n11; Court Square, 1, 138–39; Ku Klux Klan, 1–4, 262–63n1; Market Street Park, 5; monuments, xix, 1–11; public library, 121, 135–39; Unite the Right rally, 4–5; Vinegar Hill, 3, 263n12
Cheney-Lippold, John, 109
Cherokee Nation, 78, 79, 259, 273n74
Cheselden, William, 169
Christen, Kim, 188
Chief Logan, 58–59, 82, 176, 270n5
citation, xiv, xxiii–xxiv, 21, 56, 58, 169, 221, 271n13, 284n13
Cixous, Hélène, 101
Clark, George Rogers, 1–3, 5
Clark, William, 1, 5, 225. *See also* Lewis and Clark Expedition
Clarkson, Thomas, 157, 160
Cogliano, Frank, 63, 67, 68
Colden, Cadwallader: *History of the Five Indian Nations of Canada*, 178, 185
College of William and Mary, 58, 119, 127
Commager, Henry, 60
commonplace books, xi, xvi, 99, 118–119, 120, 245
common(s): xvii, xix, 37, 45, 50–51, 136, 178, 183, 239
community archives, 45, 85, 252, 254
Continental Congress, 14, 32, 62, 73
Coolidge, Ellen Randolph (TJ's granddaughter), 241
Coolidge, Thomas Jefferson, 68
Cooper, Anthony Ashley, Earl of Shaftesbury, 42
copyright, x, 72–76, 130, 251, 261n2, 272–73n59
copy press, 70, 102. *See also* polygraph
Corrêia da Serra, José (Abbé Corrêia), 79
Coulthard, Glen Sean, 18; *Red Skin White Masks*, 185
Cowan, T. L., 217
Cresap, Michael, 58
Crèvecoeur, Michel Guillaume Jean de, 128; *Letters from an American Farmer*, 163, 287–88n81
Crouch, Sara, 167
Curran, Andrew, 161, 285–86n45
Cushman, Ellen, 190

D'Alembert, Jean le Rond, 127, 142, 145–147, 278n24, 283n106, 283n120; *Preliminary Discourse to Diderot's Encyclopedia*, 125
d'Anmours, Chevalier, 127
da Silva, Denise Ferreira, 43
*Daily Progress* (Charlottesville), 1, 3, 4, 262n1
Darnton, Robert, 145, 146

Day, Ronald E., 24, 50–51, 221–22, 234, 236, 240, 267n21; "Community as Event," 50; *The Modern Invention of Information*, 12, 42
Davenport, Andrew xvii, 262n18, 299n21
De Tocqueville, Alexis: *Democracy in America*, 63
Declaration of the Rights of Man and of the Citizen, 13
Declaration of Independence. *See* Jefferson, Thomas—writings
decolonization, anti-colonialism, Indigenization, xvii, 27, 189–90, 215; Allen on, 84; Cushman on, 190; Ghaddar on, 208–9; Robinson on, 211; Snaza on, 49; Taschereau Mamers on, 239; Tuck and Yang on, 216, 289n42; Weheliye on, 18
Deer, Brian, 254
Del Lago, Enrico, 41
Deleuze, Gilles, 20
Derrida, Jacques, 51, 85, 95–96, 98, 101–3, 106–7, 110, 112, 224–25; *Archive Fever*, 96
Descartes, René, 125, 199, 224
Dewey Decimal Classification, x
Diderot, Denis, 115; *Encyclopédie*, 125, 127, 142, 145–47, 278n24, 283n106, 283n120
Dierksheide, Christa, 92, 93
Dimunation, Mark, 132
*Dingpolitik*, 37–38
dissent, xvii, xviii, 10, 45, 75, 269n59
Ditzion, Sidney, 139–40
Doctrine of Discovery, 60, 81, 205, 206–7, 293–94n45
Drabinski, Emily, xix, 266n103
Drake, Jarrett M., 13
du Moulin, Barthélémy Sernin, baron de Montlezun de Labarthette, 204, 292n33
Dugatkin, Lee Alan, 234, 235

Eaton, Joseph, 157
Edwards, Paul, 47
Ehrenpreis, Diane, 129, 272n50
Eisenstein, Elizabeth, 66
Elmborg, James, 32
Elmer, Jonathan, 55, 58, 59, 69, 82, 128, 248, 270n5
Englert, Sai, 48
Equiano, Olaudah, 160, 285n34
ethnographic refusal, Audra Simpson on, 179, 288n22
event: community as, 50–51; grief as, 106, 248; in history, 56, 83, 91, 250, 251, 254; information as, 39, 50, 239; literacy, 265n71; as memorial, 3–4, 11, 16, 25, 110; ontological, 14, 20, 25, 31, 46, 49, 161, 198, 221, 222, 240, 248, 254, 269n75; and settler colonialism, 48

Fanon, Franz, 104, 149, 167, 170
Ferguson Public Library, 140
Ferguson, Roderick, 37, 54, 55, 104, 170
Fielding, Henry, 138
Finley, Chris, 192
Fitzgerald, John, 127
Foucault, Michel, xiv, xv, 12–14, 20–21, 31, 41, 42–43, 50, 59–60, 84, 152–53, 217, 238, *Archaeology of Knowledge*, 12, 42; *The Order of Things*, 14; "What is Enlightenment?," 50
Franklin, Benjamin 118, 127, 235, 267n15, 275n40, 280n53, 291n26, 292–93n33
French Revolution, 12, 13, 14, 65, 131
Freud, Sigmund, 95–98, 102, 104
Friedrich, Markus, 85, 264n36
Frohmann, Bernd, 222
Frosio, Eugene, 187–88
Fuentes, Marisa, 151

Galison, Peter, 95, 97, 102
Garba, Tapji, 218
Gates, Henry Louis, 286
George III (of Great Britain), 33
Getting Word African American Oral History Project, 27, 247, 252–53
Ghaddar, J. J., 79, 208
Gilliland, Anne, 100
Gilmore, Ruth Wilson, 116
Gilreath, James, 177
Gilroy, Paul, 162
Gish, Dustin, 125
Glissant, Édouard, 198
Glynn, Tom, 136
Goff, Frederick, 65
Goldstein, Alyosha, 239
Gordon, Avery, 107, 109–110
Gordon-Reed, Annette, 21, 99, 161
Gray, Beverly, 252
Grégoire, Henri Jean-Baptiste (Abbé), *An Enquiry Concerning the Intellectual and Moral Faculties, and Literature of Negroes*, 157–58, 161

Habermas, Jurgen, 50
Haggerty, Kevin: *Routledge Handbook of Surveillance Studies*, xiii
Hakluyt, Richard: *The principall nauigations, voiages, and discoueries of the English nation*, 185
Halberstam, Jack, 106
Hansson, Joacim, 239
Haraway, Donna: *Simians, Cyborgs, and Women*, 16
Hardt, Michael, xix
Harney, Stefano, 20
Harris, Verne, 101
Hartman, Saidiya, 52, 79, 97, 276n70
Hatch, Frederick Winslow, 138
Haudenosaunee Confederacy, 57, 58, 79, 178, 181, 185, 259, 270n3
hauntology, 106–12
Hawkins, John Isaac, 71
Hayden, Carla (Librarian of Congress), 115, 251
Hayes, Kevin J., 107, 115, 128, 131, 132, 177, 280n53
Hazard, Ebenezer, 15, 31, 32, 55, 61–63, 76, 78; *Historical Collections*, 61, 63, 76
Head, Randolph, 35
Heidegger, Martin, 38
Holgersson-Shorter, Helena, 190
Hemings, Betty, 53
Hemings, Beverly, 100
Hemings, Eston, 100
Hemings, Harriet, 101
Hemings, John, 100
Hemings, Madison, 100
Hemings, Sally, 11, 21, 40, 52, 53, 76, 93, 100–1, 246, 247, 253, 269n90, 299n23
Hening, William W.: *Statutes at Large*, 65
Heyer, Heather, 4
Hogan, Sarah, 148
Hogarth, Rana, 168
Hogarth, William, xx, 42, 127, 162, 163, 167–69; *Analysis of Beauty*, 169
Holland, Catherine, 83, 175
Holmes, Abiel: *Memoir of the Moheagan Indians, History of Cambridge*, 178
*Homosaurus*, 253–54
Honig, Bonnie, xvii–xviii, 37, 38, 44
Hughes, Justin, 73–74
Hume, David, 156, 164
Huntington, Samuel, 78

Immigration Act of 1924, 3
information, ix; access to, as action, xix, 31–35, 37–38, 45, 49, 50, 267n2; as commodity 35, 45, 218–19, 222; as event, 39, 50; in-common, 50–51; organization of, xv, xvi, xx, 18, 19, 22, 24, 26, 36, 37, 40, 42, 49, 54, 79, 95, 96, 102, 108, 116, 121, 129, 130, 132, 133, 134, 140, 142, 150, 152, 163, 172, 179–80, 185, 187, 200, 202, 217, 252, 254, 280n53, 286n45; as technology of the self, 40–42; as thing 32, 35, 38, 200, 220, 237, 238, 239, 267n21
information architecture, xiv, xix, 15, 22–27, 42, 57, 87, 96, 98, 111
information infrastructure, 25, 46–47, 52, 88, 95, 97, 112
Institute of Museum and Library Services (IMLS), 251
intellectual property. *See* copyright
Iroquois Confederacy. *See* Haudenosaunee Confederacy
Irving, Sarah, 147, 283n120

Jefferson School African American Heritage Center. *See* Swords Into Plowshares
Jackson, Thomas J. ("Stonewall"): monument, 1, 5
Jackson, Zakiyyah, 199–200
Janzen, David, 198
Jefferson, Lucy (TJ's infant daughter), 128
Jefferson, Martha Wayles Skelton, 53, 75, 99, 100, 107–8, 121, 128–29, 244, 246
Jefferson, Thomas—archival practice and theory: xx, 12–13, 15–16, 33–34, 36, 54, 59–61, 84, 87; copying, 65–66, 70–74; and Hazard's *Historical Collections*, 31–32, 61–63, 76–77, 78; and the Hemingses, 100; Indigenous knowledges and belongings, 78–81, 181, 203, 248; and Monticello, 34, 55, 69–70, 85–86, 100; newspapers, 65; *Notes on the State of Virginia* as archive (Elmer on), 58, 128; preservation and access, 65–76; and time, 88; Virginia, 63–65, 69
Jefferson, Thomas—libraries: 1783 catalog, 121–24, 129; 1815 catalog, 134, 151, 154, 156, 158; anti-Black racial classification, 151–62; books about Indigenous peoples, 175, 177–79, 194; books and reading, 118–20; cataloging and classification of, xi, xx, 24,

49, 115, 116–117, 121–24, 128, 130–34, 135, 141–42, 144, 149, 150; influence, 14–15, 146, 202; and Library of Congress, ix, xi, xv, 49, 65, 73, 78, 116, 117–118, 121, 129–34, 141, 143, 184–87, 242, 243–44, 249; at Monticello, ix, 14, 24, 52, 141–42, 241; monumentality of, 26; preservation, 69–70; public libraries, 76, 117, 121, 135–39, 173; at Shadwell, 118, 120, 141, 198; University of Virginia, 117–118, 134–35

Jefferson, Thomas—museum practices: xxi, 24, 71, 201, 202; Indian Hall, 202–5, 215, 292–93n33; Monticello as, 249–50; Philadelphia Museum, 202, 223–24

Jefferson, Thomas—on slavery: xx, 34, 40–41, 42, 61, 83, 84, 89–94, 149, 152, 156–57

Jefferson, Thomas—writings: Bill for Establishing a Public Library, 121; Bill for the More General Diffusion of Knowledge, 121, 136; Declaration of Independence, xi, 12, 13, 14, 32, 33–34, 35, 40, 44, 51, 55, 57, 65, 67, 87, 90, 178, 246, 250, 254, 267n15, 270n1, 275n33; Farm Book, xvi, xx, 52–53, 96–97, 98, 101; Memorandum Books, 58, 98, 99, 138, 142; *Notes on the State of Virginia*, xvi, xx–xxi, 34, 58, 69–70, 72, 80, 83, 94, 98, 121, 127–29, 152–54, 156–57, 163, 169, 172, 173, 175–78, 180–82, 184, 190, 192, 194, 205, 249, 271n18, 278n23, 279n41, 284n17; 288n25; Summary Journal of Letters, 99, 108; Summary View of the Rights of British America, 32, 34–35; travel journals, 190–91

Jessup White, Gayle, 253

Jones, Peter, 179

Jordan, Daniel P., 247

Justice, David Heath, 78, 209

Kames, Lord (Henry Home), 42

Kant, Immanuel, 50, 286n45

Kauanui, J. Kēhaulani, 48

Kelley, Robin D. G., 159

Ketelaar, Eric, 12–13, 100, 264n38

Kimmerer, Robin Wall, 210; *Braiding Sweetgrass*, 185

Klinenberg, Eric, xviii, 140

Klinghard, Daniel, 125

knowledge organization systems, xvii, 18, 25, 101, 102, 133, 143

Ku Klux Klan, 1–5, 262–63n1

*Last of the Mohicans*, 81, 82, 175

LaFleur, Greta, 169, 190, 192, 233

Laporte, Joseph de: *Le voyageur françois, ou, a connoissance de l'ancien et du nouveau monde*, 185

Latour, Bruno, 38, 205–6, 207, 215, 238

Lee, Robert E.: monument, 3, 5

LeFevre, Albert, 2

LaMontagne, Leo, 31, 102

Larsen, Nella, 262n2

Laurens, Henry, 62

Lewis and Clark expedition, xxi, 1, 2, 79–80, 181, 202–3, 205–6, 208, 211, 218, 224, 226–28, 231, 249, 289

Lewis, Meriwether, 5, 79–80, 197, 203, 208, 212–13, 215, 220, 226, 228–29, 296n32. *See also* Lewis and Clark expedition

Liboiron, Max, xxiii, 216

Librarians of Congress. *See names of individual Librarians of Congress*

Library Company of Philadelphia, 166, 280n53

Library of Congress: ix–xii, xv–xvi; Copyright Office, x

Library of Congress Classification, ix, xii–xv, 22, 49, 116, 185–88, 253, 289n36

Linnaeus, Carl, 17, 42, 144, 168–69, 192, 229, 233–34, 296n12

Lloyd, David, 44, 170

Locke, John, 42, 73, 86, 125, 287n77, 292–93n33

Looby, Christopher, 184

Lorde, Audre, 116, 171

Luhmann, Niklas, 21–22, 59, 91, 104

Lyon, David: *Routledge Handbook of Surveillance Studies*, xiii; *Surveillance as Social Sorting*, xiii

Macdonald, Helen, 106

Madison, James, 10, 70, 73–75, 121, 129, 131, 223, 264n39, 279n49

Madison, James (Reverend), 127

Maldonado-Torres, Nelson, 163

Malone, Dumas, 115

Mandan Nation, 214–15, 232

Manning, Susan, 129, 163

Manovich, Lev, 286n45

Massachusetts Historical Society, 68, 202, 284n17

mastery, 24, 40, 86–88, 94, 107, 111, 116, 126, 148, 150, 153, 166, 172, 190, 199, 200, 217

Mattern, Shannon, 46, 47
Maury, James (Reverend), 119
Mazzei, Phillip: *Recherches historiques et politiques sur les États-Unis de l'Amérique Septentrionale*, 242–43, 298n6
McClintock, Anne, 189
McKittrick, Katherine, 105, 109, 116, 150, 217, 262n2, 276n88; *Dear Science*, xxiv
McLaverty-Robinson, Andy, 252
McPherson, Isaac, 72
Meriwether, William, 138
metaphor, xxi, 14, 46, 60–61, 95, 97, 102, 125, 172, 205, 216–18, 237
Mignolo, Walter, 218
Miller, Robert, 207, 294n46
Mills, Charles W., 88
Mitchell, Katharyne, 26
Monacan Nation, xxi, 176, 180, 181, 247–49, 289n30, 298n14, 299n16
Monroe, James, 93
Monticello, ix, xv, 42, 52, 67, 127, 128, 153, 198, 201, 276n70; and archives, 55, 85, 87, 107; graveyards, xxi, 1, 241, 244–48; library, xi; xiv, 24, 126, 131, 141, 172, 241, 243; Montalto, 2, 3; museum, xxi, 202–5, 215, 249, 292–93n33; plantation management, xv, 53, 92, 97, 98, 101, 111, 253; slavery, 21, 27, 53, 76, 92–93, 97, 100–1, 252–53
Monticello Association, 244
Montoya, Robert, 229, 237
monuments: burial sites as, 21, 244–49; in Charlottesville, 1–9; Declaration of Independence as, 33; to democracy, 10, 255; documents as, 11–15, 32, 63–64, 80; information architectures as, 15, 24–27, 145, 220; to Jefferson, 4, 6–8, 11, 24, 117, 241, 243; Schaefer on, 16
More, Hannah, 138
Morgensen, Scott, 193
Moses, Ezekiel, 7, 8, 264n28
Moten, Fred, 20
Murray, John, Fourth Earl of Dunmore, 58, 59, 273n74

Natural Bridge, 164–65, 286n53
Negri, Antonio, xix
Newton, Issac, 14, 42, 125
Nguyen, Mimi Thi, 212
Nord, Martin, 294n58
Nyong'o, Tavia, 94

O'Brien, Jean, 81
O'Shaughnessy, Andrew J., 67, 135
Oconostota (Cherokee chief), 78
Ogilvie, James, 141
ontology, xix, 49, 50–52, 85, 108–9, 149, 218, 198, 200, 221–23, 237; as colonialism, 52. *See also* hauntology
ontological genocide, Woolford on, 19, 265n69
ontological sovereignty, 52
Ord, George, 230
Owens, Robert, 184
*Oxford English Dictionary*, 38, 86, 94, 95, 238, 267n2

Page, John, 55–58, 79, 99, 120, 131, 198, 270n1, 298n10
Palmer, Meredith, 174, 207
paradox, xi, xv, 14, 18, 20–22, 45, 57, 84, 112, 147, 246
Patent Act (1793), 72, 261n2
Pawley, Christine, 20
Peale, Charles Willson, xxi, 42, 71, 202, 203, 204, 220, 223–24, 228–30, 232–36, 296nn11–12, 296n32
Peale, Rembrandt, 235
Peale, Titian Ramsey, 227, 236
Peale Museum. *See* Philadelphia Museum
Perlmutter, Shira, 251
Philadelphia Museum, xxi, 202, 204, 223, 224, 233, 235, 236, 296n12
polygraph, 70–71, 203. *See also* copy press
Pope, Alexander: "Elegy to the Memory of an Unfortunate Lady," 245
Popowich, Sam, 139–40
Potawatomi knowledge systems, Kimmerer on, 186–87, 210
Poulson, Zachariah, 280n53
Powell, John Wesley, 237
Pratt, Mary Louise, 179; *Imperial Eyes*, 151
primogeniture, 6, 75
Priestley, Joseph, 60
progress, 2, 14, 24, 34, 56–57, 60–61, 63, 72–73, 75–76, 83, 84, 87, 88, 92, 162, 163, 164, 174, 201, 207, 218; national, 34, 172; scientific, 74, 76, 144, 146, 148, 189, 206, 235; and time, 51, 88
pronghorn, xxi, 214, 218–19, 220–35, 237–40, 291n18, 296n32
Prospero, 120, 198–99, 201, 290n2
public libraries, xv, xix, xx, 15, 37, 44, 45, 54,

117–118, 139–40, 251, 255, 262n2; Charlottesville, 121, 135–39; in education, 121; as offices of government, 76, 117–118, 121, 131, 133, 173, 280n54, 282n80, 292n31; subscription-based, 137–38

Racial Integrity Act (Virginia), 3
racialization: as defined by Weheliye, 17; processes of, 17, 47–48, 109, 150; and sexuality, 190–92
Ramusio, Giovanni, *Delle navigazione e viaggi raccolte*, 185
Randolph, Cornelia Jefferson (TJ's granddaughter), 241
Randolph, John, 69
Randolph, Maria Jefferson (TJ's daughter), 244
Randoph, Martha Jefferson (TJ's daughter, also known as Patsy), 244, 129
Randolph, Sarah N., 244
Randolph, Thomas Jefferson, 68, 204
Rassawek, 181, 289n30
Rault, Jas, 217
Rawson, K. J., 253
Ray, William, *Horrors of Slavery*, 157, 160, 285n22
repression, xvi, xx, 94–99, 102, 111–112, 244
Rifkin, Mark, 189, 193
Robinson, Cedric, 159
Robinson, Dylan, 210, 211
*Robinson Crusoe*, 175
Rose, Jacqueline, 96
Rothman, Joshua, 3–4
Ruhleder, Karen, 46

Sacagawea, 5
Sancho, Ignatius, xx; *Letters of the Late Ignatius Sancho,* 153–56, 182, 284n14
Sayre, Gordon M., 180, 181
Schaefer, Donovan, 16–17
Schofield, Robert, 236
settler colonialism, xvii, xxi, xxiv, 20, 21, 26, 47–48, 61, 77, 83, 85, 88, 111, 188, 193, 194, 200, 209, 211, 216, 218, 235, 239, 289n42; Coulthard on, 18
Shadwell, 67, 97, 99, 107, 117, 118, 119, 141, 198, 201, 245
Shakespeare, William, 119, 199; *The Tempest*, 120, 198–99
Shannon, Edgar, 263n5
Shannon, Laurie, 199
Sharp, Granville, 160
Sharpe, Christina, 25
Shelley, Fred, 61, 65
Shogan, Colleen, 251
Silko, Leslie Marmon, 232
Simpson, Audra, 177, 288n22
Simpson, Leanne Betasamosake, 198, 239, 291n16
Six Nations. *See* Haudenosaunee Confederacy
Skipwith, Robert, 119, 162, 245
Sloane, Hans, 201
Small, David, 52
Smith, Adam, 164
Smith, John, 181, 192
Smith, Samuel Harrison, 131, 132
Smollett, Tobias, 138
Snaza, Nathan, 49, 112, 265n71
Soh, Thomas, 6
Sorentino, Sara-Maria, 218
Southall, Valentine, 138
Sowerby, Millicent, 59, 284n14
Spahn, Hannah, 14, 61, 91
Spencer, Richard, 5
Spivak, Gayatri, 20, 101
Stanton, Lucia (Cinder), 92, 252, 253
Star, Susan Leigh, 46–47, 96; *Sorting Things Out*, 266n95
Statute of Anne, 73
Sterne, Laurence, 127, 153, 284n13
Steyerl, Hito, 38
Stuchel, Dani, 107, 216
Sundstrom, Linea, 232
Swann-Wright, Dianne, 252
Swords Into Plowshares, 5–6

TallBear, Kim, 88, 173, 174, 193, 209
Tanner, Russel, 231
Taschereau Mamers, Danielle, 239
Tawil, Ezra F., 175
Tay, Endrina, 129, 132, 272n50, 284–85n20
Taylor, Hugh, 68
Thomas, Isaiah, 15
Thomas Jefferson Foundation, 132, 247, 253
Ticknor, George, 134, 203–4, 292n31
time and temporality, 11, 14, 35, 50–51, 61, 81, 83, 86–88; 174, 175, 183, 187, 189–90, 223, 250; Benjamin on "messianic time," 90, 91; Rifkin on temporal sovereignty, 189
Todd, Zoe, 52
Torquemada, Juan de, 231

Tripolitan War. *See* Barbary Wars
Trouillot, Michel-Rolph, 90
Trump, Donald J., 9, 133, 250, 251–52
Tuck, Eve, 216
Turner, Hannah, 209

United Camp of Confederate Veterans, 3
United Nations Declaration on the Rights of Indigenous Peoples (UNDRIP), 295n73
United States National Archives, 12, 251
University of Virginia: architecture, 87, 98; Black Lives Matter, 4; Confederate monuments and removal, 1–2, 3–5; Edgar Shannon Library, 1; founding of, 1, 9, 202, 246, 264n24; Jefferson monument, 6–8, 11; Karsh Institute of Democracy, 6; library collection and catalog, 54, 69–70, 116, 117, 118, 134–35, 142, 146, 284–85n20; Memorial to Enslaved Laborers, 6, 9; President's Commission on Slavery, 6; as repository, 69–70; Rotunda, 4, 6, 7, 11, 135; Unite the Right rally, 4–5, 11

van der Wel, Jack, 253
Vartija, Devin, 146–47
Vidua, Carlo, 87
*Virginia Gazette*, 59, 127

Walcott, Rinaldo, 110
Wallace, Anthony, 176; *Jefferson and the Indians*, 185
War of 1812, ix, xv, 24, 131
Washington, George 63, 155, 235, 271n22, 292–93n33
Watt, James, 70
Watterston, George (Librarian of Congress), xi, 134, 141, 243, 284–85n20
Wayles, John, 53
Weheliye, Alexander, 17–18
Wertenbaker, William, 135
Wheatley Peters, Phillis, xx, 153–56, 171, 284–85n20; *On Imagination*, 154
whiteness, xiv, xxiii, 22, 24, 25, 61, 82, 88, 93, 106, 147, 152, 168–69, 171, 174, 176, 192, 197–98, 217, 262n13
Wilberforce, William, 160
Wilson, Douglas, 118, 129, 177, 278n14, 279n41
Wilson, Michelle, 200
Wolfe, Cary, 104
Wolfe, Patrick, 47–48, 150
Wood, Gordon S., 126–27
Woodward, Augustus Elias Brevoort, 145
Woolford, Andrew, 18, 265n69
Wulf, Andrea, 164
Wynter, Sylvia, 77, 104–6, 148, 149, 162–63, 167, 198–99, 207, 268n47
Wyche, John, 135–36, 137
Wythe, George, 15, 63–64, 76

X̱wi7x̱wa Library, 254

Yang, K. Wayne, 216
Yeo, Richard, 142

Zane, Isaac, 69

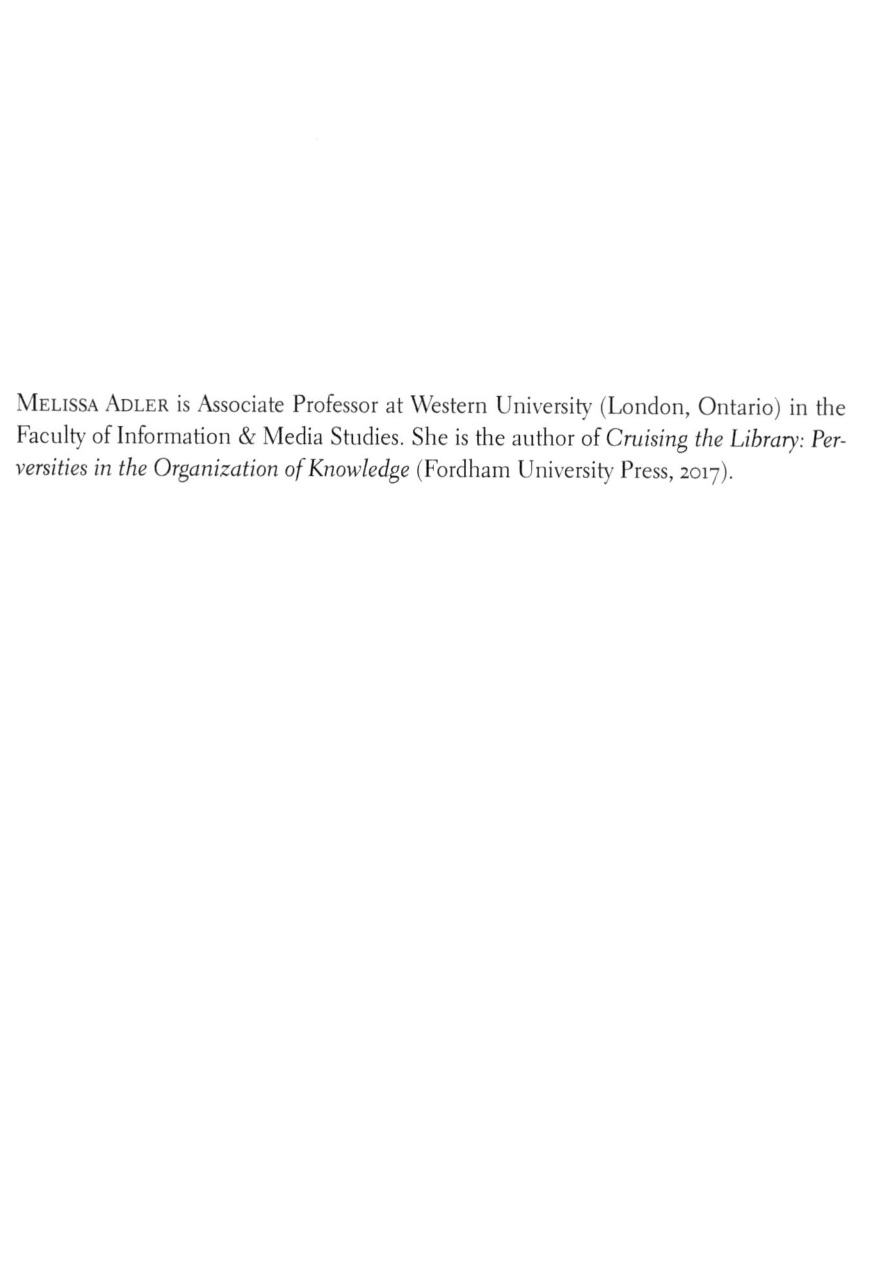

MELISSA ADLER is Associate Professor at Western University (London, Ontario) in the Faculty of Information & Media Studies. She is the author of *Cruising the Library: Perversities in the Organization of Knowledge* (Fordham University Press, 2017).